Strategic Planning for Regional Development in the UK

Strategic Planning for Regional Development covers the recent history and the current practice of strategic and regional planning in the UK, focusing on the escalation of regional powers and institutions in response to pressures such as those associated with the degradation of the environment and the atmosphere, the information revolution and the globalisation of the economy. It explores the reasons why new legislation, planning and development have been directed to the regions in the way they have and suggests why certain issues such as housing development and transport planning have become so sensitive and important.

With contributions from leading academics and practitioners, the book discusses:

- the evolution of regional planning in the UK and the strategic thinking involved,
- the spatial implications of regional economic development policies,
- the methods and techniques needed for the implementation of strategic planning for regional development, and
- how strategic planning for regional development is currently put into practice in three UK regions with different priorities.

This book takes a comprehensive approach to regional and strategic planning in all its dimensions and at all spatial levels. It examines the influence on the public sector of private and corporate sector strategic thinking and investment decisions. Detailed case studies also highlight the distinctions that exist between planning for different economic and social areas of the UK.

Strategic Planning for Regional Development is essential reading for students and academics working within strategic and regional planning, as well as providing policy makers and practitioners with a comprehensive and thought-provoking introduction to this critically important emerging field.

Harry T. Dimitriou is Bartlett Professor of Planning Studies at the Bartlett School of Planning, University College London, and previous consultant to the Hong Kong Government and the World Bank. He is also Director of the Omega Centre at UCL, where he is undertaking a comparative study of decision making in the planning of mega transport projects in ten countries.

Robin Thompson, sometime Director of Strategic Planning at Kent County Council and Past President of the Royal Town Planning Institute, has worked extensively as a local and regional planner. He was a principal author of the London Plan, the Mayor's Spatial Development Strategy, is Visiting Professor at the Bartlett School of Planning, University College London, and heads up his own consultancy firm.

The Natural and Built Environment Series

Editor: Professor John Glasson, Oxford Brookes University

Strategic Planning for Regional Development in the UK
Harry T. Dimitriou and Robin Thompson

Introduction to Environmental Impact Assessment
John Glasson, Riki Therivel and Andrew Chadwick

Methods of Environmental Impact Assessment
Peter Morris and Riki Therivel

Public Transport
Peter White

Urban Planning and Real Estate Development
John Ratcliffe and Michael Stubbs

Landscape Planning and Environmental Impact Design
Tom Turner

Controlling Development
Philip Booth

Partnership Agencies in British Urban Policy
Nicholas Bailey, Alison Barker and Kelvin MacDonald

Development Control
Keith Thomas

Forthcoming:

Regional Planning
John Glasson and Tim Marshall

Introduction to Rural Planning
Nick Gallent, Dave Shaw, Sue Kidd and Meri Juntti

Strategic Planning for Regional Development in the UK

A review of principles and practices

Edited by Harry T. Dimitriou and
Robin Thompson

Routledge
Taylor & Francis Group

LONDON AND NEW YORK

First published 2007
by Routledge
2 Park Square, Milton Park, Abingdon, Oxon OX14 4RN

Simultaneously published in the USA and Canada
by Routledge
270 Madison Avenue, New York, NY 10016

Routledge is an imprint of the Taylor & Francis Group, an informa business

© 2007 selection and editorial matter, Harry T. Dimitriou and Robin Thompson;
individual chapters, the contributors.

Typeset in Goudy by
RefineCatch Limited, Bungay, Suffolk
Printed and bound in Great Britain by
The Cromwell Press, Trowbridge

British Library Cataloguing in Publication Data
A catalogue record for this book is available from the British Library

Library of Congress Cataloging in Publication Data
A catalog record for this book has been requested.

ISBN 10: 0–415–34937–0 (hbk)
ISBN 10: 0–415–34938–9 (pbk)
ISBN 10: 0–203–53720–3 (ebk)

ISBN 13: 978–0–415–34937–6 (hbk)
ISBN 13: 978–0–415–34938–3 (pbk)
ISBN 13: 978–0–203–53720–6 (ebk)

This book is dedicated to our respective wives, Vicky Dimitriou and Margaret Roberts, whose love, support and patience helped make this publication possible.

Contents

PART 2
Theories and principles of strategic and regional planning 41

Notes on contributors

Philip Allmendinger is Professor of Planning in the Department of Real Estate and Planning at the University of Reading. He is also Director of the Centre of Planning Studies. He is a chartered planner and surveyor with interests in: planning theory, politics, regional planning and development. His teaching includes: planning policy, real estate environments, planning theory, politics and practice and property and planning studies. He is currently undertaking a number of research projects including: "Resourcing planning" for the Scottish Executive (with Arup Associates), and the ESRC-funded study: "Integrated spatial planning, multi-level governance and state rescaling" (with the Universities of Hull and Newcastle).

Mark Baker is Senior Lecturer and Head of Planning and Landscape in the School of Environment and Development at Manchester University. He is also Director of Undergraduate Studies and the Masters of Town and Country Planning. Mark is a chartered town planner with professional experience in local and regional government and research interests in: regional and strategic planning, central–local relations and the plan-making process. His current research activities include: work on stakeholder involvement in the RPG process (sponsored by ODPM/TCPA), the use of environmental and sustainability appraisal within development plans (sponsored by ESRC) and the future of sub-regional planning in England (for CPRE). He was the project manager and co-director of a recent DETR-sponsored research project on the operation and effectiveness of the English structure planning process and has been involved in a number of other research projects, sponsored by organisations including the Joseph Rowntree Foundation and the North West Regional Association.

David Banister is Professor of Transport Studies at the Oxford University Centre for the Environment. Until recently he was Professor of Transport Planning at University College London. He has also been Research Fellow at the Warren Centre in the University of Sydney (2001–2002) on the Sustainable Transport for a Sustainable City project and was Visiting VSB Professor at the Tinbergen Institute in Amsterdam (1994–1997). He is currently a visiting Professor at the University of Bodenkultur in Vienna. He is a Trustee of the Civic Trust and Chair of their Policy Committee (2005–2009). He is a geographer and transport specialist who has built up an international reputation as one of the leading UK researchers in Transport and Planning Analysis, and in particular the contribution that the social scientist can make to the investigation of these problems. His research interests include the study of: transport investment decisions and economic development, policy scenarios for sustainable mobility, transport and sustainable development – reducing the need to travel, transport planning methods and their application to policy decisions, and modelling of energy and emissions from transport modes in urban areas and regions. His teaching has covered transport planning and policy, and sustainable urban development and transport. He has been a key researcher in the EPSRC 'Sustainable Cities Initiative' and was the Director of the major ESRC programme on 'Transport and the Environment'.

Paul S. Benneworth is an Academic Fellow at the Centre for Urban and Regional Development Studies at the University of Newcastle upon Tyne. He is an economic geographer who has research interests in innovation and economic development in peripheral economic regions and who has conducted commissioned research in the role of higher education institutes in regional development in the North East, as well as skills needs for the North East renewable energies sector. He is a Board Member of both the Regional Studies Association and the Regional Science Association International – British and Irish Section, and sits on the committee of the Economic Geography Research Group of the Royal Geographical Society/Institute of British Geographers.

Harry T. Dimitriou is Bartlett Professor of Planning Studies at the Bartlett School of Planning at University College London and Director of its OMEGA Centre for Mega Projects in Transport and Development. Funded by the Volvo Research and Education Foundations, this centre has been set up as a centre of excellence to examine how complexity, uncertainty and risk are managed in the planning of future mega urban transport projects in ten countries in Europe, North America and Australasia. He is a chartered town planner and transport specialist who has had extensive international consultancy, research and teaching experience in Europe and Asia. His main areas of research and consultancy lie in: strategic urban and regional planning and policy making, urban land-use/transport interaction, urban transport policy and sustainable development, mega transport infrastructure planning and institution building for urban development and transport. He has held numerous advisory positions, including for the EC, IBRD, UNDP, UNCHS, Hong Kong government and government of Indonesia, overseas, and for SEEDA and LDA in the UK.

Nick Gallent is a Reader in Housing and Planning and Director of the MSc Spatial/International Planning Programmes at the Bartlett School of Planning at University College London. He has taught courses on planning for a changing countryside, advanced research methods and housing. As a geographer and chartered town planner, he has carried out research that is chiefly concerned with UK housing policy and, in particular, rural housing and issues relating to the provision of affordable housing through planning policy, which has been published in a range of academic and professional formats. He has also undertaken consultancy studies and applied research that has looked into: housing needs in the North of England (for local authorities and government), the reuse of airfield sites (ESRC), the geography of employment change (TCPA), the relationship between housing providers and planners (RTPI), housing pressure in rural Europe (for the Scottish Executive) and the characteristics of sustainable suburban areas (Civic Trust). Recent work on rural housing has focused on policy towards second homes in Wales (Welsh Assembly) and in England (Countryside Agency) and on categorising rural areas in South East England (SEEDA) as well as on the rural–urban fringe (Countryside Agency).

John Glasson is Associate Dean (Research and Consultancy) at the School of the Built Environment at Oxford Brookes University. He is currently Co-Director of the Oxford Institute of Sustainable Development at Oxford Brookes University and its Director of Research Development. He is an economic geographer and chartered planner, and his principal research interests and areas of teaching include: regional development and planning, environmental impact assessment, strategic environmental assessment/sustainability appraisal, economic analysis, and tourism impacts analysis. He has undertaken advisory and consulting studies for numerous bodies including ODPM, the EC, SEEDA and LGA that have focused on the socio-economic impacts of major projects, sustainability appraisal, evolving regional planning and governance, and energy and tourism impact. He has written and published widely on these topics and is joint editor of the Natural and Built Environment Series for Routledge, in which this publication is featured.

Vincent Goodstadt, who was responsible for the preparation of the Glasgow and Clyde Valley Plan: The Metropolitan Development Strategy for the Glasgow and Clyde Valley area, a government-approved 20-year plan prepared jointly by the councils in the West of Scotland, currently practises as an independent planning consultant to a range of public and private organisations. He is trained as a geographer and chartered planner, and his main research interests and expertise lie in the implementation of strategic planning, urban renewal, and heritage and countryside projects. He is Past President of the Royal Town Planning Institute, the accredited body for promoting standards in town planning with a world-wide membership, and is Honorary Professor at Manchester University Department of Planning. He is co-author of the Institute's *New Vision for Planning*, which is now widely accepted as setting the agenda for a more inclusive, integrated and sustainable approach to the future of our towns and cities, and has been an adviser to a range of international bodies including OECD, and Vice-Chair of the Hetherington Commission into the need for a plan for England, "Connecting England".

Peter Hall is Bartlett Professor of Planning and Regeneration at the Bartlett School of Planning, University College London. He has taught courses on the history of twentieth-century planning, metropolitan region planning, and urban regeneration and innovation. He was special adviser on strategic planning to the Secretary of State for the Environment, with special reference to issues of London and the South East, including the East Thames Corridor and the Channel Tunnel Rail Link, and was also a member of the Deputy Prime Minis-ter's Urban Task Force. He was knighted for his services to planning and received the Founder's Medal of the Royal Geographical Society for distinction in research. He is an honorary member of the Royal Town Planning Institute,

Fellow of the British Academy and founder member of the Regional Studies Association, as well as the first editor of its journal *Regional Studies*. He has been Chairman of the Town and Country Planning Association and Director of the Institute Community Studies (now the Young Foundation). Recent research studies he has directed/undertaken include "London's economic competitiveness and social cohesion" (for ESRC); "Social change from the individual standpoint" (for the German Ministry for Building and Planning); "The changing hierarchy of town centres in Great Britain, 1913–98" (for Chelsfield PLC); and "Transport sustainability: a study of small zone data" (for EPSRC).

Peter Roberts is Professor of Sustainable Spatial Development at the Sustainability Research Institute, University of Liverpool. He is also Chair of the Academy for Sustainable Communities, an agency of UK central government, and was appointed OBE for services to regeneration and planning. Peter also advises Addleshaw Goddard on planning, regeneration and environmental matters. He is active in a range of organisations including Urban Mines and is past Chair (now Vice-President) of the Town and Country Planning Association. He is also past Chair and Honorary Vice-Chair of the Regional Studies Association, Vice-President of the Council of Europe ISCOMET Group, Chair of the Best Practice Committee of the British Urban Regeneration Association, a member of the Scientific Committee on the Regions of Europe, Chair of the Planning Exchange Foundation and an adviser to the Local Government Association. His research has been supported by research councils and foundations, and by a wide range of UK, European and regional governments, partnerships and local authorities on matters related to governance, planning, regeneration and the spatial dimension of environmental management and sustainable development.

David Simmonds is Director of David Simmonds Consultancy. He is a chartered town planner and transport specialist especially concerned with the interface between land use and transport policy and planning, and the impacts of transport on urban and regional development. He has directed research into the effects of alternative urban land-use patterns, the regeneration benefits of improved public transport, the land-use impacts of parking policy, the possibilities for improved transport modelling methods, and the role of the coach in the economy. He has furthermore advised SACTRA and others on the methods used to assess the economic impacts of transport schemes and on the models which could be applied to such assessments. He has undertaken assignments overseas in Brazil, France, Germany, Italy and Spain, and in the UK for London and the South East, Merseyside, Edinburgh and Northern Ireland. He has also been engaged in studies of cross-Channel travel, undertaking an international market analysis of the regional impacts of the Channel Tunnel.

Mark Tewdwr-Jones is Professor of Spatial Planning and Governance at the Bartlett School of Planning, University College London, and its Director of Research and Consultancy. His research interests and teaching activities focus on: spatial planning and sub- and supra-national politics, urban and regional planning, governance and devolution, planning theory, ethics and professionalism, and certain substantive disciplines within spatial governance, including foreign direct investment, economic and spatial governance, the relationship between housing and planning, and second homes in Europe. He was a member of the DETR Roundtable on European Spatial Planning and Chairman of the Mid and West Wales Strategic Planning Forum. He has also been adviser to the DETR on the European Spatial Development Perspective; adviser to the European Union's PACTE Programme Project on Rural Change in Europe; and adviser to the Welsh Office on the development of planning guidance for Wales. He is a member of the RTPI Research Committee and the RTPI Committee on National Spatial Development Perspective for Britain; a member of the Scottish Executive/RTPI Scotland Initiative on the Future of National Planning Policy; and adviser to the Institute of Welsh Affairs on the Welsh planning system and strategic planning coordination.

Robin Thompson has been a special adviser to the Mayor of London on the policy content and processes of all stages of the London Plan and its subsequent alterations. As a geographer and chartered town planner, he is Director of his own consultancy firm, Robin Thompson Associates, which has undertaken regional planning studies in the UK for SEEDA, EEDA and LDA and in China for the China Development Bank. He is Visiting Professor of Planning at the Bartlett School of Planning, University College London, and was Chief Planning Officer and Director of Strategic Planning for Kent County Council, dealing with strategic projects such as Thames Gateway and the Channel Tunnel Rail Link. He has held senior positions in local government in London, including Director of Development in Southwark, and has been President of both the Royal Town Planning Institute (RTPI) and the European Council of Town Planners (ECTP). He was awarded the CBE for services to town planning in the UK.

Ivan Turok is Professor of Urban Economic Development and Director of Research within the Department of Urban Studies at Glasgow University. He is an economic geographer and planner, and his main research interests and areas of teaching lie in the study of the economy of cities, regional development, local labour markets and area regeneration and policy evaluation. He recently completed a four-year study of economic competitiveness, social cohesion and local governance in Glasgow and Edinburgh as part of the ESRC Cities, Competitiveness and Cohesion Programme. He has acted as an adviser to the OECD, European Commission, UK government and Scottish Executive on various aspects of economic development and employment policy.

Roger Vickerman is Jean Monnet Professor of European Economics at the University of Kent. Trained as an economist, he specialises in transport and regional economics. He founded the Centre for European, Regional and Transport Economics at Kent University and has been its Director since its inception. His major teaching interests are in regional economics and the European economy. He currently lectures on economic integration in the EU and the European spatial economy. He is Director of the Kent Centre for Europe (a Jean Monnet centre of excellence) and is Associate Dean for the Transmanche University Network. He holds visiting posts at the Universities of Münster (Germany) and Guelph (Canada) and at the Bartlett School of Planning at

University College London. He has worked as a consultant to the European Commission, the UK government and Kent County Council, and was a member of the Planning Advisory Group of the Department of the Environment and of the Standing Advisory Committee on Trunk Road Assessment, Department of the Environment, Transport and the Regions. He also currently serves on the editorial boards of *Regional Studies*, *Transport Policy* and *Les Cahiers Scientifiques du Transport*.

Geoff Vigar is Senior Lecturer in Planning and Director of Postgraduate Research at the School of Architecture, Planning and Landscape at Newcastle University. He is also Programme Director for the MA in Planning and Environment Research. Trained as a planner, he specialises in the politics of policy change and transport planning. His research interests focus on governance and spatial and transportation planning, with a particular emphasis on both environmental issues and policy process concerns. He is particularly interested in strategy development and implementation, and the ways in which different institutions and processes affect policy outcomes in varying contexts. His current research focuses on: sustainable suburbs, particularly from a transport perspective; how governance systems deal with stakeholder participation in planning and transport strategy making; renewable energy technologies and the planning system; and how UK devolution is affecting spatial planning. The latter interest is currently supported by an ESRC grant with colleagues at the Universities of Hull and Reading. His current work includes: a study of the state of Iraqi cities (for UN-HABITAT); integrated spatial planning, multi-level governance and state rescaling (for ESRC); and the sustainability of land use and transport in outer neighbourhoods (EPSRC).

Gwyndaf Williams is Professor Emeritus at the School of Environment and Development at Manchester University. He is a geographer, public policy specialist and chartered planner, and the main focus of his research and teaching has been on strategic planning, urban regeneration, urban programme and project management, and housing policy. His recent work has focused on metropolitan and regional strategic planning, city centre redevelopment and master planning with a particular interest in housing (mixed tenure communities, neighbourhood renewal, housing market niches, etc.). He is currently researching aspects of city–regional development programmes, and the implementation of housing market renewal in North West England.

Chris Yewlett is Lecturer in Planning and Course Director of the MSc in Planning and Transport in the Department of City and Regional Planning at Cardiff University. Following an initial career in operational research at the Tavistock Institute of Human Relations and in local government as Assistant Secretary of the Standing Conference on Regional Policy in South Wales, he now teaches courses on planning practice and method; transport planning; planning theory, philosophy and professional ethics; and development plan production and evaluation. He has lectured extensively internationally in Asia, Australia, Latin America and Africa. His research interests lie in the fields of planning methods, planning theory, planning policy and land-use planning and transport. He has undertaken numerous pieces of commissioned research, including two pieces of work for the Royal Town Planning Institute – one that looked into the speeding up of the delivery of development plans, and another which examined the quality of development plans (with Stephen Crow and others). He has furthermore undertaken research into completion notices for the DETR.

Preface

Many of the issues that make up the current news content of the media have a regional dimension and are perceived as needing a strategic response. We regularly read, for example, about housing shortages in some regions and relative stagnation of the housing market in others, and about acute transport infrastructure congestion problems on certain parts of our national and regional highway and railway networks and the dilemma of how to confront these effectively and in a sustainable manner. Economic performance varies substantially between regions, leading to labour shortages in some and over-supply in others. Some regions of the UK are experiencing drought and are facing the challenge of planning for sufficient supplies of water to meet demand. Climate change affects all regions, but often in different forms, and is one of the strongest examples of a phenomenon that has to be addressed by planning at a strategic level.

The origin of this book lies in a gap we perceive. We see, on the one hand, the growing importance of the regional development dimension and the increasing acceptance of the necessity of strategic planning. On the other hand, we note the paucity of skills and knowledge available to tackle the tasks of strategic planning for regional development. Unfortunately, there tends to be a lag between the emergence of new directions in public policy and the gearing up of requisite skills, knowledge and experience to tackle them. Certainly both planning practice and education became increasingly focused upon local planning and implementation during the Thatcher years, when regional and strategic planning were greatly diminished. This generally remains the case today, with the renaissance in regional and strategic planning skills proving slow to materialise. Indeed all too often there is even a lack of awareness of the strategic dimension as planning finds itself bogged down in parochial, relatively localised and time-consuming altercations, much to the frustration of the Treasury, amongst others.

The contributions to this book were chosen because they collectively offer an overview of regional and strategic planning in the recent past and in the present. A historical perspective is especially valuable because there has been a pronounced cycle of activity at the regional level from which we can and should learn lessons for the present and future. We were also certain that the book needed case studies from the different regions that reflect the very different perspectives across the UK and not least from the blossoming of regional planning in Scotland (and indeed Wales). We believe that the exceptional knowledge and expertise of the contributors has resulted in a book that offers a wide-ranging exposition of the state of regional planning in the UK and of the potential of strategic planning to address regional issues.

Harry T. Dimitriou
Robin Thompson
August 2006

Acknowledgements

There are numerous acknowledgements that need to be made for the preparation of this book. First, and foremost, the editors wish to acknowledge the support of a research grant to the Bartlett School of Planning, UCL, by ODPM for the preparation of teaching materials in strategic planning for regional development in 2002, which provided the basis for the preparation of this book.

In the case of Chapters 4 and 5 the authors would like to thank Philip Oliver, sometime Vice-President for Global Strategy at IBM, for introducing them to key publications that have influenced corporate strategy thinking. They also wish to acknowledge the help given by Professor Tony Tomanzinis, sometime of the University of Pennsylvania and long-time specialist in lessons of strategic planning from the corporate world to public sector planning. Particular thanks are due to Captain Christopher Stanger, sometime of the Royal Green Jackets, for his insight into military aspects of strategic thinking cited in Chapter 4, and to David Snowden, whose research conducted at the Cynefin Centre, when he was its Director at IBM, greatly inspired the authors when preparing this chapter.

Paul Benneworth wishes to acknowledge the support of a Research Council UK Territorial Fellowship in providing the time for contributing to Chapter 14. An earlier version of this chapter was presented as a paper at the Waseda Machizukuri Symposium, 9–10 July 2005, Waseda University, Tokyo.

Vincent Goodstadt would like to express special thanks for the advice enjoyed over many years from Professor Urlan Wannop, on whom he was dependent for much of the historical perspective provided in Chapter 16. Thanks are also conveyed to the author's colleagues Grahame Buchan, Stuart Tait and Emma Richardson for their help in preparing this contribution.

The authors and publisher gratefully acknowledge the following for permission to reproduce material in this book. Every effort has been made to contact copyright holders for their permission. The publishers would be grateful to hear from any copyright holder who is not acknowledged here and will undertake to rectify any omissions in future editions of the book.

Illustration Credits

The following material is reproduced under the terms of the Click-Use Licence: Tables 8.1, 9.2, 9.3, 9.4, 12.2, 12.3 and 12.4 and Figures 6.1, 9.1, 12.6 and 12.7.

Figures 4.1, 4.2 and 4.3 © Harvard Business School Publishing.

Figures 6.2, 6.3 and 6.4 reproduced by permission of Elsevier © 2006.

Figure 11.3 reproduced by permission of Liverpool University Press.

Figures 13.1, 13.3 and 16.1 reproduced by permission of Ordnance Survey on behalf of HMSO. © Crown copyright 2006. All rights reserved. Ordnance Survey Licence number 100045659.

Figure 14.2 reproduced by permission of Newcastle City Council.

Figure 14.3 reproduced by permission of The Northern Way.

Table 16.1 Cities for Citizens: Improving Metropolitan Governance, © OECD 2001.

Text Credits

Material in Chapter 4. Adapted with permission of The Free Press, a Division of Simon and Schuster, Inc. from STRATEGIC PLANNING: What Every Manager Must Know by George A. Steiner. Copyright © 1979 by The Free Press. All rights reserved.

Abbreviations

AEF	Aviation Environmental Federation
AESOP	Association of European Schools of Planning
AIDA	analysis of interconnected decision areas
AKSTEP	Awareness, Knowledge, Social concern, appropriate Technology, Economic resources and Political will
APEC	Asia Pacific Economic Cooperation
ARS	Alternative Regional Strategy
AST	appraisal summary table
CASE	Campaign against Stevenage Expansion
CBI	Confederation of British Industry
CEA	cumulative effects assessment
CEC	Commission of the European Communities
CES	Centre for Environmental Studies
COBA	cost benefit analysis
CPRE	Campaign to Protect Rural England (formerly Council for the Preservation of Rural England)
CSGR	Centre for the Study of Globalisation and Regionalisation
CSR	corporate social responsibility
DATAR	La Délégation à l'Aménagement du Territoire et à l'Action Régionale
DEA	Department of Economic Affairs
DETR	Department for the Environment, Transport and the Regions
DfEE	Department for Education and Employment
DfT	Department for Transport
DGXI	Environment Directorate General
DoE	Department of the Environment
DPDs	development plan documents
DTI	Department of Trade and Industry
DTLR	Department for Transport, Local Government and the Regions
DWP	Department for Work and Pensions
EC	European Commission
ECMT	European Conference of Ministers of Transport
ECTP	European Council of Town Planners
EEA	European Environment Agency
EEDA	East of England Development Agency
EERA	East of England Regional Assembly
EESC	European Economic and Social Committee
EIA	environmental impact assessment

EIP	examination in public
EIS	environmental impact statement
EMRA	East Midlands Regional Assembly
EPSRC	Engineering and Physical Sciences Research Council
ERDF	European Regional Development Fund
ESDP	European Spatial Development Perspective/European Spatial Development Planning
ESF	European Social Fund
ESPON	European Spatial Planning Observation Network
ESRC	Economics and Social Research Council
EU	European Union
EZ	enterprise zone
FUR	functional urban region
GAD	Government Actuary's Department
GBN	Global Business Network
GDP	gross domestic product
GEAR	Glasgow Eastern Area Renewal
GIS	geographical information systems
GLA	Greater London Authority
GOL	Government Office for London
GOM	Government Office for Merseyside, Manchester and Liverpool
GOMMMS	Guidance on the Methodology for Multi-Modal Studies
GONE	Government Office for the North East
GONW	Government Office for the North West
GORs	Government Offices for the Regions
GOSE	Government Office for the South East
GVA	gross value added
HBF	House Builders Federation
HIA	health impact assessment
IBRD	International Bank for Reconstruction and Development (World Bank)
IDCs	Industrial Development Certificates
IMD	Index of Multiple Deprivation
INLOGOV	Institute of Local Government Studies
INWARD	North West Agency for Regional Development
IOR	Institute for Operational Research
IPS	International Passenger Survey
IRF	integrated regional framework
IRS	integrated regional strategy
ISCOMET	International Scientific Conference of Minorities for the Europe of Tomorrow
IUCN	International Union for the Conservation of Nature
LCC	London County Council
LDA	London Development Authority
LDFs	local development frameworks
LFS	Labour Force Survey
LGA	Local Government Association
LOB	Location of Offices Bureau
LPAC	London Planning Advisory Committee

LTPs	local transport plans
MBO	management by objectives
NAFTA	North American Free Trade Area
NATA	new approach(es) to transport appraisal
NCC	Newcastle City Council
NEA	North East Assembly
NEB	National Enterprise Board
NEPA	National Environmental Policy Act
NGP	Newcastle Great Park
NHSCR	National Health Service Central Register
NORWIDA	North West Industrial Development Association
NWBLT	North West Business Leadership Team
NWDA	North West Development Agency
NWLGA	North West Local Government Association
NWMA	North West Metropolitan Area
NWRA	North West Regional Assembly
NWRAss	North West Regional Association
OAS	Organization of American States
ODPM	Office of the Deputy Prime Minister
OECD	Organization for Economic Cooperation and Development
ONS	Office for National Statistics
OPCS	Office for Population Censuses and Surveys (now ONS)
OPRAF	Office of Passenger Rail Franchising
OR	operational research
PACTE	Association in support of equal opportunities within the company for women
PAG	Planning Advisory Group
PPG	planning policy guidance
PPPs	policies, plans and programmes
PPSs	planning and policy statements
PTAs	passenger transport authorities
RAs	regional assemblies
RCU	Regional Co-ordination Unit
RDA	Regional Development Agency
REPCs	regional economic planning councils
RES	regional economic strategy
RICS	Royal Institution of Chartered Surveyors
RPG	regional planning guidance
RSDF	Regional Sustainable Development Framework
RSPB	Royal Society for the Protection of Birds
RSSs	regional spatial strategies
RTPI	Royal Town Planning Institute
RTS	regional transport strategy
SA	sustainability appraisal
SACTRA	Standing Advisory Committee on Trunk Road Assessment
SDA	Scottish Development Agency
SDD	Scottish Development Department
SDS	spatial development strategy
SEA	strategic environmental assessment

SEDD	Scottish Executive Development Department
SEEDA	South East England Development Agency
SEERA	South East England Regional Assembly
SERPLAN	South East Regional Planning Conference
SESs	strategic employment sites
SEU	Social Exclusion Unit
SIA	socio-economic impacts assessment
SME	small and medium enterprise
SPDs	supplementary planning documents
SRA	Strategic Rail Authority
SRC	Strathclyde Regional Council
TAG	transport analysis guidance
TBL	triple bottom line
TCPA	Town and Country Planning Association
TEC	Training and Enterprise Council
TEN-T	Trans-European Transport Networks
TfL	Transport for London
TPPs	transport policies and programmes
TRRL	Transport Road Research Laboratory
TWCC	Tyne and Wear County Council
TWDC	Tyne and Wear Development Corporation
UDC	urban development corporation
UDP	unitary development plan
UNCHS	United Nations Centre for Human Settlements
UNDP	United Nations Development Programme
VREF	Volvo Research and Education Foundations
VROM	Ministry for Housing, Spatial Planning and Environment
WCSP	West Central Scotland Plan
WDA	Welsh Development Agency
YHRA	Yorkshire and Humber Regional Assembly

Part 1

Setting the context

1 Introduction

Harry T. Dimitriou and Robin Thompson

Background

Strategic and regional planning has enjoyed a strong revival in recent years, both in the UK and in Europe as a whole. That revival has brought a demand for relevant knowledge and skills, which are in very short supply. This book contains a set of contributions from eminent authors: it responds to the renewed interest in these issues and the need to raise awareness of them.

At its simplest, strategic planning is the exercise of a systematic, integrated approach to policy making which takes full account of context, resources and the long term. It has its origins in military decision making and has tended to be developed more rigorously in corporate business than in public sector planning. Regional planning takes place in between the national and the local level. The book particularly evaluates regional planning policy as a form of strategic spatial planning.

A number of powerful drivers of change have generated a revived interest in the value of strategic and regional planning in the UK. These drivers all operate beyond the local level and require a policy response at a higher spatial level. They include globalisation of the economy, concerns about climate change, concerns about security, rapid advances in communications, advanced information technologies and increased migration. The challenges these powerful drivers create can be responded to at the regional level in a sufficiently strategic form. At the same time the regional level is seen to be closer and more sensitive to the local context than national government.

Both the European Union (EU) and the UK government have placed greater emphasis upon regional planning as a vehicle for longer-term and more strategic decision making in recent years. They have also promoted spatial planning, which embraces territorial policy for a much wider range of sectors in an integrated approach than does land-use planning. The greater policy range of spatial planning makes it very compatible with the comprehensive processes of strategic planning. A significant example of the promotion of these approaches is the recent legislation in England that has established regional spatial strategies (RSSs) as key statutory documents which are designed to draw together strategic and spatial planning at the regional level.

One general theme through the book is the cyclical nature of the application of both strategic planning and regional government. Both played an important role during and after the Second World War and then suffered something of a decline until a renaissance in the 1960s. They subsequently experienced a systematic dismantling by the Thatcher government before being reinvigorated in the past decade. One consequence of this lack of continuity is the absence of well-established institutions and of a strong cadre of qualified professionals in the UK. Central government in Britain has strengthened the institutions of regional government. It has assisted in the production of this book as a means of regenerating interest and skills in strategic and regional planning. The Royal Town Planning Institute (RTPI) has also placed strategic and spatial planning at the heart of its own mission statement for the profession. A number of universities are responding to the need to build capacity in these areas, and the book will contribute to this effort.

Structure of the book

A key feature of this publication is the unifying framework that underpins its content, which attempts to highlight three elements throughout: underlying concepts; main issues and challenges; and planning methods/techniques and mechanisms. The overall remit of the book is addressed through a set of chapters organised in five parts.[1]

We use Part 1 to set the context of the book: Sir Peter Hall considers the evolution of strategic planning and regional development in the UK, and Mark Tewdwr-Jones and Philip Allmendinger look at regional institutions, including the major changes made by the Blair government. Part 2 examines the theories and principles underlying strategic and regional planning, including Harry Dimitriou's review of the disciplines and theories of strategic planning thought, which were initially developed in the military and the corporate sectors. This part also contains a contribution by the editors on the importance of context in strategic and regional planning, while Chris Yewlett discusses the development of operational research (OR)-based methodologies of strategic choice in planning in the production of plans. Part 3 highlights selective substantive components of regional economics and strategic planning: Peter Roberts looks at the post-war history of regional economic development policy; Roger Vickerman considers transport policy at the regional level; and Ivan Turok considers the evolution of labour market policy. Part 4 outlines selected methods and techniques of regional analysis in key sectors: land-use/transport tools are examined by David Simmonds and David Banister, housing projections and allocation by Nick Gallent and sustainability assessment by John Glasson. Part 5 provides an insight into the practice of current strategic and regional planning in the UK through selected case studies: Robin Thompson examines the policy tensions in and between the three regions of the wider South East; Paul S. Benneworth and Geoff Vigar look at the relatively strong regional identity of the North East and its disadvantaged position in national policy; Gwyndaf Williams and Mark Baker review the sometimes troubled development of regional policy in the North West; and Vincent Goodstadt provides an example of the different approach in Scotland, where Glasgow and Clyde Valley offers a good example of inter-agency collaboration. The final chapter, "Conclusions", seeks to draw out from the preceding discussions common concepts, reoccurring issues and challenges, and generic methods, techniques and mechanisms that promote the advancement of this mode of planning practice.

Spatial planning and strategic and regional planning

Explaining what constitutes the nature and content of strategic and regional planning in the UK is very much the *raison d'être* of this book and will be elaborated by the authors. As a starting point, however, we wish to reinforce here Steiner's claim (cited in Chapter 4) that strategic planning is *not* merely a process of forecasting and subsequently determining what should be done to assure the fulfilment of these forecasts *or* the execution of a blueprint for the future (Steiner 1997). It is instead a particular type of planning that seeks to "join up" major goals, policies and actions into a cohesive entity that follows well-formulated efforts at marshalling and allocating resources into a viable planned response to a set of challenges, undertaken following a critical appreciation of competencies and shortcomings, as well as anticipated changes in the context(s) in which the strategy is formulated (Quinn 1995).

We view regional planning as a particularly complex form of strategic spatial planning, operating at a level between the national and local. Concurring with Albrechts, we see such planning as public sector led, concerned with social space and intended to influence the future distribution of activities in space through the adoption of a planning process "through which a vision, actions, and means for implementation are produced that shape and frame what a place is and may become" (2004: 746).

We understand regional planning is typically undertaken to tackle three major challenges: overcoming regional disparities, enhancing economic effectiveness, and providing effective regional planning guidance. We see a fourth rapidly coming to the forefront: namely, the environmental and climate-change challenge (see Hillman and Fawcett 2004; and RSPB and RTPI 2005), which Glasson sees as best met strategically at the regional level. Hall views strategic planning as providing a "balance" between urban regeneration and efforts at decentralisation. Roberts distinguishes between regional planning that is economic in nature, which tends to be at the national–regional interface, and regional planning that is spatial and more physical in nature, which typically operates more at the regional–local interface.

Drivers of change and components of strategic and regional planning

Strategic drivers of change

Regional developments both in recent years and in the prospective future have been/will be stimulated and affected by a number of powerful "strategic drivers of change". Discussed throughout the book by various contributors, these include:

- *The importance of globalisation* and the tendency for decision making in regional planning to operate at higher spatial levels and for global competition to require more "internationally" collaborative regions, as particularly highlighted by Tewdwr-Jones and Allmendinger, Dimitriou and Thompson, and Turok (in Chapters 3, 5 and 9, respectively).
- *The movement toward greater decentralisation of government* and the associated

attempt to reawaken and/or generate new senses of regional identity, as especially emphasised by Tewdwr-Jones and Allmendinger, and Roberts (in Chapters 3 and 7, respectively), and the authors of Chapters 13–15.

- *The increasing perceived need for strong public intervention* to address market inefficiencies and externalities, poor economic performance, and social inclusion and justice, as particularly discussed by Dimitriou and Thompson, Vickerman, Turok, and Gallent (in Chapters 5, 8, 9 and 11, respectively).
- *The engagement of private sector interest* in strategic and regional planning and the "new regionalism", as especially highlighted by Tewdwr-Jones and Allmendinger, Dimitriou, Dimitriou and Thompson, Vickerman, and Turok (in Chapters 3, 4, 5, 8 and 9, respectively).

Spatial planning as the overarching concept

The discussion and analysis of strategic and regional planning which follow take place within an overarching concept of spatial planning undertaken with the aim of its sponsors "to create a more 'rational' territorial organisation of land uses and the linkages between them" (ESPON 2005: 1). In the European Community, this vision is moulded by three fundamental aims: economic competitiveness; sustainable development; and coherence of the European continent. These are in turn reinforced by the key principles/visions of: "the pursuit of a more balanced and polycentric urban system; the parity of access to infrastructure and knowledge; and the wise management and sustainable development of Europe's natural and cultural heritage" (ESPON 2005: 5).

Strategic planning for regional development is strongly associated with schools of thought concerned about sustainable development and the need to think in the longer term and a more holistic fashion, as particularly emphasised by Glasson, Yewlett, Dimitriou, and Dimitriou and Thompson. It is also associated with the concept of collaborative planning and the use of partnerships as advocated by Healey (1997) and others, as especially discussed here by Tewdwr-Jones and Allmendinger and in the case study chapters (notably Chapter 16, the Glasgow and Clyde Valley study).

Components of strategic planning for regional development

Strategic planning for regional development may be seen to contain three essential components in face of the challenges, problems and issues it confronts:

- an underlying theory (and set of related concepts);
- a means of governance (and related governmental system); and
- methods and techniques of operation (and related institutional supporting mechanisms).

Theories and concepts

As regards the underlying theory, in this book Hall emphasises the importance of the need to distinguish between strategic and regional planning. Dimitriou, and Dimitriou and Thompson provide a strong sense that the theoretical foundations of strategic thought and planning are better embedded in other areas, including the military and the corporate worlds, than in spatial planning. Reinforced by Yewlett, they see that much potential benefit can be derived from the *careful* transfer of lessons from these other areas to the field of spatial planning, especially regarding the treatment of complexity, uncertainty and risk taking in decision making and planning, notwithstanding that the military and corporate worlds are much less democratic and employ more top-down planning approaches.

It is evident from various contributions in the book that there is a much less coherent theory of regional planning and its components than of strategic planning. Roberts especially laments the absence of an adequate theoretical base for regional planning. Turok points to the recent shift away from the emphasis upon physical to intellectual, human and social resources in regional planning, and explains that in consequence spatial planning has increasingly little control over regional developments. Hall distinguishes between economic and physical strands of regional policy and the long-standing tensions between the two, which make for "messy" plans and difficult implementation. He points to the shift away from regional policy under the Thatcher administration and the emphasis placed instead on urban policy and urban regeneration until New Labour's renewed interest in the regional agenda, albeit of a very different kind.

Issues and challenges

Glasson points to the emergence of the environmental agenda and the increasingly strong profiling of sustainability as an overarching vision for strategic and regional spatial planning. Notwithstanding this, Dimitriou and Thompson question central government's *full* commitment to this vision, highlighting contradictory government policies and actions that do not sit comfortably with the sustainability rhetoric government all too often delivers. Gallent and Vickerman point to New Labour's tendency towards top-down policy making and planning, notwithstanding the more recent attempts to strengthen bottom-up development efforts. Vickerman cites the absence of a national transport strategy and a national spatial strategy (except in Scotland, Wales and Ireland) as the source of many regional planning problems. Turok highlights challenges raised by the changing policy on labour supply. The case studies, by Thompson, Benneworth and Vigar, Williams and Baker, and Goodstadt, point to the tension between maximisation of economic growth and of the welfare of the community and the perpetuation (if not aggravation) of the North/South divide. Sectoral planning's uncomfortable fit with strategic and regional planning and other policy-related matters are illuminated by Roberts, Vickerman, Turok, Simmonds and Banister, Gallent, and Glasson.

The relative strengths of stakeholders, especially national/regional/local interests, are discussed by all the case study chapters, as is the relative commitment to regional governance and the regional planning process. The lack of integration of planned action at each level – reflected by national silos/regional fragmentation and intra-regional competition/local parochialism – is especially highlighted, as is the relative strength/weakness of identification with the region.

Tewdwr-Jones and Allmendinger raise concerns about "territorial governance" and the engagement of contributors and institutional networks. Dimitriou considers the advent of "new regionalism", in which the private sector plays a fuller and more dominant role and where more flexible approaches to regional governance are more prevalent, as a world in which the space of flows is seen by many such as Castells (1996) as more important than the space of places. The limitation of resources and powers available at regional/strategic level is highlighted by Vickerman and by Roberts. Turok refers to the low level of grants. The impact of deregulation is discussed especially by Vickerman and Gallent. Concerns about "institutional congestion" are voiced by Tewdwr-Jones and Allmendinger, Dimitriou and Thompson, and Roberts. The impacts of European policy, which according to Hall helped to keep regional planning in the UK alive, and the changing nature of EC policy from economic to political coherence are seen by the editors as key to underlying recent developments in the evolution of strategic and regional planning in the UK.

Methods, techniques and mechanisms

Finally, as regards the methodologies, techniques and mechanisms of strategic and regional planning, various contributors such as Dimitriou and Thompson, as well as Gallent, highlight the unwelcome perpetuation and reliance on "predict and provide" methodologies. Other chapters, including those by Dimitriou, and Simmonds and Banister applaud the merits of scenario planning. These contributions, together with Vickerman's, highlight the significance of making planning and policy assumptions more transparent, particularly given the institutional fragmentation and the proliferation of "agents of change" that has recently taken place. The editors see this as an important prerequisite of more rigorous strategic planning. The need to deal more effectively with complexity and uncertainty in the management of risks and the interrelatedness of decision making and network management is a reoccurring theme in a number of chapters. It is especially highlighted by Yewlett and Dimitriou, with the latter calling for the urgent need to address uncertainty much more in the practice of strategic planning for regional development in these opening years of a more uncertain and fast-globalising twenty-first century.

Note

1. The structure and content of this book have benefited from research funded by the Office of the Deputy Prime Minister (ODPM) prepared with a view to contributing to curriculum design proposals to assist future national capacity-building initiatives in strategic and regional planning in the UK.

References

Albrechts, L. 2004. Strategic (spatial) planning. *Environment and Planning B: Planning and Design* **31**, 743–58.

Castells, M. 1996. *The rise of the network society*. Oxford: Blackwell.

ESPON 2005. What is spatial planning. Home Page, European Spatial Planning Observation Network, http://www.espon.org.uk/spatialplanning.htm.

Healey, P. 1997. *Collaborative planning*. London: Macmillan.

Hillman, M. and T. Fawcett 2004. *How we can save the planet*. London: Penguin.

Quinn, J. B. 1995. Strategies for change: some useful definitions. In *The strategy process*, H. Mintzberg, J. B. Quinn and S. Ghoshal. London: Prentice Hall.

RSPB and RTPI 2005. Planning for climate change. A Royal Society for the Protection of Birds (RSPB) and Royal Town Planning Institute (RTPI) special supplement in association with *Planning*. November. London.

Steiner, G. A. 1997. *Strategic planning*. New York: Free Press Paperbacks.

2 Evolution of strategic planning and regional development [1]

Peter Hall

Introduction

It is important from the outset to distinguish between the two key concepts *regional policy* and *strategic planning*. *Regional policy* has been a major concern in the UK since the discovery of structural regional disparities in the Great Depression in the early 1930s, and culminated from 1945 in post-war policy which used a combination of controls and incentives to steer industry from the prosperous South East to the less prosperous North of England, South Wales and Central Scotland. It applied only to manufacturing (with a short-lived extension to offices in the late 1960s) and became increasingly irrelevant with the decline of manufacturing employment; the controls were removed under Thatcher in 1982, and incentives now come through EU Structural Funds. Only for a short period in the 1960s did it become conflated with an attempt at *regional planning* within the context of a national plan, and even then somewhat imperfectly.

Strategic planning has the different objective of balancing urban regeneration and planned deconcentration around the major conurbation cities; it is essentially intra-regional (while regional policy is inter-regional) and it has a strong physical planning emphasis, albeit mixed with economic and social objectives. During the Second World War and the immediate post-war period, the ground was laid in a series of plans, including the classic Abercrombie plans for Greater London and the Clyde Valley, which provided for post-war rebuilding of the cities and the construction of new and expanded towns to receive overspill from them. Another wave of strategic plans came in the 1960s impelled by population growth, with three successive plans for the South East alone between 1964 and 1970. Then, after 1977, energies and money were diverted into urban regeneration, and in the 1980s the Thatcher government officially pronounced strategic planning dead. But it has enjoyed resurgence in the 1990s, culminating in the Mayor's London Plan of 2002 and the government's Strategic Communities strategy of 2003.

This chapter will sketch the evolution of both concepts and their expression in policy, placing them in their specific historical contexts. It will conclude with speculation about their likely future evolution.

Regional policy

As Hall (1999) has argued,[2] regional policy has occupied a strange niche in British planning, separate from it but closely related to it. In essence it has sought to reshape the UK's economic geography through regulatory controls and fiscal incentives to steer economic growth from more- to less-dynamic regions. Over half a century, however – apart from a very brief and unsuccessful attempt in the mid-1960s – there has been no attempt at comprehensive regional planning, on the model successfully used in France; regional policy has been developed ad hoc, even being administered by a government department different from the ministry responsible for planning.

Further, in the high tide of Thatcherism in the early 1980s, a determined attempt was made to suppress regional policy in favour of the unfettered free market. But ironically regional policy survived, largely owing to the fact that European directives became much more significant in driving British policy formulation.

As Cameron (1974) has argued, the main aim of UK regional policy has not been economic efficiency but social equity: to correct the basic disequilibrium in regional labour markets, between regions – Scotland, Wales, northern England – suffering long-term underemployment and those – the South East of the UK – experiencing persistent labour shortages. These differences are small; some outcome measures – particularly regional GDP per capita – are even smaller. And, if migration is the ultimate measure, over the twentieth century no UK region actually suffered declining population.

The basis of regional policy for 40 years was the 1945 Distribution of Industry Act, passed by the wartime coalition government in its last days. It empowered the Board of Trade (later the Department of Trade and Industry) to provide loans and grants to firms within designated development areas and to facilitate the financing, building and leasing of trading estates. In 1947, the Town and Country Planning Act effectively made permanent a wartime system of building controls, through Industrial Development Certificates (IDCs), required for all new manufacturing establishments and extensions of over 5,000 square feet. They provided one arm of a "carrot and stick" approach which would be used, with varying degrees of enthusiasm, until the 1980s.

At first these powers were energetically used, aided by the fact that the IDC scheme adapted the wartime system of building licences and that there was a shortage of industrial premises and manpower. They brought results: during 1945–7, more than half of new industrial building in the country was in the development areas, compared with 5 per cent pre-war, though these contained less than a fifth of the population. By 1955, these buildings employed 86,000 people, mainly owing to location decisions in the immediate post-war years. Luttrell's research showed that these firms had moved in search of suitable premises and labour, and that suitable factory space owned by the Board of Trade, either newly built or converted from wartime use, was the biggest single magnet (Luttrell 1962).

But the 1951 election brought a Conservative government and a weakening of regional policy. By now, post-war shortages had eased, and the great post-war boom meant that the incentive to aid the peripheral areas was less. During 1946–9, under Labour, some £9 million a year was spent on regional policy, and

64 per cent of all job moves throughout the country went to the peripheral areas. In the eight years 1952–9, expenditure under the Act averaged only £5 million a year, and only 29 per cent of job moves were to the development areas.

In 1960, the Local Employment Act brought a major change: development areas were replaced by development districts, defined on the strict basis of unemployment rates over 4.5 per cent. But Industrial Development Certificates were retained, and government expenditure on regional policy increased seven times between 1952–9 and 1960–3, impelled partly by a recession in 1962–3. In the early 1960s, the big achievement was to steer new investment in the motor industry away from its traditional home in the Midlands (Birmingham, Coventry) and the South East (Dagenham, Luton) to Merseyside and Scotland. The impact was immediate: during 1960–3 some 25,000 new jobs a year were created in the peripheral areas and had survived by 1966 – 58 per cent of all moves nationally, and two and a half times as many as in 1952–9 (Brown 1972: 288).

But the continual changing of boundaries created uncertainty for private investment, while the stress on local unemployment made it difficult to concentrate development in growth points with good growth potential. An influential 1963 report from the National Economic Development Council, *Conditions for Faster Growth*, advocated the "growth pole" concept of the French economist François Perroux, and this was speedily accepted in White Papers on Central Scotland and the North East, which defined growth areas – in Scotland: Irvine, East Kilbride–North Lanarkshire, Cumbernauld, Falkirk–Grangemouth, Livingston and central Fife; in the North East: east Durham–south east Northumberland (building on developments earlier initiated by the Town Development Act of 1952) – and guaranteed that they would continue to enjoy assistance.

Harold Wilson's Labour government of 1964–70, continuing briefly into Edward Heath's administration of 1970–4, represented the apogee of traditional regional policy in the UK. The National Plan, launched in September 1965, represented a brief and unique attempt to create a French system of national–regional planning. But it was abandoned in a fiscal crisis within a year, reflecting an internal tension between a plan-led growth strategy espoused by the new Department of Economic Affairs and the Treasury's traditional deflationary strategy (Morgan 1980: 15).

But there were major changes nonetheless. In 1966 the much-criticised development districts were replaced by five large development areas covering 40 per cent of the area and 20 per cent of the population, embracing the then fashionable growth pole principle. Regional development strategies were prepared by new Regional Economic Planning Councils and Boards, set up by the Department of Economic Affairs. And regional aid was massively boosted from £22 million in 1962–3 to £324 million in 1969–70 (at constant 1970–1 prices). The threshold triggering IDC controls was lowered and enforced more strictly.

Importantly, for the first time the government tried to extend control from manufacturing to service industry, notably offices. The Conservative government in 1963 had established a Location of Offices Bureau (LOB) to encourage decentralisation of employment from London; during 1963–79 2,000 office firms and about 160,000 jobs left London, but 75 per cent went to the outer South East. The Control of Offices and Industrial Development Act 1965 introduced Office Development Permits for developments above 5,000 square feet in the London area, later extended to all of the South East, East Anglia, and the West and East Midlands. The government also relocated 55,000 Civil Service jobs between 1963 and 1975. In 1966 selective employment tax came in, payable by employers in the service industries, and a selective employment premium and regional employment premium for each worker employed in manufacturing in the development areas. (These were abolished by the new Conservative government in 1970, though they continued to pay regional employment premium over a seven-year term.) In 1967, special development areas were established in Scotland, the North East, West Cumberland and Wales, enjoying additional incentives, rent-free premises, percentage building grants and some operating subsidies. And in the 1970 Local Employment Act, the government accepted a recommendation for seven Intermediate Areas eligible for government-built factories, building grants and derelict land clearance grants. By then, fully one half of the area and population of the UK was regionally aided.

In 1973 the UK made its long-delayed entry into the European Economic Community, later the European Union. Henceforth, the assisted areas would have access to European financial aid. Two years later, the European Regional Development Fund was established specifically for this purpose; each member state was guaranteed a predetermined share. But the UK had to meet EEC competition policy criteria, limiting subsidies in regions like the UK Intermediate Areas and questioning the legality of direct employment subsidies like the regional employment premium, which duly came to an end in 1977.

The shift to urban policy

The incoming Labour government of 1974 made a major innovation in 1975–6 with the establishment of Scottish and Welsh Development Agencies. The SDA, in particular, received major powers to invest in industry, create new companies, provide finance and advice for industry, build and manage industrial estates, lease or sell factories, reclaim derelict land and rehabilitate the environment. This in effect gave Scotland a privileged position in relation to the peripheral English regions. Almost simultaneously, the Scottish Office abandoned a proposed new town (Stonehouse), diverting funds to a new Glasgow Eastern Area Renewal scheme (GEAR) – a model for a much wider policy shift to follow.

This reflected shifting economic reality. The "Long Boom" ended in 1973: everywhere, manufacturing employment was shrinking, and growth in services was failing to compensate, so that unemployment rose from under 2 per cent in 1966 to an average of 6 per cent in 1978–9 and to over 12 per cent by 1982 – a total of 3 million. This affected not merely the traditional assisted areas, but also regions previously thought immune: London's employment fell by 10.8 per cent, and by 30.8 per cent in manufacturing, between mid-1974 and mid-1982; the West Midlands lost a seventh of total employment and a third of manufacturing employment, and by 1976 was already recording unemployment above the national average. In these conditions, it was no longer possible to entertain a strategy of diverting industrial investment from prosperous to less-prosperous regions. David Keeble concluded that regional policy "had ceased by 1976 to exert a measurable impact on the geography of manufacturing employment change in Britain" (Keeble 1980: 955).

This precise point marked a profound policy shift: from regional policy to urban policy, signalled by the 1977 White Paper *Policy for the Inner Cities* and the 1978 Inner Urban Areas Act and representing the most important single decisive break in British regional/urban policy over this 50-year story. Expenditure on the Urban Programme was dramatically increased, from £30 million to £165 million a year; and a total of 7 partnership authorities, 15 programme areas and 14 "other" districts were designated, plus 5 "other" areas in Wales. Each had powers to provide 90 per cent loans for land acquisition and site preparation, to make loans or award grants to cooperative or common ownership enterprises, and to declare industrial improvement areas, within which grants could be awarded for improvement or conversion of old industrial or commercial property. In Scotland the arrangements were different, with the Scottish Development Agency financing GEAR.

But there was still a regional bias: in England, out of 41 designated urban areas, only 8 were in the south, all in London. Thus, regional policy was increasingly transmitted via inner-city rather than traditional regional support, and through DoE rather than DTI spending. But there remained a cumbrous divided responsibility between the DTI, which kept responsibility for IDCs and grants, and the DoE, which had charge of infrastructure and planning machinery plus housing, transport and local government, and of the new programme expenditure; the two appeared to be competing rather than complementary (Regional Studies Association 1983: 11).

Almost from the start in 1979, Margaret Thatcher further attacked traditional regional policy: regional aid was cut from £842 million in 1979 to £540 million in 1983 (at 1980 prices); regional development grants were reduced or restricted; the assisted areas were cut back from 44 to 27.5 per cent of the population; Office Development Permits were abolished, and Industrial Development Certificate controls were first eased and then (in 1982) abandoned; selective financial assistance was retained but was to be provided only where necessary for a project to proceed; and the Regional Economic Planning Councils were abolished.

Meanwhile unemployment was rising ominously, a product of recession but also continuing de-industrialisation in 1979–84, from 4.9 to 11.7 per cent nationally, 7.9 to 16.3 per cent in the Northern region, and 6.1 to 14.7 per cent in the North West. Thatcher's answer was to go even further, slashing regional aid by almost half, from £700 million to £400 million, abolishing special development areas and cutting development areas back from 22 to 15 per cent of the working population, and limiting regional development grants before abolishing them entirely in 1988. Regional policy expenditure, as a percentage of GDP, fell by three-quarters between 1970 and 1984 (Balchin 1989: 74); ironically, the savings were more than exceeded by increased expenditure on unemployment pay and other welfare payments.

All this was ideological – highly so. But it also reflected shifts in economic reality in the 1980s, underlined by recession in the early years of the decade.

First, there was a dawning acceptance that the basis of traditional policy had gone with the disappearance of manufacturing. Shifting industrial employment around was no longer an option; the challenge was now to develop the capacity for indigenous regional growth: encouraging new firm formation, helping small firms to grow, and encouraging firms to adopt new technology (Martin 1988: 28; Regional Studies Association 1983: 11; Taylor 1992: 292). But there were two problems: first, many small firms stay small or go out of business; second, many of the new dynamic firms are in the South, where the preconditions (wealth, a well-educated workforce, a tradition of small firms, developed business services, easy access to venture capital and growth of the labour force through migration) are present. New firm formation was overwhelmingly in the rural South, not in traditional industrial areas (Keeble 1997: 995).

Second, regional policy increasingly shifted from London to Brussels. By 1993/4 UK expenditure on regional industrial policy had fallen to £287 million, a quarter of the early 1980s level, while between 1994 and 1996 the UK's share of the EU's targeted regional funds totalled £980 million per year, increasing to £1,115 million if the funding of Community initiatives is added (Lloyd 1996: 61). During this time, however, there were major changes in the way this aid was awarded, culminating in 1989 when the European Regional Development Fund (ERDF) was reoriented to the Single Market ("1992") process: regional policy funds were doubled in real terms, but were henceforth allocated according to three specific policy objectives: Objective 1 (development of regions which are structurally backward); Objective 2 (the conversion of regions in industrial decline); and Objective 5B (rural areas). The 1992 Maastricht Treaty added a new Cohesion Fund to help member states with particularly serious regional problems (Armstrong and Taylor 1993: 372).

Third, during this period Thatcher continued the previous policy of diverting funds from regional to urban aid, recognising that economic decline was concentrated in the inner cities – and also, doubtless, that in any event regional aid was flowing from Brussels. But she introduced two radical institutional innovations. Urban Development Corporations were created first (in 1981) in the London and Merseyside Docklands, then (in 1987) in Trafford Park, Sandwell, Teesside, Tyneside and Cardiff Bay and then (in 1988) in Bristol, Leeds and Central Manchester, with powers to reclaim land and provide infrastructure, renovate old buildings and provide new factories. The idea was to use public money as a way of leveraging in (an American term) private investment, but the effect proved variable: by 1987 the London Docklands Development Corporation had spent £500 million to attract over £2 billion of private funds, but its Merseyside equivalent had spent £140 million to attract £20 million. Generally, UDCs failed to reduce local unemployment, and the new jobs tended to be filled by newcomers. Second, enterprise zones (EZs) were created with a simplified planning procedure; an exemption from all rates on commercial and industrial buildings for ten years from declaration; a 100 per cent first-year depreciation allowance on commercial and industrial buildings; a major reduction in government requests for statistical information; and exemption from IDC control, which however became irrelevant from 1982 when Industrial Development Certificates were abolished. By 1981, 13 EZs had been declared; a further 14 were added in 1984, but not all were in the inner cities, while all but two were in the North. They were attacked for being ineffective. Nonetheless, Thatcher pressed on with a related reform: in 1984, six freeports – enclosed zones, outside the UK customs area – were designated at various airport and dockland sites in the UK; customs duties would only be paid when goods left the freeport for the UK or EC.

Over this decade, though there was a big increase in Urban Programme spending – £165 million in 1979–80, £302 million in 1987–8 – there were corresponding cuts in grants to local authorities. The main stress was on programmes that bypassed local authorities altogether (Balchin 1989: 92). All this reflected the fundamental shift in economic geography from a regional distinction, North–South, toward an urban distinction, cities–suburbs–countryside. Regional policy proved less and less effective. The new reality everywhere was the loss of manufacturing jobs – over 3.1 million (40 per cent) in 1966–83 – and the growth of service jobs. This was bound to affect the North disproportionately, because it had more manufacturing jobs to start with, while service industry had always been highly concentrated in the South East. During 1979–87, the South increased its share from 47.5 to 48.7 per cent; the North West and Wales recorded absolute losses in services. Two service groups – distribution, hotels and catering, and business and financial services – are particularly strong in the South East. But there was a corresponding urban effect: the top 20 fastest-growing towns, except Aberdeen, were in the South East, the South West and East Anglia (Balchin 1989: 12).

Finally, therefore, de-industrialisation, "tertiarisation" and technological innovation have produced a new and more complex economic geography: job losses have been most serious in the big industrial conurbations, including London, the West Midlands, Greater Manchester and Merseyside, which suffered massive de-industrialisation and failed to compensate fully through services, while dispersal has continued to the semi-rural areas of the outer South East, East Anglia, the South West and parts of the East Midlands, assisted by better communications. Thus there are some prosperous parts of the North – the so-called "northern lights" – and non-prosperous parts of the South; terms like "core" and "periphery" no longer have a simple meaning. The North–South dividing line now runs from the Severn to the Wash, and there are only four prosperous regions; the "North" has spread south, and parts of London are really part of the North (Balchin 1989: 101; Damesick 1987: 23; Law 1980: 225–31; Martin 1988: 29–34).

There were, however, some continuing regional differences. Overseas inward investment is very strongly concentrated in the South East (Law 1980: 149). And command and control – the "centre of gravity" of firms – is concentrated here; here key decisions were made to open or close branch plants in the peripheral areas (Fothergill and Guy 1990: 170). The South benefits from access to the wealthiest markets, and from skilled labour plus suitable premises (Law 1980: 203).

But London is a special case. It lost manufacturing jobs faster, and gained service jobs more slowly, than the UK as a whole. Between 1960 and 1985 its manufacturing workforce halved, while most kinds of service employment also contracted, finance and business services excepted. London by the 1980s had the highest concentration of unemployment in the advanced industrial world, heavily concentrated in a few boroughs, and including a substantial proportion – 41.6 per cent in 1987 – of long-term unemployed. And these included not only older workers, but large numbers in the 15–24 group, who appeared to lack the necessary qualifications to enter London's highly sophisticated service economy (Balchin 1989: 110–11, 120–2).

Evaluating regional policy

During the 1960s and 1970s, there were several major attempts by economists to quantify the outcomes of UK regional policy. A. J. Brown estimated that the four high-unemployment regions improved their regional growth of employment in manufacturing, mining and agriculture, apart from structural components, in relation to the rest of the country by about 28,000 a year between 1953–9 and 1961–6 (Brown 1972: 317–18). Moore and Rhodes calculated that between 1960 and 1981 regional policy created 604,000 manufacturing jobs in the development areas, averaging almost 29,000 per annum; some 154,000, about one-quarter, were lost before 1981, leaving some 450,000 surviving jobs. A further 180,000 jobs might have been generated in service industries, giving a total of 630,000 surviving jobs in 1981. Almost half this net gain had occurred in the 1970s. The most effective instrument was the IDC, because it did not involve significant Exchequer expenditure; the regional employment premium was by far the least effective. The average Exchequer cost of each new job was some £42,000 at 1982 prices (Moore *et al.* 1986: 9–11).

Earlier Rhodes concluded that office decentralisation policies had proved successful because they reinforced market forces: an office moving out of London could expect to enjoy up to 20 per cent reduction in operating costs. But most movement had been within the South East region; of the recorded 70,000 office jobs decentralised from Central London between 1963 and 1970, only 1 per cent had gone to the development areas. To increase longer-distance moves the government would need to offer substantial incentives, though the cost would be quite small, since it would apply only to jobs created (Rhodes and Kan 1971: 98–101).

Thus, regional policy in its heyday was effective in moving inward investment into the development areas, and this investment generated substantial numbers of jobs. But it failed to create self-sustaining growth in the assisted areas (Law 1980: 232). This was still the dilemma in the 1990s, and it also was the conclusion of Gordon Cameron, who in the mid-1970s argued:

> while there is no doubt that policy did have substantial success during the sixties, especially in terms of extra employment created in the Development Areas, the task remains dauntingly large . . . In particular, far greater effort will have to be given to encouraging that part of the private service sector which is not tied to local consumption requirements to locate or to expand in the Development Areas.
>
> (Cameron 1974: 65)

Strategic planning

There have been two strong periods of regional strategic planning since 1940: the late-wartime and immediate post-war period; and the 1960s, running on into the early 1970s in Scotland. The early twenty-first century may well prove to represent the beginning of a third.

The 1940s

In the first period, a series of plans that have now achieved classic status – Abercrombie for Greater London, Abercrombie and Matthew for the Clyde Valley, Abercrombie and Jackson for the West Midlands – sought simultaneously to provide for the post-war reconstruction of outworn and often war-destroyed cities, and for orderly decentralisation to new and expanded towns (Abercrombie 1945; Abercrombie and Matthew 1946; Abercrombie and Jackson 1948). The general strategic approach was remarkably similar in all, reflecting the personality of their author: an incisive survey and analysis of the key problems – economic, social, physical – followed by a sweeping physical design, often expressed in a very strong, almost cartoon-like way. This design can be seen to have roots as far back as Abercrombie's prize-winning Dublin Plan, prepared in 1914 but finalised only after the First World War: it included inner reconstruction, urban growth limits through a green belt, and self-contained new towns or town expansions following the basic garden city principle as enunciated by Ebenezer Howard and developed by Raymond Unwin (Howard 2003 [1898]; Unwin 1912).

Abercrombie's Greater London Plan is still one of the most powerful and influential strategic plans ever conceived. Based on a belief that effective industrial location controls were possible, and on demographic projections suggesting national population growth would be negligible, Abercrombie assumed that the population of the London region could be held constant. His plan proposed massive decentralisation of people from the inner, congested part of this region to the outer rings: 600,000 from slum and blighted areas in Inner London (the old London County Council area), another 400,000 from Outer London, over 1 million in all. To end urban sprawl, a green belt would be thrown around Greater London, enclosing the built-up area of 1939; five miles wide on average, it would serve as a valuable recreational tract. Beyond that, new communities would be built to receive the overspill; because they would be beyond the then commuting range, they would be self-contained communities for living and working, the dream of garden city enthusiasts since Howard. About 400,000 people would be housed in eight more or less completely new towns averaging 50,000 people, between 20 and 35 miles from London; another 600,000 would go to expansions of existing small country towns, mainly 30–50 miles from London, some more distant.

Similar wide-ranging regional plans were prepared for the other major British conurbations: Abercrombie prepared two in collaboration, one for Glasgow and one (jointly) for the West Midlands (Abercrombie and Matthew 1946; Abercrombie and Jackson 1948). All made similarly radical proposals for planned urban decentralisation on garden city lines, though nowhere else was the geographical scale as extensive as in London. They required a new administrative organisation, proposed by a committee headed by former BBC Director John Reith (Ministry of Town and Country Planning 1946): new towns, typically with a size range of 30,000 to 50,000 or 60,000, should each be built by a Development Corporation, responsible to Parliament, but free of detailed day-to-day interference, with direct Treasury funding.

In Scotland, Abercrombie's Clyde Valley Plan was realised through new towns at East Kilbride, just south west of Glasgow, and at Cumbernauld, a little farther out to the east. The latter was the only new town designated in Britain between 1951 and 1961, reflecting the power of the Scottish Office. Even then, as Urlan Wannop's study shows, the Office was unable completely to stop Glasgow's invasions of the green belt through its huge peripheral estates, driven by the pressing need to clear the city's slums after clearance began again in earnest in the mid-1950s (Wannop 1995: 118).

The 1960s and 1970s

The 1960s brought the sudden realisation that, contrary to earlier demographic forecasts, Britain's population was increasing rapidly through an upsurge in births. *The South East Study*, published in 1964, caused surprise and even controversy: it concluded that, even with measures to restrain growth in the London region, the pressures for expansion made it necessary to house a further 3.5 million people during the 20 years 1961–81 (Ministry of Housing and Local Government 1964). This growth came not from the much publicised "drift south" from the North and Scotland, but from natural increase, Commonwealth immigration and movement of retired people to South Coast resorts. To accommodate it, the report recommended a second round of new towns for London farther out than the first round, outside London's commuter range: Milton Keynes, 49 miles (80 kilometres) from London, Northampton, 70 miles (110 kilometres) out, Peterborough, 81 miles (130 kilometres) distant, and Southampton–Portsmouth, 77 miles (120 kilometres) from London, were among the key projects which finally went ahead in one form or another. Significantly, only Milton Keynes among these was a greenfield new town on the old model, albeit with a bigger population target than any previously designated town; the others represented a new departure in being new towns attached to major existing towns or cities. To cope with the development nearer London which might still depend to some degree on commuting, the *Study* was much less clear; this, it implied, was a matter for local planners.

In 1965, further regional studies, produced in the same way by official ad hoc teams, appeared for two other major urban regions: the West Midlands and the North West. Recognising the challenge of population growth and the continuing slum clearance programme, they concluded that provision must be made for planned overspill on an enhanced scale – even though the North West was experiencing net out-migration. To accommodate it, the reports called for an accelerated new towns programme, though neither region had received any new towns before 1961. By 1965 two new towns had already been designated in the Midlands: Dawley (1963) and Redditch (1964); later (1968), as the result of the *Study*'s conclusions, Dawley was further expanded and renamed Telford. In the North West, Skelmersdale (1961) and Runcorn (1964) had been established for Merseyside overspill; the report suggested similar developments· for Manchester, and this was eventually met by new towns at Warrington (1968) and Central Lancashire (1970). In Central Scotland, further overspill pressures from Central Clydeside (Greater Glasgow) resulted in the designation of Livingston (1962) and Irvine (1966). Finally, south of Newcastle the new town of Washington (1964) was created to receive overspill from Tyneside and Wearside. Thus, in addition to the new towns for London, the major provincial conurbations had no fewer than nine new towns designated between 1961 and 1970 to house overspill problems. Like Northampton and Peterborough, several – notably Warrington and Central Lancashire – attached a new town to an old-established older town possessing a full range of urban services.

These reports of 1963–5 mark an important stage in the evolution of British post-war planning. They recognised that population growth – even in regions of continued out-migration – demanded bold regional strategies, covering wide areas around the conurbations, and extending in some cases to the limits of the economic planning region. Essentially, they applied to these regions the old Howard–Abercrombie formula: planned decentralisation, green belt restrictions, and new communities outside commuting range. They were physical plans in a traditional British mould.

These regional reports were the work of ad hoc teams of central government officials – a reflection of the very high level of professional capacity then found in the old Ministry of Housing and Local Government. They had to be: local government was not structured for the task, though in the South East planning authorities had cooperated to set up a Standing Conference on London and South East Regional Planning. But during 1965–6 the gap was partially filled by the new Regional Economic Planning Councils and Boards. Originally created to develop French-style economic development planning, they found themselves immersed in spatial planning for city regions. In a development area like the North East of England it was impossible to produce a development strategy without a physical component – main roads, major new industrial areas and associated housing schemes, ports and airports. In the prosperous and rapidly growing areas like the South East or the West Midlands, economic planning would require physical planning to control and guide the directions of expansion. Thus, the councils and boards found themselves heavily involved with the internal disposition of investment within their regions – in other words, spatial planning.

This came to a head in the South East Planning Council's report of November 1967, which recommended a development strategy based on broad corridors following the radial transportation lines from London (South East Economic Planning Council 1967). The report ran into predictable opposition from the Regional Standing Conference of local authorities, which argued that spatial planning was their prerogative. In 1968 the government resolved the problem for the South East: another ad hoc team was set up, including both central and local government officials and commissioned jointly by the Standing Conference and the Planning Council. The outcome was the 1970 Strategic Plan for the South East, which evaluated two alternative strategies – one the Planning Council's, the other from the Standing Conference – and emerged with a third, based on a number of large multi-centred growth areas of between 0.5 million and 1.5 million people at varying distances from London (South East Joint Planning Team 1970). This was accepted by central and local government as a framework for regional development. By 1971, the same formula was being applied again to another heavily urbanised region, the North West.

Such a new scale of planning, for broadly based city regions that might even approximate to entire economic planning regions, logically suggested a new scale of regional or provincial government. In 1969 a Royal Commission on Local Government for England, under Sir John Redcliffe Maud (later Lord Redcliffe Maud), recommended reorganisation based on city regions (Royal Commission on Local Government in England 1969). Efficiency suggested a large average size of unit; effectiveness and respect for community demanded the same units for all services; planning needed rather large units. The Commission's answer was unitary authorities capable of running all local services for England, except for the three biggest conurbations, Greater Manchester, Merseyside and the West Midlands, which would have a two-tier structure: a metropolitan authority for strategic physical and transport planning, plus metropolitan districts for the more personal services – the structure already adopted in the 1963 Act for London. In 1970 a Labour government accepted this, but in 1971 the Conservative government replaced the English proposals by a two-tier system based on the existing county structure plus amalgamations of existing county district authorities. In the conurbations it retained the metropolitan principle, and extended it to West and South Yorkshire, but cut back the boundaries, thus ignoring the city region principle.

This reorganisation was in many ways a second-best solution that failed to recognise the realities of contemporary urban geography, and created powerful, often contraposed, planning bureaucracies. It precluded further fundamental reorganisation for many years. During the 1990s, another Conservative government carried through a piecemeal tinkering that resulted in a strange patchwork quilt of local government, with larger cities and towns breaking away as all-purpose unitary authorities (as with the old County Boroughs before 1972–4), the abolition of two 1970s counties (Avon and Cleveland), and even the dismemberment of the Royal County of Berkshire. The effect was to make it almost impossible to use local government as an agent of strategic planning. But this might have required much larger units than even Redcliffe Maud were willing to contemplate. Their report had recommended a structure of provincial units for England, above the unitary and metropolitan authorities, for just this purpose; but nothing came of it.

In Scotland a separate Royal Commission recommended a different structure of local government based on very broadly defined regional councils, and this was duly enacted (Royal Commission on Local Government in Scotland 1969). At its very inception Strathclyde, the most populous of these new units, was the object of one of the most ambitious regional strategic plans ever undertaken in Britain. This, the West Central Scotland Plan of 1974, was successfully implemented – because the Strathclyde Regional Council was just coming into existence. Wannop's account shows that the Plan was drawn up in the confident expectation of the new structure, which gave Scotland a 20-year experiment in effective regional governance that was unique in the UK until a Conservative government inexplicably abolished it in the 1990s. And, as Wannop reminds us, Strathclyde and its equivalents were doubly unique, because – unlike the equivalent English Metropolitan County Councils – they were responsible for a huge range of services, from strategic planning to social work, and from public transport and roads to education, police and fire. That meant that these policies – both those directly relevant to planning, like transport, and those less directly related, like social services and education – were coordinated within one authority (Wannop 1995: 126–7).

Ironically, the Strathclyde Council used these powers to follow a policy that was directly contrary to that of the 1946 Plan: it persuaded the Scottish Office, against its better judgement, to abandon plans for a new town at Stonehouse and divert the funds into the Glasgow Eastern Area Renewal project, and it did so largely by refusing to support the infrastructure necessary for the new town's existence. This might be called the belated triumph of Glasgow over the spirit of Abercrombie, but that would be unfair: as already seen, there was a major shift of policy across the UK, out of planned deconcentration and into urban regeneration, reflecting the new realities of massive de-industrialisation and inner-city decay that dominated from the mid-1970s. The point is that, as in the post-1946 era, there was a strategic plan and there was a mechanism to achieve that plan, limited only by the resources that central government could supply.

The 1980s: strategic planning officially pronounced dead

But that again made Scotland special. Some time after 1979 the Thatcher government famously declared that there had been a "heyday of a certain fashion for strategic planning, the confidence in which now appears exaggerated" (Secretary of State 1983: 2). Strategic planning was thus officially declared dead. So it was perhaps remarkable that in the later stages of Mrs Thatcher's administration, from 1987 onward, there developed a remarkably effective system of regional advice from Regional Standing Conferences of local planning authorities followed by regional guidance from government, fortified in 1994 by the establishment of Government Offices in each region which took over responsibility for producing the regional guidance. In effect, though under Conservative governments the word could never be used, this was a system of regional physical planning, effective in handling the politically delicate matter of housing allocations, though less so in developing the bold approaches characterised by the 1970 Strategic Plan and similar exercises in other regions.

The John Major government did two other things, one massively unhelpful to the cause of strategic regional planning, the other potentially helpful: it instituted a piecemeal reform of English local government which left a chaotic patchwork quilt of two-tier county and district councils punctured by all-purpose unitary councils, and perversely abolished the highly successful Scottish Regional Councils; but it did create English Partnerships, the "roving Development Corporation" recommended by Michael Heseltine as a way of continuing the work of the Urban Development Corporations on a more flexible basis.

The 1990s: miraculous reincarnation

The incoming Labour administration, in 1997, at first intended to replace this system by one of directly elected regional authorities, but – with the sole exception of Greater London – this step was postponed until a second term of office. Instead, the government proceeded to create Regional Development Agencies, essentially to promote inward investment: a step which in many ways recalled the 1965 establishment of the Regional Economic Planning Councils, though – unlike them – the RDAs were provided with real funds and backed by the regionalisation of English Partnerships, to provide a kind of development arm, a major implementation agency for physical development, for their work.

The government also first proposed to give the Regional Standing Conferences "ownership" of regional planning guidance through a shared responsibility with the government regional offices, though it remained clear that it intended to reserve final powers of decision – for reasons that became clear when, for a time in 1998, the South East Regional Conference refused to accept the government's figures for housing provision contained in the government's own projections. Then, in its second (2001) term, it announced that these Standing Conferences (which went under various names in different English regions) would be transformed into regional planning bodies or "regional assemblies", with a strong local authority representation as well as outside experts, pending their democratic legitimation via referenda in each regions; the first three such referenda would be held in the three northern regions in 2004. But this step proved much more controversial than at first seemed possible: the government first scaled down the three to only one referendum, in the North East, but then – in November 2004 – lost this by a large margin, followed by abandonment of the entire idea, perhaps for a generation, perhaps for ever.

This created a looming and immediate problem of democratic legitimacy. For, in the 2004 Planning and Compulsory Purchase Act, the government had fundamentally reshaped the entire planning system, replacing county structure plans – a feature of the system ever since the late 1960s – by regional spatial strategies to be prepared by the new bodies. Indeed, these strategies were in active preparation at the time the North East referendum was lost (and as this chapter was being written).

For South East England, in particular, this creates a problem (see Chapter 13). For in 2003 – reacting again to a crisis of housing supply, as in the late 1940s and in the mid-1960s – the government launched a bold new strategic planning initiative: the Sustainable Communities strategy, with proposals to build hundreds of thousands of new houses in three major growth corridors radiating from London – Milton Keynes–South Midlands, London–Stansted–Cambridge and Thames Gateway – plus an outlier of the last at Ashford[3] (ODPM 2003). This proposal, which took shape in 2004 and was approved in broad outline by both the South East and East of England assemblies in late 2004, would then become embodied in regional spatial strategies, which would in turn be binding on district and unitary authorities as they prepared their local development frameworks.

In London, the Mayor's London Plan, issued in final and definitive form in early 2004 after examination in public, is thus the only regional spatial strategy produced by a body with true democratic legitimacy (Mayor of London 2004). Outside London, the equivalents are being prepared by assemblies which at best have only very partial legitimacy, and besides divide the Wider South East region arbitrarily in two (with parts even in a third, the East Midlands). There are parallel problems in the North of England, where the other half of the government's strategy, labelled the Northern Way, emerged in late 2004 as centred on the development of eight city regions: six of them contiguously clustered along the parallel axes of the M62 and M55/M65/A59 from Liverpool and Preston to York and Hull, and two others isolated in the North East (ODPM 2004) (see Chapters 14 and 15). These seem to suggest a parallel reorganisation of local government on a city region basis, reviving the Redcliffe Maud proposals of 35 years earlier, as a basis for a different kind of regional spatial strategy. But, as this chapter closes, it seems that nothing as specific as this may be intended: at most, the outcome may be elected mayors for the provincial conurbations on the

London model, who – again following that model – may try to steer development out of the favoured central business districts of the core cities into some of the less favoured locations in the old one-industry towns around them.

A concluding speculation: towards French-style *Aménagement du Territoire?*

Thus the conclusion has to be that British planning has never succeeded in integrating the concepts of regional policy and sub-regional planning into some wider and all-embracing planning concept resembling the French *Aménagement du Territoire*. The closest attempts came in the ill-fated National Plan of 1965 but after its failure all such attempts were scaled back and have never been resuscitated. Indeed, it would have required an integrated national and regional planning mechanism, actually created under the 1964 Wilson government but effectively abandoned in stages soon after. In particular, the traditional strength of the Treasury, as evident as ever 40 years later, would have made it unlikely that a rival structure could effectively operate for long.

The intriguing question in 2007 is the possible effect of European Union policy – in particular, the 1999 European Spatial Development Perspective (ESDP). Though not officially emanating from the Commission, which has no direct formal responsibility in the area, it has been agreed by member governments and it uses language derived from French planning experience, clearly mediated through French officials from DATAR (La Délégation à l'Aménagement du Territoire et à l'Action Régionale) (Faludi 2003: 130–1, 2004a: 160). Further, though the ESDP is non-binding on member states, in the UK the Office of the Deputy Prime Minister (ODPM) appears to have embodied key concepts in its 2003 Sustainable Communities strategy and the 2004 Planning and Compulsory Purchase Act. They include:

* the recognition of *spatial–economic imbalance* as a consequence of economic competitiveness, which should be combated;
* the notion (implicit in the ESDP itself, and only made specific subsequently) of promoting *territorial cohesion*, embodied in the Amsterdam Treaty by Michel Barnier when Commissioner for Regional Policy (Faludi 2004a: 161), with the aim of promoting spatial equity by maintaining key services, even in remote areas, in order to achieve a harmonious allocation of economic activities (Faludi 2004a: 159, quoting Chicoye 1992; Faludi 2003: 133);[4] and
* the promotion of *polycentric development* "to ensure regionally balanced development . . . to avoid further economic and demographic concentration in the core area of the EU" (EC 1999: para. 67), specifically "the pentagon defined by the metropolises of London, Paris, Milan, Munich and Hamburg" (EC 1999: para. 68), by developing:

> several dynamic zones of global economic integration, well distributed throughout the EU territory and comprising a network of internationally accessible metropolitan regions and their linked hinterland (towns, cities and rural areas of varying sizes) to improve spatial balance in Europe.
>
> (EC 1999: para. 70)

- As Davoudi points out, here polycentricity is regarded as a norm, despite lack of supporting evidence (Davoudi 2003: 991–5).

By signing up to the concept of "regional spatial strategies", embodied in the 2004 Planning and Compulsory Purchase Act, it appears that the UK government has accepted a French-style integrated regional planning that goes far beyond the traditional UK emphasis on land-use planning. What is far less clear, given that separate departmental structures are still strong in the UK government system, is how it is to be delivered. Possibly, the increasing emphasis on "regionalising" public expenditure through the Regional Development Agencies may provide the clue. But the devil as usual is in the details, and some well-publicised decisions, notably the Department for Transport's failure to fund light rail schemes viewed as essential for regeneration in Manchester, Liverpool and Leeds, suggest that integration will prove hard to achieve.

Notes

1. This chapter is dedicated to the memory of John Barry Cullingworth, who made such significant academic contributions to the subject, and who died just as the final draft was being completed.
2. The argument in this half of the chapter essentially summarises the more detailed historical treatment in the earlier contribution to the definitive symposium edited by John Barry Cullingworth (Cullingworth 1999).
3. This strategy rather uncannily resembles parts of the South East Economic Planning Council's 1967 *Strategy for the South East*, except that it omits all the southern and western corridors and adds a new one, up the M11.
4. Territorial cohesion appeared in Article 3 of the ill-starred EU Constitution on a par with economic and social cohesion, as a competence shared between the Commission and the member states through the "community method" (Faludi 2004b: 1019, 2005: 2).

References

Abercrombie, P. 1945. *Greater London Plan 1944*. London: HMSO.

Abercrombie, P. and R. H. Matthew 1946. *The Clyde Valley Regional Plan, 1946: a report prepared for the Clyde Valley Regional Planning Committee*. Edinburgh: HMSO.

Abercrombie, P. and H. Jackson 1948. *West Midlands Plan*, Interim confidential edn, 5 vols (mimeo). London: Ministry of Town and Country Planning.

Armstrong, H. and J. Taylor 1993. *Regional economics and policy*, 2nd edn. New York: Harvester Wheatsheaf.

Balchin, P. N. 1989. *Regional policy in Britain: the North–South divide*. London: Paul Chapman.

Brown, A. J. 1972. *The framework of regional economics in the United Kingdom*. Economic and Social Studies 27. Cambridge: Cambridge University Press.

Cameron, G. C. 1974. Regional economic policy in the United Kingdom. In *Public policy and regional economic development: the experience of nine Western countries*, N. M. Hansen (ed.), 65–102. Cambridge: Ballinger.

Cullingworth, J. B. (ed.) 1999. *British planning: 50 years of urban and regional policy*, 76–90. London: Athlone.

Damesick, P. J. 1987. Regional economic change since the 1960s. In *Regional problems, problem regions and public policy in the United Kingdom*, P. J. Damesick and P. A. Wood (eds), 19–42. Oxford: Clarendon Press.

Davoudi, S. 2003. Polycentricity in European spatial planning: from an analytical tool to a normative agenda. *European Planning Studies* **11**, 979–99.

EC 1999. *ESDP – European spatial development perspective: towards balanced and sustainable development of the territory of the European Union*. Brussels: European Commission.

Faludi, A. 2003. Unfinished business: European spatial planning in the 1990s. *Town Planning Review* **74**, 121–40.

Faludi, A. 2004a. Spatial planning traditions in Europe: their role in the ESDP process. *International Planning Studies* **9**, 155–72.

Faludi, A. 2004b. The open method of co-ordination and "post-regulatory" territorial cohesion policy. *European Planning Studies* **12**, 1019–33.

Faludi, A. 2005. Territorial cohesion: an unidentified political objective. *Town Planning Review* **76**, 1–13.

Fothergill, S. and N. Guy 1990. *Retreat from the regions: corporate change and the closure of factories*, Regional Policy and Development 1. London: Jessica Kingsley and Regional Studies Association.

Hall, P. 1999. The regional dimension. In *British planning: 50 years of urban and regional policy*, J. B. Cullingworth (ed.), 76–90. London: Athlone.

Howard, E. 2003 [1898]. *To-morrow: a peaceful path to real reform*, facsimile edn, with an editorial commentary by P. Hall, D. Hardy and C. Ward. London: Routledge.

Keeble, D. E. 1980. Industrial decline, regional policy, and the urban–rural manufacturing shift in the United Kingdom. *Environment and Planning A* **12**, 945–62.

Keeble, D. E. 1997. Small firms, innovation and regional development in Britain in the 1990s. *Regional Studies* **31**, 281–93.

Law, C. M. 1980. *British regional development since World War I*. Newton Abbot: David & Charles.

Lloyd, P. 1996. Contested governance: European exposure in the English regions. In *Regional development strategies: a European perspective*, J. Alden and P. Boland (eds), 55–85. Regional Policy and Development Series 15. London: Jessica Kingsley.

Luttrell, W. F. 1962. *Factory location and industrial movement: a study of recent experience in Great Britain*. London: National Institute of Economic and Social Research.

Martin, R. 1988. The new economics and politics of regional restructuring: the British experience. In *Regional policy at the crossroads: European perspectives*, L. Albrechts, F. Moulaert, P. Roberts and E. Swyngedouw (eds), 27–51. London: Jessica Kingsley.

Mayor of London 2004. *The London Plan: spatial development strategy for Greater London*. London: Greater London Authority.

Ministry of Housing and Local Government 1964. *The South East Study 1961–1981*. London: HMSO.

Ministry of Town and Country Planning 1946. *Interim Report of the New Towns Committee* (Cmd. 6759) (B.P.P., 1945–46, 14). London: HMSO.

Moore, B., J. Rhodes and P. Tyler 1986. *The effects of government regional economic policy*. London: HMSO.

Morgan, K. 1980. *The reformulation of the regional question, regional policy and the British state*. Urban and Regional Studies, Working Paper 18. Brighton: University of Sussex.

ODPM 2003. *Sustainable communities: building for the future*. London: Office of the Deputy Prime Minister.

ODPM 2004. *Making it happen: the Northern Way*. London: Office of the Deputy Prime Minister.

Regional Studies Association 1983. *Report of an inquiry into regional problems in the United Kingdom*. Norwich: Geo Books.

Rhodes, J. and A. Kan 1971. *Office dispersal and regional policy*, University of Cambridge,

Department of Applied Economics, Occasional Papers 30. Cambridge: Cambridge University Press.

Royal Commission on Local Government in England 1966–69 1969. *Report* (the Redcliffe Maud Report) (Cmnd 4040). London: HMSO.

Royal Commission on Local Government in Scotland 1966–69 1969. *Report* (the Wheatley Report) (Cmnd 4150). London: HMSO.

Secretary of State for the Environment 1983. *Streamlining the cities: government proposals for reorganising local government in Greater London and the metropolitan counties* (Cmnd 9063). London: HMSO.

South East Economic Planning Council 1967. *A strategy for the South East: a first report by the South East Planning Council*. London: HMSO.

South East Joint Planning Team 1970. *Strategic Plan for the South East: a framework report by the South East Joint Planning Team*. London: HMSO.

Taylor, J. 1992. Regional problems and policies: an overview. In *Regional development in the 1990s: the British Isles in transition*, P. Townroe and R. Martin (eds), 288–96. Regional Policy and Development Series 4. London: Jessica Kingsley.

Unwin, R. 1912. *Nothing gained by overcrowding! How the garden city type of development may benefit both owner and occupier*. London: P. S. King. Reprinted 1998 in R. LeGates and F. Stout, *Selected essays (early urban planning 1870–1940*, vol. I), n.p. London: Routledge.

Wannop, U. 1995. *The regional imperative: regional planning and governance in Britain, Europe and the United States*. Regional Policy and Development Series 9. London: Jessica Kingsley.

3 Regional institutions, governance and the planning system

Mark Tewdwr-Jones and Philip Allmendinger

Introduction

The (re-)emergence of the regional level of governance and planning within Britain has occurred partly by changes outside the UK, including the "hollowing out" of the nation state (Ohmae 1997), globalisation (Brenner 1999), changes in governance (Stoker 1990), resurgent national and regional identities (Keating 1997) and developments within the European Union. Policies aimed at creating a "Europe of the Regions" (Jonas and Ward 1999), together with proposals on spatial planning and the EU Structural Funds (Bachtler and Turok 1997) and inter-territorial cooperation at the regional level through the INTERREG III initiative and the European Spatial Development Perspective (ESDP) (EC 1991, 1994, 1999), have directly and indirectly promoted the regional level. Within Britain, changes in regional policy and governance have been a priority of the New Labour government since its election in 1997. A mass of constitutional reforms, including devolution to the Scottish Parliament, the Welsh Assembly and the Northern Ireland Assembly, the introduction of Regional Development Agencies (RDAs) and regional chambers, and the faltering introduction of elected regional assemblies within England, have all added an impetus to the more modest institutional changes towards enhanced regional planning introduced under the Major governments between 1990 and 1997, as explained in the previous chapter.

The political determination to enhance regional competitiveness and bolster regional economic growth drove the push towards this institutional restructuring, but the degree to which particular regions could become successful is dependent not only on the existence of advantageous physical assets or resources, but also on "the emergence of socially and institutionally mediated forms of selective co-operation between actors" (Raco 1999: 951). These networks of institutions conform to the emerging structures of regional planning and policy that the government's various approaches seek to modify. However, as Amin and Thrift point out, "It should be remembered that institutional thickness is not always a boon as it can produce resistance to change as well as an innovative outlook" (1995: 103). The individual characteristics of a region may therefore shape or impact upon the degree to which regions becomes more competitive. Di Maggio (1993) classifies networks as structural (spatially concentrated and resistant to change), strategic (less spatially concentrated and more open to change), and cognitive-aesthetic (not spatially concentrated and fluid). For planning purposes, regions are likely to fall into the first two of these categories, as there is undoubtedly an element of spatial concentration by definition. This does not, however, exclude other forms of institutional networks from simultaneously existing. Consequently, it cannot be guaranteed that existing networks will automatically embrace new forms of regional initiatives despite their general welcome; a good example of this scepticism was found in the North East of England in November 2004, where the public voted overwhelmingly against the establishment of a regional assembly in a referendum, and thereby frustrated not only regional institutional accountability in the North East but the government's final phase of English regionalisation. Of critical importance in the success of new regional planning and governance mechanisms in integrating with existing regional institutions and networks, therefore, will be the attitude and dispositions of those currently involved in regional policy making and those members of the public who interact with policy-making institutional structures.

This chapter seeks to explore the evolving nature of regional planning and governance across the UK. The renewed emphasis upon regional planning, or strategic planning as Peter Hall calls it in Chapter 2, has produced a new impetus and direction for planning after the antipathy of the 1980s and 1990s. Yet this resurgence should not be taken as an uncritical endorsement of planning by the Labour government. The emphasis in change is as much on delivery of central policy objectives (especially economic competitiveness and growth) as feeding resurgent identities and cultural affiliations. As a consequence, regional planning is "on trial". This requires an even greater need to "get it right" on the part of new and evolving institutions and practices.

As we hope to demonstrate, while widely welcomed the impact of these new regional arrangements is likely to be thwarted by the complexity and large degree of change involved.

The rescaling of regional governance and planning

The institutional restructuring processes under way since 1997 have directly affected the role of planning and its relationship with economic development within the regional agenda. There is, for the most part, a consensus that the emphasis on regional planning and policy has been welcomed by academics (see, for example, Roberts 1996; Roberts and Lloyd 1999; Mawson 1997; Baker 1998; Goodstadt and U'ren 1999; Murdoch and Tewdwr-Jones 1999; Hayton 1997), regional stakeholders (CBI 1997; BCC 1997; TEC National Council 1997) and others (TCPA 1997; CPRE 1994), but a number of questions remain unanswered. Such questions revolve around, for example, the ability of these proposed arrangements to integrate with existing institutional networks that evolved during the "fallow period" of regional planning (Baker 1998), and the extent to which the new governance and policy-making processes do offer something relatively different and workable.

Yet there is also a debate about how "new" these arrangements are. Those with experience of previous incarnations of regional planning (there are some still around!) see the regions once again taking their rightful place in the spatial hierarchy of planning. However, such views tend to underplay significant differences. There is a tendency to confuse regional *policy* and regional *planning* (as explained in Chapter 2). The rebirth of the region as a level of planning is about economic competitiveness and growth but within a neo-liberal framework of supporting the market rather than supplanting it. There is also the addition of the prefix "spatial" to planning. As pointed out in Chapter 1, spatial planning involves integration and coordination across different spatial scales and institutional and sectoral boundaries. The nature of government that dominated regional planning in the 1960s (referred to by some as the "command and control" understanding of government) has been replaced by fragmented governance. Government requires the coordination and integration of a range of public and private bodies, and planning (at the regional and local level) has been given a primary role as the spatial expression of this co-regulatory environment.

Enough is now known about Regional Development Agencies and the varying experiences of the devolved administrations to lead some to conclude that issues such as the future scale of governance and the spatial policy dimension of the state (Jones and MacLeod 1999; MacLeod and Goodwin 1999) and accountability and coordination remain potential problems (Baker *et al.* 1999; Roberts and Lloyd 1999; Murdoch and Tewdwr-Jones 1999). In the context of increasing government modernisation, a fragmented public sector attempting to work to private sector efficiency alongside the continued centralisation of power, and the confusion caused by "institutional congestion" of the ad hoc bottom-up arrangements currently in place, together with the lack of direct accountability, some commentators have already gone as far as to call the changes in England a "missed opportunity" (Mawson 1997). Nevertheless, the evolving forms of governance have released "a real tide of imagination and optimism . . . to plan the development path of this small nation" (Hague 1990: 296). What we are witnessing is either sets of teething problems – inevitably perhaps with any new process of governance – or the apparent disappointment caused by heightened expectations of radical changes to the way Britain is governed.

The shift in institutional relations and policy processes is certainly welcome as being a vast improvement on the situation during the Thatcher years. There is a possibility that the new arrangements for economic and land-use regional planning and regional governance will be embraced as a relative rather than absolute advance. There remains heated debate as to whether the creation of new regional institutions alone is able to generate successful economic strategies for the English regions similar to the regional "success stories" in other parts of the European Union (cf. Cooke and Morgan 1998; Lovering 1999) without a deeper consideration of and sensitivity to "path-dependent regional economic and political geographies" (Jones and MacLeod 1999). More fundamentally, questions emerge on the scale of this new regional level of governance and its relationship to the existing national and local levels of governance, including whether the regional level is the most appropriate spatial scale to "solve" wider policy concerns in the country, if indeed that is one of the premises of the new arrangements.

The ongoing changes to regional planning and governance, meanwhile, have been examined from a number of different perspectives, with the emphasis being largely on England. However, one missing element in such analyses has been the fusion of existing and evolving regional institutions and procedures across the three nations of Britain. Of critical importance to the success of evolving forms of land-use and economic planning and new governance are the attitude and cooperation of existing agencies, or "stakeholders" in New Labour terminology, institutions and policy networks that evolved during the 1980s and 1990s. As institutional and network theory demonstrates, there are important and powerful existing interests that have the ability to facilitate or thwart the new regional policy initiatives.

Regional planning, policy making and governance before 1997

The push towards regional governance

Regional planning in England, Scotland and Wales was, to all intents and purposes, suppressed under the market-orientated ethos of the Thatcher years. Strategic and regional planning was viewed by the government at the time as an unnecessary bureaucratic tier, and this attitude reached its peak when the Conservatives proposed the abolition of structure plans in 1989 (DoE 1989). The market orientation had an impact upon attitudes towards planning and the ability of planners and others to coordinate change, with the result that planning, urban regeneration and economic development issues were tackled at the local level through a combination of central government-imposed project-led development and financial incentives. This led to a more site-specific approach to planning (if it could be termed "planning" at all) but it was the less direct changes associated with the changing nature of government and the decline of the welfare state that made regional planning increasingly difficult. Privatisation of public utilities such as telecommunications, electricity and water, and transport agencies, the establishment of numerous agencies on a semi-commercial footing such as health boards and trusts, the creation of new quangos charged with the provision of public services, and the increased centralisation of power to Westminster all led to fragmentation of strategic coordination amongst a disparate group of "providers", with the responsibility for services divided between different public and private bodies at the strategic level (Hayton 1997; TCPA 1997; Mawson 1997). A further round of local government reorganisation in all three nations in 1986 (of the metropolitan counties) and again in 1996 (with a slide towards unitary authorities) led to the abolition of the two-tier system throughout Scotland and Wales and in some parts of England (Clotworthy and Harris 1996).

The reaction to this perceived strategic policy vacuum was the emergence of "bottom-up" forms of regional coordination and planning, especially for the purposes of economic development (Dicken and Tickell 1992; Lynch 1999). The emergence of these new forms of partnerships – ad hoc groupings meeting as and when required – led in some cases to "institutional congestion" (Roberts and Lloyd 1999), which only highlighted the complex and inefficient division of responsibilities and functions in this new realm of governance. The strategic vacuum was partly the motivation behind the growing demands for greater coordination of regional policy and planning (CBI 1997; BCC 1997; TEC National Council 1997), but other issues were also significant. Baker (1998), for example, identifies a number of other factors that led to the renewed interest in regional planning, including:

- the recognition that many policy concerns can only be adequately addressed on a regional scale;
- the realisation that local government reorganisation had effectively removed a level of strategic overview in certain areas;
- the increasing role of the European Union in spatial planning and development that is more focused at a regional level; and
- the path paved by the creation of regional Government Offices in creating a similar institutional regional framework for other stakeholders.

Tewdwr-Jones and McNeill (2000) also highlighted four factors influencing the emergence of a stronger form of regional policy making: central government funding opportunities through "innovative" partnerships; the emergence of regional planning; the creation of regional development organisations and/or agencies with both an urban regeneration and an economic development remit; and opportunities provided by European Union funding mechanisms.

In opposition, the Labour Party had begun to explore possible forms for such regional planning and governance, and this had culminated in referenda on devolution in Scotland and Wales and a consultation document on the form of regional governance in England entitled *A choice for England* (Labour Party 1995). The emphasis in the proposals was on economic and land-use planning but with a more accountable framework along the lines of regional assemblies, which would be adopted only if a referendum in the region returned a yes vote. Once in power, New Labour has proceeded with the broad approach and effectively combined the three dimensions of its regional proposals – planning, governance and economic development – into tailored packages for the three separate countries. The distinctive social, economic and political backgrounds in each country, combined with elements such as electoral pragmatism in regional politics (Lynch 1999) and cultural and linguistic differentiation, have necessitated distinctive approaches that place more or less emphasis on the three elements.

The regional voice in England, Scotland and Wales

In respect of England, Harvie (1991) has compared the lack of a coherent regional voice with the situation in both Scotland (Paterson 1998) and Wales (Tewdwr-Jones 2002). Scotland, meanwhile, has historically had a far greater demand for greater responsibility for its affairs, including its own Parliament. But with its own form of regional administration through the Scottish Office and economic development policy through Scottish Enterprise and Highlands and Islands Enterprise, the emphasis for Scotland has been on accountability, coordination and distinctiveness (Allmendinger and Tewdwr-Jones 2000). This was certainly the agenda of planners in Scotland who had been critical of the fragmented, centralised and unaccountable approach to planning (Goodstadt and U'ren 1999; Tewdwr-Jones and Lloyd 1997; Hayton 1997) – an agenda of expectations that was fuelled by the Scottish Office itself (Scottish Office 1999). Although greater coordination and distinctiveness could be achieved through alterations in policy guidance, Scotland also had the ability to pass primary legislation. Within Wales, the situation was slightly different, since the country has historically been far more integrated into the Union than Scotland, and there was less demand for accountability, as the failed referendum vote of 1979 indicates (Kendle 1997). Similarly to what had happened in Scotland, the Welsh Office had provided regional administration with limited accountability, while the Welsh Development Agency (WDA) had provided effective economic development policy (see, for example, Morgan 1997, but cf. Lovering 1999). The package of regional measures was tailored towards providing accountability through an Assembly, with greater coordination of policy and the ability to alter policy guidance.

The English regions started from a far less advanced position. The Government Offices for the Regions (GORs), introduced in 1994, provided a much needed form of regional administration and coordination but were far more limited in their ability to enter into debate and partnership with the fragmented and congested landscape of institutions that were seeking to provide some form of land-use and economic regional planning (Mawson and Spencer 1997a, 1997b; Mawson 1997). They also lacked accountability at Cabinet level, since different ministers represented the different departmental interests that were all included within each Government Office. The decentralisation package for England was skewed in New Labour's first government towards an economic emphasis through the creation of Regional Development Agencies to "level the uneven playing field" for institutional presence, to match the situation in both Scotland and Wales (Tewdwr-Jones and Phelps 2000); the accountability issue, through the creation of regional chambers and possibly at a later stage regional assemblies, would only be addressed in Labour's second election term.

The White Paper on regional government published in 2002 (ODPM 2002) advocated regional assemblies for the English regions. But rather than imposing tiers of government on to territories, Labour decided to arrange referenda in each of the regions to gauge whether assemblies were desired. The North East of England was the first region selected, and a postal-vote referendum was organised in November 2004. The region was chosen mainly because it was considered to be the one territory where there was a strong desire for a newly elected tier of governance. The result proved embarrassing for the government, with a clear no vote expressed in the poll. This had the effect not only of rejecting the prospect of a North East Regional Assembly, but also of throwing out the government's regional democracy plan, as ministers did not want to risk further no votes in other parts of the country. The final phase of the regional governance policy of New Labour has therefore had to be abandoned, at least for the foreseeable future.

One element that has been common to all three countries, even in those agencies sceptical about new institutions of democracy, is the need for emerging governance institutions and policies to work and cooperate with the plethora of existing formal and informal institutional arrangements and networks. Ironically, it is this need that has generated a desire for enhanced strategic and regional coordination, to ameliorate "silo mentalities" on the part of the different service providers and to ensure joined-up government. Many of the agencies and networks that emerged in the strategic vacuum of regional planning and policy in the 1980s and 1990s were a pragmatic response to the need for coordination and promotion. However, "These agencies performed an important role in facilitating national policy priorities into a sub-national agenda whilst seeking to organise local authority activities and resource commitments" (Roberts and Lloyd 1999: 517). Similarly, the Scottish Parliament and Scottish Executive, and Welsh Assembly and Assembly Government in Wales have emphasised the cooperative nature of government approaches to existing institutional arrangements. This cooperative approach is in stark contrast to the more "top-down" and confrontational perspective of the Thatcher years (Allmendinger and Tewdwr-Jones 2000). It is therefore likely, despite the North East Regional Assembly referendum "no" result and the government abandoning the plan across the rest of England, that the English regional governance and democracy issue will return to the political agenda, since there remains a clear need for regional policy and regional planning coordination. The task of "joined-up government" at the strategic level is now more important than it has ever been, and New Labour will not wish to leave a half-finished process in place that only speaks at the present time of territorial partial-democracy.

Regional planning and spatial strategy making

Turning attention to the nature of regional planning rather than democracy, one can see Labour's reforms to planning have been ambitious. The Planning and Compulsory Purchase Act 2004 completely reforms the planning policy and strategy-making function at not only regional level but also national, sub-regional, local and community levels: Regional Planning Guidance Notes are replaced with "Regional Spatial Strategies"; "Sub-Regional Strategies" are introduced for the first time; Structure Plans, Local Plans and Unitary Development Plans are replaced with "Local Development Frameworks", "Action Area Plans" and "Masterplans"; "Community Strategies" are to find implementation at neighbourhood level within Local Development Frameworks; and "public consultation" is to be replaced by enhanced public participation.

The second aspect of the reforms concerns scale and uniqueness. Prior to devolution, the UK government expected planning to be devised and implemented uniformly across all parts of Britain: one country, one system. But such an ethos lies counter to processes of devolution and regionalisation. It also contributed to the notion that planning was failing to deliver development in the right locations or to cater for the desires and expectations of local and regional actors, and produced standardised plans and policies that did not deliver. Planning is now becoming increasingly differentiated in different parts of the UK as a consequence of devolution, decentralisation and regionalisation (Tewdwr-Jones 2002; Haughton and Counsell 2004). With the impetus provided by devolution and a planning reform agenda, Scotland, Wales and Northern Ireland are developing their own spatial strategies separate to England, with a desire for differentiation (Allmendinger 2002; Berry et al. 2001; Harris et al. 2002).

A further issue to bolster the case for regional planning concerns the expectation of change, particularly that of economic development and policy integration. There is now a new role for regional spatial strategy making in achieving coordination between disparate actors and strategies. New forms of planning are being explored as tools to help resolve community, sub-regional and regional problems (Counsell and Haughton 2003), alongside a renaissance for planning as the means of achieving policy integration and coordination and the promotion of sustainable development (Tewdwr-Jones 2004). The emphasis here is to look at planning not as a delivery process per se, in the style of planning under the welfare state, but rather as a strategic capacity and political integration mechanism intended to cement the increasingly fragmented agents of the state, all of whom possess their own agendas, political objectives, strategies and resources, but who need to cooperate in order to deliver projects and developments. Planning is being looked at to ensure compatible working and strategic coordination when desired. This process, dubbed "spatial planning" rather than town and country planning, extends the remit of planning beyond mere land-use development and the 1980s/1990s regulatory rump into a coordinative process where professional planners' duties concern management of agency integration (Healey 1997; Lloyd and Illsley 1999).

These three characteristics of change – complexity, scale and expectation of change – within regional spatial plan making are transforming the activity and scope of planning, across scales and across territories in varied ways and at varied times. The recent focus on devolution in UK planning is not limited to, for example, a potential shift from one form of spatial planning to another. Planning is a contributor to and a reflection of a more fundamental reform of territorial management that aims to, *inter alia*, improve integration of different forms of spatial development activity, not least economic development. So, at one level, devolution and its implications for spatial planning must be analysed in respect of other aspects of New Labour's regional project, particularly the government's concern with business competitiveness. At another level, the current reforms which privilege regional scale policy interventions will inevitably require changes in the divisions of powers and responsibilities at local and national levels. In other words, devolution and decentralisation involve a major rescaling of both planning and spatial development, which is unfolding rapidly and unevenly across Britain.

Consequently, planning is deeply implicated in the re-territorialisation of the British State, and a number of related significant issues and areas of interest arise from such changes, including:

- the need and opportunity to integrate spatial development through new regional strategies, including activities such as economic development, transport, sustainable development, energy, water and biodiversity;
- the scope for and implications of policy divergence and inter-regional rivalry;
- the tension between regional autonomy and national interest, including wider questions concerning the balance between the two and the role of the centre;
- the relationship between the evolving new regionalist agenda and existing institutions, processes and stakeholders; and
- the role and extent of "region building" and the ways in which the region is discursively constructed, being politically, socially and symbolically shaped and contested in various ways.

The objective of this spatial transformation is to widen the trajectory of planning, or spatial strategy making, in the modernisation and governance agendas at both the regional level and the local level within the UK. Although this is resulting in new participatory processes and greater contestation on the form and trajectory of regional and local spatial plan making, it is nevertheless occurring within a planning legislative framework that remains firmly rooted within the agenda of and context provided by the central and local government state and within professional planning duties. Here, the tension surrounding the form of spatial plan making occurs at the level of the state between the broader form of and relationship between governance and government. It should be an interesting arena of policy conflict to watch.

Conclusions

In marked contrast to the situation in planning before New Labour was elected to office, the creation and promotion of governance styles at the regional level since 1997 have led to the welcomed reduction in the role of the nation state in determining the fortunes of sub-national territories. But such decentralisation and devolution processes, structurally and institutionally, have been overlaid by simultaneous policy-making transfers from the centre to both the region and the locality. This twin process of institutional decentralisation and policy transfer has created a fusion of different styles of government and governance across the UK territory that remains fluid and difficult to comprehend. Different government styles and structures are now apparent in England, Scotland, Wales and Northern Ireland; very soon, a similar mix of styles will be apparent within planning processes within the three nations. The partial and, in all probability, temporary abandonment of the regional democracy push in England will leave the English territories in a sort of democratic limbo, but that does not mean that the task of regional strategy making and regional spatial coordination stops. That process will continue, and new forms of planning and new partnerships will continue to evolve in very different ways in very different places.

One of the problems for new institutions is to demonstrate their worth against a backdrop of growing complexity and upheaval in UK governance. Not only do new regional arrangements have to "bed in" and take their place among the plethora of bodies that constitute the landscape of governance, but they have to account for the changing nature of the landscape itself. Nevertheless, as many of the actors within governance arrangements are beginning to discover, the promotion of regional spatial planning and participatory governance within each scale is a goal worth pursuing, but it still requires a form of strategic direction to set some sort of political vision if agreement by lowest common denominator is to be avoided. What regional governance within spatial strategy making seems to be creating is greater discretion and autonomy within particular scales and across particular territories. Such moves within planning may serve a useful role to provide a perspective that is reflective of the disparate interests with regard to the economy, transport and housing. If the new forms of regional spatial planning and coordination are to stand any chance of success, a great deal of commitment and vision will be required to ensure all vested interests buy into the process.

References

Allmendinger, P. 2002. Prospects for a distinctly Scottish planning in a post-sovereign age. *European Planning Studies* **10**(3), 359–81.

Allmendinger, P. and M. Tewdwr-Jones 2000. Spatial dimensions and institutional uncertainties of planning and the "new regionalism". *Environment and Planning C: Government and Policy* **18**(6), 711–26.

Amin, A. and N. Thrift 1995. Globalisation, institutional "thickness" and the local economy. In *Managing cities: the new urban context*, P. Healey, S. Cameron, S. Davoudi, S. Graham, A. Mandani-Pour (eds). Chichester: John Wiley & Sons.

Baker, M. 1998. Planning for the English regions: a review of the Secretary of State's regional planning guidance. *Planning Practice and Research* **13**(2), 153–69.

Baker, M., I. Deas and C. Wong 1999. Obscure ritual or administrative luxury? Integrating strategic planning and regional development. *Environment and Planning B: Planning and Design* **26**.

Bachtler, J. and I. Turok 1997. *The coherence of EU regional policy*. London: Jessica Kingsley.

BCC 1997. *Regional policy*. London: British Chambers of Commerce.

Berry, J., L. Brown and S. McGreal 2001. The planning system in Northern Ireland post-devolution. *European Planning Studies* **9**(6), 781–91.

Brenner, N. 1999. Globalisation as reterritorialisation: the re-scaling of urban governance in the European Union. *Urban Studies* **36**, 431–51.

CBI 1997. *Regions for business: improving policy design and delivery*. London: Confederation of British Industry.

Clotworthy, J. and N. Harris 1996. Planning policy implications of local government reorganisation. *British planning policy in transition: planning in the 1990s*, M. Tewdwr-Jones (ed.). London: UCL Press.

Cooke, P. and K. Morgan 1998. *The associational economy: firms, regions and innovation*. Oxford: Oxford University Press.

Counsell, D. and G. Haughton 2003. Regional planning tensions: planning for economic growth and sustainable development in two contrasting English regions. *Environment and Planning C* **21**(2), 225–39.

CPRE 1994. *Greening the regions: regional planning guidance – a review and assessment of current practice*. London: Council for the Preservation of Rural England.

Dicken, P. and A. Tickell 1992. Competitors or collaborators? The structure and relationships of inward investment in Northern England. *Regional Studies* **26**, 99–106.

Di Maggio, P. 1993. On metropolitan dominance: New York in the urban network. In *Capital of the American century: the national and international influence of New York City*, M. Shelter (ed.). New York: Russell Sage Foundation.

DoE 1989. *The future of development plans*. White Paper, Department of the Environment. London: HMSO.

EC 1991. *Europe 2000*. European Commission. Luxembourg: Office for Official Publications of the European Communities.

EC 1994. *Europe 2000+*. European Commission. Luxembourg: Office for Official Publications of the European Communities.

EC 1999. *European Spatial Development Perspective*. European Commission. Luxembourg: Office for Official Publications of the European Union.

Goodstadt, V. and G. U'ren 1999. Which way now for Scottish planning? *Planning* **22**, January, 11.

Hague, C. 1990. Scotland: back to the future for planning. In *Radical planning initiatives: new directions for urban planning in the 1990s*, J. Montgomery and A. Thornley (eds). Aldershot: Gower.

Harris, N., A. Hooper and K. Bishop 2002. Constructing the practice of "spatial planning": a national spatial planning framework for Wales. *Environment and Planning C* **20**(4), 555–72.

Harvie, C. 1991. English regionalism: the dog that never barked. In *National identities*, B. Crick (ed.). London: Blackwell.

Haughton, G. and D. Counsell 2004. *Regions, spatial strategies and sustainable development.* London: Routledge.

Hayton, K. 1997. Planning in a Scottish Parliament. *Town and Country Planning* **66**, 208–9.

Healey, P. 1997. *Collaborative planning.* Basingstoke: Macmillan.

Jonas, A. and K. G. Ward 1999. Toward new urban and regional policy frameworks for Europe: competitive regionalism "bottom up" and "top down". Paper presented to the Regional Association Studies Sixth International Conference: Regional Potentials in an Integrating Europe, University of the Basque Country, Bilbao, Spain, September.

Jones, M. and G. MacLeod 1999. Towards a regional renaissance? Reconfiguring and rescaling England's economic governance. *Transactions of the Institute of British Geographers*, New series, **24**(3), 295–314.

Keating, M. 1997. The invention of regions: political restructuring and territorial government in Western Europe. *Environment and Planning C: Government and Policy* **15**, 383–98.

Kendle, J. 1997. *Federal Britain: a history.* London: Routledge.

Labour Party 1995. *A choice for England.* A consultation paper on Labour's plans for English regional government. London: Labour Party.

Lloyd, M. G. and B. Illsley 1999. Planning and developed government in the United Kingdom, *Town Planning Review* **70**(4), 409–32.

Lovering, J. 1999. Theory led by policy: the inadequacies of the "new regionalism" (illustrated from the case of Wales). *International Journal of Urban and Regional Research* **23**, 379–95.

Lynch, P. 1999. New Labour and the English Regional Development Agencies: devolution as evolution. *Regional Studies* **31**(1), 73–89.

MacLeod, G. and M. Goodwin 1999. Space, scale and strategy: rethinking urban and regional governance. *Progress in Human Geography* **23**, 503–27.

Mawson, J. 1997. New Labour and the English regions: a missed opportunity? *Local Economy*, November, 194–203.

Mawson, J. and K. Spencer 1997a. The Government Offices for the English Regions: towards regional governance. *Policy and Politics* **25**, 71–84.

Mawson, J. and K. Spencer 1997b. The origins and operations of the Government Offices for the Regions. In *British regionalism and devolution: the challenges of state reform and European integration*, J. Bradbury and J. Mawson (eds), 158–79. London: Jessica Kingsley.

Morgan, K. 1997. The regional animateur: taking stock of the Welsh Development Agency. *Regional and Federal Studies* **7**(2), 70–94.

Murdoch, J. and M. Tewdwr-Jones 1999. Planning and the English regions: conflict and convergence amongst the institutions of regional governance. *Environment and Planning C* **17**, 715–29.

ODPM 2002. *Your region, your choice: revitalising the English regions.* White Paper, Office of the Deputy Prime Minister. London: Stationery Office.

Ohmae, K. 1997. *The end of the nation state.* London: HarperCollins.

Paterson, L. J. 1998. Scottish home rule: radical break or pragmatic adjustment? In *Remaking the Union: devolution and British politics in the 1990s*, H. Elcock and M. Keating (eds). London: Frank Cass.

Raco, M. 1999. Assessing "institutional thickness" in the local context: a comparison of Cardiff and Sheffield. *Environment and Planning A* **30**, 975–96.

Roberts, P. 1996. Regional planning guidance in England and Wales: back to the future? *Town Planning Review* **67**(1), 97–109.

Roberts, P. and M. G. Lloyd 1999. Institutional aspects of regional planning, management and development: models and lessons from the English experience. *Environment and Planning B* **26**, 517–31.

Scottish Office 1999. *Land use planning under a Scottish Parliament*. Edinburgh: Scottish Office.

Stoker, G. 1990. Regulation theory, local government and transition from Fordism. In *Challenges to local government*, D. King and J. Pierre (eds), 242–64. London: Sage.

TCPA 1997. *Regional Development Agencies: ensuring sustainable regional planning and development*. London: Town and Country Planning Association.

TEC National Council 1997. *Regional development principles*. London: Training and Enterprise Council National Council.

Tewdwr-Jones, M. 2002. *The planning polity: planning, government and the policy process*. London: Routledge.

Tewdwr-Jones, M. 2004. Spatial planning: principles, practice and culture. *Journal of Planning and Environment Law* **57**(5).

Tewdwr-Jones, M. and M. G. Lloyd 1997. Unfinished business. *Town and Country Planning*, November, 302–4.

Tewdwr-Jones, M. and D. McNeill 2000. The politics of city-region planning and governance: reconciling the national, regional and urban in the competing voices of institutional restructuring. *European Urban and Regional Studies* **7**(2), 119–34.

Tewdwr-Jones, M. and N. A. Phelps 2000. Levelling the uneven playing field: inward investment, inter-regional rivalry and the planning system. *Regional Studies* **34**(5).

Part 2

Theories and principles of strategic and regional planning

4 Strategic planning thought: lessons from elsewhere

Harry T. Dimitriou

Introduction

Strategic planning is composed of two important elements: the planning process (i.e. the plan to plan) and the substantive information regarding the context(s) and object(s) of planning (Steiner 1997). While it is sometimes difficult to disentangle the two, in that one is a product of the other, this chapter primarily pays attention to the planning process and the next chapter to the planning context and objects of planning.

The discussion which follows explores and reviews many of the main concepts, issues and methods that underlie or are embedded within the generic strategic planning process. In so doing, it draws extensively and unashamedly from George Steiner's seminal book entitled *Strategic planning: a step-by-step guide* (1997), with a view to identifying possible lessons of parallel significance for strategic spatial planning, especially regional planning. The chapter commences with an examination of the fundamental meaning of strategic planning as employed in *any* complex planning exercise and calls on ideas of strategic thinking from the world of the military (this being very much the origin of strategic thought), commerce and knowledge management. It concludes by pointing to potential new avenues of planning thought and practice that more explicitly deal with decision making in climates of uncertainty that emerge from recent corporate experiences. The chapter also sets the scene for the following chapter, which explains the importance and impact of "context" on strategic thought and regional planning.

What is strategic planning?

What it is not

There is considerable diversity in the use of the term "strategy". Some include goals and objectives as part of a strategy; others make a firm distinction between the two (Quinn 1995: 5). It is taken as read here that goals and objectives are an integral part of strategy making and that strategic planning is *not* merely a process of forecasting and then determining what should be done to assure the fulfilment of these forecasts or the execution of a blueprint for the future (Steiner 1997: 15). A strategy is instead the plan that "joins up" major goals, policies and actions into a cohesive entity. "A well-formulated strategy helps to marshal and allocate an organisation's resources into a unique and viable posture based on its relative internal competencies and shortcomings, anticipated changes in the environment and contingent moves by intelligent opponents" (Quinn 1995: 5).

Military strategies

To make more sense of the meaning of "strategy" we need to go to the origins of its use, which have their roots in the Ancient Greek word *strategos*, which means "a general". The term "strategy" thus literally means "the art of the general" and, in this sense, strategies may be seen as offering "directional decisions" that "provide purpose and missions to planned actions" (Steiner 1997: 348).

Military strategists, such as von Clausewitz (1835) and Jomini (1838) (see Osgood 2000), postulate that an effective strategy should concentrate on a few central principles that "can create, guide and maintain dominance despite the enormous frictions that occur as one tries to position or manoeuvre large forces in war" (Quinn 1995: 5). Here, "friction" refers to uncertainties, errors, accidents, technical difficulties and the unforeseen and their effect on decisions, morale and actions (Shy 1986). These include many of the Ancient Greek (Macedonian) principles of warfare, such as "spirit or morale, surprise, cunning, concentration in space, dominance of selected positions, use of strategic reserves, unification over time, tension and release" (Quinn 1995: 9).

Stanger (2004) argues that military strategy teaches us that, in certain circumstances, particular goals need to be achieved (sacrificed even) in order to gain other objectives. This implicit acknowledgement of a hierarchy of aims is inherent in *all* strategy formulation and planning exercises. He also claims that, because war is chaotic by its very nature, the simpler the strategy the more likely it is to succeed, and that the fewer in the command structure the less frequent the difference in interpretations of directives. Jomini (1838) (Osgood 2000) adds that military cum diplomatic strategies should be bold, simple and clear but seek to always retain the initiative.

An appreciation of these different qualities of military strategy formulation provides essential insights into the fundamental parameters, nature and design of both formal and informal strategies for many other fields. According to Quinn (1995: 11) formal strategies should contain three essential elements: "the most important goals to be achieved; the most significant policies guiding or limiting actions; and the major action sequences that accomplish the defined goals". He also insists that "effective" strategies develop around selected concepts and thrusts that give them cohesion, balance and focus, with some thrusts being of a temporary nature and others carried through to the end of the strategy. Strategy deals with the unpredictable and the unknown, and acknowledges that "no analyst can predict the precise ways in which all impinging forces could interact with each other" (Braybrooke and Lindblom 1970).

While military strategies offer an excellent framework for strategy formulation and appraisal in a variety of contexts and at different levels, Quinn warns that too often one encounters what is claimed to be strategies when in fact "they are little more than aggregates of philosophies or agglomerations of programmes . . . [that] lack the cohesiveness, flexibility, thrust, sense of positioning against intelligent opposition and other criteria that historical analysis suggests effective strategies must contain" (Quinn 1995: 11).

Corporate strategies

Steiner takes a broader view of strategy formulation than that offered by the military and diplomats. Drawing from the corporate world, he refers to strategic planning as a formal planning process that involves "the systematic identification of opportunities and threats that lie in the future, which in combination with other relevant data provide a basis for . . . making better current decisions to exploit the opportunities and to avoid the threats" (Steiner 1997: 13–14). He points out that in the business world the level of formality of the strategic planning processes varies according to the size of the organisation, so that the larger the organisation the more formal the planning process typically employed, and the smaller the organisation the more ad hoc is the planning process used. Interestingly, a number of large multinational corporations such as IBM have recently argued in favour of using smaller units of production and employing "looser strategies", claiming that these smaller groups yield higher levels of productivity (see Kurtz and Snowden 2003), a position also supported by Gladwell (2003) and Surowiecki (2004).

Steiner presents formal strategic planning from four perspectives (1997: 13–15):

- From the *perspective of the future*, where "planning deals with the futurity of current decisions . . . and . . . the chain of cause and effect consequences over time of an actual or intended decision . . . [so that] if what is seen ahead is not liked then planning presumes a capability to change these future events by looking at the alternative courses of action that are open".
- As a *systematic process*, whereby strategic planning "begins with the setting of aims, defines strategies and policies to achieve them, and develops detailed plans to make sure that the strategies are implemented so as to achieve the ends sought". This is "a process of deciding in advance what kind of planning effort is undertaken, when it is to be done, how it is to be done, who is going to do it, and what will be done with the results". It is systematic in the sense that it is organised and undertaken on a continuous basis.
- As a *philosophy*, in so far as strategic planning is a kind of "attitude" that "necessitates dedication to act on the basis of contemplation of the future . . . as more of a thought process, an intellectual exercise, than a prescribed set of processes, procedures, structures, or techniques".
- Finally, as a *structure*, in that the concept of a structure of plans adopted by a strategy implies a hierarchy of linked planned actions and major types of plans, including strategic plans, medium-range programmes, and short-range budgets and operating plans.

As indicated in the introduction to this chapter, Steiner (1997: 18–20) also suggests that the premises of strategic planning are of two kinds: the plan to plan, and substantive information needed in the formulation and implementation of plans. The first can be said to be reflective of how a planning system works and is typically articulated in the form of guidance, whereas the latter is reflective of four other considerations which together constitute what may be called the "situation (context) audit". These include: a summary statement of the major outside interests to the plan; a summary statement of the expectations of major inside interests of the plan; a database of past performance, current situation and forecasts of the object of the plan; and evaluations of the context of the plan, including the opportunities, threats, strengths and weaknesses of the subject matter of the plan.

Building on the above premises, the formal strategic planning process thus proceeds from the formulation of a hierarchy of planning actions, which include basic mission (and vision) statements, a statement of purposes and (normative and operational) objectives, and policies, to associated programmes of action. In addition to the above, other types of planning exercises typically incorporated in strategic plans include (Steiner 1997: 32):

- *Project plans* – which may be described as detailed plans for specific undertakings, which vary in their dimensions, time frame and resource base.
- *Contingency plans* – which are "associated with strategic plans but are *not* an integral part of them" in that strategic plans are considered more probable, while contingency plans are associated with low probabilities of realisation. Contingency plans are developed more as a precaution to help management meet crises.
- *Scenario/exploratory planning* – which is concerned with "possible future combinations of events". While some scenarios overlap with the typical planning periods there is a tendency to develop them around distant time horizons. They are often employed to stimulate senior management thought about what *could* or *might* happen in the future; on other occasions, they represent the very basis of a strategic plan.
- *Management by objectives (MBO)* – which is a process where parties work with one another in complex organisations to "identify common goals and coordinate their efforts (and resources) toward achieving them".

Steiner concludes that all the above need to be accompanied by annual monitoring processes as part of the implementation process and that the flows of information here are critical to the strategic planning process. While these will significantly differ according to which part of the planning process they serve, he emphasises that they will often be coloured by the values of senior management and policy makers.

Spatial planning strategies

Spatial planning is a set of policies and tools of intervention at different levels and for different horizon dates, designed to assist the management of strategic change taking place within territories, their economies and societies, directed largely (but not exclusively) by the public sector. It is an exercise ostensibly undertaken in the public interest to protect civil society against failures of the market system, problems of unsustainable development and concerns of equity as they affect land use and the spatial distributions of activities in cities and regions. If we accept the European Spatial Planning Observation Network's (ESPON) definition of spatial planning cited in Chapter 1, it is moulded by goals of economic and social cohesion, sustainable development, and coherence of the European continent (ESPON 2005).

Reflecting these values, spatial planning, as promoted by the Royal Town Planning Institute (RTPI) in its *New vision for planning* (RTPI 2001), seeks to bring the management of the spatial dimension of planning in the UK up to speed with a pace and scale of social, technological, economic and political change never experienced before. It is a strategy that is based on a core set of ideas, many of which draw directly from European experiences (see Chapter 5) that present planning as:

- spatial – dealing with the unique needs and characteristics of places;
- sustainable – looking at the short-, medium- and long-term issues;
- integrative – in terms of knowledge, objectives and actions involved; and
- inclusive – recognising the wide range of people involved in planning.

Perhaps the most thorough recent examination of the application of strategic thought to spatial planning that provides an invaluable critical overview is provided by Louis Albrechts in an article entitled "Strategic (spatial) planning re-examined" (2004). In this publication he explains that "solutions to complex problems (such as regional development challenges) depend on the ability to combine the creation of strategic (long-term) visions with short-term actions" (2004: 743). Implied in this, however, is a presumed ability by government (or appointed/elected public sector agencies acting on its behalf) to successfully identify, design and deliver "shared futures" that are capable of expression in spatial forms and agreed by major stakeholders. Herein, unhappily, often lies a level of expectation (especially) from those in industry and commerce that is unrealistic, particularly if judged against the kind of (more controllable) criteria with which they are more familiar.

Spatial planning involves strategic processes of decision making that are by their very nature, necessarily, more democratic and transparent. They are more difficult and more complex in character and often (therefore) slower to arrive at agreement than their equivalent in the corporate and military worlds. This is so because, among other things, spatial planning typically involves a larger number of stakeholders, many of whom have greater expectations of their views being taken into account than is often realistically possible. While this increased complexity, demand for accountability and resultant delay can reduce the sharpness of the strategic qualities of spatial planning, this very fact ironically highlights even more the importance and need for strategic thought and expertise for a spatial plan to prove successful.

Reflecting on the challenges spatial planning faces generally and the experiences accumulated thus far, Albrechts sees spatial plans as strategic frameworks for action. Like Kunzmann and Healey (Albrechts *et al.* 2003), he views these plans as largely public-sector-led, and socio-spatial in terms advocated by Healey (1997b). He considers strategic spatial planning to be essentially "about building ideas" (Mintzberg *et al.* 1998) and processes that can carry them (the ideas) forward, and ways of organising and mobilising for the purpose of exerting influence in different arenas (Healey 1997a; Albrechts 2004: 747). Albrechts does not see spatial planning as a single concept, procedure or tool but instead as a set of concepts, procedures and tools that may be tailor-made to specific contexts and circumstances, orientated to the achievement of different visions. While acknowledging that many planners may view this interpretation as too broad, he is adamant that there is ample evidence in planning literature that backs up this position, as this and the following chapter confirm.

Overcoming anti-planning bias

A challenge that strategic planning often encounters in many different contexts, whether in spatial planning or corporate planning, is that of an anti-planning bias, especially among those closely associated with booming free market developments and activities. To overcome this bias, whether in the corporate or public sector world, Steiner argues it is *imperative* that the planner understands its source and cause. According to Steiner (1997: 96–101), resistance to strategic planning emerges from one or more of the following:

- *The alteration of relationships* – brought about, for example, by the introduction of a new planning system into an organisation or within a planning framework for several organisations. This can contribute to the break-up of established groups and to the setting up of new groups, as well as contribute to residual problems, including frustrations, misunderstandings and insecurities which, although over time they may evaporate, can become chronic.
- *The change of information flows, decision making and power relationships* – which creates new decision-making patterns that inevitably introduce new information flows. This often changes power relationships and even resource allocations, which in turn can bring a new apprehension about decision making whether or not it introduces a more coordinated formal planning system.
- *The highlighting of conflicts* – brought about by new relationships and resource allocations created by the new strategic plan. These can pitch parties at different levels or in different areas of activity against each other in a bid to gain influence or access to resources under the new regime. The resultant conflicts can be transitional or become structural depending upon how well they are dealt with and the flexibility of the system to absorb them.
- *The conflict between operational problems and planning efforts* – created by the clash of influence between those in operations who have power and satisfaction acquired through their track record of effectively coping with operational problems, and the newly acquired influence of strategic planners. The fact that the latter typically have no equivalent track record and are looking into more long-term and speculative futures too often has strategic planning tasks perceived to be less important than resolving more short-range operational problems.
- *The new demands placed on (new) decision makers* – often generated by the introduction of strategic planning in contexts where it was previously either too weak or absent. The new perspectives brought in by strategic planning often demand different ways of perceiving and doing things that require a mastery of new concepts, methods and techniques, and a capability of thinking in *both* the short term and the long run, as well as from the specific to the complex whole. There is typically a need also to be more intuitive and

creative in problem solving rather than rely on old standardised approaches.

- *The risk and fear of failure* – often increased by the introduction of strategic planning. This is because it involves "flirting with possible error" and because wrong strategic choices can incur heavy penalties. Indeed, some parties associate planning with negative concerns of how to avoid error and buck-passing.
- *The desire to avoid uncertainty* – often generates a great deal of anxiety (and friction), especially for those more accustomed to achieving more finite goals and being in more control of outcomes. To be "strategic" a plan needs to convey an understanding of how well it might fare, not knowing how its contexts might change. Strategic planning deals with this uncertainty in a variety of ways and on different levels, more often by the use of different scenarios. Failure to do this means that it is not a "strategic" plan. Finally, an important task of strategic plans is not only to confront uncertainty but to do this with confidence. A fuller account of how this may be achieved follows immediately below.

Strategy formulation under conditions of uncertainty

Treatment of uncertainty in urban and regional planning

Citing traditional principles of strategic planning of the kind advocated by Mintzberg (1994) and Mason and Mitroff (1981), three McKinsey and Company consultants (Courtney, Kirkland and Viguerie) wrote in the *Harvard Business Review* in 1999 that "at the heart of the traditional approach to strategy lies the assumption that by applying a set of powerful analytical tools, executives can predict the future of any business accurately enough to allow them to choose a clear strategic decision", *whereas*, in environments of uncertainty at levels so high that no amount of such analysis allows confident predictions, a totally new approach is needed (Courtney *et al.* 1999: 1).

This very significant call for greater sensitivity in the treatment of uncertainty (and risk) in strategic planning is today emerging from a number of quarters. It derives from the widespread appreciation that we now live in an increasingly fast-changing world, arising from many new technological and globalisation forces. The fact that these changes are so dramatic makes the experience of the corporate world in undertaking strategic planning potentially very valuable for the more public sector-orientated field of strategic and regional planning if any parallels can be established. Before attempting to draw out any lessons, however, a brief historical review follows of the treatment of uncertainty and risk in urban and regional planning in the UK since the Second World War, drawn from previous research conducted by the author (see Dimitriou 2005).

During the post-war period, up to say the mid-1970s, uncertainty as a concept and risk taking as an outcome did not feature greatly in planning in Britain. This was a period when uncertainties were seen to have been dissipated by a combination of knowledge and power (see Benveniste 1970) and where planning projects were conceived and implemented by professionals more confident of their capabilities and expertise. Acknowledged uncertainties were seen to have been prematurely transformed and dispersed by planning procedures and techniques, whereas in reality they merely postponed risk taking and latent conflicts (see Christensen 1983).

While a certain amount of attention was drawn to the issue of uncertainty in the context of strategic planning and corporate planning in the 1970s (see Friend and Jessop 1969; Edison 1975), it was during the 1980s that uncertainty, and responses to it, came to be more systematically studied in physical and spatial planning (see Hall 1980). During that period, the procedural school of "strategic choice" further developed planning methodologies and techniques for decision makers to cope with uncertainty (see Friend and Hickling 1987, 2005). Others in response argued for an adjustment of planning aspirations and techniques to accommodate the existence of uncertainty rather than seek to bypass or hide it (see Christensen 1983) in a manner more akin to the approach presented by Courtney et al. (1999) (see "Coping with different types and levels of uncertainty", pp. 50–3).

Subsequent attempts to better understand and respond to uncertainty and complexity (also see Chapter 5) have sought to reduce the risks to which projects (rather than plans) are exposed. These are based on the premise that this can be achieved by means of increasing the knowledge of the project "content" and (more especially) "context", and then identifying scarce resources to resolve uncertainty. These "knowledge-generating responses" to uncertainty, of the kind outlined by Steiner (1997) and Mason and Mitroff (1981), seek to fill the gap between "present knowledge" and "future information" required to fulfil a project's objectives. They typically depend on the use of sophisticated dynamic prediction models and seek to manage uncertainty by exploring simulated performance in relation to a series of possible scenarios.

Numerous policy analysts have since been engaged in making uncertainty the focus of their research, on the assumption that uncertainty is the norm rather than the exception (see Dror 1986; Innes 1990; Beck 1992, 1999; Lash et al. 1998; Courtney et al. 1999). As we entered the twenty-first century, more attention had also been given to the impacts on uncertainty and risk taking arising from changing forces of globalisation (see Castells 1991, 1996, 2004; Held et al. 1999; Beck 2000; Seitz 2002), an aspect discussed further in Chapter 5 ("New regionalism as a context for strategic planning", pp. 74–5). This is especially significant as some see the world as only just now being "tipped over" into being constituted by agencies operating at a global scale rather than by predominantly national governments (see Shaw 2003), which has major impacts on regional planning and spatial development, not only in the UK but elsewhere throughout the world. It is *imperative* that an understanding of these circumstances and developments is acquired for effective future strategic (spatial) planning and regional development in Britain.

Coping with different types and levels of uncertainty

Returning to the corporate world and the work of Courtney et al. (1999) and their claim that present-day environments of high uncertainty require the abandonment of the traditional binary view of the concept, where uncertainty is *either* underestimated *or* overestimated, and where analysis is sometimes even abandoned. The new approach advocated by the three McKinsey consultants offers a useful framework which explicitly helps policy makers decide which analytical tools can inform decision making under uncertainty and which cannot.

It begins by differentiating among four levels of uncertainty (see Figure 4.1) and, within this, presents three generic strategies that can be used in each level. The four levels of uncertainty include (after Courtney *et al.* 1999: 4–5):

- *level 1* – which represents the most likely outcomes based on clear trends that can help define potential demand for products and services;
- *level 2* – which includes outcomes that are currently unknown but knowable in the future assuming that the right analysis is undertaken of performance attributes for current developments that are predictable to certain levels of confidence;
- *level 3* – which incorporates currently unknown but not entirely unknowable variables on the premise that there are certain performance attributes for current technologies, and trends in stable conditions that reveal these; and
- *level 4* – which represents "residual uncertainty outcomes" that reflect the uncertainty that remains *after* the best possible analysis has been conducted and/or as a result of incomplete/inconclusive developments.

The last categorisation, deemed by the authors to pose the highest risks, can be further sub-categorised into four situations: situations representing a "clear-enough" future that enables planners to develop a single forecast that is precise enough for strategy development; those requiring consideration of alternative futures whereby the future may be seen as one of a few discrete alternative scenarios;[1] those warranting an examination of a range of potential futures defined by a limited number of key variables with an "actual" outcome lying on an identified known continuum but with no discrete scenarios;[2] and those representing the state of "true ambiguity" where multiple dimensions of uncertainty interact to create a context that is virtually impossible to predict. Unlike the position with level 3, the range of potential outcomes here cannot be identified, let alone scenarios within that range. Courtney *et al.* explain that not only is the last level in reality rare but over time it tends to move toward one of the other levels. They claim that at least 50 per cent of all strategy problems in the corporate world fall within levels 2 and 3, with most of the remainder falling within level 1. The most uncertain of contexts – where true ambiguity is believed to exist – is the rarest of situations, albeit on the increase (1999: 6–11).

The conclusion then is that different strategic planning exercises warrant different types of approaches, depending on the level of uncertainty (and risk) reflected in their decision making and their decision-making contexts. The fact that most current planning practices in both the corporate and the public sector worlds, including spatial planning for regional development, fail to recognise this but instead pursue strategies that are more suited to level 1 (and maybe level 2) represents one of the most significant obstacles to effective strategic planning. Aspects of this are further alluded to in Chapter 5, where reference is made to Baghai *et al.*'s (1999) three horizons of sustainable growth.

Responding to the above-identified situations, the McKinsey consultants offer three strategic postures for strategic planning (see Figure 4.2), where "posture defines the intent of a strategy relative to the current and future state of any industry" (or region in the case of regional planning). They include postures that:

How to Use the Four Levels of Uncertainty

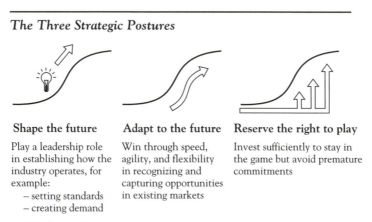

	A Clear-Enough Future	Alternate Futures	A Range of Futures	True Ambiguity
What Can Be Known?	• A single forecast precise enough for determining strategy	• A few discrete outcomes that define the future	• A range of possible outcomes, but no natural scenarios	• No basis to forecast the future
Analytic Tools	• "Traditional" strategy tool kit	• Decision analysis • Option valuation models • Game theory	• Latent demand research • Technology forecasting • Scenario planning	• Analogies and pattern recognition • Nonlinear dynamic models

Figure 4.1 Four levels of uncertainty in the highest-risk situation
Source: Courtney *et al.* 1999: 6–7

The Three Strategic Postures

Shape the future

Play a leadership role in establishing how the industry operates, for example:
 – setting standards
 – creating demand

Adapt to the future

Win through speed, agility, and flexibility in recognizing and capturing opportunities in existing markets

Reserve the right to play

Invest sufficiently to stay in the game but avoid premature commitments

Figure 4.2 Strategic postures
Source: Courtney *et al.* 1999: 16

* *shape the future* – where strategies are about creating new opportunities either by shaking up relatively stable "level 1 activities" or by attempting to control the direction of the market in circumstances with higher levels of uncertainty;
* *adapt to the future* – where planners take the existing situation and its future evolutions as given, and adapt strategies to react to the opportunities that the market offers; and
* *reserve the right to play* – which is a special form of adapting, and relevant only to levels 2 and 4 of uncertainty, that involves the making of investments step by step in an attempt to place an operation in an advantageous position (Courtney *et al.* 1999: 15–17).

Courtney *et al.* then identify three types of "moves" that can be employed to implement a strategy as part of a *portfolio* of actions in a climate of uncertainty (see Figure 4.3). These include:

- *Big bet moves* – which are major commitments to strategies, such as large investments or major acquisitions. Not unusually, shaping strategies typically involve making "big bets", whereas adapting and reserving the right to play postures do not.
- *Option moves* – which are designed to tie down the major pay-offs of the best-case scenarios, while minimising losses in the worst-case scenarios. Those adopting a reserving the right to play posture rely heavily on options, although *shapers* also use them.
- *No-regret moves* – which are destined to "pay off" no matter what transpires. These include initiatives that reduce costs in highly uncertain contexts, taking strategic decisions like investing in capacity in advance of a market and the decision to enter certain markets in advance of them becoming apparent to competitors (1999: 18–19).

The choice of strategic posture *and* accompanying follow-up portfolio of strategic actions outlined here is almost entirely reliant upon the level of uncertainty confronted/addressed by the strategy. In this way, the four levels of uncertainty assist in helping provide a framework for designing an appropriate strategy for any given situation.

Planning as learning and dangers to avoid

Planning as learning

Through the use of scenario planning, Shell International has done much to highlight the importance of strategic planning as a learning process (see GBN 2004). The company has even argued that strategic planning is ultimately more

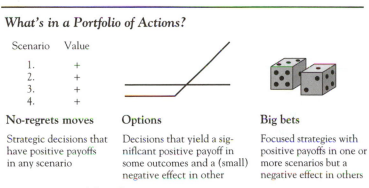

What's in a Portfolio of Actions?

Scenario	Value
1.	+
2.	+
3.	+
4.	+

No-regrets moves	**Options**	**Big bets**
Strategic decisions that have positive payoffs in any scenario	Decisions that yield a sig-niflcant positive payoff in some outcomes and a (small) negative effect in other	Focused strategies with positive payoffs in one or more scenarios but a negative effect in others

Figure 4.3 Portfolio of actions
Source: Courtney *et al.* 1999: 18

valued as a learning process than a plan-making one. The basis of this claim is explained by de Geus first in his book entitled *The living company* (1997) and later in the *Harvard Business Review* (1999). It rests on the belief that the key to the adaptability of any organisation to continuous change is the institutional learning process it acquires over time, "with switches from expansion to self-preservation and back again to growth". Institutional learning in this context refers to the "process whereby management teams change their shared mental modes of their company, their markets, and their competitors" (de Geus 1999: 52–3); clearly, the labels would need to change for application to the public sector.

The lessons of the above for strategic planning for regional development in the UK are immense given the waxing and waning of national and regional economies in the country over the years, and the dramatically different emphasis placed by respective governments on regional planning efforts (see Chapters 2, 3 and 7). In the business world, it is estimated that for "every successful turn-around there are two ailing companies that fail to recover" (de Geus 1999: 54). If one was to conduct a similar analysis of the performance of regional development and planning agencies in the UK, the rate of failure of "turnaround" could be *very much* higher. An important institutional question that needs to be asked (and answered) here is why are some organisations better able to survive than others?

In de Geus's *Harvard Business Review* publication he reminds us that it is pain that makes people and living systems change, although he also points out that "pain management" (crisis management) is a "dangerous way to manage change" (1999: 54). He warns that crisis situations typically offer little time and few options to resolve problems, and that the deeper one is in crisis the fewer options to resolve them that remain. Having said this, it is clear that one of the positive attributes of crisis management is its speedy decision making but the track record of crisis management is *not* good.

Ultimately, it is best then to acknowledge and react to change *before* crisis points are reached. The most effective way to do this, de Geus argues, is for those involved in planning to be continuously engaged in a learning process about both the context of strategic planning *and* the planning process itself. This requires, however, managers and decision makers to review and change their own mental models on a *continuous* basis and to be willing to enter into joint amendments to their models as they engage in dialogue and learn from past experience. The difficulty here is that the speed of this (institutional) learning process is often too slow for "a world in which the ability to learn faster than competitors may be the only sustainable competitive advantage". The issue then is not whether a company will learn but "whether it will learn fast and early enough, and how institutional learning can be accelerated". De Geus adds a very significant rider to this conclusion. He makes it very clear that "the only relevant learning in a company is the learning done by those people who have the power to act", and this does *not* typically include the planner (1999: 55–6).

The method employed by Shell to trigger institutional learning is by the use of scenarios that include some "out of the box" models of the future, i.e. scenarios not within the normal probability range of expectancy (Shell International 2003). Their use enables the development of mental models for decision makers of what might/could happen to be extended and changed, with planners taking on the role of facilitator, catalyst and accelerator of the learning process. There are, however, according to de Geus (1999: 57) several potential pitfalls of this approach that need to be taken into account. Firstly, planners sometimes start with a mental model that is unrecognisable to those whom they seek to influence. Secondly, they often take too many steps at once and in so doing lose credibility among those they seek to influence. Finally, planners also have a tendency of communicating their information/guidance through instruction rather than persuasion.

Perhaps the most significant of all observations made by de Geus is that, because planners do not typically hold the same level of influence in the board-room as they do in the seminar room, it is of utmost importance that the institutional learning is completed *well before* the board meeting at which key strategic planning decisions are made. The failure to do this has major negative ramifications where (as in regional planning) the institutional learning exercise needs to take place not only within one agency but in association/partnership with a number of other stakeholders from the community and industry.

Dangers to avoid in strategic planning

The perils of strategic planning highlighted by Steiner on the basis of findings of a survey conducted more than 30 years ago in the corporate world (see Steiner 1972) still resonate today. Among the most basic perils that he cites are: the selection of the "wrong" subject to examine; the making of the "wrong" type of analysis; the drawing of the "wrong" conclusion from reliable data; senior management delegating the entire planning function to a planner; and assuming that a simple linear extrapolation of past data will provide acceptable forecasts for the future (Steiner 1997: 287–98). Drawing from the same survey results, he identifies four sub-groups of strategic planning pitfalls. These include: pitfalls in getting started; pitfalls related to a misunderstanding of the nature of strategic planning; pitfalls in doing strategic planning; and pitfalls in using strategic plans (1997: 290–2).

While Steiner's list pertains to strategic planning dangers to avoid in a corporate world, those involved in strategic planning in the public realm will *not* find it difficult to closely identify with most if not all of these potential shortcomings. Many planning and regional development and local planning agencies in the UK, for example, are so preoccupied with ongoing challenges on a day-to-day-basis that they are unable in reality to allot sufficient resources to conduct effective long-range planning. This is in large part because central government exerts so much pressure on them to address immediate issues, such as social exclusion, acute housing shortages, major transport infrastructure inadequacies, etc., and yet simultaneously ensure that their region/city retains a competitive advantage over other regions/cities that resources are spread too thinly. The tendency for many public sector planning agencies to declare broad long-term goals and promise sustainable visions of development that fail to easily translate into meaningful operational targets can *add* to the problem by generating frustration among those less sympathetic to the complexities of the situation and who expect more immediate "solutions".

The failure of top management to communicate their confidence in strategic thinking to lower management tiers can also unwittingly undermine the capability of an organisation to think *both* long-term and short-term, and link strategy to tactics. "Line managers at low levels in an organization will not spend time on projects that they do not believe top management is thoroughly committed to doing" (Steiner 1997: 293). The spread of this lack of belief (trust) in strategic planning can be encouraged by high levels of bureaucracy associated with much government planning legislation and the complicated planning procedures they insist must be followed. These situations often engender a lack of flexibility and an absence of looseness and simplicity in plan making which excessively restrain creativity in problem solving and kill off many of the important prerequisites of good strategic planning (so much valued by military strategists). Circumstances become even more problematic and complicated if this lack of belief in strategic planning infects both the communities and the private sector interests the planning system is intended to serve, contributing to cynicism and distrust, and possibly aggressive calls by various vested interests for the further dismantling of planning legislation (and the planning process) and the introduction of more speedy market-led solutions with potentially less equitable outcomes.

The new dynamics of strategy

Order, rational choice and execution

Notwithstanding the advantages of pursuing a formal strategic planning process along the lines outlined by Steiner, as well as others such as Johnson and Scholes (1999), it is important to report here that, in addition to IBM advocating the promotion of smaller decentralised units in its recent corporate global strategy, it has also recently recognised that excessively tight and formal strategic planning based on large organisational units can often suffocate innovative thinking, a conclusion believed to have potentially significant implications for strategic planning for regional development.

In recognition of this concern, IBM has turned to the findings of its one-time research arm – the Cynefin[3] Centre for Organisational Complexity – which developed a new strategic planning framework intended, among other things, to replace earlier applauded scenario planning approaches pioneered by Shell (see Kurtz and Snowden 2003). Following on from Aristotle's assertion that to understand an event or an entity one *must* consider "ordered" *as well as* "un-ordered" factors (see Loomis 1971), the Cynefin researchers (Kurtz and Snowden) who developed this framework challenge three basic assumptions that underlie the formal strategic planning process in the corporate world. These are the assumptions of the necessity for order, the practice of rational-choice decision making, and the ability to execute intentional capability.

Kurtz and Snowden believe that strategic planning assumptions of order incorrectly presume that there are *always* explainable underlying relationships between cause and effect in human interactions and markets that enable, ultimately, the production of prescriptive and predictive interventions. They further argue that planning assumptions of rational choice, based for example on minimising costs or maximising benefits (see Heap *et al.* 1992), erroneously imply a capability that collective behaviour can be successfully managed by "sticks and carrots" and disseminated through formal education/information networks. They also suggest that assumptions of intellectual capability within the planning process wrongly presume its acquisition *automatically* leads to an intention of its use, and that choices/decisions/actions taken by competitors, populations, governments, communities, etc. are the result of intentional collective behaviour rather than ad hoc happenings.

This challenge to the conventional wisdom of ordered science sees the growth of technological determinism and the dominance of certain engineering cum business management paradigms in the planning process arise from two related developments: firstly, a greater and more widespread automation and standardisation that reinforces the preference for (and assumption of) certain kinds of order; and, secondly, an order that is propelled by the increasing market-led forces of globalisation (see Chapter 5). Despite these developments, and reflecting the thoughts of Poincaré a century ago (see Adams 1994), Kurtz and Snowden see no overall planner or designer in control of *all* change. Instead, they see a development of phenomena that in *certain circumstances* emerge (almost organically) and/or evolve without direction through the interaction of many entities over time and space to create what they have termed an "emergent order".

Emergent orders and patterns

Kurtz and Snowden point out that these "emergent orders/patterns" are not unique, for they are found in many natural situations (such as snowflakes). Most significantly, they contrast greatly with those fabricated by complex planning systems employing considerable computing power to simulate complex patterns of behaviour, population movements, traffic flows, land-use interactions, etc. used by public sector planning agencies. The Cynefin researchers' position is quite simply that the latter more complex strategic planning tools are valuable *only* in certain contexts and *not* in others, and that the basis for deciding which approach is best suited to what circumstances, and when, depends very much on the "sense making" of the context in which the planning is to be undertaken of the kind discussed below and in further depth in Chapter 5.

What these authors argue is that the conventional kind of strategic thinking and planning advocated by Steiner and others is actually of "more limited applicability when it comes to managing people and knowledge", a conclusion that has major implications for strategic planning for regional development. Kurtz and Snowden highlight at least three important contextual differences in sense-making the complex world we live in. According to them, the differences are as follows (2003: 3–4):

- *Humans are not limited to one identity.* Individually, people can be parents, spouses or children but will behave differently depending on the context they find themselves in. Collectively, they can, therefore, be part of a community or a wider group, with the result that it is not always possible to know which unit of analysis to plan for/with.
- *Humans are not limited to acting in accordance with predetermined rules.* They are also able to impose (or disrupt) structure on their interactions through

collective agreements (such as partnership agreements) and enforcements (such as planning measures) as well as individual acts of free will, shifting a system from complexity to order and in so doing making it become more predictable. Furthermore, where group agreements, consensus finding and political bargaining are important components of the planning process (as in public sector planning) it is very difficult to simulate free will and complex intentionality (including duplicity, self-deception, manipulation, etc.). This reduces the certainty presumed in many of our plans.

- *Humans are not limited to acting on local patterns of decision making.* People today have a capacity to comprehend (and respond to) large-scale developments as a result of enhanced communications and technologies. This means that all scales of awareness (local, regional, national and global) *should* be considered simultaneously in contemporary planning exercises. Successfully achieving this can produce very important unexpected outcomes and changes in behaviour and decision making compared to conventional strategic planning approaches.

Directed order and emergent order

The essence then of the Cynefin Centre findings is not only that strategic planning should entail more sensitive sense making of the context of a planning exercise but *also* that planners should become more aware of the complexity of these planning contexts by differentiating between "directed order" and "emergent order". The latter, incidentally, is *not* to be regarded as "disorder" but a very different kind of order ("un-order") rarely considered in conventional strategic planning that is just as legitimate in its own way. Its use challenges the premise that any order that has not been planned or designed is either invalid or unimportant (Kurtz and Snowden 2003: 4).

It should be emphasised that, in practice, many planners and decision makers implicitly acknowledge the existence of "emergent order". They attribute this to such things as "cultural factors", "inspired leadership" and/or "gut feelings" – moulded over time (and space) by the interaction of various entities and experiences. It should also be pointed out that not only do both "un-ordered" and "ordered" contexts exist (with their own dynamics) but they interact and intertwine, a fact that is well illustrated for example in any credible description and analysis of cities and regions (see Chapter 6). They explain that for the domain of "emergent order" "the whole is *never* the sum of the parts". Kurtz and Snowden see the analysis of the seeds of "emerging patterns of order" offering the added value of revealing potential new ways of thinking, learning and, ultimately, acting. To use the authors' own words, "learning to recognize and appreciate the domain of 'un-order' is liberating, because we can stop applying methods designed for 'order' and instead focus on (and legitimate) methods that work well in 'un-ordered' situations" of "emerging order" (2003: 5).

The Cynefin framework has its origin in the practice of knowledge management as well as the analysis of formal and informal communities, and the interaction of both with structured processes. It is a "sense-making" framework intended to provide decision makers with enhanced capabilities to better understand a wide spectrum of unspecified problems. It is especially useful in tasks of collective sense making in that it facilitates outcomes to emerge from shared understandings and through multiple discourses among decision makers, all of which are common to strategic and regional planning in the public realm. The main value of the framework is to help decision makers "consider the dynamics of situations, decisions, perspectives, conflicts, and changes in order to come to a consensus for decision-making under uncertainty". In the context of their new strategic planning framework, "every intervention is seen as a potential opportunity . . . that can change the nature of the system so that to optimize the whole one has to allow a degree of sub-optimal behaviour of each of its constituent parts" (Kurtz and Snowden 2003: 6–7).

Sense-making and categorisation frameworks

The Cynefin approach, however, makes an important distinction between "sense-making" and "categorisation" frameworks. In the latter case, five quadrants are presented in a two-by-two matrix of domains (complex, knowable, chaos and known domains) (see Figure 4.4), with the most desirable situation typically believed to be in the upper right-hand quadrant, and with the main challenge being how to get to this destination from any of the other quadrants. The fifth domain is the central area, which is described by Kurtz and Snowden as the "domain of disorder", with the right-hand domains representing "order" and the left-hand "disorder". Another way to look at the Cynefin framework is to understand the types of connections that each domain promotes (see Figure 4.5), which incidentally has significant governance and management implications. The authors conclude that in most circumstances:

> a reasonable strategy is to capitalize on the stability afforded by strong connections without allowing them to harden so much that they destroy flexibility; and to capitalize on the freedom and renewal afforded by weak connections without allowing them to permanently remove useful patterns.
>
> (Kurtz and Snowden 2003: 7–9)

This new approach is summarised here not only to highlight the innovative and potentially important nature of this kind of strategy formulation for strategic and regional spatial planning but also to emphasise the complex relationship (and dynamics) that exists between a strategic planning process and the contexts it is applied to. Over time, this relationship can mutate new contextual outcomes that call for different planning approaches not perhaps considered before. In this regard, notwithstanding the themes of this and the following chapter, the division between the planning process and the planning context (with all its substantive challenges) is ultimately artificial in that one ultimately moulds/reflects the other, as Chapter 5 suggests, with common challenges of complexity, uncertainty and risk taking prevailing throughout.

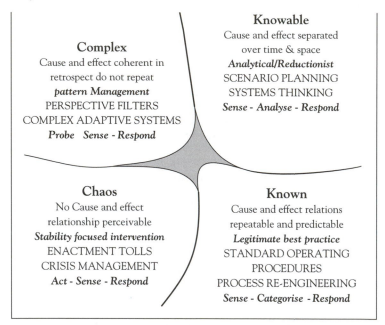

Source: Kurtz and Snowden, 2003:7

Figure 4.4 Cynefin domains
Source: Kurtz and Snowden 2003: 7

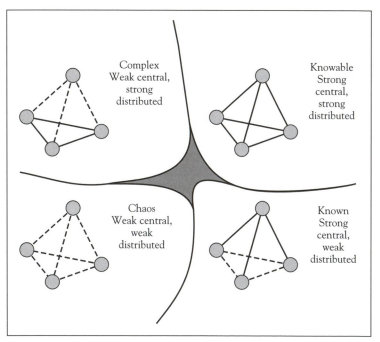

Figure 4.5 Cynefin connection strength
Source: Kurtz and Snowden 2003: 9

Conclusions

Notwithstanding the broad scope of the above discussion and on occasions its complexity, there are certain generic lessons regarding the strategic planning process that offer valuable insights and conclusions for the regional planner engaged in strategic spatial planning in the UK and elsewhere. These are summarised below within five sets of lessons, of which some act as bridgeheads for discussion points in Chapter 5:

- *Lesson set 1: Regarding the definition of strategic planning:*

  - Strategic planning contains both "the plan to plan" and the substantive information needed in the formulation and implementation of plans.
  - Strategic planning is *not* a process of forecasting and then determining what should be done to assure the fulfilment of these forecasts.
  - Goals and objectives are an integral part of *any* strategy.
  - A strategy marshals and allocates an organisation's resources into a unique and viable posture based on its relative internal competencies, concentrating on a few central principles that can create, guide and maintain dominance despite the frictions it may encounter.
  - A strategy implicitly acknowledges a hierarchy of aims and benefits and the transparency of decision making. It benefits from being bold, simple and clear, and being developed around selected concepts and thrusts that give it cohesion, balance and focus.

- *Lesson set 2: Regarding analysis in the strategic planning process:*

  - No analyst can predict the *precise* ways in which impinging forces interact with each other in pre-analysis for strategy making.
  - Strategic analysis entails the systematic identification of opportunities and threats that lie in the future, which in combination with other data provides a basis for making better current decisions.
  - The larger the organisation, the more formal the strategic planning process.
  - Complex strategic planning tools are valuable *only* in certain contexts; the basis for deciding which approach is best suited to what circumstances depends on the "sense making" of the context in which planning is to be undertaken.
  - Strategic planning *must* be capable of differentiating between "directed order" and "emergent order", where the latter is often attributed to cultural factors, "inspired leadership" and/or gut feelings, and recognising the benefits of the use of both at the appropriate time/place.
  - To optimise the value of an overall strategy one has to allow a degree of sub-optimal behaviour of each of its constituent parts.

- *Lesson set 3: Regarding the treatment of risk and uncertainty:*

  - Strategic planning *must* be engaged in greater sensitivity analysis of risks and uncertainties.

- Uncertainties in strategic planning can no longer be seen as being dissipated by a combination of knowledge and power, i.e. by increasing the knowledge of the project "content" and "context" and then identifying scarce resources to resolve the uncertainties.
- Planning and planning projects in the past were conceived and implemented by professionals more confident of their capabilities and expertise than is the case today.
- No longer can uncertainties be seen as being dispersed by planning procedures and techniques, for what this does in reality is merely to postpone risk taking and create latent conflicts.
- Many new strategic policy analysts now place uncertainty (and risk) in the milieu of their research, on the assumption that uncertainty is the norm rather than the exception.
- Different strategic planning exercises warrant different types of approaches, depending on the level of uncertainty (and risk) reflected in their decision making and their decision-making context.

- *Lesson set 4: Regarding public sector planning agencies:*

  - The tendency for public sector planning agencies to declare broad long-term goals and promise visions of development that fail to translate easily into meaningful operational targets adds to the frustration of those who expect immediate "solutions".
  - The failure of top management to communicate to their lower management tiers *their* confidence in strategic thinking can unwittingly undermine the capability of an organisation to think long-term and short-term *and* link strategy to tactics.
  - Much of the lack of trust in strategic planning arises from the high levels of bureaucracy associated with government planning legislation and the complicated planning procedures it often insists must be followed. These can engender a lack of flexibility and an absence of looseness and simplicity in plan making which excessively restrain creativity in problem solving.
  - When the lack of belief in strategic planning infects the communities and private sector interests the planning system is intended to serve, the resultant cynicism and distrust can lead to aggressive calls by vested interests for the further dismantling of planning legislation and the introduction of more market-led solutions with potentially less equitable outcomes.

- *Lesson set 5: Regarding the importance of recognising "emergent order":*

  - Excessively tight and formal strategic planning based on large organisational units can often suffocate innovative thinking.
  - The formal strategic planning process can be challenged in terms of its assumptions of the necessity for order, the practice of rational-choice decision making, and the ability to execute intentional capability.
  - The growth of technological determinism and the dominance of certain engineering/business management paradigms in the planning process

arise from greater/more widespread automation and standardisation, propelled by increasing globalisation.

– To understand an event or an entity one *must* consider "ordered" *as well as* "un-ordered" factors, as certain phenomena emerge in circumstances almost organically without direction to create "emergent order".

– Planners should become more aware of the complexity of the differing planning contexts and differentiate between "directed order" and "emergent order". For the domain of "emergent order" the whole is *never* the sum of the parts.

– Complex planning systems are valuable *only* in certain contexts. They are especially ineffectual in contexts associated with emergent order and when it comes to managing people and knowledge.

– The basis for deciding which planning approach is best suited to what circumstances, and when, depends on the "sense making" of the context. The Cynefin approach makes a distinction between "sense-making" and "categorisation" frameworks, with a reasonable strategy seen as one that capitalises on the stability afforded by strong connections between the planning process and the context, without allowing them to harden so that they destroy flexibility.

Notes

1. What is most important here is that some, if not all, elements of the strategy would change if the outcome were predictable.
2. As in level 2, some, and possibly all, elements of the strategy would change if the outcome were predictable.
3. The name Cynefin is a Welsh word whose translation into English as "habitat" or "place" does not do it justice, as it should, according to Kurtz and Snowden (2003), be more correctly understood as the place of multiple belongings.

References

Adams, C. C. 1994. The Poincaré Conjecture, Dehn Surgery, and the Gordon-Luecke Theorem. In *The knot book: an elementary introduction to the mathematical theory of knots*, 257–63. New York: W. H. Freeman.

Albrechts, L. 2004. Strategic (spatial) planning re-examined. *Environment and Planning B: Planning and Design* **31**, 743–58.

Albrechts, L., P. Healey and K. R. Kunzmann 2003. Strategic spatial planning and regional governance in Europe. *Journal of the American Planning Association* **69**.

Baghai, M., S. Coley and D. White 1999. *The alchemy of growth: kick-starting and sustaining growth in your company*. London: Texere.

Beck, U. 1992. *Risk society: towards a new modernity*. London: Sage.

Beck, U. 1999. *World risk society*. Cambridge: Polity Press.

Beck, U. 2000. *What is globalization?* Cambridge: Polity Press.

Benveniste, G. 1970. *The politics of expertise*. London: Croom Helm.

Braybrooke, D. and C. Lindblom, 1970. *A strategy of decision: policy evaluation as a social process*. New York: Free Press.

Castells, M. 1991. *The informational city*. Oxford: Blackwell.

Castells, M. 1996. *The rise of the network society*. Oxford: Blackwell.

Castells, M. 2004. *The power of identity*. Oxford: Blackwell.

Christensen, K. 1983. Coping with uncertainty. *American Planners Association Journal*, Winter edn.

Clausewitz, Carl von 1835. On war. *Military and Naval Magazine of the United States* **V** (August), **VI** (September). Originally appeared in *Metropolitan Magazine* (London) 1835, **13** (May, 64–71, and June, 166–76).

Courtney, H., J. Kirkland and P. Viguerie 1999. Strategy under uncertainty. In *Harvard Business Review on managing uncertainty*. Cambridge, MA: Harvard Business School Press.

Dimitriou, H. T. 2005. Globalization, mega transport projects and the making of mega places. Paper presented to session on Social and Economic Factors of Transportation, 84th Annual Meeting of Transportation Research Board, Washington, DC, January.

Dror, Y. 1986. *Policymaking under adversity*. New Brunswick, NJ: Transaction.

Edison, T. 1975. *Local government: management and corporate planning*. Leighton Buzzard: Leonard Books.

ESPON 2005. What is spatial planning. Home Page, European Spatial Planning Observation Network, http://www.espon.org.uk/spatialplanning.htm.

Friend, J. K. and W. N. Jessop 1969. *Local government and strategic choice*. London: Tavistock Publications.

Friend, J. K. and A. Hickling 1987. *Planning under pressure*. Oxford: Pergamon Press.

Friend, J. K. and A. Hickling 2005. *Planning under pressure*. Amsterdam: Elsevier.

GBN 2004. *Scenarios come to Davos: a GBN conversation with Ged Davies*. Emeryville, CA: Global Business Network.

Geus, A. de 1997. *The living company: growth, learning and longevity in business*. London: Nicholas Brealey Publishing.

Geus, A.P. de 1999. Planning as learning. In *Harvard Business Review on managing uncertainty*. Cambridge, MA: Harvard Business School Press.

Gladwell, M. 2003. *The tipping point*. London: Abacus.

Hall, P. 1980. *Great planning disasters*. Harmondsworth: Penguin.

Healey, P. 1997a. An institutional approach to spatial planning. In *Making strategic spatial plans: innovation in Europe*, P. Healey, A. Khakee, A. Motte and B. Needham (eds), 21–36. London: UCL Press.

Healey, P. 1997b. *Collaborative planning: shaping places in fragmented societies*. London: Macmillan.

Heap, S. H., M. Hollis, B. Lyons, R. Sugden and A. Weale 1992. *The theory of choice: a critical guide*. Oxford: Blackwell.

Held, D., A. McGrew, D. Goldblatt and J. Parraton 1999. *Global transformations: politics, economics and culture*. Cambridge: Polity Press.

Innes, J. E. 1990. *Knowledge and public policy*. New Brunswick, NJ: Transaction.

Johnson, G. and K. Scholes 1999. *Exploring corporate strategy: texts and cases*. Harlow: Prentice Hall and Financial Times.

Jomini, A.-H. de 1838. *Précis de l'Art de la Guerre: Des Principales Combinaisons de la Stratégie, de la Grande Tactique et de la Politique Militaire*. Brussels: Meline, Cans.

Kurtz, C. F. and D. J. Snowden 2003. The new dynamics of strategy: sense-making in a complex-complicated world. *IBM Systems Journal*, Fall.

Lash, S., B. Szersynski and B. Wynne 1998. *Risk, environment and modernity: towards a new ecology*. London: Sage.

Loomis, L. 1971. *Aristotle: on man in the universe*. New York: Gramercy Books.

Mason, R. O. and I. I. Mitroff 1981. *Challenging strategic planning assumptions: Theory, cases and techniques*. New York: John Wiley & Sons.

Mintzberg, H. 1994. *The rise and fall of strategic planning*. London: Prentice Hall and Financial Times.

Mintzberg, H., B. Ahlstrand and J. Lampel 1998. *Strategy safari: the complete guide through the wilds of strategic management*. London: Prentice Hall and Financial Times.

Osgood, J. 2000. *Carl von Clausewitz and Antoine-Henri Jomini and military strategy,* http://pw2.netcom/~jrosgood/w12.htm (accessed by C. Stanger on 31 October 2001).

Quinn, J. B. 1995. Strategies for change: some useful definitions. In *The strategy process,* H. Mintzberg, J. B. Quinn and S. Ghoshal. London: Prentice Hall.

RTPI 2001. *A new vision for planning: delivering sustainable communities, settlements and places,* May/June. London: Royal Town Planning Institute.

Seitz, J. L. 2002. *Global issues: an introduction.* Oxford: Blackwell.

Shaw, M. 2003. The state of globalisation. In *State/space: a reader,* N. Brenner, B. Jessop, M. Jones and G. Macleod (eds). Oxford: Blackwell.

Shell International 2003. *Exploring the future – scenarios: an explorer's guide.* Global Business Environment. London: Shell International.

Shy, J. 1986. Jomini. In *Makers of modern strategy from Machiavelli to the nuclear age,* P. Paret (ed.), 143–85. Princeton, NJ: Princeton University Press.

Stanger, C. 2004. Unpublished notes on strategic planning from a military perspective provided to the author.

Steiner, G. A. 1972. *Pitfalls in comprehensive long range planning.* Oxford, OH: Planning Executive Institute.

Steiner, G. A. 1997. *Strategic planning: a step-by-step guide.* New York: Free Press Paperbacks.

Surowiecki, J. 2004. *The wisdom of crowds.* London: Little, Brown.

Further recommended readings

Risk and uncertainty

Adams, J. 1995. *Risk.* London: UCL Press.

CABE (ed.) 2004. *What are we scared of? The value of risk in designing public space.* London: Centre for Architecture and the Built Environment, Space.

Lupton, D. 1999. *Risk.* London: Routledge.

Lupton, D. (ed.) 1999. *Risk and socio-cultural theory: new directions and perspectives.* Cambridge: Cambridge University Press.

Mythen, G. *Ulrich Beck: a critical introduction to the risk society.* London: Pluto Press.

Strategy, strategic thought and strategic planning

Berhhout, F. and J. Hertin 2002. Foresight futures scenarios: developing and applying participative strategic planning tool. *GMI,* Green Leaf Publishing, Spring.

Hargreaves Heap, S., R. Sugden and A. Weale 1994. *The theory of choice: a critical guide.* Oxford: Blackwell.

Harvard Business Review 1999. *Corporate strategy.* Boston, MA: Harvard Business School Press.

IBM 2000. *IBM's deep dive strategy development process,* Section II. London: Corporate Strategy Board, Corporate Executive Board.

Ohmae, Kenichi 1982. *The mind of the strategist: the art of Japanese business.* New York: McGraw-Hill.

Rittel, H. W. J. and M. Webber 1973. Dilemmas in a general theory of planning. *Policy Sciences* 4(2), 155–69.

River Path Associates 1999. Revenge of the nerds: how companies dream the future. Research note for BT corporate clients, River Path Consultants, Dorset.

Snowden, D. 2004. Multi-ontology sense making: a new simplicity to decision making. *Management Today Yearbook,* Richard Havenga (ed.), **20**(10).

5 Strategic thought and regional planning: the importance of context

Harry T. Dimitriou and Robin Thompson

Introduction

This and the preceding chapter's attempt to conceptually outline the main planks of strategic thought and planning may be seen by some, particularly "practitioners", to be too theoretical and detached, *even* perhaps impractical. However, as Mintzberg *et al.* (1995: xi) point out, theories and conceptual guidelines are useful since "it is easier to remember a simple framework about a phenomenon than it is to consider every detail you have ever observed". These authors claim that theoreticians and practitioners differ in their outlook on strategy formulation and planning because the latter typically believe they understand the world the way "it is" rather than the way it "should be", and because in some cases prescriptive theories can become the problem rather than the solution. Even when a strategic prescription "seems" effective in a given context, they argue, it requires a full appraisal of the new context to which it is to be applied and how it may function before it can be deemed effective.

This need to focus on "context" in strategic planning is very much the theme of this chapter and follows on from observations made in the preceding chapter. It seeks to further highlight the importance of contextual "sense making" as advocated by Kurtz and Snowden (2003) and examines "the power of context" on decision making and strategic planning practices. The chapter also investigates the dynamics of the substantive issues raised by regional change as the "object" of their planning efforts, and the relationship and interplay between these considerations. This is done with a view to exposing the considerable intricacies involved in effectively matching appropriate strategic planning practices with the contexts they are designed to serve, drawing on a variety of sources, including:

- Basil and Cook (1974) on the management of change;
- Mason and Mitroff (1981) on the relationship between complexity and strategic planning;
- Spindler (2002), Burfisher *et al.* (2003) and others on the new regionalism agenda and its requirements of strategic and regional planning;
- *The Economist* (2005) on private enterprises as the driver of new regional growth, corporate social responsibility and the role of public intervention;
- Baghai *et al.* (1999) on the importance of the public and private sector pursuing simultaneously different horizons of growth to achieve sustained economic change;

- Gladwell (2000) on the emerging rules of the epidemics of ideas that significantly influence change; and
- Surowiecki (2004) concerning the growing significance of the decentralisation of decision making and the use of non-specialised expertise in planning.

The chapter concludes by relating the above fields to the practise in the UK of spatial planning in general and regional planning in particular. The ideas in this chapter are explored with the help of examples from regional planning practice, especially from London and the South East, which form a fuller case study in Chapter 13.

Components of managing change

Origins of change

Strategies are often developed as a means to manage change within *and* between contexts. An extremely useful book which emphasises this conceptually and which in hindsight has proven highly prophetic was written by Basil and Cook in 1974 entitled *The management of change*. Their message read today reinforces the conviction that time does not age the truth. The authors of this relatively unknown publication argue that, "while change is readily apparent, its magnitude and consequences are relatively unknown" and that the "dysfunctions" of change in planning mainly lie in inadequate environmental (read contextual) scanning, the lack of change responsiveness capabilities in organisations, and/or the excessive reliance on crisis management. The authors' diagnosis suggests it is *imperative* for strategic planning to have regard to three facets of change management: the origins of change; the transitional responses to change; and the development of new strategies for change responsiveness (1974: ix–x).

As regards the "origins of change", Basil and Cook identify these primarily as structural-institutional, technological, and social-behavioural. They cite the expansion and growth of the influence of the European Union (EU) as having been particularly pervasive here, to which we would add the collapse of the Communist Bloc and the dramatically improved economic fortunes of Asia, especially China and India (see Dimitriou 2006). Even more consequential have been the impacts of globalisation on the nation state and local industries (especially manufacturing) and the move to market-driven economies (Buarque 1993; Lechner and Boli 2004; Kay 2003), as well as the reduced reliance on government intervention, and the threat to (and partial dismantling of) the welfare state (Ohmae 1990, 1995; Hutton 2002; Palast 2002).

Most significant of all in the last two decades has been the phenomenal change in "technological developments", especially those associated with communications, including transport and information technology. These have fuelled globalisation, brought tremendous new opportunities, and spawned many new sociological and behavioural impacts (Castells 1996, 1998; Dicken 1999; Graham and Marvin 2001; Dimitriou 2005). According to Basil and Cook, the feeding of such forces one upon the other produces complex reactive forces in "an additive or multiplicative manner to create even greater change" (1974: 28). These forces are discussed later in this chapter in the context of the new regionalism agenda and strategic and regional planning in the UK.

With their emphasis upon physical characteristics and tenuous linkages to economic planning, regional plans in the UK have tended in the past (see Chapter 2) to have a rather weak understanding of the origins of change: an example is the failure to anticipate the growth in car ownership in early post-war planning. It is notable that the recent London Plan (GLA 2004) explicitly starts from an analysis of "drivers of change". These drivers are broadly based, including economic, social, environmental and technological change. The Plan's objectives are shaped to manage the spatial impacts of these drivers in an effective and sustainable way. In this approach the planner does not seek to impose a strategy upon the region (as Abercrombie tried to do), but rather tries to identify and influence underlying forces that are seen as too powerful for the instruments of strategic and regional planning to shape in any significant way.

Strategic gaps

Another imperative of contextual analysis for strategic planning is the capacity for agencies (and regions) to accommodate "transitional responses" to change. Basil and Cook explain that this concerns how (well) institutions (including national, regional and local governments), other organisations *and* individuals have developed a capacity for "change responsiveness", including measures to introduce decentralisation and developments that engender greater coordination and transparency. Here the authors identify "strategic gaps" that can develop in both industry and government "as a result of organizational inflexibility, ignorance of complexity and open systems effects", where such gaps represent "the shortfall between the actions of organizations and institutions and the objective of an orderly adaptation to change" (1974: 133). Basil and Cook see these gaps significantly contributing to the misallocation and waste of resources, and producing an urgent need for proactive strategic action on many critical fronts.

This may be currently witnessed in the transport sector in the UK, which has become over the years increasingly automobile dependent, with annual motor vehicle purchases and use having now reached record levels and increased consecutively for the last five years (DfT 2005a). It may also be observed in the long-term failure of central government to reinvest in rail transport infrastructure (up until the second term of the New Labour government), which has jeopardised the sustained economic growth of the country (Glaister 2001). These developments have been further aggravated by a return to road building on a scale not seen since the Thatcher era (Brown 2005). In the environmental field, another "strategic gap" has developed from the painfully slow (and very belated) measures taken to effectively tackle the country's growing emission problems. The resultant pollution, made worse by the government's national and regional airport development policies, with no immediate prospect of a reversal in sight, is predicted to impact especially negatively on climate change given the traffic forecasts (Hillman and Fawcett 2004). These policies have largely pursued a "predict and provide" trajectory and contradict government proclaimed aims of promoting sustainable development (Friends of the Earth and AEF 1999; CPRE 2004).

Change agents and change responsiveness

The third imperative of contextual analysis highlighted by Basil and Cook is the development of new strategies for "change responsiveness". These rely heavily on "environmental scanning" (i.e. contextual analyses) and the need to create "change agents" that are more independent rather than dependent on the forces of change. The authors emphasise that the cost of traditional crisis management as a result of the failure to introduce is unaffordable and that "the case for 'change responsiveness' is one that society, organizations and individuals cannot ignore" (1974: 158).

The creation of the Greater London Authority (GLA) in 2000 partly reflects the recognition that the capital lacked a strategic authority with the mandate to manage spatial change since the dissolution of the Greater London Council (GLC). Although London's economy performed quite strongly under the Thatcher government, the reliance upon market mechanisms also produced growing personal and spatial inequalities and an inability to deal adequately with major change such as fast-rising traffic congestion, the spread of out-of-centre retailing and the overall decline in the quality of urban design. Against this backcloth, the new Mayor has in effect acted as a critical "change agent" for London, bringing a fresh perspective to a city subject to immense change (illustrated by the fact that today one in four of London's residents is born outside the UK). As an entirely new institution, the GLA has been able to exercise a fresh mandate. Its senior management like to be seen not to be weighed down by the conventional wisdoms and institutional inertia that can attach to older institutions. Whether this capacity to act as a "change agent" can be retained as the Mayor and the GLA become longer established remains to be seen, but the organisation was deliberately designed to be far smaller, more strategic and more flexible than its predecessor, the GLC. The challenge of how to make such "change agents" become more responsive is as important today as it was when first discussed by Basil and Cook, as the GLA example demonstrates. It remains one of the most formidable challenges currently facing society in the UK.

These authors insightfully concluded their work by expressing a desire to see "twenty-first-century man" "educated to accept and manage ambiguity, uncertainty and complexity" (1974: 158). They argue that the only way to do this effectively is to introduce a series of new "proactive strategies" that cope better with ambiguity, risk, uncertainty and complexity of the kind advocated by post-modernist sociologists and geographers such as Adams (1995), Beck (1992, 1999, 2000) and Lash *et al.* (1998) *some thirty years later.* Given that the preceding chapter discussed the first of these four concerns at some length, the following section focuses on the importance of understanding complexity as part of context analysis and "sense making" in support of more effective strategic planning for regional development.

Complexity, "wicked" problems and strategic planning

Complex contexts of decision making

A question that needs to be posed by anyone engaged in strategic planning early on in the exercise is whether the solution to one problem is in any way related to the solution of other problems. Confirming that this is often indeed the case, Mason and Mitroff (1981: 3–4) argue that a major problem with connected systems of complexity is that deviations in one element can be transmitted to others. They claim that these deviations "can be magnified, modified, and reverberated so that the system takes on an unpredictable life of its own" (1981: 6). The outcome can be that policies developed to resolve one problem spawn others and generate many unintended impacts as the dynamics of the problem(s) unfold, a phenomena only too common in regional planning.

Accepting this premise, this requires of the strategist two things: firstly, the appreciation of the concept of complexity as the *context* of his/her strategy making – where "complexity" may be defined as "the condition of being tightly woven or twined together" (Mason and Mitroff 1981: 5); secondly, the development of a "sense-making" capability of complexity in the strategic plan-making process (Snowden 2004).

Mason and Mitroff see a fundamental characteristic of the complexity of major problems to be that they are typically "organised" in so far as they tend to possess "an illustrative structure to underlying problems that give pattern and organization to the whole" (1981: 5). They suggest that organised complexity can in fact become a major obstacle to problem resolution, because, while there is a range of techniques available for taming simple problems, there are only a few methodologies for tackling complex ones. This is a view shared by Kurtz and Snowden (2003), who in their research undertaken for IBM advocate simplicity to decision making in complex environments.

Complexity and wicked problems

Problems of organised complexity are referred to by Rittel and Webber (1973) as "wicked problems" in the sense that the more one attempts to tackle them the more complicated they become. Paraphrasing Mason and Mitroff (1981) they claim that such problems have no definitive formulation and that every formulation of a wicked problem corresponds to a statement of solution and vice versa. They see no single criteria system or rule that determines whether the solution to a wicked problem is correct or not and liken the task of tackling such problems to a "Faustian bargain, requiring eternal vigilance". There is, furthermore, no exhaustive, enumerable list of permissible operations for solving a wicked problem. Instead, they have many possible explanations for the same discrepancy; depending on which explanation one chooses, the solution takes on a different form. Each wicked problem can be considered as a symptom of another problem that has no identifiable root cause, and once a solution is attempted one can *never* undo what has been done. They finally see every wicked problem as essentially unique with no way of knowing when a wicked problem is solved (1981: 10–11).

Drawing from the same source, such problems exhibit six characteristics:

- *interconnectedness* – whereby strong connections link each problem to other problems so that "solutions" aimed at one problem have the potential to generate important opportunity costs and side effects;
- *complicatedness* – characterised by "feedback loops" through which change can multiply itself or even cancel itself out;
- *uncertainty* – in that wicked problems typically emerge in dynamic and highly uncertain environments that require of change agents a flexibility to respond to unexpected outcomes with the assistance of contingency plans;
- *ambiguity* – as a result of the fact that problems can be seen in quite different ways by different parties, depending on their interests, loyalties and perspectives;
- *conflict* – resulting from competing claims and interests, colliding visions and values of development warranting compromises, creating "winners" and "losers" of planned (and unplanned) outcomes;
- *social constraints* – exerted by prevailing social, political, technological and political forces and capabilities (1981: 12–13).

These characteristics have two major implications for policy makers and strategic planners working in environments of complexity. Firstly, they require a broader participation of parties affected either directly or indirectly by planned outcomes. Secondly, they need to rely on a wider spectrum of data from a larger and more diverse set of sources (1981: 13–14). The former conclusion concurs very much with the findings of Gladwell (2000) and Surowiecki (2004) outlined later in this chapter, and the latter with the conclusions of Courtney *et al.* (1999) discussed in Chapter 4.

The first major implication confirms the now widely acknowledged fact that policy making is essentially political, in the sense that it involves forming individuals into groups to discuss, formulate and pursue common interest.[1] The second major implication presumes that much of the information necessary for dealing with complex problems rests in the minds of a large number of individuals, and that special efforts are needed to extract this information from them to disseminate it to others, reinforcing the need to utilise (and thus identify) as many different "objectified" sources of information as possible for collective decision making so as to facilitate the exchange and comparison of views.

Complexity and strategic planning

Yet another important observation that emerges from the work of Mason and Mitroff (1981) is the need for the strategic analysis of contexts both to incorporate a healthy respect for "doubt" and as a method of identifying *and* assessing it. They see the systematising of the analysis of doubt as a critical part of the strategic planning process, best provided through dialectics and argumentation that entail:

- making information and its underlying assumptions explicit;
- raising questions and issues toward which different positions can be taken;
- gathering evidence and building arguments for and against each position; and
- arriving at some final conclusion (1981: 15).

Over and above their requirement for broader participation in the planning process, the use of diverse sets of data, and the incorporation of doubt in strategy analysis and formulations, the same source emphasises the importance of employing a holistic *and* systematic approach to analysis and synthesis. This is particularly necessary, they claim, in light of the need to break down the complex problem into understandable elements and on this basis "determine the linkages that give organization to its complexity and to understand the problem as a whole" (1981: 15). Mason and Mitroff suggest that these requirements call for a new set of criteria with which to design, appraise and evaluate strategies that are:

- *participative* – given that the required knowledge to solve such problems is drawn from a variety of sources;
- *adversarial* – on the assumption that doubt in the context of opposition is seen to be the guarantor of the best judgements;
- *integrative* – so as to ensure the bringing together of diverse knowledge as a basis of coherent action; and
- *supportive* – of a managerial predisposition in such a way that efforts to expand insights into the nature of complexity and developing holistic views at problem solving are undertaken as continuous process (1981: 16).

Regional planning faces particularly complex and often wicked problems. These reflect the breadth of the decision-making field and the size and diversity of the regions for which decisions are being made. The regional institutional context is also complex (as verified by Chapters 3 and 7), so that decision making itself is a very complicated and often unpredictable process. Yet from this complexity, relatively straightforward decisions are *ultimately* required. Should a new airport be built? Should a town be expanded? The strategic challenge is to achieve the most "effective" decisions by managing the way in which complex problems are identified, analysed and addressed in the most systematic and inclusive way.

The demand for additional (and affordable) housing is a prime example of a wicked issue faced by many regional planning authorities in the UK. It exhibits all of Rittel and Webber's six characteristics. It is *highly interconnected* with other major and complex issues such as the labour market and the quality of transport. It is *complicated*: demand in one part of a region may result in (perhaps unintended) pressures to compensate by increasing demand in another part of the region. Housing demand is subject to great *uncertainties*, depending, for example, on economic cycles. There is *ambiguity*, for instance in the different perspectives of the existing resident wishing to protect the immediate environment and the first-time buyer wishing to see choice and availability in the housing market. Demand for housing (see Chapter 11) has long been an area for *conflict*, notably between cities that have tended to "export" population and their hinterlands that have tended to receive incomers from the city. The whole issue encounters high levels of *social constraint*: for example, some political constituencies are highly mobilised to minimise additional housing and employ a great deal of expertise to justify their position; this has certainly been the case in the wider South East of England, where the resistance of many political establishments to new growth has been seen as one of the reasons for the creation of the new regional assemblies.

One of the weaknesses of regional planning in the UK has been that its instruments have often seemed too simplistic and insufficiently strategic to address the complexity of the matters they have to deal with. Until the recent infusion of spatial planning into the theory, practice and legislative base of planning, the main instruments related to the regulation of land use. Moreover, the discretionary nature of the UK planning process, whilst offering the opportunity to relate proposals to their individual context, nevertheless has encouraged a mindset and procedure that lack rigour. Decision making is often reflective of a set of implicit values rather than of a disciplined process of examination of evidence and systematic appraisal of alternatives. The new system of regional spatial strategies (RSSs) does offer much greater potential for a broader spatial perspective and for a systematic appraisal of options, including the requirement to engage with the community in considering these, although there remains much development work to be done.

New regionalism as a context for strategic planning

New regionalism and globalisation

Spatial planners, whether working at the city or the regional scale, are continually reminded that they are today operating in a new context, a context where the world is made up of a new global political economy, divided into new (often trans-national) "regions" such as the European internal market, the North American Free Trade Area (NAFTA), the Asia Pacific Economic Cooperation (APEC) area, etc. These are seen by many to present "the re-emergence of the region as a unit of [global] economic analysis and the territorial sphere most suited to the interaction of political, social and economic processes in the era of 'globalization' " (Tomaney and Ward 2000: 471), where globalisation is characterised by the unimpeded flow across national borders of investment, industry, information technology and individual consumers (Ohmae 1995).

This reconfiguration of the region very much highlights the role and impact of international trade on regional development and its spatial outcomes, and reflects an increasingly "innovation-led economy" with entrepreneurship and competition as its main sources of economic growth (Porter 1990). The likes of Ohmae (1995) and Webb and Collis (2000) argue that globalisation has made the nation state an inappropriate level at which to formulate and coordinate economic policy because regional development becomes increasingly organised at the international level in a manner whereby sub-national regions give way to regions of the global economy (Smith 1988). While there is no doubt that the recent interest in "the region" in the UK has been greatly stimulated by the development of devolved political institutions in Scotland, Wales and (to a lesser extent) Northern Ireland, this new regionalisation is taking place very much as part of a "Europe-wide" process in a larger global context. In this respect, local developments of the new regionalism agenda in the UK represent only one dimension of a "broad set of [critical] economic, social, cultural and political changes that are transforming territorial relationships" (Tomaney and Ward 2000: 471).

New and old regionalism

The growing literature on new regionalism both as a concept and as a reality presents to the strategic and regional planner new highly complex and dynamic presumed contexts within which and for which to plan territories and space (Jones and MacLeod 2004). Structurally, many of these new contexts incorporate and pose the epitome of "wicked problems", as they have strong associations (through globalisation) with features of interconnectedness, complicatedness, uncertainty, ambiguity, conflict and social constraints. Employing Burfisher *et al.*'s (2003) notion of a continuum of levels of integration among countries – from "shallow" to "deep" – new regionalism is correlated with "deep integration", while "old regionalism" is associated with "shallow integration". Whereas "old regionalism" is "based on the logic of the welfare state that prescribed an interventionist, protectionist role of the state, thus constraining market forces" (Spindler 2002: 5), "new regionalism" involves "additional elements of harmonising national policies, and allowing or encouraging internal factor mobility" (Burfisher *et al.* 2003: 2) and the reduction or elimination of barriers to trade in commodities.

"New regionalism is not only *new* in terms of a renaissance of regional tendencies and in terms of the fashionable creation of regional institutions" but is also new because of its new *purpose* and *content* and the new underlying *logic* of regionalism that is changing (Spindler 2002: 3). What is most important about these developments is that they demonstrate how increasingly (global) business creates (and promotes) new concepts of development which envision a regionalised world "that sharply contrasts to the role so far played by regions" and that this concept of new regionalism has "tipped" into the political acceptance with so little resistance (2002: 5). This is notwithstanding the blistering and very persuasive critique of the concept provided by Lovering (1999) and the rejoinder offered by MacLeod (2001).

Lovering claims that, however attractive and persuasive a story new regionalism might tell, it is seriously compromised by numerous practical and theoretical limitations and "is largely a fiction" (1999: 380). MacLeod in his rejoinder, while sympathetic to Lovering's stance, claims that a more in-depth "understanding of the social and political construction of regions, the uneven geography of growth, and the moments of re-scaled regionalised state power that now enframe the process of economic governance" would provide a clearer idea of what could be salvaged from the range of new regionalist ideas on offer (2001: 804).

New regionalism in the UK

It is certainly true that regional planning in the UK has sought to accommodate a new regionalism agenda, as in the case of the inclusion of private enterprise in the planning decision-making processes. Regional assemblies have a separate constituency for business representatives, and many of the government's favourite policy-oriented partnerships have a business (and voluntary) sector presence, for example the Local Strategic Partnerships responsible for Community Strategies. To an important extent, this does facilitate the ownership of regional and strategic policy by the bodies that will have the powers to implement them. Regional planning authorities in the UK are, however, particularly deficient in powers and resources. They are now required to formulate policy for a wide set of sectors, and the only serious prospect for delivery is not compulsion but the generation of a sense of shared ownership of the issues. This can only be achieved if the "delivery agents" and local communities have themselves formed some part of the policy process.

The Mayor of London, for example, surprised many by his apparent embrace of the forces of global business and finance in his London Plan. This rested in considerable part upon the support of these forces as the keystone of London's continuing growth. The role of the Plan was to introduce a relatively strong and clear set of policies for the spatial management of growth – and for the mediation of economic growth with environmental, social and transport consequences. However unpalatable this approach may have been to some, it did create the potential to enlist the resources of business whilst mitigating the less desirable effects of this empowerment.

One impact of the new regionalism agenda has been the elevation of economic development and enhanced competitiveness as the prime objectives of policy. Driven by the Regional Development Agencies (RDAs), regions across the country have sought to maximise growth and competitiveness. One consequence is that the accumulative economic aspirations of individual regional plans far outstrip any reasonable projection of future economic performance at a national level. The government's refusal to contemplate a national spatial strategy means that there is, furthermore, no agency with a remit to reconcile the economic (and other) strategies of each region or to encourage a more effective form of regional collaboration and specialisation as an alternative to inter-regional competition. In this situation, the hope of mitigating differences in wealth and economic potential between the regions through regional policies of redistribution is a slim one indeed.

Regional identity

Notwithstanding the preceding discussion, whether we talk of old or new regionalism, the term "region" in reality remains an inconclusively defined geographical unit (Jones and MacLeod 2004). Geographers referring to the regions of old regionalism most commonly inferred from them that they had some physical basis of similarity, a fact that is increasingly untrue today as boundaries are frequently defined as a matter of political and/or administrative convenience, as in the case of the regions of East and South East England in the UK (John and Whitehead 1997; Murdoch and Tewdwr-Jones 1999).

For others, the regional hypothesis was derived from a degree of cultural affinity or the sharing of common economic problems or possibilities (Robertson 1965). Again, this premise is less valid today, although it is truer in certain places (for example, Wales and Scotland) than others. Cooke and Morgan (1994: 91) argue that "regional identity" is an especially important facet in today's fast-globalising world because "contemporary regional economic success is inseparable from cultural, social and institutional accomplishment", a point also discussed at some length by Castells in his seminal book *The power of identity* (2004).

Ohmae (1995: 5), on the other hand, asserts that what defines a region in the era of new regionalism is not its location or its political borders "but the fact that [regions] are the right size and scale to be the true, natural business units in today's global economy". In support of this vision of "region states" (of which perhaps Hong Kong and Singapore are theoretically archetypal), he claims these regions make "effective ports of entry to the global economy because the very characteristics that define them are shaped by the demands of that economy" (1995: 89). He goes on to argue that they need to be large enough to provide an attractive market for the brand development of leading consumer products and possess a population range of 5–20 million so as to enable their citizens to share interests as consumers, and be large enough to justify the economies of scale of key services that are essential to participation in the global economy.

Private enterprise as the driver of new regional growth

Private enterprises and public intervention

Current challenges to strategic planning within the realities of the new regionalism agenda clearly bring with them two significant developments. The first, as already indicated, is "the growing importance of global business as a [major] non-state actor in governing the political economy . . . [with the knowledge that] business actors increasingly interact 'outside the market' " (Spindler 2002: 5) and thereby reduce the transparency of decision making. The second is the influence and limitations of "corporate social responsibility" (CSR) as a potential antidote to unrestrained market forces and profit making, with scepticism growing as to the sincerity with which this is practised.

The Economist (2005: 3–4) concludes that while "It would be a challenge to find a recent annual report of any big international company that justifies the firm's existence merely in terms of profit rather than 'service to the community' " and although the prevalence of CSR among so many companies in the UK sometimes represents a success in the "battle of ideas", "the winners [of CSR], oddly enough, are disappointed [and] . . . are starting to suspect that they have been conned". According to this source, an important aspect in understanding *why* some firms promote CSR, as opposed to why many parts of civil society are sceptical of its sincerity, lies in the fundamental fact that private enterprises are *ultimately* dependent upon a supporting infrastructure of laws and permissions to succeed, infrastructure that can only be provided by the state with the consent of the electorate. *The Economist* quite rightly argues that the effective formulation of these "sticks and carrots" relies on an understanding by the public sector of "how capitalism best works to serve the public good" but concludes that this understanding not only appears to be in short supply but also sometimes suffers from a presentation of this understanding that is "downright false" (2005: 4).

The same source suggests that the private sector serves the public good *only* if certain of its conditions are met and that, therefore, in order to extract the *most* benefit from capitalism, (strategic) public intervention of different types (and a great deal of it) is necessary in different areas of business activity. Remembering that this advice comes from a newspaper cum journal not known for its liberal leanings, its conclusion that in order to improve capitalism and for the state to intervene more effectively in market failures "you first need to understand it"

(2005: 4) may come as a rude surprise to many. It is a message that is at the heart of the kind of strategic planning advocated for regional development in the conclusions to this chapter.

The three horizons of growth

A relevant piece of research regarding what it takes for private business ventures, as important drivers of regional growth and change, to achieve sustained profitable growth and turn around failing businesses in today's climates of increased deregulation, competition and globalisation was published in a book entitled *The alchemy of growth* by Baghai, Coley and White in 1999. In this publication, the authors, who are consultants to one of the world's leading consultancy firms (McKinsey and Company), report on a number of critical conclusions from a two-and-a-half-year study conducted in the 1990s. The main conclusions include: executives must discuss as much about future aspired horizons as where they have been; very few companies sustain above-average growth for their industry year after year; and sustained economic growth can only be achieved by the pursuit of "three horizons" of growth simultaneously and a "staircase to growth strategy".

Baghai *et al.* (1999) make it clear that understanding growth is a prerequisite to achieving sustained development and that the principles underpinning the three horizons analysis of economic growth they present are crucial to effective strategic decision making and planning. These three horizons (see Figure 5.1) represent a different stage in the creation and development of business, each of which, the authors argue, calls for radically different initiatives and poses very different management challenges. Together they allow one to "distinguish between the embryonic, emergent, and mature phases of a business life cycle" (1999: 4) whereby:

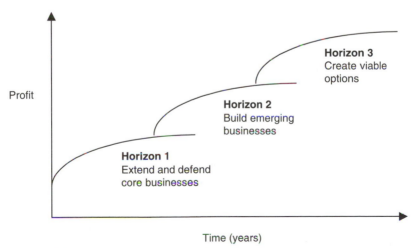

Figure 5.1 The three horizons and growth staircase

Source: Baghai *et al.* 1999: 130

- Horizon 1 is preoccupied with the extension and defence of the core businesses;
- Horizon 2 is focused on the building of emerging businesses; and
- Horizon 3 is concerned with the creation of viable alternative options to current businesses.

It is not necessary to dwell too long here on the detailed analysis of each of these horizons, but what Baghai *et al.* argue are three important things. Firstly, it is very significant to understand that each horizon pay offs over *different* time frames. Secondly, successful industries are much better at tackling the challenges of Horizon 1, are less skilled at addressing the challenges of Horizon 2, and are distinctly poor at confronting the challenges of Horizon 3 (which is why the culture of short-term thinking prevails so much in the private sector). Finally, the art of achieving sustained growth is to engage in the challenging of the three horizons concurrently and *not* sequentially.

The implications of this "staircase to growth strategy" for strategic planning for regional development are profound. This is because the traditional expertise of most public sector change agencies has been in Horizon 3 rather than Horizon 1. This has contributed to the creation of "strategic gaps" developing between the different planning horizon emphases of the two sectors. With many public bodies entering into partnership relationships with the private sector, the public sector has felt obliged to increasingly "fall in line" with Horizon 1 priorities and synchronise its activities more with those of the short-term focus of private enterprise. Paradoxically, this has taken place at a time when business gurus such as Baghai *et al.* are discovering the importance of more forward-thinking strategies. The public sector, on the other hand, has recently gone through a period (since the 1980s especially) of shedding its institutional capacity for forward thinking at the very time it is needed most and is in short supply in industry. This mismatch does not bode well for either the public or the private sector, as the problems of recent planning, finance and delivery efforts of public transport in the UK (railways in particular) suggest. These experiences demonstrate that the private sector *needs* a strong public sector to succeed and deliver what is expected of it, a conclusion supported by *The Economist* and one that is contrary to much of the conventional thinking about globalisation and new regionalism.

An atypical but remarkable example of private and public sector collaboration in the UK can be found at Kent Thames-side, one important sub-region within the Thames Gateway. There the major landowners and developers (now Land Securities) have worked with planning authorities in a formal partnership for over a decade. In this instance, the private sector partner has acted as an agent of long-term strategic planning on the lines advocated by Baghai *et al.* On occasions, it has seemed more strategic than the planning authorities, for the philosophy of Land Securities is that long-term (Horizon 3) collaborative strategic planning can raise the value of the asset. If the area's economy prospers then the developer's businesses benefit. It also understands, however, that a much better physical and social environment will raise the perception of the area and eventually translate into higher land values and thus higher profits.

This approach tallies with a growing and much more common private sector belief that longer-term planning is beneficial as it can generate a degree of certainty within the development market and so enable more effective management of assets and a secure environment against which to generate proposals. It was on this basis that the business lobby in London largely supported the London Plan's relatively specific targets for jobs and housing. A firm decision about Crossrail would yield similar advantages.

Tipping points and the battle for ideas

But where, in the first place, did the notion come from that the private sector does *not* need a strong public sector to assist it attain sustained growth? And where is the evidence for this position? Furthermore, how were politicians (and the public) convinced (if indeed they were) that minimum public sector intervention in territorial and regional development is to be preferred? And how in today's climate of realpolitik do these notions sit with stated government aims to achieve sustainable environmental development and more equitable growth? The fact of the matter is that these and other ideas, notions and visions, all of which impact on policy making and planning (see Albrechts 2004), each have their own ideological and theoretical roots, and their own heyday of rhetoric and influence that waxes or wanes over time (and even space).

Gladwell's book *The tipping point* (2000) does much to help one understand how to address the above questions, for it alerts the world to the process by which certain products, ideas and ways of behaving cross the threshold or "tip" and "take off". It also reveals the inconsistencies, incompatibilities and constituencies of some ideas which are otherwise intended to be complementary. This is most important for the strategic planner and policy maker to understand for, while many of the examples Gladwell cites have to do with marketing products, several of the principles he identifies are transferable to the practice of spatial planning and regional policy making. For example, an analysis and understanding historically of how corporate industry persuaded governments of the Western world, Latin America and now Asia to adopt a vision of automobile-dependent cities and regions (and the associated lifestyles this implies), over and above other options, can shed a great deal of light on how to successfully promote/market new ideas and policies in the future that can effectively introduce alternative visions.

The unexpected "take-off" of the concept of sustainable environmental development and its growing acceptance by national and local governments, and the international development community alike is a more positive example (perhaps against the odds) of how an idea/vision has "tipped" and is now beginning to be seen as a possible antidote to the motorised vision for the future. The widespread acceptance of the notion that increased global pollution related to automobile dependency is contributing very significantly to climate change with potential devastating implications is a good illustration of how ideas "tip" into global acceptance and stimulate the introduction of new thinking, policies and action. The adoption and pursuit, however, of policies by the UK government that simultaneously promote automobile dependency *and* sustainable development confirm the presence of ongoing battles for visions of the future and of a race between visions that ultimately manifest themselves as policy conflicts and planning contradictions, creating new sets of "wicked problems".

Gladwell's invaluable insights into the pivotal role certain parties and individuals can have in changing or perpetuating trends, ideas and policies – so important to policy makers and planners anywhere – shed light on the rules of what he calls "the epidemics of ideas" that make certain ideas and visions (such as new regionalism) ignite and stick, and others fade. In all these insights, what is critical to appreciate is "the power of context" and "the influence of the few" in defining context. The argument forwarded by Gladwell is that the word-of-mouth epidemic that contributes to the "sticking factor" of an idea – such as the case for privatisation of public transport in the railway industry and the separation of ownership of the track from the operation and ownership of the franchised train services – requires not only what he calls "Connectors, Mavens and Salesmen"[2] but also an effective dissemination network capable of "spinning" (on a sustained basis) the benefits of the idea among those who matter. Failure to do this leads to the fading away of the perceived legitimacy of an idea, sometimes temporarily; it may return in a modified form at a later date (even several decades later) in a changed, more welcoming context.

It can be argued that the office of Mayor has been introduced in London to create community leadership and that it is designed to enable connections. Certainly the current Mayor is a highly skilled salesman, supported by some mavens and connectors. His campaign to introduce the congestion charge demonstrated the arts of tipping public opinion in favour of a scheme that was initially characterised as both impracticable and unpopular. This was done by the promotion of alternatives to the private car and, especially, a major expansion of bus passenger mileage, and the generation of longer-term hope that schemes such as Crossrail would be successful. It demonstrated, furthermore, skilful implementation by introducing the scheme in the school holiday when traffic flows were lower.

However, the "soft" processes by which concepts such as sustainable development reach a tipping point and become accepted wisdom carry some major difficulties. It has been argued that this and other strategic concepts in city planning (such as sustainable communities) are ideas which have emerged without sufficient rigorous analysis and testing. Sustainable development, so the argument goes among such sceptics, manifestly means different things to different people. For most people within the community, they argue, the concept carries little or no meaning. It has been introduced into conventional wisdom through the domain of policy makers and professionals. However, even those within these groups are likely to have different understandings: many approach the concept through their own fields of social or economic or environmental action, whereas sustainable development seeks to achieve a balance between all of these dimensions. For example, the London Plan was attacked by various groupings as being insufficiently sustainable in, respectively, social, economic and environmental terms. The expectations of the protagonists were clearly different, whereas sustainability seeks to promote all three characteristics of development.

The wisdom of crowds

Another recent influential publication that acknowledges the importance of the "power of context" in strategic decision making and policy making is Surowiecki's book entitled *The wisdom of crowds* (2004). The controversial premise of this publication is that, if you want to make a "correct" decision or solve a strategic problem, *under the right circumstances* large groups of people are often smarter than a few experts. If true, this premise has profound implications for how we plan and run our cities and regions, and how we structure our political systems and think about the future. It also, incidentally, "has the potential to make a profound difference in the way companies do business" (2004: xiv). Interestingly, some of the ideas presented by Surowiecki lend support to Gladwell's critique of the current ways by which new products, ideas, visions and policies are promoted and allegedly rely on "a few that matter".

Whereas conventional wisdom has it that when we want something done "right" we turn to a leader or expert, Surowiecki demonstrates quite convincingly (by citing a variety of examples) that this need not be true, and indeed is often not the case. He argues that "chasing the expert is a mistake . . . and a costly one at that" (2004: xv). He also claims that, although non-specialists have less information at hand than the specialist, and possess limited foresight into the future, "when their imperfect judgements are aggregated in the right way, their collective intelligence is often excellent" (2004: xiv). While there are many who clearly would have poured scorn on the idea that a crowd has *any* collective intelligence (see Macay 1841; Menschel 2002 on Baruch, Thoreau and Carlyle; Nietzsche 1966; Le Bon 1982), a recent event that it could be argued dramatically reinforces Surowiecki's premise (especially if one holds Euro-sceptic or Euro-reformist views) is the outcome of the French and Dutch referenda on the proposed EU constitution which rejected the newly proposed constitution.

The conclusion, that *under certain circumstances* large groups of people are often smarter than a few experts, has amazing implications for city and transportation planning and environmental management and for those involved in efforts to make regional policy making more effective, democratic and decentralised. The recent introduction by central government of regional assemblies in the UK (and national assemblies in Wales and Scotland), in an effort to further devolve regional government and decision making, is more in harmony with Surowiecki's belief in collective intelligence. However, one of the striking considerations about the "wisdom of crowd" thesis is that, "even though its effects are all around us, it's easy to miss, and, even when it's seen, it can be hard to accept" (Surowiecki 2004: xiv). The rejection by the populace of a North East Regional Assembly in the UK is a case in point.

While most planning experts will unsurprisingly be sceptical of Surowiecki's views, it is difficult to deny that his provocative stance rings true in a number of instances. If we return to the challenges in the UK of public transport planning and delivery, and the railways in particular, we cannot but conclude that Surowiecki's position makes a great deal of sense. Here, followers of neo-liberal economic thinking, who appear at present to dominate much of the expertise of the UK's transportation sector and advice given to New Labour, have recommended an increase in the price of peak-hour travel as a means of reducing railway patronage to more "manageable levels". Following earlier (relatively successful) efforts by government to encourage the public to transfer their preferred mode of commuter travel from the car to the train in the name of achieving enhanced sustainable development, it is hard *not* to foresee that Surowiecki's premise will be vindicated. For if the recommended price hike is indeed introduced, it is likely to be only a matter of time before the "wisdom of the crowds" is strongly expressed in the political arena and will lead either to a policy reversal or to a return by many commuters to the wider use of the motor car.

The desire to subject regional and other forms of planning to public participation and focus group analysis has been a significant feature of government policy making in recent years. Under the new Planning and Compulsory Purchase Act 2004, planning authorities in England are now required to produce a statement of community involvement to show that the community has indeed been engaged in the process. However, the process has always been one in which the wisdom of some of the crowd is articulated. Surowiecki emphasises that wisdom comes from the aggregate of individual opinions. It can be distorted, however, by groupings within the population that tend to influence and steer individual views. This is often the case in planning consultation where interest groups either orchestrate or strongly influence individual opinion.

In the case of housing growth discussed earlier, government's advocacy of higher numbers of houses has relied on an assumption (for better or worse) that the heavily organised NIMBY groupings do not represent the true wisdom of all people in the wider South East. There are many groups such as lower-paid workers and first-time buyers whose opinions are rarely articulated in consultation exercises because the relevance of plans and policies is not obvious to them. It may well be the case that their desire for more housing outweighs the focused lobbying of NIMBYs. However, there is very little evidence to demonstrate whether or not this is the case.

Regional planning deals with very large crowds indeed. Some of them are very disparate with little sense of collective interest of identity. It is unsurprising therefore that strategic planning for regional development is a highly politicised process in which elected representatives aspire to identify the balance of public interest in a situation in which direct expression of all individual opinions is impracticable. The "wisdom of the crowd" is most likely to be effectively assessed by long-term efforts at community engagement across a whole range of issues, such as, for example, the city of Vancouver has made and cities with strong leadership like Manchester have made, especially at times of collective crisis.

Challenges and lessons for strategic planning for regional development

The challenges ahead

Accepting for the moment the underlying premise of the new regionalism agenda, notwithstanding Lovering's reservations, three fundamental questions need to be posed to those engaged in strategic spatial planning in the UK, especially regional planning. The first, in light of the preceding extensive discussion, is whether strategic planning practices today adequately address the current issues and challenges of new regionalism or whether in reality (putting aside rhetoric) they are more reflective of old regionalism or indeed some fusion of the two. Secondly, on the assumption that there is indeed a new regionalised order in the making, what changes should be made to past regional planning practices for them to better fit today's needs, given both the logic of market expansion *and* the need for some political control (protectionism) against its excesses? Thirdly, how do strategic planners go about simultaneously planning for, managing and addressing these two important (sometimes conflicting) major sets of forces?

If we look back, regional planning in the context of old regionalism is described by Friedman (1963) as a process of formulating and clarifying social objectives in supra-urban space and in areas that are larger than a single city. Describing regional planning more broadly, Martins (1986: 3) argues it is "a type of public planning (state activity) which is specifically concerned with social space; with the 'ordering' of activities and facilities in space at a scale greater than a single local authority and smaller than the state". Wood (1989), again in the context of old regionalism, suggests there are two reasons for undertaking regional planning. The first is to tackle regional disparities and the second to address economic effectiveness. A third important purpose, especially in recent years in the UK, has been the task of producing regional guidance (see Cullingworth and Nadin 1997).

Benefiting from the preceding discussion, a good starting point to enhancing strategic planning for regional development in the UK would be the abandonment of the separation between regional economic planning and regional spatial planning. A second consideration has to be the injection of greater diversity and flexibility in strategic planning practice in order to enable planning practice to better adapt to different regions and their different exposures to globalisation forces. Greater flexibility is also needed so as to better cope with changing national, regional and local priorities and visions of sustainable development as they emerge. A fourth important consideration is the need to build an institutional capacity that has both the political mandate to address regional issues and sufficient expertise to effectively handle trans-national, national, regional *and* local issues, simultaneously. This same organisation (or group of agencies) must also possess a capability of effectively engaging in dialogue and collaborating with the private sector on all Horizon growth levels. It should also be in a position (with the support of government infrastructure) to provide protectionism against failures of the market system.

Spatial planning and regional planning redefined

The extent to which the above qualities are already incorporated in the concept of spatial planning that has relatively recently been introduced into the UK and elsewhere in Europe may be examined if we accept ESPON's definition of spatial planning cited in Chapter 1 (ESPON 2005: 5) and refer to Albrechts's excellent re-examination of strategic (spatial) planning cited in Chapter 4 (Albrechts 2004). In the former case, spatial planning is perceived and carried out with the intention of arriving at a better "balance" of environmental, economic and social demands on development, relying on (strategic) measures to "co-ordinate the spatial impacts of other sector policies to achieve a more even distribution of economic development between regions than would otherwise be created by market forces, and to regulate the conversion of land and property uses" (EC 1997: 24).

Spatial planning in this context is very much a phenomenon with European roots. It has been much influenced by the work of Kunzmann and Wegner (1991), who to counter a trans-national regional system dominated by a few large cities, advocated the planning of a polycentric system of cities across Europe.

Spatial planning has also been promoted by the Dutch National Physical Planning Agency which (again in 1991) published *Perspectives in Europe* and developed the concept of supra-national spatial planning that ultimately led to the adoption of the European Spatial Development Perspective (ESDP) by the planning ministers of EU member states at Potsdam in May 1999 (see EC 1999).

The resultant two-part report, which developed a series of 60 policy options accompanied by appropriate rationales, was the product of a long dialogue among representatives from the European Commission (EC) member states over the best part of ten years (see Faludi 2001; Tewdwr-Jones and Williams 2001). The fundamentals of the ESDP are reinforced by an earlier EC idea of developing a pan-European network of transport infrastructure (TENs), agreed at the Maastricht Treaty of 1992, which the EC estimates requires an investment of €400 billion by 2010 (DfT 2005b).

As recently promoted and practised in the UK, spatial planning draws considerably from the European Commission's *Compendium of European spatial planning systems* (EC 1997). It has also been greatly influenced by the Community's movement towards the Single Market, subsequent regional development concerns arising from this, and the coordination of its Structural Funds to address these concerns. The EC's Directorate-General for Regional Policy and Cohesion has taken a dominant role in promoting and disseminating an understanding of spatial planning, as reflected in its *Europe 2000* (EC 1991) and *Europe 2000+* (EC 1994) reports. Together, these documents analyse pressures on Europe's territory arising from both socio-economic developments and national and regional Community interventions, overall making the case for inter-regional cooperation in spatial planning across the Community.[3]

This overall vision is reflected in the British government's new planning legislation which promotes more spatially aware and sustainable planning strategies, as is evident from the content of the new planning and policy statements (PPSs) for all regions in England, apart from London, where the Mayor is responsible for preparing a spatial development strategy (see Chapter 13). These efforts constitute part of the 2004 Planning and Compulsory Purchase Act's intention to strengthen the role and importance of regional planning as a replacement of past regional planning guidance (RPGs) by statutory regional spatial strategies (RSSs) (see ODPM 2004).

These new government initiatives are claimed to provide the pillars of a new planning practice in the UK in which strategic spatial planning is expected to have a critical impact on future regional development and how strategic decisions are to be taken regarding transport, housing, health and the environment, and how they will work together (Forum for the Future 2004). In some respects, the new measures offer an "acid test" of whether the advocated sustainable approaches to regional development are to be truly placed in the milieu of strategic planning for the regions, and whether strategic thinking will finally replace the "predict and provide" mantra of much past planning practice, a concern expressed earlier in the book by several of the contributors and especially highlighted by Haughton and Counsell in their recent publication entitled *Regions, spatial strategies and sustainable development* (2004).

For the new RSSs to be successful, it is imperative that they are clearly understood by regional organisations; especially in light of the findings of a recently completed survey conducted by *Regional Futures* in 2003 which revealed confusion among various regional organisations as to what an RSS is supposed to be and do (Forum for the Future 2004). This survey concluded that:

> For most people the RSS is a new concept, with a consensus around what it is not . . . but little consensus about what it should look like and the role it should have. Coupled with this, a lack of shared vision of what "sustainable development" means for a particular region threatens to undermine the spatial strategy's potential to deliver sustainable development.
>
> (Forum for the Future 2004: 2)

Concurring with this fear, Haughton and Counsell (2004) raise a number of more specific challenges that the new planning system must address if central government is to improve upon its past "mixed" success in attaining sustainable development through earlier regional planning guidance. These include the challenges of whether regional planning (2004: 213–14):

- meets the needs of the present generation and the principle of *intra-generational equity* – past experiences suggest that the main losers in regional development in the UK have been the lower-income groups;
- addresses *geographical equity* or trans-frontier responsibility and is geared to address global issues – in the past (with certain exceptions such as plans for London and the South East) regional planning practices in the UK have been largely an introspective affair;
- promotes and advances the principle of *procedural equity* which advocates that regulatory and participatory processes treat all people openly and fairly – while changes to the planning system since 1997 have to varying degrees led to greater involvement by stakeholders in the planning process, it remains some way from full engagement;
- contributes to *environmental or inter-species equity* whereby the survival of species of plants and animals is placed on a more equal footing to that of humans – while there is evidence of a weakening of this aspect, recent developments have resulted in stronger policies of biodiversity within, however, an overall more anthropocentric approach.

Conclusions

Regional planning emerges from this discussion as a particularly complex form of strategic spatial planning in which "context" and (competing) visions are all important. A plan such as the London Plan or the regional spatial strategy (RSS) for any of the regions in England has to address the spatial dimensions of a very wide range of activities over a relatively long time span, in a context of considerable uncertainty and of doubt about the powers and resources available to implement strategy. In these circumstances, substantial resources are needed in order to enable strategic choice to be informed about the relative consequences of alternative actions, the likely responses of different interest groups and the potential impacts of change in related fields. Unfortunately, the resources available to regional planning in the country are currently very limited in terms of expertise, funding, data and powers of influence and implementation. It was this gap between the aspirations of (city) planning and the actual capacity to realise them that led Wildavsky to reflect: "If planning is everything, maybe it is nothing at all" (1973).

Sustainable development is now a statutory purpose of the UK planning system. Excellent though its objectives undoubtedly are, as indicated above the lack of clear definition or common understanding of the concept in too many instances appears likely to reinforce the difficulties of achieving rigour in the regional planning process. Worries about capacity for strategic plan making are exacerbated by the lack of a strong current tradition of and skills in long-term policy making and planning in the public sector as a result of the Thatcherite purge of this expertise in the 1980s. Many of today's senior officers in local and strategic planning authorities are the products of the Thatcher era, when Nicholas Ridley heaped scorn upon the very word "strategy" and when the instruments of long-term policy were systematically eroded or weakened. The effect of this fed through into planning education so that strategic planning lost its place within the syllabus. As a result, there has been a time lag during which the planning profession has struggled to adapt to the government's desire for a more strategic approach, and although this skills gap is now beginning (slowly) to be filled it remains in critical short supply.

There are, nevertheless, some grounds for optimism, not least in the present government's will to promote strategic and regional planning. The introduction of spatial planning provides a more effective instrument for the management of change. The focus upon spatial planning encourages an approach that is wider than the earlier land-use model, but which concentrates upon the spatial dimension in which the regional planning agencies do have some significant delivery tools such as development control and transport planning. The new planning system, which provides a hierarchy of plan making with a clear relationship between strategy at the regional level and specificity at the local level, should be better suited to tackling the complexity of the problems it confronts. The real challenge is how this process can be further enhanced by incorporating the major lessons highlighted in the preceding discussion in the context both of the new long-term RSSs and of the local development frameworks (LDFs) spawned by them.

Planning is, for the first time in England, given a statutory purpose in the Planning and Compulsory Purchase Act 2004 and this is fundamentally for the purpose of managing strategic change. Regional planning has new agencies that should be highly responsive to introducing such change. The Office of the Deputy Prime Minister (ODPM) talks about "mainstreaming planning" through a process that introduces it into the main channels of decision making and resource allocation. Certainly examples such as the collaboration between the ODPM and the Treasury on the stimulation of more housing developments suggest that there is some degree of success in this endeavour. At the regional level, planning is able to align itself both with the Regional Development Agencies (RDAs), which possess substantial resources and powers, and with Government Offices in the regions, offering access to national government.

There is also room for hope that some fusion of the strengths of old and new regionalism is possible. New regionalism offers planning a much greater probability of harnessing the delivery power of the private sector towards the goals of regional policy, whilst the public sector authorities retain overall management of the regulatory instruments of planning and can use these to balance economic against social and environmental objectives. The Kent Thames-side model of private and public sector collaboration described earlier (p. 78) could emerge as a common response to the need for a clear long-term spatial planning context against which business and the development sector can plan their own decisions and investments. The challenge to strategic and regional planning in this scenario will be to exploit the financial and other powers of the private sector, whilst simultaneously managing development in ways that are sustainable and equitable. The status of RSSs as statutory documents gives them greater weight as the place at which the balance of the public and private interest is struck.

Notes

1. Here both Gladwell and Surowiecki have something to say about the optimum size of such groups, citing 150 persons as the upper limit of effective group decision making and dialogue.
2. Gladwell describes "Connectors" as individuals whose social circle is four or five times the size of that of other people, sprinkled in every walk of life, and who "have an extraordinary knack of making friends and acquaintances" (Gladwell 2000: 43). Their importance however goes beyond the number of people they know and has much to do with the kinds of persons they know. Connectors learn new information in an entirely random manner and access it wherever it emerges. The term "Maven" refers to a person who accumulates knowledge that has been tested, proven and accurately ascertained, often collected as part of a quality control monitoring process (ibid.: 60). Such parties are typically passive collectors of information, since they collect it in order to inform. They are "information brokers" sharing and trading what they know (ibid.: 69). Gladwell sees "Salesmen" as persons who possess persuasive skills and who apply these skills to parties who are unconvinced of what they are hearing, thereby making them as critical to the tipping of word-of-mouth epidemics as the Connector and the Maven (ibid.: 70).
3. It should be noted that this directorate's thinking has been greatly influenced by French ideas of *aménagement du territoire* through French civil servants and senior officials seconded to the Commission or working there, whose expertise dates back to domestic planning in France and the golden age of national planning in the 1960s as well as, more recently, the early 1980s which saw the establishment in France of a shared competence in spatial planning between central government and other levels of government (Colomb 2005).

References

Adams, J. 1995. *Risk*. London: UCL Press.

Albrechts, L. 2004. Strategic spatial planning re-examined. *Environment and Planning* B **31**, 743–58.

Baghai, M., S. Coley and D. White 1999. *The alchemy of growth: kickstarting and sustaining growth in your company*. London: Texere.

Basil, D. C. and C. W. Cook 1974. *The management of change*. London: McGraw-Hill.

Beck, U. 1992. *Risk society: toward a new modernity*. London: Sage.

Beck, U. 1999. *World risk society*. Cambridge: Polity Press.

Beck, U. 2000. *What is globalization?* Cambridge: Polity Press.

Brown, P. 2005. Trouble at the Department. In Analysis, *Guardian*, 16 February. London.

Buarque, C. 1993. *The end of economics: ethics and the disorder of progress.* London and New Jersey: Zed Books.

Burfisher, M. E., S. Robinson and K. Thierfelder 2003. Regionalism: old and new, theory and practice. Paper presented at the International Agricultural Trade Research Consortium Conference on Agricultural Policy Reform and the WTO: Where Are We Going? Capri, 23–26 July.

Castells, M. 1996. *The information age: economy, society and culture*, vol. I: *The rise of the network society.* Oxford: Blackwell Publishers.

Castells, M. 1998. *The information age: economy, society and culture*, vol. III: *End of millennium.* Oxford: Blackwell Publishers.

Castells, M. 2004. *The information age: economy, society and culture*, vol. II: *The power of identity.* Oxford: Blackwell Publishers.

Colomb, C. 2005. Notes provided to authors on 23 September.

Cooke, P. and K. Morgan 1994. Growth regions under duress: renewal strategies in Baden Wurttemberg and Emilia Romagna. In *Globalization, institutions and regional development*, A. Amin and N. Thrift (eds). Oxford: Oxford University Press.

Courtney, H., J. Kirkland and P. Viguerie 1999. Strategy under uncertainty. In *Harvard Business Review on managing uncertainty.* Cambridge, MA: Harvard Business School Press.

CPRE 2004. *Policy position statement: aviation.* London: Campaign to Protect Rural England.

Cullingworth, B. and V. Nadin 1997. *Town and country planning in the UK.* London: Routledge.

DfT 2005a. *National road traffic survey.* London: Department for Transport.

DfT 2005b. www.dft.gov.uk/stellent/groups/dft.

Dicken, P. 1999. *Global shift: transforming the world economy*, London: Paul Chapman Publishing.

Dimitriou, H. T. 2005. Globalization, mega transport projects and the making of mega places. Paper presented to session on social and economic factors of transportation, 84th Annual Meeting of Transportation Research Board, January, Washington, DC.

Dimitriou, H. T. 2006. Urban mobility and sustainability in Asia and the power of context. Paper presented to session on transportation and sustainability, 85th Annual Meeting of Transportation Research Board, January, Washington, DC.

EC 1991. *Europe 2000: views on the development of the territory of the Community.* European Commission. Luxembourg: Office for Official Publications of the European Communities.

EC 1994. *Europe 2000+: co-operation for the spatial development of Europe.* European Commission. Luxembourg: Office for Official Publications of the European Communities.

EC 1997. *Compendium of European spatial planning systems.* European Commission. Luxembourg: Office for Official Publications of the European Communities.

EC 1999. *European Spatial Development Perspective: towards balanced and sustainable development of the territory of the EU.* European Commission. Luxembourg: Office for Official Publications of the European Communities.

Economist, The 2005. The good company: a survey of corporate social responsibility, *The Economist*, 22 January, 3–17. London.

ESPON 2005. What is spatial planning. Home Page, European Spatial Planning Observation Network, http://www.espon.org.uk/spatialplanning.htm.

Faludi, A. 2001. The European Spatial Development Perspective and the changing institutional landscape of planning. In *The changing institutional landscape of planning*, A. da Rosa Pires, L. Albrechts and J. Alden (eds), 35–55. London: Jessica Kingsley Publishers.

Forum for the Future 2004. Spatial planning in the regions. Research report. *Regional Futures*, October. Cheltenham: Forum for the Future.

Friedman, J. 1963. Regional planning as a field of study. *Journal of the American Institute of Planners* **29**.

Friends of the Earth and AEF 1999. Plane crazy: airport growth in the UK. Friends of the Earth and Aviation Environmental Federation, http://www.foe.co.uk/resource/reports/plane_crazy.pdf.

GLA 2004. *The London Plan*. London: Greater London Assembly.

Gladwell, M. 2000. *The tipping point: how little things can make a big difference*. London: Abacus.

Glaister, S. 2001. UK transport policy 1997–2001. Paper delivered to the Beesley Lectures Regulation, Royal Society of Arts, 2 September.

Graham, S. and S. Marvin 2001. *Splintering urbanism: networked infrastructure, technological mobilities and the urban condition*. London: Routledge.

Haughton, G. and D. Counsell 2004. *Regions, spatial strategies and sustainable development*. London: Routledge.

Hillman, M. and T. Fawcett 2004. *How we can save the planet*. London: Penguin.

Hutton, W. 2002. *The world we're in*. London: Little, Brown.

John, P. and A. Whitehead 1997. The renaissance of English regionalism in the 1990s. *Policy and Politics* **25**, 7–17.

Jones, M. and G. MacLeod 2004. Regional spaces, spaces of regionalism: territory, insurgent politics and the English question. *Transactions of the Institute of British Geographers* **29**, 433–52.

Kay, John 2003. *The truth about markets: their genius, their limits, their follies*. London: Allen Lane, Penguin.

Kunzmann, K. R. and M. Wegner 1991. The pattern of urbanization in Western Europe: 1960–1990. Internal report to European Commission, Brussels.

Kurtz, C. F. and D. J. Snowden 2003. The new dynamics of strategy: sense-making in a complex-complicated world. *IBM Systems Journal*, Fall.

Lash, S., B. Szerszynski and B. Wynne (eds) 1998. *Risk, environment and modernity: towards a new ecology*. London: Sage.

Le Bon, G. 1982. *The crowd: a study of the popular mind*, trans. anon. Cambridge: Blackwell.

Lechner, F. J. and J. Boli (ed.) 2004. *The globalization reader*. Oxford: Blackwell.

Lovering, J. 1999. Theory led by policy: the inadequacies of the "new regionalism" (illustrated from the case of Wales). *Journal of Urban and Regional research* **23**, 379–95.

Macay, A. 1841. *Memoirs of extraordinary popular delusions*. London: Richard Bentley.

MacLeod, G. 2001. New regionalism reconsidered: globalization and the remaking of political space. *International Journal of Urban and Regional Research* **25**(4), 804–29.

Martins, M. 1986. *An organisational approach to regional planning*. Aldershot: Gower.

Mason, R. O. and I. I. Mitroff 1981. *Challenging strategic planning assumptions: theory, cases and techniques*. New York: John Wiley & Sons.

Menschel, R. 2002. *Markets, mobs and mayhem*. New York: John Wiley & Sons.

Mintzberg, H., J. B. Quinn and S. Ghosal (eds) 1995. Introduction. In *The strategy process*, ix–xvii. London: Prentice Hall.

Murdoch, J. and Tewdwr-Jones, M. 1999. Planning and the English regions: conflict and convergence amongst the institutions of regional governance. *Environment and Planning C* **17**, 715–29.

Nietzsche, F. 1966. *Beyond good and evil*, trans. Walter Kaufmann. New York: Random House.

ODPM 2004. *Planning Policy Statement 11: regional spatial strategies*. Office of the Deputy Prime Minister. London: HMSO.

Ohmae, K. 1990. *The borderless world: power and strategy in the interlinked economy*. London: HarperCollins.

Ohmae, K. 1995. *The end of the nation state: the rise of regional economics*. London: HarperCollins.

Palast, G. 2002. *The best democracy can buy*. London: Pluto Press.

Porter, M. 1990. *The competitive advantage of nations*. New York: Free Press.

Rittel, H. W. J. and M. Webber 1973. Dilemmas in a general theory of planning. *Policy Sciences* **4**(2), 155–69.

Robertson, D. 1965. A nation of regions. *Urban Studies* **2**(2).

Smith, N. 1988. The region is dead: long live the region! *Political Geography Quarterly* **7**, 141–52.

Snowden, D. 2004. Multi-ontology sense making: a new simplicity to decision making. In *Management Today Yearbook*, Richard Havenga (ed.), **20**(10).

Spindler, M. 2002. New regionalism and the construction of global order. CSGR Working Paper 93/02, March. Centre for the Study of Globalisation and Regionalisation, University of Warwick, Coventry.

Surowiecki, J. 2004. *The wisdom of crowds: why the many are smarter than the few*. London: Little, Brown.

Tewdwr-Jones, M. and R. H. Williams 2001. *European dimensions of British planning*. London: Spon Press.

Tomaney, J. and N. Ward 2000. England and the new regionalism. *Regional Studies* **34**(5), 471–8.

Webb, D. and C. Collis 2000. Regional Development Agencies and the new regionalism in England. *Regional Studies* **34**(9), 857–73.

Wildavsky, A. 1973. Planning is everything, maybe it's nothing. *Policy Sciences* **4**, 151–2.

Wood, P. 1989. United Kingdom. In *Regional Development in Western Europe*, H. D. Clout (ed.). London: David Fulton.

6 Strategic choice and regional planning

Chris Yewlett

Introduction

One may note from the history of regional and strategic planning in the UK that there have been three distinct periods since the mid-twentieth century during which "the Plan" itself has achieved particular prominence: the years immediately following the 1947 Town and Country Planning Act; those immediately following 1972; and those from 1991 to date (Yewlett 2001a). This interest in "the Plan" led inevitably to a parallel interest in appropriate methods of plan production. As John Muller put it:

> historically, the pre-requisite for planning has been access to tenable methods which are responsive to the needs of society . . . [T]he ongoing quest of the [planning] profession to maintain social relevance and disciplinary legitimacy . . . has required of planning that it modify its methods to accommodate the changes that have occurred in society from time to time.
>
> (Muller 1992: 125)

Following the initial post-war enthusiasm for planning associated with the 1947 legislation, a number of important practical problems were identified, most notably the time taken to produce plans, more than ten years in some cases. This slow production process, further compounded by the plans' inflexibility in practice, in turn discouraged any further review, leading to a set of excessively outdated, and thus unrealistic, Development Plans. The resulting concerns, which had by the early 1960s eroded confidence in the existing planning system, were heightened by the anticipation at that time of high rates of population and economic growth. These latter factors led inevitably to an increased level of interest in the strategic end of land-use planning, and in regional planning. Regional planning in particular was seen as both the means for reconciling national government economic plans with land-use proposals – the latter traditionally the responsibility of local government (Alden and Morgan 1974) – and also for tackling the perennial knotty problems of population balance (Stilwell 1972).

The consequence of these concerns was the establishment in 1964 of the Planning Advisory Group, or PAG (Delafons 1998). Their revolutionary report (PAG 1965), which was subsequently implemented by the government through the 1968 and 1971 Town and Country Planning Acts, recommended a completely new approach to statutory land-use planning, involving a "two-tier" Development Plan, comprising the Structure Plan and the Local Plan. Whilst the Local Plan continued many elements of the old "Master Plan" and "Urban Design" traditions, the "Structure Plan" was a completely new, intrinsically strategic, concept, and therefore one which needed a completely new methodological approach.

This revolutionary new approach to planning did not just launch a major wave of activity; it also impacted fundamentally on the very way in which plan preparation was undertaken. The new Structure Plans were essentially written expressions of strategic land-use policies, with graphical expression of spatial policy restricted to an impressionistic "key diagram". This was in direct contrast to all previous plans, which had been presented graphically, superimposed on an accurate underpinning Ordnance Survey base map, with supporting text. This change in turn gave rise to a pressing need to develop appropriate new methods for Structure Plan production. The previous approach had been very much in the architectural design tradition, whereby plans had been developed largely by application of the "professional planner's mystique", and formal policies emerged implicitly from the resultant designs. This also meant that the underlying assumptions remained largely hidden; the political decision makers often had no alternative other than to accept or to reject a detailed proposed plan in its entirety.

Operational research and planning

One important consequence of these developments was a very productive synergy between practising professional planners and researchers working in the increasingly influential field of operational research (OR), at the interface between traditional scientific and social science approaches (Yewlett 2001a, 2001b). OR ideas, originating in the 1930s, had proved particularly useful during and immediately after the Second World War (Kirby 2003a). During the war, significant contributions had been made to both strategic and tactical actions (Waddington 1973). Subsequently, OR ideas had been extensively deployed in the then publicly owned industrialised sector, notably steel and coal. Exemption from military service requirements for workers in these fields, a continuation of wartime policy, helped these industries recruit very strong graduate operational research teams, which became world leaders in their field. However, by the 1960s the industrial problems now being tackled in industry were at a much less strategic level, whilst use of OR ideas to tackle governmental problems had declined, a situation of concern to several members of the governing council of the UK Operational Research Society, many of whom had themselves been personally involved in the historic wartime studies.

The outcome of extensive deliberations at that time, and subsequent discussions at Russell Ackoff's suggestion with the Tavistock Institute of Human Relations – an independent social science research institution (Kirby 2003b) – led to the creation in 1963 of a new Institute for Operational Research (IOR) as part of "the Tavi" (Trist and Murray 1993), with Neil Jessop as its initial Director (Friend 1980; Friend *et al.* 1988). The IOR was founded with a mandate:

- to extend the field of usefulness of OR;
- to bring it into closer relationship with the social sciences;
- to carry out fundamental research; and
- to help in setting a standard of training.

(Operational Research Society 1962)

A modest start followed, tackling the inevitable problems of any new organisation: generating funds; recruiting staff; balancing the two. The three initial projects secured were concerned respectively with communications in the building industry; with processes of adaptation and change in hospital management; and with policy making in local government. Previous OR work had always assumed, explicitly or implicitly, that there was a single "decision maker" to be advised, a unitary perspective which carefully excluded any such messy "real life" issues as conflict within and between organisations, or internal organisational politics, from the analysis. Work in the building industry quickly confirmed that this was a gross oversimplification, leading to the novel concept of the "multi-organisation" (Stringer 1967), in essence the intersection of parts of several organisations, and consisting of a range of participants drawn from them. This concept, which with hindsight proved ground-breaking (Yewlett 2000), led to major breakthroughs in effectiveness in dealing with certain kinds of tasks, especially in fields where the developing technical expertise of OR needed to be married effectively to issues of public policy, including land-use planning, regional development and health.

The birth of strategic choice

Attempts to model the decision processes in such situations, undertaken as part of this early work on communications in the building industry (Crichton 1966), led to the development of the method known as "analysis of interconnected decision areas", subsequently referred to by the acronym AIDA (Luckman 1967). The essence of this now well-known approach lies in structuring relationships between decision problems in terms of patterns of distinct "decision areas", each made up of a set of two or more mutually exclusive options. The power of the method lies not only in the possibility of generating "solutions" by selecting sets of a single option from each decision area, but also in the ability to express the structure of the decision graphically, in a way which facilitates discussion, first as a structure of interconnected decision areas or a "decision graph" (see Figure 6.1) and then in more detail displaying options as well as an "option graph" (see Figure 6.2).

This kind of approach has been characterised by Rosenhead (1980) as "consequence display" in contrast to the more common "optimising approach". Contemporary critics who suggested (mathematically) that AIDA could be reduced to a "zero-one integer programming" calculation (Openshaw and Whitehead 1977) had perhaps missed this point, as well as overlooked the benefits of graphical display. In subsequent years, computer support was developed for AIDA, incorporating both analytical and problem-structuring aspects (STRADSPAN n.d.).

These ideas were further developed in the context of engineering design

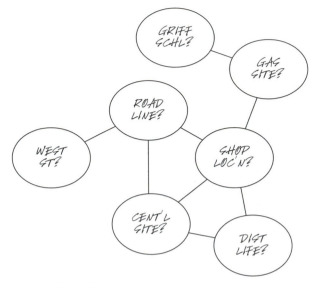

Figure 6.1 Example of a decision graph
Source: After Figure 12, Friend and Hickling 2005: 28

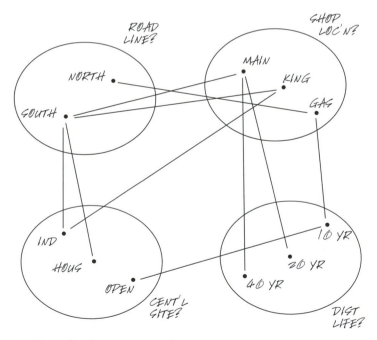

Figure 6.2 Example of an option graph
Source: After Figure 16, Friend and Hickling 2005: 36

(Morgan 1971). However, the most significant developments for planning occurred when the Nuffield Foundation supported a four-year in-depth study of decision processes in Coventry City Council. This major project provided the foundations for what later became known as "strategic choice" (Friend and

Jessop 1969). The term was adopted to reflect the process through which decision makers continually confront uncertainties of various types, and try to agree strategies for the management of uncertainty. This formed a key central concept, implying recognition that uncertainty (as opposed to quantifiable risk) is inevitable and cannot simply be ignored. The active management of uncertainty allows some key decisions to be taken on a piecemeal basis, whilst keeping options open in other areas.

The work led to the evolution of the renowned threefold classification of uncertainties: those involving the decision maker's operating environment (UE); those involving value judgements or policy issues (UV, later UP); and those which entailed anticipating choices in related areas of decision (UR). The classification was derived from an analysis of the content of policy documents, coupled with interpretations of observed group behaviour in key meetings, with the threefold categorisation respectively reflecting observed demands for "more research", "more policy guidance" or "more coordination" in order to resolve deadlocks (see Figure 6.3). Extensive subsequent researches in a number

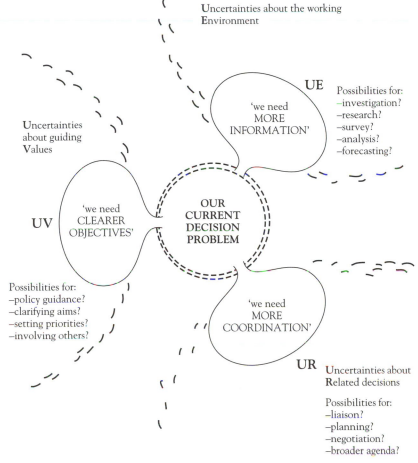

Figure 6.3 The threefold classification of uncertainty

Source: After Figure 3, Friend and Hickling 2005: 8

of different contexts have led to considerable further developments of these ideas, including the idea that the output of a planning process should not be a "plan" as such – certainly not in the historical, primarily graphic, form – but rather a defined set of current actions, further explorations and contingency arrangements: a "commitment package" in the terminology adopted.

There was also considerable emphasis on the cyclic and iterative nature of the process, and the need to constantly review earlier stages, indeed often to reformulate the perceived problem in the light of insights and further knowledge gained, rather than simply to plough straight through an assumed linear process. Moreover, the cyclic approach provided a practical means of managing the inevitable pressures to expand the formulation, thus coping with complexity, without simultaneously causing an exponential increase in the ensuing analytical phase.

This research involved the pursuit of two complementary strands of thought, distinct but intertwined. The first concerned the appreciation and analysis of the structure of relationships between decisions, and the way these relationships change over time, so as to assist in the selection of preferred courses of action. The second related to the appreciation and analysis of the structure of social and organisational relations which form the context of these decisions. The latter of these two strands also built on important insights emerging from the building industry project, and was to be developed further in subsequent researches into wider development activities involving several local authorities as well as aspects of central government and other agencies.

Work on further development (and, de facto, dissemination) of the first strand was aided through support from the then Centre for Environmental Studies (CES) for a collaborative project with several local authorities (CES 1970). A pilot project into progressing the second strand identified the West Midlands overspill town of Droitwich as a promising field site (Friend and Hunter 1970). Subsequently this work was expanded into a major study of the networks of inter-organisational decision making involved in managing the different aspects of the Droitwich expansion scheme. This research resulted in a set of general concepts about the management of such networks of decision makers, which arose across a number of formally independent corporate entities. It also led to a set of propositions designed to be tested in other contexts of "inter-corporate" decision making (Friend *et al.* 1974; Friend 1976), introducing a number of additional concepts useful for structuring, analysing and, vitally, subsequently operating in such multi-organisational contexts. The first was that of the "policy system", essentially comprising a set of relationships between actors involved in a decision process. A policy system would be identified by the actors' legitimate concern in some specific identifiable class of problem situations, and a nominal allegiance to some set of policy guidelines. This organisational concept was complemented by that of the "decision network", a wider, more flexible and adaptable set of arrangements between decision makers who, whilst sharing a direct or indirect concern with some identifiable class of problems, did not necessarily subscribe to any shared policy guidelines. Effective strategic planning in such contexts depended largely on the skills of the actors involved in managing these networks, especially those involved in important "boundary roles" between otherwise formally separate organisations. The need to describe these skills led to the third key new concept: that of network management or "reticulist judgements". It was recognised at the time that the developments in the contemporary planning environment would imply significant changes in the role of the professional town planner, who would be increasingly called upon to exercise policy design skills, including effective reticulist judgements, rather than the spatial design skills which had formed the traditional skills base (Friend 1976).

Strategic choice: a method for structure and regional planning

The increasing dissemination of these "blue skies" research efforts led the then Department of the Environment (DoE) to commission research into developing methods for the analysis of policy options in structure plan preparation (Sutton *et al*. 1977), which proved very influential in planning practice at the time (Faludi and Mastop 1982). This research entailed a team consisting of both planners and IOR scientists working jointly with a number of local planning authorities on their ongoing Structure Plan preparation problems, focusing simultaneously on the related facets of plan generation and plan evaluation. The project report took the novel form of a document which interlaced "how to do it" sections with specific case illustrations and constructively annotated facsimiles of actual material outputs from the various participants. This collaboration contributed significantly to the ensuing "golden age" of strategic planning, which lasted from the initial implementation of the PAG ideas until the election of a UK Conservative government ideologically unsympathetic to planning in 1979 (Thornley 1991).

Although the concept of strategic choice made significant contributions to the production of the initial round of Structure Plans, it should be noted that it was not generally the practice to report "methodology" in final statutory documents, and therefore published practice examples are few and far between. There are some more or less ephemeral illustrations around, as well as discussions of the case studies concerned in the key research reports. Indeed, whilst some items are fairly explicit about the role played by strategic choice, as in the case of the Berkshire study (Bather *et al*. 1976), in other cases, whilst the influence of the concepts is clear to the informed reader, explicit mention is absent (see Hertfordshire County Council 1976). Officers employed at the time in the key Local Government Implementation Project (LOGIMP) from local authorities in Cheshire, Coventry, Hampshire, Hertfordshire, the London boroughs of Barking (and Dagenham) and Havering, and Teesside had a major impact (CES 1970), whilst the DoE work mentioned above (Sutton *et al*. 1977) also introduced participants from Avon (Greater Bristol), Hereford and Worcester, Leicestershire, Tyne and Wear, Cleveland and Lancashire. Such exercises tended to attract the more dynamic local government officers, and the tradition of regular promotions between authorities as part of a "national local government service" played a considerable part in disseminating the ideas, as did the fact that the regular project meetings included "interested observers" from other authorities, as well as active "action research" participants. (Sutton *et al*. (1977) mention Cambridgeshire, Dorset, Gloucestershire, Greater Manchester, Humberside, Merseyside, Northamptonshire, Staffordshire, West Glamorgan and West Midlands in this latter category, alongside a number continuing from the previous exercise.)

The underlying philosophy of this style of research is particularly noteworthy. The approach was rooted in the "Tavistock" tradition of "action research", involving working with individuals faced with problems on those problems. As well as adopting the "consequence display" rather than the "optimising approach" discussed above, the starting assumption was not a normative assumption that there is "one right way" to tackle problems, regardless of any factors arising from the specific situation (a failing of much contemporary OR and indeed other technocratic planning work). Neither, however, did the approach accept the pessimistic conclusion that the complexities of public administration are such as to render any attempts to engage comprehensively, rather than by incremental adjustments within the existing bureaucratic structure, ultimately futile (Braybrooke and Lindblom 1963). Rather the approach is "one of taking best present practice and seeking to refine it systematically", one which has been described, perhaps rather fancifully, as "polishing practice" (Yewlett 1984: 497). Whilst this characteristic is not unique – Etzioni's (1968) "mixed scanning" has similar participant observation roots – it is one of the factors which help to explain its contemporary resonance with the actual practice of structure, and later regional, planning by practitioners.

The development of strategic choice ideas has also been contemporaneous with the enormous recent explosion of information technology. From the start, in the days when computers were large mainframes, IT was adopted to help AIDA analyses, using remote teleprinter technology and extensive Fortran programming by J. M. H. Hunter. Although this format was valuable in dealing with complex analyses, it was found that it tended to inhibit the cyclic nature of the approach, as any reformulation effectively required the re-entry of all data. It was not until much later, with the proliferation of personal computers and intensive further programming undertaken by David Friend, that effective IT support (discussed further below) was achieved.

Also at this time, the anticipation of substantial economic and population growth, coupled with the continuing unresolved problems of inter- and intra-regional inequality, stimulated an interest in extending these ideas to the sphere of regional planning. Moreover, the very nature of Structure Planning required a regional context in which to set the plans. A number of key projects researching into aspects of regional planning were set in hand. The initial project examined organisational influences in the regional strategy process (Carter et al. 1975). This pilot study, undertaken by IOR with Ken Carter, a colleague from Lanchester Polytechnic (now Coventry University), drew on experiences from ongoing regional strategy work in the North West and East Anglia, and was designed to help the DoE appreciate the way in which "decisions about the organisational setting of a regional strategy team can influence the outcome of the team's work" (Carter et al. 1975: Summary). The research was further developed into a wider study focusing on the development of policy guidelines in regional strategies (DoE 1976). The key output was "a systematic framework . . . which future strategy teams . . . can use to understand better the way discretion is exercised at national, regional and local levels within any selected field of governmental policy" (DoE 1976: 6), exploring such matters as established guidelines, accountability to relevant interests and other forms of expertise.

These initial studies led into a subsequent full methodological study undertaken jointly with the Institute of Local Government Studies (INLOGOV) at

Birmingham University (Hart *et al.* 1978a). This latter work focused on the process of planning, and methods by which it might be improved. The broad working position was that methodological decisions could usefully be described under the four headings of technology, products, organisation and process. The conclusions reached included a need to be sensitive to the specific social, economic and political context of the region – "context-relevant" planning (a concern highlighted by Chapter 5) – and to adopt a process of continuous planning, covering updating, monitoring and review, described as "planning continuity". The third key methodological issue concerned the inter-corporate dimension of coordination between numerous agencies' planning exercises: at that time including structure plans, local plans, housing investment plans and the regional water authority's rolling investment plans.

The study pointed out that, although considerable research work had taken place into substantive elements of planning, such as population projections or employment surveys, much less effort had been devoted to "considering how the dynamics of the overall planning activity could be more effectively and consciously designed" (Hart *et al.* 1978a: para. 1.1). The work built on a number of previous studies by both IOR and INLOGOV, including the pilot project outlined above, and some further developments of it intended to move on from examining structures to exploring how "regional strategy teams might exert influence over the processes of policy formation and change" (IOR 1978). INLOGOV contributed the fruits of their parallel "Exploratory study in strategic monitoring" (Wedgwood-Oppenheim *et al.* 1975), which had also been commissioned by the DoE. Undertaken following the publication of the Strategic Plan for the North West, this study argued the need for a considerably wider activity than had traditionally been understood by traditional planning; indeed, after Etzioni's (1968) classic "mixed scanning" approach, it was argued that a strategic monitoring team required a capability for both continuous scanning of the problems of the region and analysis in-depth where appropriate. More fundamentally, the role of a monitoring group was seen as essentially involved in the development of influence, rather the mechanistic collection of monitoring data. A further INLOGOV study (INLOGOV 1976; Hart *et al.* 1978b) looked at the use of objectives in regional planning work to investigate, *inter alia*, whether it might be possible to draw up a set of regional objectives which could apply with different weightings in different regions. However, after reviewing the work undertaken in East Anglia and the North West, and the development of the Strategic Plan for the South East, the conclusion reached was that substantive objectives had been of limited practical use to teams in guiding them towards their final outputs.

One other input into the full methodological study was some work undertaken into Scottish Regional Reports. This grew out of the slightly different implementation of the Structure Plan system in Scotland, where Scottish regions at the time were the functional equivalent of counties in Wales and England (albeit much larger in area in some cases). The Scottish regions had been invited to prepare a "Regional Report" containing the data and policy decisions underpinning their Structure Plans, and thus the Plan itself would be a very strictly land-use-focused document. One advantage of this was that, unlike the Structure Plan itself, the Regional Report did not require governmental approval (and thus implicit approval for any consequential expenditure – a constant battleground south of the border).

Alas, following the presentation of the findings as a draft report in September 1978 (Friend *et al.* 1978), the May 1979 election of the radical Conservative government, and the consequential different emphases, meant that this work was never formally published. The new Thatcher government showed little enthusiasm even for the statutorily required "review" of Development Plans, an attitude exacerbated by a continuation of the excessive time still being taken. This was further compounded by an economic recession, resulting in less pressure even to accommodate growth, let alone continue the voluntary production of regional strategies (see Chapter 2). This was the start of a period of greatly reduced plan production activity; by 1984 the government was explicitly advising that full coverage of all areas by Local Plans was not necessary (DoE 1984).

However, subsequent environmental concerns led to a revival of interest in plans as such, with the rehabilitation of the long-established town and country planning system, which was expressly cited as a key vehicle for achieving environmental objectives in the government's ground-breaking multi-departmental environmental White Paper entitled *This common inheritance* (DoE 1990a: 80). Unfortunately, this specific role for development planning was not one of the points selected for emphasis in the executive summary (DoE 1990b), still less in contemporary press releases, meaning that it was widely overlooked outside the immediate planning profession. Nevertheless, following extensive subsequent professional and political debate, the Planning and Compensation Act of 1991 inaugurated the current plan-led system (by introducing the key section 54A into the 1990 Town and Country Planning Act).

Unfortunately, the intervening decade following the 1979 election was "a dark age" for planning, particularly strategic planning, during which "a generation of planners came into being with little or no experience of plan preparation, and relevant skills were largely lost" (RTPI 1997: 28). Providing a contribution to redressing this skills gap is one of the primary objectives of this publication.

Strategic choice spreads abroad

Despite the history of the lack of UK governmental enthusiasm for strategic thinking in planning since the late 1970s, strategic choice ideas continued to be developed elsewhere, both in a wider context and for planning in other jurisdictions, as Chapter 4 demonstrates. Whilst the basic concepts of strategic choice continued to be applied elsewhere, considerable development work took place on problems and opportunities provided in developing applications in new contexts. Of particular interest to regional planners is work undertaken on "capacity building" in the context of sustainable development, both in developing countries and in areas of relative deprivation in particular regions of more developed countries. Some of this ongoing work included a major project arising in 2001 which sought to promote capacity building in Venezuela, in the context of a national policy development. Its aim was "[to focus] development resources in special economic zones which combined present conditions of rural deprivation with future opportunities for significant economic growth" (Friend 2002: 20).

Work also continued on the development of computer support for strategic choice as a method, rather than simply on the "analytical" side. A noted specific problem in the UK context has been the failure, with a few noted exceptions, of others outside the IOR cadre of specialists to take up and develop strategic choice ideas. Dutch society, with its pluralistic open debate traditions has provided some fertile soil for new developments in strategic choice-based planning both in land-use planning (Faludi 1987) and in other related fields such as environmental safety planning (Hickling 1989). A number of interesting cases are reported in some detail in the third edition of *Planning under pressure* (Friend and Hickling 2005).

In addition to the Dutch work mentioned above, there have been applications of strategic choice approaches to planning in the Netherlands to national environmental policy development (Evers 2005), nature conservation (Bregman 2005) and planning education (Van der Valk and Carsjens 2005). Sweden has seen the development of a strategic choice-based project to address problems of unrented apartments, comparing the use of strategic choice workshops in one town with an alternative approach using futures studies methods in another (Khakee and Strömberg 1993). Subsequent applications have been applied to Agenda 21 and local waste management (Strömberg and Kain 2005). Other experiences elsewhere in Europe include an illustrated discussion of the scope for use of strategic choice methods in developing and evaluating integrated local transport plans in the face of uncertainty, drawing on experiences in Dublin and in British local authorities using the STRAD software (Swanson 1994), and applications to neighbourhood renewal in a Rome suburb (Giangrande and Mortola 2005).

On the wider international scene, strategic choice concepts have been applied to a wide range of planning activities, including rural community development through enhanced information technology in South Africa (Phahlamohlaka 2005), rural community development in Belize (White 1994) and airport planning in Hong Kong (Ling 1990). As mentioned earlier, strategic choice-based planning has been particularly well received in Venezuela, where from the early 1990s a number of planners had been exploring it as an alternative to traditional comprehensive planning. In 1999, one of its key protagonists in Latin America, Professor Jorge Giordano of the Central University, was appointed Minister of Planning and Development by the incoming President Chavez, leading to the capacity-building exercise discussed above, and a number of projects concerned with topics as diverse as public services management, economic issues and reconstruction following the 1999 mud slide disaster (Vila and Benaiges 2005). Strategic choice as a basis for planning appears to have captured the imagination of the Venezuelan president to the point of explicit advocacy of *Planificando bajo presión: el enfoque de escogencia estratégica* (Friend and Hickling 2002) on Venezuelan television (Vila n.d.)!

As well as this Spanish translation, accounts of strategic choice planning have been translated into: Dutch (Hickling *et al.* 1976; Hickling and de Jong 1990); French (Hickling *et al.* 1980); Swedish (Strömberg 1986); Portuguese (Hickling 1985); Japanese (Hirotaka Koike *et al.* 1991); and Bahasa Indonesia (Ismail *et al.* 1989). Another novel innovation in connection with the third edition of *Planning under pressure* is the launch of a "companion website" (Elsevier 2005) with additional bibliographical material and relevant updates, and further linkages to a new Strategic Choice website (SCW n.d.) offering further reading materials and opportunities to interact with other users.

Parallel developments took place in the field of IT, with the successful creation and launch of the STRAD (for STRategic ADviser) program (Friend 1992), now available in Windows format as STRAD 2 (STRADSPAN n.d.). The availability of this software has in fact inspired its inclusion in an online course developed by Ray Wyatt at Melbourne University (1999).

Strategic choice: potential for revival?

Advocates of strategic choice spoke from the outset of the development of a new language for problem solving. Increasing internationalisation of research, and involvement of researchers with primary languages other than English have since raised some interesting cross-fertilisations of concepts. This is potentially an important development as the European Union expands and the challenges of securing effective working relationships among the many individually autonomous states loom ever more significant. At the opposite end of the political (if not geographical) scale, sub-nation states are also developing increasing autonomous discretion: in the UK, for example, with devolution of important powers to Wales (Tewdwr-Jones 2001a), Scotland (Tewdwr-Jones 2001b) and (subject to satisfactory resolution of sectarian issues), ultimately, Northern Ireland. These political developments have already led to distinctive changes, both in planning procedure and practice and in substantive policies, as outlined in the case of Scotland in Chapter 16. In contrast, proposals to extend devolution to the English regions have foundered, at least for the time being, following rejection of the flagship North East Regional Assembly scheme, and the associated local government restructuring, in the 2004 referendum, perhaps because the new structure on offer was essentially not local autonomy within a defined range of powers, as in Scotland and Wales, but rather merely an advisory role to UK national government on key issues. Nevertheless, it is apparent that some kind of effective arrangement to legitimise at least regional planning, if not wider spatial policy formulation, will eventually be required within England. All these innovations will clearly increase the demand for effective methods for strategic choice for inter-organisational working, as well as for tackling "messy" planning problems.

Another interesting development in recent years has been the increasing signs of convergence between the British "discretionary" planning tradition, under which the Development Plan is one of many "material considerations", and the "legal" tradition prevalent on the European continent, whereby the adopted Development Plan has, at least in principle, total authority. In reality, of course, this dichotomy has never been so absolute in practice, as the original Oxford–Leiden studies demonstrated back in the 1970s (Oxford Polytechnic 1978; Thomas 1983); the need to respond to changing events has meant that the "European" tradition incorporated considerable flexibility. More recently, this convergence has been stimulated by the introduction of the "plan-led" system in the UK, reinforced by closer working between UK and continental academic planners, both practically through the increasing numbers of multi-country European Union-funded research projects, and theoretically through the creation of the European academic forum the Association of European Schools of Planning (AESOP) (Healey *et al.* 1997).

As interest in the preparation of plans for spatial and territorial development grows in the UK, effective methods of plan production are increasingly likely to be sought after; strategic choice-based planning clearly offers one valuable tool. However, there is an explicit recognition, especially given the hiatus in UK planning referred to earlier, that, as the IOR cadre of planning specialists (including the author) ages and increasingly withdraws from the active research and practice arenas, there is a need to promote and propagate these ideas to the rising generation of planners. The fact that, in recent years, John Friend has received more of the formal recognition due to him, including the receipt of an honorary doctorate in planning from the University of Amsterdam in 1998 and, on the OR front, election as Vice-President of the UK Operational Research Society, may help here. In the latter capacity, in his plenary paper at the UK OR Society 2000 Annual Conference (Friend 2000), John explored some of the problems inherent in institution-building initiatives designed to push outwards the frontiers of OR and, especially, in bridging "academic" and "consultancy" archetypes.

Another key contribution to the revival of strategic choice in planning, combining both recognition and academic discussion, has been the recent symposium on the work of John Friend, published as a special edition of *Planning Theory* (Mandelbaum 2004). As well as containing contributions reflecting on the history of strategic choice ideas (Burns 2004), this edition placed the "Tavi" and the impact of strategic choice philosophy on planning practice in their wider context (Faludi 2004). The symposium also addresses wider theoretical concerns from both OR (Bryson *et al.* 2004) and planning (Needham 2004) perspectives, rounded off by a response from John Friend himself (Friend 2004). This work reflects on some of the more theoretical points as well as practical, commencing with the distinctive "Tavistock" culture of "action research" (traced back to Lewin's clinical model of social research), the group relations perspective and systems thinking – with the latter evolving into a "decision-centred" rather than "synoptic overview" – paving the way to the wider multiple-actor inter-organisational perspective. In the wider context, the revised edition of *Rational analysis for a problematic world* (Rosenhead and Mingers 2001) not only contains a valuable brief introduction to strategic choice ideas, but also looks at a number of other "softer" methods emerging from the OR community.

Autonomous professional practitioners and academics in the planning world are of course free to accept, adapt or reject such ideas; but it is incumbent on educators and researchers to ensure that they are at least aware of the possibilities offered by such an approach; reinventing wheels is a waste of everyone's time and effort and, of course, of valuable resources. The present offering is one small contribution towards achieving this awareness and promoting the revival of strategic choice-based planning.

References

Alden, J. and R. Morgan 1974. *Regional planning: a comprehensive view.* Leighton Buzzard: Leonard Hill.

Bather, N. J., C. M. Williams and A. Sutton 1976. Strategic choice in practice: the West Berkshire Structure Plan experience, Department of Geography, University of Reading, Reading.

Braybrooke, D. and C. E. Lindblom 1963. *A strategy of decision.* New York: Free Press.

Bregman, L. 2005. Commitment is the key: building inter-agency agreement over the future of an historic estate. Chapter 13.15 in *Planning under pressure: the strategic choice approach*, 3rd edn, J. K. Friend and A. Hickling (eds), 357–60. Oxford: Elsevier Butterworth-Heinemann.

Bryson J., F. Ackerman and C. Eden 2004. Contributions of planning under pressure. *Planning Theory* **3**(3), 201–10.

Burns, T. 2004. A practical theory of public planning: the Tavistock tradition and John Friend's strategic choice approach. *Planning Theory* **3**(3), 211–23.

Carter, K. R., J. K. Friend, J. de B. Pollard and C. J. L. Yewlett 1975. *Organisational influences in the regional strategy process.* IOR/846. Coventry: Institute of Operations Research.

CES 1970. *The LOGIMP experiment.* CES Information Paper 25. London: Centre for Environmental Studies.

Crichton, C. 1966. *Interdependence and uncertainty: a study of the building industry.* London: Tavistock.

Delafons, J. 1998. Reforming the British planning system 1964–5: the Planning Advisory Group and the genesis of the Planning Act of 1968. *Planning Perspectives* **13**, 373–87.

DoE 1976. Regional planning and policy change: the formulation of policy guidelines in regional strategies. Consultancy report prepared by J. K. Friend, M. Norris (IOR) and K. Carter (Lanchester Polytechnic) for Department of the Environment, London.

DoE 1984. *Memorandum on structure and local plans.* Circular 24/84 (Welsh Office 43/84). London: Department of the Environment, HMSO.

DoE 1990a. *This common inheritance: Britain's environmental strategy.* White Paper. London: Department of the Environment, HMSO.

DoE 1990b. *This common inheritance: a summary of the White Paper on the environment.* London: Department of the Environment, HMSO.

Elsevier 2005. http://books.elsevier.com/companions/0750663731 (accessed 28 July 2005).

Etzioni, A. 1968. *The active society: a theory of societal political processes.* London: Collier-Macmillan, and New York: Free Press.

Evers, F. 2005. Delving into the toolboxes: national environmental policy-making and strategic choice. Chapter 13.3 in *Planning under pressure: the strategic choice approach*, 3rd edn, J. K. Friend and A. Hickling (eds), 308–11. Oxford: Elsevier Butterworth-Heinemann.

Faludi, A. 1987. *A decision-centred view of environment planning.* Oxford: Pergamon Press.

Faludi, A. 2004. The impact of a planning philosophy. *Planning Theory* **3**(3), 225–36.

Faludi, A. and J. M. Mastop 1982. The "IOR school": the development of a planning methodology. *Planning and Design: Environment and Planning B* **9**, 241–56.

Friend, J. 1976. Planners, policies and organizational boundaries: some recent developments in Britain. *Policy and Politics* **5**, 25–46.

Friend, J. K. 1980. From IOR to COOR: a brief history. In *OR, social science and strategic choice: a discussion of themes emerging from the work of IOR, 1963–1979.* London: Tavistock Institute of Human Relations.

Friend, J. K. 1992. New directions in software for strategic choice. *European Journal of Operational Research* **61**, 154–64.

Friend, J. K. 2000. Sustaining innovation in OR: opportunities and obstacles. Plenary paper at OR42 – OR in the 21st Century: Communications and Knowledge Management, UK OR Society Annual Conference, 12–14 September, University of Wales, Swansea.

Friend, J. K. 2002. Building linked capacities for environmental planning. International Conference on Strategic Planning and Environmental Governance, Ministry of Environment and FORMEZ, Rome, November. Subsequently published in Italian in 2005 as: Creare competenze collegate per la pianificazione ambientale. In *Pianificazione strategica e governabilità ambientale*, Franco Archibugi and Antonio Saturnino (eds). Firenze: Alinea.

Friend, J. K. 2004. Response from John Friend: a future for the non-academic planning theorist? *Planning Theory* 3(3), 249–62.

Friend, J. K. and W. N. Jessop 1969. *Local government and strategic choice*, 2nd edn. London: Tavistock, and Oxford: Pergamon.

Friend, J. K. and Hunter, J. M. H. 1970. Multi-organisational decision processes in the planned expansion of towns. *Environment and Planning* 2, 33–54.

Friend, J. K. and A. Hickling 2002. *Planificando bajo presión: el enfoque de escogencia estratégica* (Spanish translation of *Planning under pressure: the strategic choice approach*, 2nd edn, 1997), trans. E. Vila. Caracas, Venezuela: Iveplan – Instituto Venezolano de Planificación.

Friend, J. K. and A. Hickling 2005. *Planning under pressure: the strategic choice approach*, 3rd edn. Oxford: Elsevier Butterworth-Heinemann.

Friend, J. K., J. M. Power and C. J. L. Yewlett 1974. *Public planning: the inter-corporate dimension*. London: Tavistock. Reprinted in 2001 in the Taylor & Francis Classics from the Tavistock Press series, London.

Friend, J. K., G. Lind and S. McDonald 1978. Future Regional Reports: a study of form and content. Report IOR/926R. Edinburgh and Coventry. Tavistock Institute of Human Relations, London.

Friend, J. K., M. E. Norris and J. Stringer 1988. The Institute for Operational Research: an initiative to extend the scope of OR. *Journal of Operations Research Society* 39, 705–13.

Giangrande, A. and E. Mortola 2005. Neighbourhood renewal in Rome: combining strategic choice with other design methods. Chapter 13.7 in *Planning under pressure: the strategic choice approach*, 3rd edn, J. K. Friend and A. Hickling (eds), 322–6. Oxford: Elsevier Butterworth-Heinemann.

Hart, D. A., D. A. Hickling, C. K. Skelcher and M. E. Norris 1978a. Regional planning: a report to the DoE. COOR/4 2T 194. Centre for Organisational and Operational Research, Tavistock Institute of Human Relations, Coventry.

Hart, D., C. Skelcher and F. Wedgwood-Oppenheim 1978b. Goals and objectives in regional planning. *Public Administration Bulletin*, April.

Healey, P., A. Khakee, A. Motte and B. Needham 1997. *Making strategic spatial plans: innovation in Europe*. London: UCL Press.

Hertfordshire County Council 1976. Hertfordshire County Structure Plan: report of studies 2. Hertfordshire County Council, Hertford.

Hickling, A. 1985. *Abordagem de Escolha Estrategica*. Sao Paulo: Fundacao do Desenvolvimento Administrativo.

Hickling, A. 1989. Gambling with frozen fire. In *Rational analysis for a problematic world*, J.V. Rosenhead (ed.). Chichester: John Wiley.

Hickling, A. and A. de Jong 1990. *Mens en Beleid*. Leiden/Antwerpen: Stenfort Kroese.

Hickling, A., R. Hartman and J. Meester 1976. *Werken met Strategische Keuze*. Alpen aan den Rijn: Samson Uitverij.

Hickling, A., L. Wilkin and F. Debreyne 1980. *Technologie de la Décision Complexe*. Brussels: Université Libre de Bruxelles.

Hirotaka Koike et al. 1991. A Japanese edition of *Planning under pressure*, with translation by Hirotaka Koike and colleagues of Utsunomiya University, Gihodo, Tokyo.

INLOGOV 1976. Definition of regional objectives. Final report to DoE. Summarised in: D. Hart, C. Skelcher and F. Wedgwood-Oppenheim 1978. Goals and objectives in regional planning. *Public Administration Bulletin*, April.

IOR 1978. Regional planning and policy change. IOR draft report to DoE, May, IOR/950R. Institute for Operational Research, Coventry.

Ismail, M., T. Setiabudi and F. van Steenbergen 1989. *Modul Pendekatan Pilihan Strategis*. Aceh: Bappeda Provinsi Daerah Istimewa.

Khakee, A. and K. Strömberg 1993. Applying futures studies and the strategic choice approach in urban planning. *Journal of Operations Research Society* **44**(3), 213–24.

Kirby, M. W. 2003a. *Operational research in war and peace: the British experience from the 1930s to 1970*. London: Imperial College Press.

Kirby, M. W. 2003b. The intellectual journey of Russell Ackoff: from OR apostle to OR apostate. *Journal of Operations Research Society* **54**(11), 1127–40.

Ling, M. 1990. Making sense of planning evaluations: a critique of some methods. *Planning and Development* **6**(1), 14–20, Hong Kong.

Luckman, J. 1967. An approach to the management of design. *Operations Research Quarterly* **18**, 345–58.

Mandelbaum, S. 2004. A symposium on the work of John Friend: introduction. *Planning Theory* **3**(3), 199–200.

Melbourne University n.d. Computer-aided policymaking (course home page), http://www.capolicy.unimelb.edu.au/ (accessed 28 July 2005).

MHLG 1970. *Development plans: a manual on form and content*. Ministry of Housing and Local Government, Welsh Office. London: HMSO.

Morgan, J. R. 1971. *AIDA: a technique for the management of design*. Coventry: Institute of Operations Research.

Muller, J. 1992. From survey to strategy: twentieth century developments in Western planning method. *Planning Perspectives* **7**, 125–55.

Needham, B. 2004. John Friend: advising and theorizing. *Planning Theory* **3**(3), 237–47.

Openshaw, S. and P. Whitehead 1977. Decision making in local plan: the DOT methodology and a case study. *Town Planning Review* **48**, 29–41.

Operational Research Society 1962. A proposal for an Institute for Operational Research. Recommendations of the Joint Working Party with the Tavistock Institute of Human Relations. CR/115/1962 (as cited in Friend 1980).

Oxford Polytechnic 1978. Leiden–Oxford: a comparative study of local planning in the Netherlands and England (5 project papers). Department of Town Planning with Planning Theory Group, Delft University of Technology, Delft.

PAG 1965. *The future of development plans: a report*. London: HMSO.

Phahlamohlaka, J. 2005. Building commitment in a rural community: use of commitment packages in empowerment through information technology. Chapter 13.14 in *Planning under pressure: the strategic choice approach*, 3rd edn, J. K. Friend and A. Hickling (eds), 353–6. Oxford: Elsevier Butterworth-Heinemann.

Rosenhead, J. 1980. Planning under uncertainty: the inflexibility of methodologies. *Journal of Operations Research Society* **31**, 209–16.

Rosenhead, J. and J. Mingers 2001. *Rational analysis for a problematic world revisited: problem structuring methods for complexity, uncertainty and conflict*, 2nd edn). Chichester and New York: John Wiley.

RTPI 1997. Slimmer and swifter: a critical examination of district wide local plans and UDPs. Research report from Cardiff University for the Royal Town Planning Institute by S. Crow, A. Brown, S. Essex, H. Thomas and C. Yewlett, RTPI, London.

SCW n.d. Strategic Choice website, http://www.stratchoice.net/ (accessed 28 July 2005).

Stilwell, F. J. B. 1972. *Regional economic policy*. London: Macmillan.

STRADSPAN n.d. STRADSPAN website, http://www.btinternet.com/–stradspan/ (accessed 28 July 2005).

Stringer, J. 1967. Operational research for "multi-organisations". *Operations Research Quarterly* **18**, 105–20.

Strömberg, K. 1986. *Planera met Osakerheter!* Stockholm: Byggforskningsradet.

Strömberg, K. and J.-H. Kain 2005. Communicative learning, democracy and effectiveness: facilitating private–public decision-making in Sweden. Chapter 13.2 in *Planning under pressure: the strategic choice approach*, 3rd edn, J. K. Friend and A. Hickling (eds), 303–7. Oxford: Elsevier Butterworth-Heinemann.

Sutton, A., A. Hickling and J. K. Friend 1977. *The analysis of policy options in structure plan preparation*. Coventry and London: Institute for Operational Research.

Swanson, J. 1994. Sending out the right packages. *Surveyor*, 18 August.

Tewdwr-Jones, M. 2001a. Planning and the National Assembly for Wales: generating distinctiveness and inclusiveness in a new political context. *European Planning Studies* **9**(4), 553–62.

Tewdwr-Jones, M. 2001b. Grasping the thistle: the search for distinctiveness in a devolved Scottish planning system. *International Planning Studies* **6**(2), 199–213.

Thomas, D. 1983. *Flexibility and commitment in planning: a comparative study of local planning and development in the Netherlands and England*. London and The Hague: Martinus Nijhoff.

Thornley, A. 1991. *Urban planning under Thatcherism: the challenge of the market*. London: Routledge.

Trist, E. and H. Murray (eds) 1993. Historical overview. In *The social engagement of social science: a Tavistock anthology*, vol. 2: *The socio-technical perspective*, 1–34. Philadelphia, PA: Pennsylvania University Press.

Van der Valk, A. and G. J. Carsjens 2005. Feet on the ground: engaging planning students with political realities. Chapter 13.5 in *Planning under pressure: the strategic choice approach*, 3rd edn, J. K. Friend and A. Hickling (eds), 315–18. Oxford: Elsevier Butterworth-Heinemann.

Vila, E. n.d. Network news, cited on www.stratchoice.net (accessed 1 August 2005).

Vila, E. and A. M. Benaiges 2005. Capacity building in Venezuela: using strategic choice methods with policy-makers and students. Chapter 13.12 in *Planning under pressure: the strategic choice approach*, 3rd edn, J. K. Friend and A. Hickling (eds), 345–8. Oxford: Elsevier Butterworth-Heinemann.

Waddington, C. H. 1973. *OR in World War 2: operational research against the U-boat*. London: Elek.

Wedgwood-Oppenheim, F., D. Hart and B. Cobley 1975. An exploratory study in strategic monitoring: establishing a Regional Performance Evaluation and Policy Review Unit for the North West. *Progress in Planning*, vol. 5, part 1. Oxford: Pergamon Press.

White, L. 1994. Development options for a rural community in Belize: alternative development and operational research. *International Transactions in Operational Research* **1**(4), 453–62.

Wyatt, R. 1999. *Computer-aided policymaking: lessons from strategic planning software*. London: E & FN Spon.

Yewlett, C. J. L. 1984. Polishing practice: the reconciliation of scientists and practitioners. *Journal of Operations Research Society* **35**, 487–98.

Yewlett, C. J. L. 2000. A commentary on: Stringer, J. (1967). Operational research for "multi-organisations" (*Operations Research Quarterly* **18**, 105–20). *Journal of Operations Research Society* **51**, 135.

Yewlett, C. J. L. 2001a. Theory and practice in OR and town planning: a continuing creative synergy? *Journal of Operations Research Society* **52**, 1304–14.

Yewlett, C. J. L. 2001b. OR in strategic land-use planning. *Journal of Operations Research Society* **52**, 4–13.

Part 3

Regional economics and strategic planning

7 Regional economic planning and development: policies and spatial implications

Peter Roberts

Introduction

As already emphasised in earlier contributions to this volume, regional economic planning and development policy in the UK has its origins in the actions taken during the 1920s and 1930s to address the structural regional disparities which became ever more evident during the Great Depression. Two lines of analysis, argument and policy were introduced during this period, many elements of which persist to the present day: firstly, various planning policies, restrictions on location and financial assistance schemes designed to guide the location and development of economic activities; secondly, measures intended to promote the occupational and physical mobility of labour. The former have been described as "taking work to the workers", whilst the labour market and inter-regional migration policies have been typified as "taking workers to the work" (Richardson and West 1964).

A further set of theories and justifications for the presence of regional economic planning and development can be identified. The Report of the Royal Commission on the Distribution of the Industrial Population (the Barlow Report), when published in 1940, addressed the causes and consequences of the increasingly divergent regional distribution of economic activity growth and population change. In discussing these matters, it made reference to the "social, economic or strategic disadvantages of concentration" (1940: 5), and also described and analysed in considerable detail what we now refer to as the environmental and spatial difficulties associated with excessive urbanisation and with the physical degradation and virtual abandonment of some of the older industrial areas located in the disadvantaged regions. As will be seen later in this chapter and in Chapter 12, the traditional triad of reasons used to support and justify the presence of regional economic planning and development policy – social, economic and political (McCrone 1969) – has in recent years been joined by what can be called the environmental and spatial capacity arguments.

Whilst the origins of regional economic planning and development as a discrete policy area can be traced back to the 1920s, it is also important to acknowledge the significance of the relationship between this area of activity and what is now normally called regional spatial or land-use planning. Other authors make a similar distinction between the two connected disciplines: Hall (1974) has described regional economic planning and development as "national/regional planning", because it chiefly considers the development of regions as contributions to the national economy, and regional spatial planning as "regional/local" planning because it is mainly concerned with the more physical aspects of the development of regions. Equally, Baker *et al.* (1999) refer to "regionally-based economic development" and "regional land-use planning". A similar, but more detailed, set of definitions is provided by Diamond's (1974) six broad objectives of regional policy, which include the objectives of reducing regional unemployment differentials, reducing population pressure in congested areas, and achieving a better balance between the population and the environment. As will be discussed in the next section, what is more important than the specific application of the terminology is the nature of the relationship between these two policy fields or, to be more precise, for most of the period from 1945 to the present day the *absence* of such a relationship. This lack of a meaningful relationship between economic and land-use planning is not unique to the UK, although it has persisted longer in the UK than in many other countries, and it reflects the complexity and opaque nature of the link between the two activities in the UK (Burns 1964).

Having established the origins of regional economic development and planning, three other points of introduction are necessary. First, it is essential to appreciate the essentially reactive nature of much of regional economic planning and development policy, especially prior to 1997; this performance at regional level contrasts with the presence of a number of attempts to provide explicit national economic planning and guidance, on the one hand, and with the efforts of some local authorities and their partners to intervene proactively in the local economy, on the other hand.

Second, it is also important to recognise that domestic regional economic planning and development policy has increasingly become intertwined with the operation of the European Union's Structural Funds (Roberts 2003). The regional plans and programmes supported by the Structural Funds were initially introduced in the UK regions during an era when many other forms of regional planning and development were dormant or discouraged, and they have grown considerably in recent years in terms of both their spatial coverage and their value.

Third, it is necessary to acknowledge the interrelationship between the design and operation of regional economic planning and development and the politics of the UK devolution "project". The modern devolution project, which can trace its origins to the failed attempts to introduce devolution to Scotland and Wales in the 1970s, has as its starting point the *Alternative Regional Strategy* report published in 1982 (Parliamentary Spokesman's Working Group 1982). As alluded to in Chapter 3, the project has seen the establishment of directly elected territorial governments for Wales, Scotland, Northern Ireland and the Greater London region, the introduction of formal non-elected regional assemblies (RAs) in the other eight English regions and the establishment of Regional Development Agencies (RDAs) in all nine English regions. The implications of this series of institutional transformations for the content, structure and operation of regional economic planning and development should not be underestimated and are discussed in greater detail later.

All of the above points are discussed in the following sections of this chapter. The next section offers some reflections on the origins, evolution and changing characteristics of regional economic planning and development, and may be studied alongside consideration of the more extensive historical review presented by Peter Hall in Chapter 2. A third section examines the various roles and areas of competence of regional economic planning and development policy, with particular reference to its role as a means of stimulating and supporting national and regional economic growth, and its secondary function as an agent of decentralisation. The fourth discusses the search for ways of ensuring the integrated and coordinated development of regions and examines the various contributions made by regional economic planning and development activities in helping to satisfy this objective. The final section reflects on the achievements of regional economic planning and development and considers the possible future evolution of the policy area.

Evolution and characteristics

It has been claimed that regional policy is "the oldest form of industrial policy" in the UK (Grant 1982: 53) but it equally could be claimed that it has long been observed that the practice of this important area is sometimes hampered, confused or restricted because no adequate theory of regional development exists (Hilhorst 1971). This was considered to be the situation some 30 years ago, and it can be argued that it is even more the case nowadays (see Chapter 5). It has also been suggested that it is difficult, or even impossible, fully to measure and evaluate the success or failure of regional economic planning and development activities. In part this difficulty can be considered to be a consequence of the dynamic nature of regional economies and an outcome of the problems that are encountered in attempting to isolate or attribute the effects and eventual outcomes of individual policy actions. Equally, this difficulty can be seen as a reflection of the absence, inconsistency or inadequacy of relevant and sufficiently wide-ranging regional and national information systems, especially those which cover a long time period. The simplest example of this problem can be illustrated by reference to the frequent changes that have been made to the definition of unemployment between 1979 and the present day.

A further set of problems is encountered when discussing or assessing the content and consequences of individual aspects of regional economic planning and development policy. This set of problems reflects the inherent difficulties associated with any attempt to define the target or goal of a specific regional economic planning and development initiative, and to then measure the level of achievement. In the past, one of the commonly stated aims of policy was to promote the achievement of "regional balance". This term was used by the Barlow Commission, but was never adequately defined or fully explained. As a consequence, in the view of one commentator, the term has been "flung around as an all-purpose phrase in lieu of thought" (Hall 1968: 292). Other equally vague goals, aspirations and targets have been advanced, including ideas such as "balanced growth" ("fine rhetoric, but the term 'balance' is somewhat confusing" – Glasson 1974: 14), "balanced regional structure" and "sectoral balance" (Holland 1976) and, more recently, the idea that regional economies can or should realistically set a target of attaining "world class" status across a vast array of functions and activity areas at some, frequently undefined, point in the future.

Developing the discussion of the origins of regional economic planning and development which was initially presented in the introduction to this chapter, it is evident that the basis for much of post-1945 policy was established by the Barlow Commission. In particular, but unfortunately frequently ignored for much of the subsequent period, the Barlow Commission made what it considered to be an essential connection between the regional (economic) problem and the difficulties associated with the physical growth of the major metropolitan areas, especially those located in the South East and Midlands regions. However, subsequently the relevance and implications of this connection were not fully analysed or introduced into policy (see, for example, the earlier discussion of "regional balance"). More importantly, in one sense, many elements of the Barlow orthodoxy remained substantially unchallenged for many years; this, as will be demonstrated later, has tended to fossilise policy and practice.

The importance of the Barlow Report was that it placed the arguments for post-1945 regional policy at the centre of its analysis and policy prescriptions. In particular, it argued that regional policy was required in order to reduce high and persistent unemployment in the depressed regions and to alleviate congestion in the growing metropolitan areas. What was more contentious was how best to deliver regional policy. Accepting that "no democratic government could direct people where to live" (Hall 1974: 97) and the experience of the 1920s and 1930s, it was acknowledged that the means of control would have to be through the location of industry. On this point a number of the Commissioners agreed with the view of the majority report, which recommended that a central authority should be established in order to influence the distribution of industry and population, and that this authority should take the form of a national board that should have power in London and the Home Counties to regulate the development of industry (McCrone 1969). A note of reservation by three of the Commissioners argued in favour of the establishment of regional or divisional bodies linked to the national board, and the preparation of a report on positive measures to promote regional development, and that the power of negative control over the location of industry should cover the entire country, even though it should be applied in London in the first place. Three other Commissioners were unable to support the majority report and recommended the creation of a new central government department to be responsible for a range of regional matters, together with the introduction of more general controls on the location of economic activities throughout the UK. The authors of the minority report also suggested that the new central government department should prepare a national plan for the distribution of economic activities and that regional boards should be established to oversee the elaboration and implementation of policy.

In a number of senses the Barlow Report represents a landmark in the history of regional economic planning and development policy in the UK. First, it offered a comprehensive analysis and assessment of the origins and consequences of the "regional problem". Second, it linked the regional (economic) problem to the problems associated with excessive and often unmanaged urbanisation. Third, it provided a basis for much of post-war regional policy. In particular, the Barlow Report provided an overarching logic and rationale for regional policy: to reduce chronic unemployment in the depressed regions, to achieve a better balance in the geographical distribution of economic activity in order to help reduce congestion in the growing regions, and to reduce the strategic vulnerability of the major centres of production (Balchin and Bull 1987). Even though some of the evidence and interpretations upon which this logic was based have subsequently been called into question as "outdated . . . tendentious and inconclusive at the time" (Hall 1974: 96), its overall contribution and influence to this day cannot be doubted.

The Distribution of Industry Act of 1945 introduced a selective and substantially modified version of the recommendations of the Barlow Report. In relation to the administrative structure, many of the proposals contained in the majority report (to create a central authority or national board), in the note of reservation (to establish regional or divisional bodies of the national board) and in the minority report (to introduce a new central government department) were not implemented. Instead the Board of Trade (subsequently the Department of Trade and Industry – DTI) was given responsibility for the development and operation of regional policy. The powers provided in the Act allowed for the introduction of development areas – initially broadly similar in spatial coverage to the pre-war special areas – and for a series of measures designed to encourage economic development in the designated areas. Key elements of the selective assistance programme included powers:

- to construct, finance or lease industrial buildings and trading (industrial) estates;
- to make provision for basic public services;
- to reclaim derelict land; and
- to provide grants or loans to firms located in designated areas.

In addition to these powers, the Board of Trade was also given powers to restrict the building of new industrial premises; this was enabled initially through the continuation of a wartime control measure (building licences) and subsequently through the use of the Industrial Development Certificate (IDC). Introduced under the Town and Country Planning Act of 1947, an IDC was required for any industrial scheme in excess of a specified limit (originally set at 5,000 square feet). Any proposed development was required to have an IDC before planning permission could be granted; the grant of the certificate indicating that "development was consistent with the 'proper' distribution of industry" (McCallum 1979: 7). As has been noted by a number of authors, this procedure established a double hurdle for any proposed industrial development and also reflected the inherently fragmented nature of the administrative regime which was established in 1945, especially at regional–local level. For much of the period from 1945 to the present day this division of function and responsibility has hindered the managed development of regions.

Alongside the measures administered by the Board of Trade, a number of other important elements of policy were introduced during the immediate post-war years. Chief among such initiatives were the building of new towns – initially developed mainly to rehouse displaced urban dwellers, but also intended in a limited way to promote a linkage between the processes of economic development and urban regeneration (McCrone 1969) – and the redevelopment of towns and cities both through the powers introduced in the Town and Country Planning Act of 1947 and as a consequence of the implementation of a range of other measures and the direction of general public expenditure in order to deal with the task of post-war reconstruction.

In offering a summary and some points of conclusion on the first great era of policy, which occurred during the late 1940s, it is important to be aware of a number of significant weaknesses in the structure and operation of the system of regional economic planning and development introduced under the 1945 and 1947 Acts. The weaknesses reflect, in part, the faults in analysis and inter-pretation that were associated with the Barlow Report, especially the failure to analyse and manage the development of the service sector – both the Barlow Report and much of post-war legislation concentrated on the manufacturing sector – and the inherent limitations of the controls on industrial floor space to deal with many regional economic problems. With regard to the latter point, the focus on investment in fixed assets (floor space and equipment) as a basis for determining the provision of financial support led to the relative absence of incentives for the support of economic innovation.

A more serious defect in the post-war package of measures was the separation of the land-use and economic elements of regional planning and development through the division of functions between the Ministry of Town and Country Planning and the Board of Trade. Ignoring the great strength of the analysis contained in the Barlow Report, which "saw the problems of the depressed regions as the inseparable complement to the concentration of growth in other areas, especially the London city-region" (Regional Studies Association 1983: 2), the organisation and structure of the post-war administrative machinery strengthened the divide between the two elements of the policy system. This institutional divide, with a number of notable exceptions, has persisted through-out the post-1945 period. As a consequence, the ability of policy makers and practitioners to introduce a comprehensive and integrated approach to the management of regional development has been restricted. As will be seen in the next section, evidence now exists which suggests that it is essential that the various elements of regional planning and development, including regional economic policy, are designed and managed as part of a single territorial pro-gramme guided by an agreed regional spatial strategy (Roberts 2000).

Moving beyond the origins of modern regional economic planning and development policy that are associated with the work of the Barlow Com-mission, the remainder of the post-1945 history is chiefly dealt with herein by reference to other sources. In particular, the material covered in this section emphasises the often neglected administrative and organisational elements of the regional economic planning and development debate, rather than concentrating on the details of the frequently discussed economic and other consequences of the design and implementation of policy. Part of the reason for this emphasis is a reflection of the inherently political nature of much of regional policy. As Wyn Grant has observed, "regional aid is a highly evident form of location-specific benefit" (1982: 57); this characteristic is frequently visible in both local and national political behaviour. A further reason for the choice of emphasis is the difficulty inherent in any attempt to provide a simple but authoritative assessment of the effectiveness of regional policy. As Armstrong and Taylor have argued, "without clarifying the objectives of regional policy, evaluation degenerates into measuring the effects of regional policy rather than measuring the effectiveness – and there is a world of difference between the two" (Armstrong and Taylor 1978: 12). Even if sufficient space was available herein to deal fully with the precise measurement of policy effectiveness, the absence of adequate data, together with the complexity of the continually evolving regional policy portfolio, militates against the provision of a straightforward assessment. Although it was a relatively simple matter from the 1940s to the 1970s to assess the progress of regional policy, especially when judged against standard objectives such as those outlined by Diamond (1974), this has not been the case over the past three decades. The problem for the potential analyst is that the detailed objectives and tasks associated with regional policy have varied considerably since the 1970s (Taylor and Wren 1997).

The previous discussion of the organisation of regional affairs can be extended, and it would appear that the political-economic emphasis evident in much of post-war regional economic planning and development policy is further reflected in the many struggles for control over the policy area which have occurred within central government. As was noted earlier, once the logic of the Barlow institutional recommendations had been rejected responsibility for the management of regional affairs was split between two ministries; this division of power, responsibility and function has continued to hinder the integrated planning and management of the United Kingdom space. Despite attempts by Labour administrations during the 1960s and 1970s to introduce institutional reforms that would help to foster integrated territorial planning and management at national and regional levels – through Regional Economic Planning Councils and Boards working with the Department of Economic Affairs (in the 1960s) or the National Enterprise Board (in the 1970s) – such reforms failed to take root and become effective agents of change.

During the 1980s and early 1990s there was little or no evidence of any attempt to promote comprehensive positive working between the land-use and economic components of regional planning and development. The election of a Labour administration in 1997 which was committed to political devolution to Wales, Scotland, Northern Ireland and London, the establishment of RDAs, the creation of other new institutional arrangements at regional level in England and the reform of the land-use planning system marked the first real attempt to forge a permanent link between the two elements of policy. A more detailed discussion of these reforms is provided in the section "Integrated regional development" (p. 126).

A consideration of the history of regional economic planning and development from 1945 to the present day indicates that many features of policy are enduring. The most immediately observable point of coincidence between the situations then and now is the relatively static nature of the regional assistance map. Many of the regions and localities designated as eligible for assistance under the 1945 Act are still eligible today. Equally, even though the definition of eligibility for assistance has now been extended in order to cover the service sector, considerable emphasis is still placed upon the provision of support for the introduction or retention of manufacturing activities. In addition, despite the prominence nowadays of various special regional agencies and devolved governments endowed with considerable powers and resources to assist regional economic development, the essential defining characteristic of UK regional economic planning and development policy – that it is in effect a national policy which has been and still is principally designed and applied separately from many other aspects of regional planning and development – still holds true. These three features – the relatively unchanged nature of the regional assistance map, the continuing emphasis on support for manufacturing activity, and the national and administratively separate nature of much of regional policy – can be regarded as constant themes in any attempt to analyse and assess the post-war history of UK regional policy.

From the Distribution of Industry Act 1945 until 1950 the package of measures described earlier – the development of industrial premises, the provision of basic services, the reclamation of derelict land, and the distribution of grant in aid and loans – was applied to development areas, which were extended in terms of their spatial coverage in 1946 and 1948. The fifth major policy instrument – IDC control – was applied in the congested areas. Fears of recession and the worsening economic situation in some regions prompted the government to strengthen the powers available in development areas; this strengthened package of measures was contained in the Distribution of Industry Act 1950. A change of government in 1951 initially did little to alter the package of measures available. The Conservative administration did, however, relax IDC controls, encourage the growth of export industries irrespective of their locations, and introduce measures to encourage the migration of labour – the Key Workers Scheme was launched in 1951 and was intended to assist the migration of workers who had skills in short supply (Prestwich and Taylor 1990).

By the late 1950s recession threatened again, and this prompted the government to tighten controls over economic development in the prosperous regions. In addition, government acted to extend the other powers available to provide assistance through passing the Distribution of Industry (Industrial Finance) Act 1958. With three exceptions, this general cyclical pattern of the extension and subsequent contraction of the powers available to encourage economic development in the less prosperous regions and to control growth in the congested areas has continued to the present day. For a fuller account of the history and effectiveness of regional economic development policy the reader is directed to the many standard sources, including McCrone (1969), Regional Studies Association (1983), Moore *et al.* (1986), Balchin and Bull (1987), Prestwich and Taylor (1990), Taylor and Wren (1997), MacKay (2003) and, last but not least, the successive editions of Armstrong and Taylor (1978 onwards).

The first of the three exceptions to the general cycle of extension and subsequent contraction in regional policy noted in the previous paragraph has already been referred to; this exception refers to the two experiments conducted during the 1960s and 1970s, which saw the introduction of attempts to establish a system of national and regional economic planning and development intended to provide an integrated framework for policy making and implementation. In both cases the objective was to establish a national organisation, similar in some respects to the national board proposed by the Barlow Report, which would work in tandem with regional bodies to design and deliver assistance packages "tailored to fit" the circumstances obtaining in each region. Although neither the ill-fated Department of Economic Affairs (DEA) of the 1960s nor the National Enterprise Board (NEB) (established under the Industry Act 1975) survived for sufficient time to allow for the long-term effectiveness of their operations to be tested, the reform of the 1970s did give birth to two more lasting arrangements. These were the development agencies for Scotland and Wales – the Scottish Development Agency (SDA) was subsequently renamed Scottish Enterprise, whilst the Welsh Development Agency (WDA) has recently been merged with the department responsible for economic planning and development in the

Welsh Assembly Government. In essence, the problems encountered by both the DEA and the NEB were in part a reflection of the fact that they were superimposed upon the existing institutional framework; neither the Board of Trade (or DTI) nor the Ministry of Town and Country Planning (or Ministry of Local Government/Department of the Environment) relinquished their powers and responsibilities for, respectively, regional economic development and strategic spatial planning.

This superimposition of new agencies on an already congested institutional platform resulted in the "crowding out" of the newcomers. A substantially different and far more positive relationship was established between the SDA and WDA and their respective institutional partners, but these exceptions are more a reflection of the presence and strength of territorial central government departments (the Scottish Office and Welsh Office) than of the willingness of the DTI to devolve responsibility for regional economic policy. It should also be noted here that similar institutional arrangements were established in Northern Ireland.

Although the experiments of the 1960s and 1970s failed to take root and evolve to maturity, the lessons from these experiments have informed subsequent policy making and more recent attempts at political and administrative devolution. Some of these lessons were isolated and evaluated at the time of the initiatives or soon after; one such example of early evaluation can be seen in the suggestion that the economic and land-use elements of regional policy should be "brought together at the regional level as integrated parts of a set of coherent regional strategies" (Regional Studies Association 1983: 126). Other lessons took much longer to reach maturity and achieve implementation, such as the devolution of powers and responsibilities to Wales, Scotland, Northern Ireland and London, or the establishment of the RDAs and other regional institutions in the English regions, including the London region.

The second exception to the general pattern of evolution of regional economic planning and development policy is associated with the changes introduced by the Conservative government after 1979. In 1979 over 60 per cent of the land area of the UK was designated as eligible for regional assistance (Prestwich and Taylor 1990). The stated objective of the new administration was to reduce the amount of funding available by 38 per cent and to concentrate assistance on the areas with the highest unemployment. Although criticised at the time as a break with the traditional consensus on regional policy, the new policy package as a whole, and especially the objective of concentrating resources on the areas of greatest need, was broadly consistent with the pattern of intervention which had been evident under previous administrations.

What was less consistent was the scale of the reduction in expenditure which was proposed, especially at a time of recession and rapidly rising unemployment, and the abolition in 1981 of IDC controls. However, in reality, expenditure on regional assistance had been falling since the mid-1970s (Taylor and Wren 1997) and, in the event, the scale of the reduction in both the spatial extent of assisted areas and expenditure was less than originally stated. The spatial coverage of assisted areas was reduced, but not by much, for fear that the removal from the UK map of designated areas would also exclude such areas from eligibility to receive support from the, then, newly introduced European Regional Development Fund (ERDF). In fact, the introduction of the ERDF went some considerable way to replacing the reduction in domestic expenditure on regional assistance as well as providing a number of other important opportunities for policy innovation (Talbot 1977; Roberts 2003). A further change to the regional policy portfolio took place in line with one of the recommendations made by the Regional Studies Association (1983); that was that the level of support for the service sector should be increased substantially. Such a recommendation would once have been regarded as unwelcome and unhelpful, but in the difficult economic circumstances encountered in the early 1980s, with a rapid decline in manufacturing employment and the absence of any significant potential for employment growth in the sector (Morgan 1986), jobs in service activities were seen as offering the greatest potential for reducing regional unemployment. During the 1990s and through to the present day, the level of support for the establishment of service sector activities and employment has been increased in amount and extended in terms of the range of interventions.

The third and final exception to the general pattern of policy evolution reflects the increasingly important role played by local authorities and other agencies in the promotion of regional economic development. Needham (1982) identified and evaluated a number of the key roles performed by local authority-sponsored economic development; one of the most important of these was described as "gap filling". In the context of the operation of regional economic planning and development policy during the 1970s and 1980s, this gap-filling role included the provision of specialist local and regional facilities, such as "starter" and "incubator" units designed to offer both premises and support facilities for new enterprises, specialist training services and the provision of industrial finance. The latter initiative was associated especially with the (later abolished) metropolitan county councils, but was also extended to other local authority areas as the success of pioneer organisations, such as the West Midlands Enterprise Board (which has survived to the present day), became apparent (Roberts *et al.* 1990).

The roles performed by local authorities and other agencies have extended in terms of their scope and expenditure in recent years as a consequence of the increased emphasis placed upon the local and neighbourhood "tailoring" of policy and upon the integrated delivery of services. Included among the growing list of roles is what the Audit Commission (1999) has identified as the crucial "understanding complexity" role; this is an essential function in a policy field which has seen an explosion of direct initiatives and delivery mechanisms and which also engages with mainstream local authority expenditure in order to "bend" it in support of wider economic development objectives.

From these three exceptions to the general pattern of policy evolution, as well as the identification and evaluation of the general lessons from the operation of mainstream regional economic planning and development policy, it would appear that many of the institutional and policy reforms of the past ten years reflect issues and aspirations which would not have been out of place in the Barlow Report. First, a number of the modern academic assessments and evaluation studies of the operation of regional policy have pointed to the need for regional policy to "not only create jobs in areas of persistently high unemployment, but also to reduce the excess demand for labour and other resources, such as land and infrastructure, in areas where these demand pressures are excessively high" (Taylor and Wren 1997: 846). Second, it has increasingly been recognised that regional economic planning and development policy should extend beyond its previously somewhat politically constrained agenda and set of instruments of implementation, in order to deal with the problem of the uneven distribution of opportunity, income and expenditure; this again suggests the reintegration of the two elements of regional policy, because:

> public expenditure in London is well above its "expected level". Providing public services of an acceptable standard is difficult in the national capital with its increasingly dominant political, corporate and financial elements. This problem is purely due to growing congestion costs.
>
> (MacKay 2003: 315)

A third matter of concern has been the presence of duplication and fragmentation in regional economic policy making and implementation, exacerbated by the absence of adequate regional institutional infrastructure in the English regions outwith London. It has been argued that much of regional policy suffers from "a 'Humpty Dumpty effect'. Efforts to promote economic growth . . . fracture when they hit the ground in departmental silos" (Audit Commission 2004: 53). The absence of adequate regional governance is mirrored by the continuing dominance of central government, which can result in individual initiatives underperforming at regional and local level, or even cancelling each other out (RCU 2002). Fourth, it has been acknowledged that regional economic planning and development policy cannot stand alone: it is an essential element in the design and delivery of strategic spatial policy, on the one hand, and it is also considered that regional economic planning and development policy should be the subject of democratic control and accountability, on the other hand (Morgan 1999; Roberts 2000).

The above lessons from the history of the operation of regional policy have been important in informing the recent review and revision of the regional economic planning and development system. Most of the lessons were already evident by the 1960s, and this awareness of the weaknesses inherent in the system prompted the reforms which took place at that time, including the establishment of the DEA. The failure of the reforms of the 1960s to take root led to a second attempt at reform during the 1970s, again with few lasting results in England. From 1979 onwards few positive changes were introduced, although the strategic policy vacuum left, initially by the abandonment of the Regional Economic Planning Councils and, later, by the abolition of the metropolitan county councils and Greater London Council, did, somewhat ironically, stimulate later reforms. It was during this period of policy reversal and the decay of strategic planning that the foundations were laid for the recent package of policy innovation and institutional reform. The keystone event in this process of innovation was the publication of the *Alternative Regional Strategy* (ARS) (Parliamentary Spokesman's Working Group 1982), which argued the case for the devolution of a wide range of central government powers and functions, the election of regional governments and the establishment of a series of regional executive agencies, including regional economic development agencies. It is appropriate at this point to shift consideration to the next topic: an analysis of the roles and functions associated with regional economic planning and development activities.

Roles and functions

Although this chapter is principally concerned with the formulation and implementation of regional economic planning and development policy, in practice it is virtually impossible, and certainly undesirable, to attempt to separate this aspect of regional planning and development from the wider system of strategic territorial management and governance, hence the overlap of coverage with the contents of Chapters 2 and 3. This was recognised by the Barlow Commission and has figured prominently as a central idea in a succession of other research studies and official inquiries, including the ARS. As noted earlier, the adoption of such an approach to regional planning and development is an essential prerequisite for effective and integrated territorial management and governance: regional economic development and strategic land-use planning are best considered as two sides of the same coin. So why has responsibility for these two aspects of policy been divided between two or more departments of state and why has it taken so long to produce an institutional solution which reflects the fundamental logic espoused by the Barlow Commission more than half a century ago?

In part the answer is to be found in the deep-rooted dominance of departmentally based central government, a form of government which in the past has frequently appeared to regard the characteristics and requirements of the nations and regions of the UK as of less importance than ensuring the design and delivery of a uniform package of policies, instruments and measures. Although there have been clear exceptions to this rule, such as the presence of the (former) Welsh and Scottish Offices, even these territorial departments of central government were allowed only limited discretion in their administration of centrally determined policy. As Kellas (1991) has observed, the indirect rule exercised in Wales and Scotland prior to devolution was a form of central control through locally recruited managers. This central domination has been eroded significantly in recent years as a consequence of the establishment of directly elected governments in Wales, Scotland, Northern Ireland and the Greater London region, although the latter body only exercises power over a restricted set of functions and has a limited resource base (see Chapter 13). As for the other eight English regions, they still lack elected assemblies, whilst their economic development agencies – the RDAs – are non-departmental public bodies answerable to the DTI. Although the present situation in the English regions represents substantial progress when compared with that which obtained eight years ago, the asymmetric model of devolution which has been followed to date has not yet delivered a decisive shift in the balance of power between the centre and the regions.

Put simply, whilst the establishment of the RDAs and RAs has allowed the English regions to assist in the shaping and delivery of regional economic development policy, this shift in power has not yet extended to the control of expenditure in associated policy areas such as education, housing, training, and infrastructure and transport provision. The definition and assignment of power over the associated policy areas, many of which are fundamental to the successful design and operation of regional economic planning and development policy, are a matter of considerable concern. In addition, it is now generally accepted that the professional-technical dimension of regional economic planning and development policy *cannot* be divorced from questions of government, accountability and governance; as one author has concluded, the establishment of the RDAs is "not the final frontier" (Harman 1998: 194).

The main reason advanced in support of greater territorial integration, coupled with the introduction of better governance and accountability, is relatively easy to identify: one of the fundamental prerequisites for effective regional economic development is the presence of the full range of agencies and facilities required to support business and other economic activities, and in order to ensure the effective provision of these services it is necessary both to "bend" public sector budgets and to ensure the cooperation of private investors. To be successful this collaborative approach requires that the contributors of resources are given a say in how their resources are allocated and managed. This is the model of "new territorial governance" which is emerging in the English regions (Roberts 2000; Stephenson and Poxon 2001).

So what are the core areas of regional economic planning and development activity, and which of the adjacent policy fields can be considered essential to the effective design and delivery of managed regional adjustment? There are few comprehensive assessments of the full range of regional activities. One of the most insightful of these was prepared in the mid-1990s by Breheny (1996). As part of his analysis of the scope of regional planning, Breheny argued that the collaborative and coordinative aspects of regional organisation are fundamental to the success of planning and development policy, irrespective of whether the focus of such policy is social, environmental or economic. In a similar manner, Raco *et al.* (2003) have identified the importance of securing the commitment of all stakeholders and actors to mobilising resources in support of local development, whilst White (1998) has discussed the need to treat each element of regional development equally.

The great merit of Breheny's (1996) analysis is that his approach is based on the linked consideration of the "degree of coverage" of a regional activity – i.e. the scope of the activity which is determined by reference to its aims and the "degree of responsibility" – and the powers available to change or influence the substantive issues that a regional activity deals with. With regard to the latter point, it is evident that the "scope" is chiefly determined by the control exercised over the means which are at the disposal of the resource holder, policy maker or practitioner. Although Breheny's principal concern was to determine the scope and competence of regional land-use planning, his analysis can equally be applied to other aspects of regional activity (see Figure 7.1).

Tunnelling through Breheny's (1996) regional competences system, it is apparent that the twin considerations of "coverage" and "responsibility" can be applied to a number of defined clusters of regional activity. It is, for example, equally valid to determine the coverage and responsibility of regional social welfare policy or regional economic planning and development policy as it is to define the scope of regional land-use planning. Herein lies the value of Breheny's approach, because, as well as defining the scope of any individual cluster of regional activity, the analysis also allows for the identification and promotion

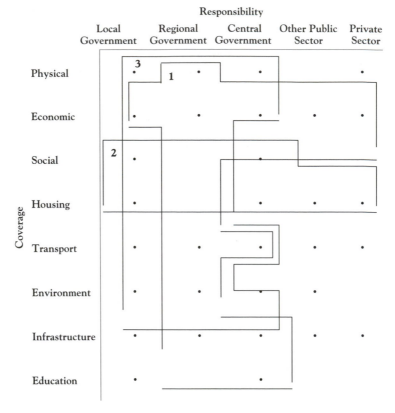

Illustrative Clusters of Activity:

    Cluster 1 - Regional Economic Development

    Cluster 2 - Regional Social Provision

    Cluster 3 - Regional Land-use Planning

Figure 7.1 Regional competences and illustrative clusters of activity

Sources: Breheny 1996; Roberts and Lloyd 1999; Baker *et al.* 1999

of the linkages between clusters. Furthermore, if the total activity system is considered as a whole, then what he describes is, in effect, the list of competences associated with an entire integrated system of territorial governance.

The Breheny model stands in stark contrast to the confused and confusing fragmentation that is presented in Harding's (2000) analysis of the arrangements for the planning and governance of the English regions, what he refers to as the "missing middle". The logic which underpins the Breheny model, and which is currently only partly developed in the management of affairs in the English regions, would appear to be central to the arrangements adopted by the devolved administrations in Wales and Scotland. In these two nations, the general approach to territorial planning and management which has been adopted can best be described as an "integrated competence" model (Roberts and Beresford 2003).

Glasson (2002) takes these arguments further and identifies what he describes as the various "layers" of influence on regional policy. These layers, in the case of regional economic planning and development, include the European Union (through general policy and the Structural Funds), UK central government (through the content and operation of general policies, the guidance exercised over the RDAs and the presence of assisted areas policy), regional governance (through the parallel policy systems responsible for regional land-use planning, transport, infrastructure provision and other issues) and local governance (through a wide range of policies and interventions). The challenges to be confronted in resolving the conflicting demands of the various "layers" include the relaxation of "constraints on content", the "better integration of economic development, and land-use planning and transport" and the "better co-ordination of area-based initiatives" (Glasson 2002: 261)

Having determined the "scope" of regional economic planning and development, and having identified the desirability of establishing a positive relationship between regional economic planning and development as well as associated areas of policy and action, the final part of this section considers the linked issues of governance and accountability also addressed in Chapter 3. Whilst it is well established that accountability for general national economic development policy and assisted areas policy should be exercised at UK level through the formal processes of Parliamentary scrutiny and reporting, a more difficult issue is how best to exercise such functions at regional level.

At present, in the English regions, outwith Greater London, the powers and competences of the non-elected RAs are limited to the scrutiny of the activities of the RDAs and Government Offices. Although the RAs have no formal powers of control over the operation of mainstream regional economic planning and development policy, they are able to influence the structure, form, content and mode of delivery of policy through a variety of means, including guiding the actions of local authorities (many members of RAs are elected members of local authorities), influencing the activities of RDAs through participation in the production of regional economic strategy (RES), and producing other regional and sub-regional plans related to the delivery of specific aspects of policy, and encouraging policy integration and coordination. This suggests that a new form of territorial governance is emerging in the English regions which extends beyond the normal limits of elected government (Healey 1997; Roberts 2000). In order to enhance the development of this new territorial governance, and thereby more closely coordinate the various activities which make up the "cluster" of regional economic planning and development policy, central government proposed that elected regional assemblies should be established in the English regions (DTLR 2002).

It is evident from the above discussion that defining the scope and institutional structure of regional economic planning and development is as important as establishing the map of assisted areas or introducing a set of policy instruments. The inherent limitations of a "one size fits all" approach to policy formulation and implementation have been demonstrated at frequent intervals since 1945. In order to address some of these weaknesses, central government has devolved significant powers and responsibilities to the elected territorial governments in Wales, Scotland, Northern Ireland and Greater London, and has now extended the case for devolution to the other eight English regions. In the interim, RDAs, RAs and other regional institutions have been established in order to help to deliver the decentralisation of key aspects of policy design and their implementation. The penultimate section of this chapter considers, first, the contributions made by these new institutions to the coordinated and integrated management of regions and, second, the role played by regional economic planning and development in helping to deliver regional restructuring.

Integrated regional development

Building on the discussion presented in the previous sections, and reflecting the views expressed by the major stakeholders and actors who are engaged in the design and delivery of regional economic planning and development policy, this section briefly reviews and assesses the contributions of the various institutions to the overall management of the English regions. Whilst it would be incorrect and potentially misleading to suggest that all elements of regional planning, development and management are of equal importance, it is essential to recognise that the economic dimension of policy cannot stand apart or alone. If for no other reason than ensuring the most effective overall utilisation of public and private resources – although there are many other reasons connected with aspirations, such as ensuring a high quality of living, promoting social justice or protecting the environment, that help to shape the overall policy landscape – it is essential to view regional economic policy as a component part of a wider regional system. As Breheny's (1996) model demonstrates, the various regional policy clusters are best treated as connected elements of a single regional system, rather than as isolated or individual activities.

The growing range and maturity of the various regional activities in England represent the outcome of a series of incremental additions to the regional portfolio. These additions to regional capacity have been described as "part of a broader programme of state modernisation" (Benneworth and Dabinett 2001: 1) and, more particularly, as a means of addressing the economic management deficit in the English regions (Caborn 2000). By creating new regional institutions, on the one hand, and by decentralising functions previously discharged by Whitehall departments, on the other hand, the administrative landscape of the English regions has been transformed (Roberts and Lloyd 1999; Roberts and Benneworth 2001; Goodwin *et al.* 2002). But has this transformation resulted in better governance of all aspects of regional life, or has it created new tensions and resource competitions between the various actors occupying the overcrowded regional "platform"?

Following Stöhr's (1990) analysis of the positioning and role of regional economic development and governance, the region or small nation can be seen to have a crucial role to play in mediating the demands of top-down and bottom-up policy through establishing a "meso" level of management and governance which can promote the effective mobilisation of the indigenous institutional resources present in a region. As the present author has observed elsewhere, this process of mobilisation provides the potential to utilise the full range of skills and abilities present within a region (Roberts and Lloyd 1999). In other words, once the twin processes of devolution and decentralisation have commenced, they begin to develop a capacity to both sustain their own growth and enhance their momentum; as has been argued, the establishment of the RDAs was only a starting point in the creation of complete regional governance (Harman 1998).

In some regions the processes of policy integration and coordination are more advanced than elsewhere. One way of testing the strength of policy linkage is to assess the extent and depth of partnership working between regional organisations, together with the resulting quality of the connections evident between the various plans and programmes produced by the partners. Examining the extent of partnership working and collaboration in the production of the first round of RDA strategies, it was evident that "The establishment of the RDAs and the process of developing Regional Economic Strategies have proved a catalyst for enhanced co-ordination" (Bridges *et al.* 2001: 65). Another source of evidence, and one which provides outputs in the form of integrated or coordinated policy statements and strategies at regional level, is to be found in the stance adopted by regional institutions when faced with the task of preparing a strategy. Given the presence of many "actors" on the regional "stage" (Harding 2000; Roberts 2000; DTLR 2002), it is evident that the potential for policy or operational divergence is considerable. Using the common set of objectives adopted by central government to represent the achievement of sustainable development – including the environmental, social and economic dimensions – it is possible to test the conformity of economic, land-use, cultural, transport and other regional strategies with the adopted Regional Sustainable Development Framework (RSDF).

The task set by central government for regional actors was to agree "a high-level vision for promoting sustainable development at regional level" (DETR 2000: 7). By testing the conformity of the RES with the RSDF, it is possible to identify convergence or divergence in both policy making and implementation (Benneworth *et al.* 2002). Whilst the evidence suggests that it is difficult to "retrofit" the integration or coordination of the various separate policy streams, it would appear to be easier to introduce an integrated approach at the start of the process. In one English region, the East Midlands, an overarching integrated regional strategy (IRS) was negotiated by the regional actors in advance of the preparation of the various individual, topic-specific regional strategies (East Midlands Regional Assembly 2000).

Two barriers to the integration of regional strategies exist: first, there is no requirement for regional organisations to produce an overarching strategy and, second, there is no indication as to which strategy, if any, should be considered to be the superior document (Benneworth *et al.* 2002). A further difficulty, which is not insurmountable if an integrated approach is established at the outset, is that some regional strategies are aspatial in nature; this problem can be overcome by introducing a spatial dimension into the preparation of an IRS. In the absence of such reforms, and reflecting the division of powers and responsibilities between regional organisations, it is unlikely that an integrated approach to the design and delivery of regional economic planning and development can easily be achieved. Although it would be incorrect to simply assume that the establishment of an elected regional assembly with powers of guidance or direction over other regional organisations and their strategies would solve the above-noted problems, it would appear that the creation of elected governments in Wales and Scotland has allowed for the preparation of "corporate" spatial strategies for these nations (Roberts and Sykes 2005). Equally, but in a much more constrained and networked form of governance, the strategic coordination arrangements for the Greater London region appear to be more satisfactory than those obtaining in the other eight English regions (Syrett and Baldock 2003).

A final point of observation in this section is that many of the above ideas are neither new nor revolutionary. Rather, they reflect established theory and best

practice, including the adoption of an integrated sustainable regional development model by the New Deal pioneers in the USA during the 1930s (Friedman
and Weaver 1979) and, as was seen earlier, the suggestions made in the minority
report prepared by three of the Barlow Commissioners (Barlow Report 1940)
that a new central government department should be established to allow for
the coordinated management of regional affairs, together with the creation of
associated regional boards or offices. This search for a means of ensuring the
integration of regional economic planning and development with other aspects
of regional policy has proved to be an enduring feature of the post-war institutional history of the UK. Despite the efforts made in the 1940s, 1960s and
1970s to introduce reforms which would encourage, support and enforce the
integration of the various policy streams associated with regional economic
planning and development, few lasting or significant results were achieved.

Whilst the reform programme which commenced in 1997 has achieved some
notable results, especially in Wales, Scotland, Northern Ireland, the London
region and through the establishment of new institutions the other eight English
regions, to date the impact of such reforms on the governance of regional
economic planning and development has been limited. Although the general
management of regional economic issues is now better coordinated than in the
past, a number of key matters of concern remain, outwith the responsibility or
competence of the devolved governments or the English regional organisations,
especially with regard to the form and content of the UK-wide assisted areas
programme and, by implication, the UK component of the EU Structural Funds
Programme (Roberts 2003). Despite the promise of further decentralisation of
regional policy beyond the level already achieved (HM Treasury 2003), there
are significant obstacles to the future integration of the full range of regional
economic planning and development policies and processes of implementation.

Conclusions: future prospects

Although the overall story of the attempts made since 1945 to integrate the twin
disciplines of regional economic planning and development and regional
strategic (or spatial) planning is essentially a tale of "false starts", failed initiatives
and missed opportunities, there have been a number of notable successes, especially since 1997. In part some of these recent successes can be considered as
accompanying benefits associated with the current government's devolution
project. However, a number of recent changes represent planned outcomes from
a specific programme of reform of the way in which the nations of the UK are
governed. One line of policy development can be traced from the Alternative
Regional Strategy (Parliamentary Spokesman's Working Group 1982) to the
creation of the devolved administrations and the RDAs, another line can be seen
in the progress which has been made from the "strange death of strategic
planning" (Breheny and Hall 1984: 95) to the introduction of new arrangements
for regional spatial and economic planning in the English regions, whilst a third
strand of evolution can be followed from early attempts at national and regional
integrated spatial management to the production of the present-day "corporate"
spatial plans which now exist for Wales, Scotland, Northern Ireland and Greater
London.

The essential learning point from this brief history and analysis of regional economic planning and development is that the triple forces of inertia, over-centralisation and political expediency have frequently overwhelmed attempts at regional reform. Most importantly, previous episodes of reform have failed to take root, principally because of the lack of an adequate resource base controlled at regional level, combined with the absence of a regional level of government and governance. As was observed some years ago in relation to attempts made to introduce strategic and regional planning, "it has been the incomplete, constrained and discontinuous way in which it has been attempted which has been at fault, not its purpose" (RTPI 1986: iii).

To these forces of resistance to regional reform should be added the inherent traditional compartmentalism of many central government departments. This is the so-called "silo" approach to the management of public policy, the weaknesses of which have been discussed at length elsewhere. This compartmentalism created or exacerbated the institutional fragmentation which has traditionally pervaded the English regions, with each central government department sponsoring its own regional organisations and arm's-length agencies (Mawson 1997). Remnants of this situation have continued, with the Regional Co-ordination Unit complaining in 2002 that the proliferation of compartmentalised area-based initiatives had resulted in a "lack of integration between initiatives" which has been associated with the growth of bureaucracy and "partnership overload" (RCU 2002: 1). Further evidence of the continuing danger of fragmentation was provided when responsibility for the RDAs was transferred from the Department for the Environment, Transport and the Regions (DETR), where RDAs were within the same portfolio as regional land-use planning, transport, housing and environmental matters, to the Department for Trade and Industry (DTI).

Reforms to both the policy system and the structure of territorial governance have brought about much-needed improvements in Wales, Scotland, Northern Ireland and Greater London, but even here, as was noted earlier, a number of UK-wide priorities continue to be imposed irrespective of the particular requirements of these areas. In the English regions there is less evidence of deep and lasting change, with the fear that "the increasing autonomy of regional governance" might generate scope for conflict between the centre and the regions as regions "begin to diverge from centrally formulated policies" (Murdoch and Tewdwr-Jones 1999: 726). In this situation it is unlikely that a genuinely integrated form of territorial development and planning will be introduced at regional level in the near future, especially given that the prospect of the introduction of elected regional assemblies has recently receded.

A more hopeful sign, however, has emerged, with the publication of a growth strategy for the three northern regions. The Northern Way strategy (Northern Way Steering Group 2004) argues in favour of the elaboration and implementation of an integrated approach to the economic, social, environmental and physical development of the North East, North West, and Yorkshire and the Humber regions. The primary purpose of the strategy is to establish the North of England as "an area of exceptional opportunity, combining a world-class economy with a superb quality of life" (Northern Way Steering Group 2004: 1); a key factor in realising this vision is identified as the determination of cross-sector expenditure priorities within the three regions rather than nationally.

Some aspects of the content and certain of the intentions of the Northern Way strategy are reminiscent of the proposals contained in the Barlow Report: the linkage made between economic development and spatial planning, the emphasis placed on providing excellent economic and social infrastructure, the priority attached to producing a clear strategic vision and a robust approach to implementation, and the stated aim of stimulating enhanced regional performance in the national interest. What is very different is that few of the traditional levers of economic and political control and enforcement are available to a modern government. It is almost impossible to imagine the reintroduction of IDC or building licences in a post-Thatcher era, whilst the notion of using nationalised industries as locomotives of regional development is currently regarded as belonging to the past.

Modern regional economic planning and development activities rely on new instruments of policy (see Table 7.1), including market-based incentives and controls, voluntary contributions to economic and social infrastructure, and the operation of public–private partnership in relation to many aspects of policy making, investment and implementation. Other significant additions to the policy agenda include the role now performed by regional economic policy as a delivery vehicle for social and environmental measures (Roberts 2003), the emphasis placed on support for the service sector, and the presence of a multi-tier funding and management structure for regional economic planning and development. This latter point is a reflection of the extensive engagement of EU, UK, sub-national and local interests and actors in the various aspects of regional development. It also suggests that it is now essential to attend to both the vertical and the horizontal dimensions of policy design and delivery. Whilst in the past

Table 7.1 Past and present characteristics of regional economic planning

Feature of characteristic	Traditional model	New model
Dominant direction of policy	Top-down	Top-down and/or bottom-up
Model of government	Centralised	Some functional devolution
Method of approach	Public sector dominated	Partnership
Key strategic objective	Promoting growth	Sustainable development
Style of planning	Hierarchical "family of plans"	National direction, local variation
Type of regional plan	Comprehensive and multi-sector detail	Strategic with spatial focus
Regional economic policy	Subsidies to firms, economies of scale, role of nationalised industries	Emphasis on competitiveness, innovation and research
Policy instruments	Bureaucratic regulation, financial inducements, public sector provision	Greater autonomy, reduced financial support, mixed public/private/voluntary provision

Source: Roberts and Lloyd 1999

national government principally concerned itself with the location and funding of individual enterprises, modern regional policy is a much more complex and fluid exercise (HM Treasury *et al.* 2004)

So, has regional economic planning and development policy since 1945 been successful, and what lessons can be identified that might guide future policy? Not unexpectedly, the response to the first part of the question is mixed: as one seasoned observer has stated, regional policy in the UK "had a major impact in the years up to 1975, but little effect subsequently" (MacKay 2003: 315). One set of explanations for this reversal of fortunes can be found in the changed nature and distribution of economic activities in an era dominated by globalisation and driven by rapid technological change (see Chapter 5). Other explanations reflect the breakdown of the traditional cross-party consensus on the role and operation of the public sector in relation to national and regional economic planning.

A further level of analysis might seek to consider why regional policy has been less successful than it might have been: here the general consensus is that this reflects the underfunding and inconsistency of policy (Taylor and Wren 1997), rather than its original intentions. In addition to the strict economic performance of regional initiatives, it is also important to acknowledge the administrative and organisational achievements of regional policy, especially at local level (Audit Commission 1999): its role as one of the driving forces behind the current devolution project, and its contribution to the promotion of greater coordination and integration between adjacent policy fields, especially as a consequence of the operation of EU Structural Funds regional programmes (Roberts 2003). Although the devolution project is far from completed, it is evident that a new form of integrated regional policy has now started to emerge.

Three themes are likely to dominate the future shape and content of regional economic planning and development policy: the creation of ever more flexible and better targeted instruments of policy; the establishment of organisational, administrative and governance structures which can provide for greater account-ability and coherence between policy fields; and the full incorporation of regional economic policy into the wider sphere of sustainable regional develop-ment – the environmental, social and economic dimensions of strategic spatial policy are now inextricably intertwined and should be guided by an agreed single spatial strategy in each region. In many ways this wider, better coordinated and more spatially sensitive approach to regional economic planning and develop-ment is in accord with the aims expressed by the Barlow minority report. In retrospect, perhaps the most disappointing feature of post-war UK regional economic planning and development policy is that it has taken over 50 years to realise the merits of what Abercrombie and his two fellow dissenting Commissioners advocated.

References

Armstrong, H. and J. Taylor 1978. *Regional economic policy.* Oxford: Phillip Allan.
Audit Commission 1999. *A life's work.* London: Audit Commission.
Audit Commission 2004. *People, places and prosperity.* London: Audit Commission.
Baker, M., I. Deas and C. Wong 1999. Obscure ritual or administrative luxury? Integrating strategic planning and regional development. *Environment and Planning B* **26**, 763–82.

Balchin, P. N. and G. H. Bull 1987. *Regional and urban economics*. London: Harper and Row.

Barlow Report 1940. Report of the Royal Commission on the Distribution of the Industrial Population (Cmnd 6153). London: HMSO.

Benneworth, P. and G. Dabinett 2001. English devolution and regional development: your region, your choice. *Local Work* **46**.

Benneworth, P., L. Conroy and P. Roberts 2002. Strategic connectivity, sustainable development and the new English regional governance. *Journal of Environmental Planning and Management* **45**, 199–217.

Breheny, M. 1996. The scope of regional planning. Paper presented at the RGS-IBG Conference, Glasgow, January.

Breheny, M. and P. Hall 1984. The strange death of strategic planning and the victory of the know-nothing school. *Built Environment* **10**, 95–9.

Bridges, T., D. Edwards, J. Mawson and C. Tunnell 2001. *Strategy development and partnership working in the RDAs*. London: Department of the Environment, Transport, Local Government and the Regions.

Burns, L. S. 1964. The relationship between physical and economic planning. *Town Planning Review* **34**, 269–84.

Caborn, R. 2000. Introduction. In *Towards a new regional policy*, E. Balls and J. Healy (eds). London: Smith Institute.

DETR 2000. *Guidance on regional sustainable development frameworks*. London: Department of Environment, Transport and the Regions.

DTLR 2002. *Your region, your choice*. Department for Transport, Local Government and the Regions. London: Stationery Office.

Diamond, D. 1974. The long-term aims of regional policy. In *Regional policy and planning for Europe*, M. Sant (ed.). London: Saxon House.

East Midlands Regional Assembly 2000. *England's East Midlands integrated regional strategy*. Melton Mowbray: EMRA.

Friedman, J. and C. Weaver 1979. *Territory and function*. London: Edward Arnold.

Glasson, J. 1974. *An introduction to regional planning*. London: Hutchinson.

Glasson, J. 2002. Some interim conclusions. In *Contemporary issues in regional planning*, T. Marshall, J. Glasson and P. Headicar (eds). Aldershot: Ashgate.

Goodwin, M., M. Jones, R. Jones, K. Pett and G. Simpson 2002. Devolution and economic governance in the UK: uneven geographies, uneven capacities? *Local Economy* **17**, 200–15.

Grant, W. 1982. *The political economy of industrial policy*. London: Butterworths.

Hall, P. 1968. Regional balance. *Town and Country Planning* **36**, 292.

Hall, P. 1974. *Urban and regional planning*. Harmondsworth: Penguin.

Harding, A. 2000. *Is there a "missing middle" in English governance?* London: New Local Government Network.

Harman, J. 1998. Regional Development Agencies: not the final frontier. *Local Economy* **13**, 194–7.

Healey, P. 1997. The revival of spatial planning in Europe. In *Making strategic spatial plans*, P. Healey, A. Khakee, A. Motte and B. Needham (eds). London: UCL Press.

Hilhorst, J. G. M. 1971. *Regional planning*. Rotterdam: Rotterdam University Press.

HM Treasury 2003. *A modern regional policy for the United Kingdom*. London: Stationery Office.

HM Treasury, Office of the Deputy Prime Minister and Department of Trade and Industry 2004. *Devolving decision making: meeting the regional economic challenge*. London: Stationery Office.

Holland, S. 1976. *Capital versus the regions*. Basingstoke: Macmillan.

Kellas, J. 1991. The Scottish and Welsh Offices as territorial managers. *Regional Politics and Policy* **1**, 87–100.

McCallum, J. D. 1979. The development of British regional policy. In *Regional policy: past experience and new directions*, D. Maclennan and J. B. Parr (eds). Oxford: Martin Robertson.

McCrone, G. 1969. *Regional policy in Britain*. London: Allen & Unwin.

MacKay, R. R. 2003. Twenty-five years of regional development. *Regional Studies* **37**, 303–17.

Mawson, J. 1997. The origins and operation of the Government Offices for the English regions. In *British regionalism and devolution*, J. Bradbury and J. Mawson (eds). London: Jessica Kingsley.

Moore, B., J. Rhodes and P. Tyler 1985. *The effects of government regional economic policy*. London: HMSO.

Morgan, K. 1986. Re-industrialisation in peripheral Britain: state policy, the space economy and industrial innovation. In *The Geography of De-industrialisation*, R. Martin and B. Rowthorn (eds). Basingstoke: Macmillan.

Morgan, K. 1999. England's unstable equilibrium: the challenge of the RDAs. *Environment and Planning C* **17**, 663–7.

Murdoch, J. and M. Tewdwr-Jones 1999. Planning and the English regions: conflict and convergence amongst the institutions of regional governance. *Environment and Planning C* **17**, 715–29.

Needham, B. 1982. *Choosing the right policy instruments*. Aldershot: Gower.

Northern Way Steering Group 2004. *Making it happen: the Northern Way*. London: Office of the Deputy Prime Minister.

Parliamentary Spokesman's Working Group 1982. *Alternative Regional Strategy: a framework for discussion*. London: Labour Party.

Prestwich, R. and P. Taylor 1990. *Introduction to regional and urban policy in the United Kingdom*. London: Longman.

Raco, M., I. Turok and K. Kintrea 2003. Local development companies and the regeneration of Britain's cities. *Environment and Planning C* **21**, 277–303.

RCU 2002. *Review of area based initiatives*. London: Regional Co-ordination Unit.

Regional Studies Association 1983. *Report of an inquiry into regional problems in the United Kingdom*. Norwich: Geo Books.

Richardson, H. W. and E. G. West 1964. Must we always take work to the workers? *Lloyds Bank Review*, January.

Roberts, P. 2000. *The new territorial governance*. London: Town and Country Planning Association.

Roberts, P. 2003. Partnership, programmes and the promotion of regional development: an evaluation of the operation of the Structural Funds regional programmes. *Progress in Planning* **59**, 1–69.

Roberts, P. and G. Lloyd 1999. Institutional aspects of regional planning, management and development: models and lessons from the English experience. *Environment and Planning B* **26**, 517–31.

Roberts, P. and P. Benneworth 2001. Pathways to the future. *Local Economy* **16**, 142–59.

Roberts, P. and A. Beresford 2003. European Union spatial planning and development policy: implications for strategic planning in the UK. *Journal of Planning and Environment Law* **31**, 15–26.

Roberts, P. and O. Sykes 2005. *Regional spatial strategy for the North West: learning the lessons from elsewhere*. Wigan: North West Regional Assembly.

Roberts, P., C. Collis and D. Noon 1990. Local economic development in England and Wales. In *Global challenge and local response*, W. Stöhr (ed.). London: Mansell.

RTPI 1986. *Strategic planning for regional potential*. London: Royal Town Planning Institute.

Stephenson, R. and J. Poxon 2001. Regional strategy making and the new structures and processes for regional governance. *Local Government Studies* **27**, 109–24.

Stöhr, W. 1990. Introduction. In *Global challenge and local response*, W. Stöhr (ed.). London: Mansell.

Syrett, S. and R. Baldock 2003. Reshaping London's economic governance. *European Urban and Regional Studies* **10**, 69–86.

Talbot, R. B. 1977. The European Community's Regional Fund. *Progress in Planning* **8**, 183–281.

Taylor, J. and C. Wren 1997. UK regional policy: an evaluation. *Regional Studies* **31**, 835–48.

White, G. 1998. *Regional development: can RDAs make a difference?* Cambridge: Segal Quince Wickstead.

8 Regional planning, regional development and transport markets

Roger Vickerman

Introduction

Transport has always been both a key element in strategic planning at the regional level and a key instrument in the promotion of regional economic development. However, neither of these is a simple relationship; they generate considerable controversy, and consequently policy towards transport often appears confused and inconsistent. Despite the recognition of the importance of transport in regional development it is difficult to identify coherent development in thinking. This is at least in part because policy towards transport in general has been dominated by political dogma, especially, for many years, through the debates over nationalisation/privatisation and road building and, more recently, by debates over road pricing/congestion charging.

Transport is, however, central to an understanding of the way a spatial economy works (see Chapter 10). Without efficient transport a region's economy could not function. This applies both to the internal transport system of the region, which provides the key linkage between inputs and outputs for regional markets, and to the external transport links which enable a region to trade with other regions. Transport thus has been a key element in regional structure plans and is one of the areas for which it is the responsibility of regional assemblies to develop coherent regional plans.

Transport planning is thus not *just* about planning an appropriate infra-structure network to meet a region's economic needs – a plan which can be bolted on to the regional development and spatial plan. It is an integrated part of the overall strategy for a region's development. Thus the future demographic and employment structure of a region will have certain transport requirements; an ageing population has different demands for transport from a working-age population, but also older residents will have very different demands from those of a similar age in previous generations. The core spatial structure will imply certain transport needs; the current interest in polycentric development will imply different patterns of movement from the more traditional structure of dominant urban centres. This is particularly relevant where there are questions surrounding the allocation of future housing needs. Strategic planning also requires consideration of the sustainability of future development; since transport is a major contributor to environmental damage the sustainability proofing of transport policies is a critical issue. Health and social development are matters of increasing concern in the development of regional planning; access to facilities as well as promoting healthier modes of transport is a key issue in delivering such objectives. However, changes in transport provision which are made can induce changes in any of these areas and potentially destabilise the strategic plan if not incorporated as an integral part of the planning process.

Strategic plans in England are presently the product of planning exercises being undertaken by the English regional assemblies to provide strategic guidance for 20 years to 2026. Long-term planning is needed where major shifts in transport provision are to be made, but at the same time the detailed modelling of transport demands over such a long period is fraught with dangers. Most transport forecasting exercises have been shown to be very unreliable. To some extent this is because forecasts of demand for new infrastructure do not fully take into account the changing circumstances of the surrounding economy, and hence more integrated planning should help to set the parameters right. However, where the focus of a strategic plan is to shift the behavioural parameters of the system, conventional models based on past responses may be inadequate. New approaches to strategic planning imply new approaches to the basic toolkit of the transport planner.

The key conceptual issues which will be raised here are:

- The two-way link between regional economic development and the transport needed to support it.
- Understanding that improving accessibility does not always lead to improved economic performance; transport costs interact with market size and structure such that improving links to poor regions may benefit richer regions more. Furthermore, improving accessibility by developing access to high-level networks may be more effective than just improving the high-level networks.
- Recognising that transport planning is not just about the provision of infrastructure and services, but also about how that infrastructure is managed and allocated, including the way it is charged for and who pays, and how transport markets are organised to serve the needs not just of the transport markets but also of the wider economy.
- Transport improvements in one region may have both positive and negative spillover effects on other regions, both adjacent regions and those some distance away, for example where transit traffic is diverted into a neighbouring region or where congestion in one region has a negative effect on access to markets for another region.
- The appraisal of transport projects requires a clear and consistent methodology to ensure that wherever and by whomever decisions are taken they are transparent and consistent, hence the need for very clear government guidance.
- Because transport is planned and organised at several different levels there is considerable scope for confusion and conflict between the policies of these different levels and also between different authorities at the same level.

In this chapter we examine, first, the nature of the role which transport plays in the development of the regional economy, considering both the development of infrastructure and the operation of the markets for transport services. Secondly, we consider the way in which transport policy has developed at national level in the UK and the implications this has had for regional planning. Thirdly, we look at the development of regional transport plans and the prospects for consistency.

Transport in regional development

It is clear that efficient transport is a necessary prerequisite for regional development. Without good transport a region cannot trade with other regions, nor can its internal markets function properly to bring together resources such as labour and materials and supply local markets. We have to be careful however that we do not assume from this that any improvement in transport will have a positive impact on a region's economy. Nor must we assume that transport is always a sufficient prerequisite for economic development (see Quinet and Vickerman 2004).

At the simplest level, if we were to move from a situation where there was no effective transport system in a region to the provision of a basic network, the likely return would be enormous, as it would enable the development of markets to take place – this is the situation which arises in undeveloped regions when, for example, all-weather roads are built for the first time. At a more advanced level, the completion of a high-level network, such as a motorway network or high-speed rail network, may have similar impacts, enabling the wholesale restructuring of market areas. However, the impact of marginal changes to a network may have a much less than proportional impact. Moreover this impact may be ambiguous; improving a link between two regions could have positive benefits on both or could lead to a redistribution of economic welfare between the two regions. This redistribution may frequently be in favour of the already more advantaged region, so using transport infrastructure investment as a development tool for lagging regions could be counter-productive (see SACTRA 1999; Vickerman 2002; Vickerman *et al.* 1999).

What is meant by efficient transport? There are two aspects to this: first, there has to be an infrastructure network (or networks) with a sufficient capacity and maintained to an adequate level to meet the needs of a region's markets; secondly, there has to be efficient operation of services on these networks. Efficiency implies that the services of both the infrastructure network and the operational network are provided at a price which reflects the full resource cost. This implies that on the one hand there should be no monopoly rents. Transport, and particularly transport infrastructure, has strong tendencies towards the creation of monopoly. Standard examples of natural monopoly use transport, particularly rail transport, where it is typically impractical (if not impossible) to create competing networks. On the other hand, the relatively low barriers to entry and exit in transport services markets mean that there is potential for destructive competition, by which new entrants cream off profits on routes with high demand by entering with lower fares than incumbent operators, but then leave when profits are no longer available. The impact is to destroy the long-term profitability of operators and reduce their ability to invest, and ultimately some form of public intervention will be required to maintain minimum levels of service. To prevent this, some form of regulation is often imposed on transport markets. Whatever form of competition is in place, transport markets for both infrastructure and services impose significant externalities which are often not included in the prices charged. These externalities include both the external impacts of one user on another, such as congestion and accidents, and the impacts of users on non-users, such as noise, local air pollution and global environmental impacts through greenhouse gases.

If the correct price is not charged for transport because of these market imperfections then the wrong amount of transport will be demanded. Hence, before we identify the correct level of capacity provision for a region we have to ensure that the prices are correct. If prices are too low, and there is clear evidence that the long-run relative price of transport, especially road transport, has been too low for most of the past half-century, then the economy will demand too much transport: this implies that the transport intensity of the economy (the amount of transport needed to produce one unit of GDP) will rise. For much of the period to the early 1990s, most developed countries based their provision of transport infrastructure not on a sound assessment of what the correct level of provision should be but on a "predict and provide" basis which ignored the appropriate level of prices and simply forecast likely usage and then aimed to provide transport capacity accordingly.

In the absence of "correct" prices it is much more difficult to make an adequate appraisal of transport investment projects. The basic approach has been to make an evaluation of the transport investment case on the basis of the benefits to users, mainly through time savings and reductions in accident risk, compared with the costs of the project. Any wider impacts of projects have to be dealt with rather carefully, since there could be a tendency to double-count some perceived wider benefits already accounted for in terms of user benefits. For example, if land rents were to rise in a given location as a result of improved accessibility following the provision of a new link, at least some of this rise would already have been taken into account in the implicit willingness to pay of users. In a sense, landowners can expropriate part of the increased accessibility benefits; how much will depend on the relative power of landowners and land users. Similarly, if the profits of companies in a region which benefits from lower transport costs through improved infrastructure were to rise, some of this would already be implicit in the time savings enjoyed by transport users.

But this does not mean that there are never circumstances in which there may be wider benefits. Economists have sought to identify if there are ways in which transport infrastructure may act rather like a public good and raise the returns to factors of production in an area, in that it acts rather like an autonomous shift in productivity. The argument here is that the savings in time spent in transport can free up that time to be spent in other productive activities. For individuals, this can be work-related activity: the savings in time reduce commuting time and enable workers to be more productive when arriving at work. Equally, the time saved could be spent in non-work activities, which may raise the level of demand for such activities, with a positive impact on aggregate demand. If so, this would imply that better infrastructure would raise the rate of economic growth. More-over, it could also be used as the justification for the use of public money to invest in enhancing infrastructure. Although there is a long history of discussion of this issue, it is only relatively recently that both the data and the econometric techniques have been capable of providing some real evidence. Unfortunately for the policy maker, the evidence is not clear cut. Some early studies suggested that the provision of more and better infrastructure could have a significant positive impact on economic growth, implying very high rates of return on investment. However, the accumulation of further evidence suggests that, although generally positive, the impact of infrastructure investment on economic growth may be only modest, and there is no guarantee that any particular investment will automatically produce positive returns over and above those to the user (SACTRA 1999; Vickerman 2002).

One of the particular difficulties is that of defining the appropriate study area for a specific investment. A given investment may have a generally positive impact on a country or large region, but this may mask a positive impact on one region and a negative impact on another as the infrastructure leads to a redistribution of economic activity between two regions. This so-called "two-way road" effect may mean that a new road built to improve accessibility for a peripheral region, with the objective of promoting economic growth, may result not in firms within the region benefiting from lower transport costs and access to markets in other regions, but rather in the firms in those regions with existing competitive advantages being better placed to exploit the improved accessibility and widen their own markets into the peripheral region. In some circumstances, therefore, a region could lose from the construction of new infrastructure. The key point here is that we cannot easily predict a priori which of the effects is likely to dominate. This will depend on: the existing industrial structures in the two regions, the current market sizes of firms in the two regions, the existence of scale economies and the level, and the share in total costs and the degree of change in transport costs. It is recognised that in certain circumstances quite substantial changes in transport costs could occur without having any significance on the relative economic performance of the two regions, whilst in other circumstances quite small changes in transport costs could result in a significant movement in the core–periphery relationship.

This suggests that there can be no simple definition of an economic development multiplier which relates a particular level of investment or change in accessibility to an expected change in productivity or GDP of a region. Moreover, there is no guarantee as to the direction of change in GDP resulting from a particular project, since it is possible as suggested above that improved accessibility will lower GDP, especially in the case of small areas or regions. Each project will have to be considered on its merits. Some quite large projects, in terms of the size of investment and impact on accessibility, time savings, etc., may have minimal wider economic impacts. All of the benefits can be captured in users' willingness to pay. Some smaller projects may not generate such large user benefits, but as a result of their ability to unlock economic potential have a disproportional impact on economic performance.

Thus far we have concentrated on the infrastructure investment case. What other aspects of transport efficiency can impact on economic performance? Other than the possibility that the availability of high-quality infrastructure creates a positive image for a region, the real impact of infrastructure is in enabling the provision of lower-cost transport services. The cost at which such services are provided to the user also depends on the efficiency of the operators on the infrastructure. That efficiency will depend in part on the market organisation of such operators and on the relationship between the infrastructure and the service providers.

This is most clear in the provision of rail services, where it is possible to have a vertically integrated industry in which a single organisation controls both the infrastructure and the services operated on it. This is the traditional structure of the nationalised railway company. More recently there has been a general move to the separation ("unbundling") of infrastructure and service provision in railways, as in a number of other network industries such as energy. The UK is among the countries that has carried this out to the greatest degree; on privatisation of the former British Rail, a new private infrastructure company – Railtrack – was established to own and manage the national rail network, whilst passenger services on that network were provided by (initially) 25 different franchisees. Initially, there was to be little or no direct competition between operators, except where parallel routes were allocated to different franchises, but eventually it was anticipated that some on-track competition could take place via the effective auctioning of "slots", rather like the process for allocating take-off and landing slots at airports.

The unbundling was expected to lead to increased efficiency through greater transparency, with franchised operators purchasing slots from the track provider and differences in performance between operators leading at least to what is usually referred to as "yardstick" competition. Franchised operators were also expected, as part of the franchise contract, to seek greater efficiency, which would lead to an eventual reduction in the level of subsidy. At the same time the private sector operators would be expected to be more innovative in investment and freed from public sector expenditure controls, which would bring forward long-overdue investments in infrastructure and rolling stock to modernise the railway system using increasing amounts of private finance. The whole system was subject to regulation by the Office of the Rail Regulator to ensure that the monopoly power of Railtrack was not abused, and the franchises were monitored for performance against various targets.

This is not the place to develop a full critique of the deregulated, privatised transport system which emerged between the mid-1980s and mid-1990s (see Quinet and Vickerman 2004). For our purposes it is sufficient to note first that what was absent from this new structure was any planning either at the overall level of the national rail network or, more significantly, at the regional or local level. Thus the existing responsibilities of the passenger transport authorities (PTAs) in the major metropolitan regions or the attempt to build up an integrated network for London and the South East were largely lost. Coupled with the deregulation of local bus services outside London, this meant that any attempt to plan integrated public transport services, including integrated ticketing, was essentially abandoned in favour of a market-driven system. Secondly, the new system failed to deliver all the improvements in service which had been promised. Outside London bus usage fell continuously after deregulation. In London, the alternative route franchising system was more successful in promoting bus usage (Mackie and Preston 1996; Preston 2001). Rail usage, on the other hand, grew significantly. In part this was due to the even greater supply of train services as franchisees sought to meet franchise commitments; in part the growth on the intercity routes was also related to the increasing congestion on the motorway network. Thirdly, for various reasons, investment in the rail network, both infrastructure and rolling stock, failed to meet the levels or pace of expansion necessary to meet this increased demand. A particular example of this is the problems surrounding the renewal and upgrading of the West Coast main line from London to the West Midlands, the North West and Scotland (Vickerman 2004a). This could be seen as a critical development from the point of view of regional development in three core regions of the UK in terms both of providing a rail network comparable to those being developed on the basis of new high-speed infrastructure in other EU countries and of relieving congestion on the M6 motorway linking these regions. The problems surrounding this development have led to the even greater growth of low-cost air services between cities such as Manchester, Glasgow and London.

Thus, it has to be concluded that the great benefits promised from deregulation and privatisation have not been realised. Some would argue that this is because the system was still too regulated, with insufficient direct competition to promote greater efficiency; others claim that the system is still coping with the consequences of a long period of underinvestment in the British Rail days (which is the official position of the government). The experience of Railtrack highlighted the difficulties of leaving the planning and management of the core rail network in a purely private sector company which had the relevant experience neither of long-term infrastructure planning nor of managing the effective maintenance and renewal of a decaying network, reinforcing similar more generic observations made earlier by Dimitriou and Thompson in Chapter 5. Attempts by the Labour government since 1997 to shore up the system they inherited, first by the imposition of a Strategic Rail Authority (SRA) to provide strategic planning and oversight of the system and, secondly, by the replacing of the fully private sector public limited company Railtrack with the not-for-profit (more strictly not-for-dividend) company Network Rail, have not been effective in reducing the level of criticism of the rail system (see Glaister 2002 for a fuller analysis).

The government has recognised this in its latest policy statements. The 2004 White Paper (DfT 2004b) contains an entire chapter on "making choices locally and regionally", which proposes further devolution of powers to the local level, giving local authorities greater financial freedom to develop projects of essentially local or regional interest. The Welsh Assembly Government, the Scottish Executive, Transport for London and the PTAs are to be given increased powers over franchising and the right to buy rail services as well as flexibility to transfer funding between rail and other modes. On the national rail network the SRA has been seen to be ineffective, and in its latest plans (DfT 2004a) the government has proposed abolishing the SRA, giving more overall management power to Network Rail and bringing the strategic direction back into the Department for Transport. In the next section we outline the current structure of transport planning at the national level in more detail.

National transport planning

It could be argued that there is in effect no real transport planning which takes place at the national level. Despite two major transport policy White Papers in six years (DETR 1998; DfT 2004b), the first of which led to a ten-year plan (DETR 2000b), the real national strategy for transport policy remains unclear. What has emerged is a set of inconsistent policies towards each of the main modes, inconsistent both through time with respect to each mode and across modes at any one time. Two issues have dominated national transport priorities during this period, with shifting emphases. One is the problem of road congestion; the other is the continuing problem of the railways.

The road congestion problem occurs in a number of guises: there is the continuing problem of congestion in most urban areas, particularly in peak hours, but notable during the 1990s had been the increasing problem of all-day congestion on major inter-urban routes. The current Labour government came to power in 1997 with a generally pro-public transport stance. Its initial move was to place a moratorium on most road schemes and to favour the development of innovative public transport solutions in urban areas whilst exploring the potential for road pricing of various forms. This ostensibly marked a formal end to the "predict and provide" philosophy which had dominated road planning for the preceding 30 or more years. In this approach the road planning problem had simply been seen as forecasting the likely demand for road use and then planning the provision of the necessary capacity to cater for this. Initially, the only constraint on road development was the availability of finance, but a number of high-profile public inquiries had led to increasing environmental constraints (see Chapter 12).

In urban areas, the initial preference was for bus-based systems, but pressure to commit resources to new light rail or tramway schemes, which were seen to have a better chance of inducing motorists to abandon their cars, allowed the completion of the first stages of the West Midlands and Croydon tramways, the extension of the Manchester Metrolink and the initial phase of the Nottingham tramway. A number of others remain in the planning stage, but generally the revealed cost of these schemes and the rather less-than-forecast traffic and revenues have led to nervousness on the part of the necessary private sector partners and reluctance on the part of the government to fund the increasing gaps between revenues and costs. The pendulum has swung back in favour of bus priority schemes and guided bus-ways. The government also made a commitment in principle to urban road pricing by allowing local authorities to devise and develop congestion charging schemes in which they would be permitted to retain the revenues thus raised as long as they were used for public transport enhancement. Thus revenues from the London congestion charge, so far the only one to have been introduced, are designated for enhancements to the bus network; those from the proposed (but aborted) Edinburgh congestion charge were allocated to the development of a third line in the proposed Edinburgh tram network.

Outside urban areas, the government faced a severe problem. The national motorway network had largely been completed, but sections of this network, such as the main radial approaches to London, the M25 London Orbital motorway, and the M6 north of Birmingham, were operating daily at well over design capacity. Options included widening key sections of route, an expensive and disruptive option, building parallel routes (including the potential for alternative toll routes) and the introduction of direct user charging through tolls. Capacity enhancement had increasingly been criticised by expert commentators as being self-defeating owing to the problem of induced demand. Evidence had mounted that the official forecast for road schemes had underestimated the potential for a new road to induce extra traffic in addition to that diverted from existing routes (SACTRA 1994). This arose because the official forecasting method assumed a fixed trip matrix. A given origin–destination (O–D) matrix of trips was allocated between alternative routes according to an algorithm based on journey times. This did not allow for the possibility that reduced journey times might both redistribute trips around the O–D matrix and generate completely new trips. The most efficient economic solution would involve first the introduction of tolls to ensure efficient use of the existing capacity (DfT 2003a, 2004c). This would enable some of the existing taxes on road users, vehicle excise duty and fuel tax, to be shifted to those using the roads most, especially at peak congested times. The scheme could thus be revenue neutral and involve a fairer distribution of the tax burden on road users.

The government took a decision in principle to move towards toll charging for heavy goods vehicles (see HM Treasury *et al.* 2004), but there was some discussion as to whether it should apply only to the motorway network. This was objected to by environmental lobbyists, who feared that it would simply divert significant volumes of heavy traffic to parallel national roads where both overall and local environmental damage would be even greater. Secondly, the government decided to wait for experience with the proposed introduction of the Toll Collect system for heavy goods vehicles in Germany, wisely as it turned out given the technical and financial problems with this system, which was initially cancelled by the German government but then reinstated albeit with a potential delay in introduction of three to four years. Clearly the more widespread charging becomes, the greater the potential efficiency in fitting more sophisticated charging devices to vehicles (and the more worthwhile for the individual user) as long as there is compatibility between systems. This is of particular importance for the effective introduction of local charging since it may remove the so-called "hassle factor" which has been identified in the London scheme, where users have to pay remotely by telephone or internet (TfL 2004).

In practice, therefore, the government has adopted a mixed strategy towards roads. It has been reluctant to adopt a stance which could be interpreted as anti-car/lorry on political grounds, as a nationwide protest on fuel taxes in 2001 and the continuing threat of renewed action have led to caution over more widespread introduction of road user charging and a commitment to a fairly significant road construction/motorway widening programme. Leaving the introduction of local congestion charging to local authorities shifted the political fallout to the local level and away from the national government. Nevertheless, the one scheme introduced so far, in London, has been generally regarded as successful. The reduction in all traffic of 15 per cent is rather higher than forecast (especially the 30 per cent reduction in car traffic), although this has produced a lower-than-forecast revenue stream. Generally the scheme has been accepted, and the widespread forecasts of chaos did not materialise (TfL 2004).

Turning to rail planning, we have already outlined some of the problems the government inherited with the fragmented rail system created under privatisation in the mid-1990s. The government has been struggling to get on top of this problem ever since. The failure of the SRA and the significant battles between the government, the Rail Regulator and Network Rail over the latter's proposed investment and maintenance programmes have blown the targets set out in the government's ten-year plan well off course.

The nub of this problem has lain in the continuing fact that despite the increasing patronage of the railways – passenger-kilometres on national rail rose by 25 per cent in the period 1992/3–2002/3, and by almost 30 per cent including light rail and urban metros – the system was also requiring increasing financial assistance from government. Despite an initial fall in subsidy envisaged in the original privatisation of British Rail, and bid for in the various passenger franchises, the franchisees started to need increasing aid to meet track charges and other investment requirements. The average subsidy per passenger-kilometre required reached 5.0p in 2003/4, requiring a total subsidy to train operators of over £2 billion. This figure had only ever been reached once in British Rail days, in 1992/3, and this was exceptional (Gourvish 2002). Both Network Rail, in its attempt to recover the quality problems of the infrastructure, and the SRA, in its requirement both to assist the franchise operators to meet track charges and to provide a long-term framework for investment in both track infrastructure and rolling stock, have needed to go back to government for increased finance. If this was to be the case, the government eventually took the view in its 2004 policy paper on the railways that it should reassume direct responsibility for strategy rather than having an independent authority determining this and letting contracts which implicitly relied on government guaranteeing a substantial part of the downside risk.

In this the rail situation has been less satisfactory than the use of an arm's-length authority for the road network in the form of the Highways Agency. This has been effective in both planning the national road network and managing investment and maintenance with increasing use of private finance. However, the situation is simpler. The Highways Agency manages only a fraction of the total network (i.e. the motorways and national trunk roads); it has been able to identify effective contractual arrangements for tractable parts of the network, and it does not have to deal with the complication of separate infrastructure providers, service providers and end users. Even here, though, the nature of contracts has been criticised by the National Audit Office (2003) as being more expensive than it needs to be, as private capital has sought protection against various risks, including that of the imputed revenue from shadow tolls or availability fees.

Risk, more specifically the need to insure against the downside risk of escalating capital costs and uncertain revenues, has become the major factor in the ongoing problem of using private finance to support government investment policies in transport. The ten-year transport plan (DETR 2000b) identified a significant gap between the investment needs and the government's ability to provide funds, which was expected to be filled by the private sector. The private sector's involvement would be encouraged by the wider benefits expected to flow from the increased efficiency of the transport system. However, the costs of major projects have continued to rise, and much of that rise is due to the private sector's desire to protect the risks in such projects where the government has not been prepared to give clear underwriting guarantees. One area where this has become most significant is in the development of urban light rail (tramway) systems. The hesitancy of government in approving schemes in principle and then delaying commitment has led to significant cost escalation and then essentially an abandonment of a number of schemes, most significantly the major expansion of the Manchester Metrolink network.

Such vacillation over the commitment of government funds has led to increasing frustration at the regional and local levels. Clear regional strategies in favour of public transport, often using new technologies, especially in the larger cities and metropolitan areas, have been thwarted, often *after* the expenditure of significant sums of money and effort in gaining acceptance of proposals. This includes the political capital expended in persuading local residents of the value of investing in public transport schemes at the expense of roads. In the latest policy statements the government appears to be moving to a position where rather more control can be exerted at local level, but given the degree of control which central government maintains over local finances it is unlikely that this can signal a major shift in policy at the local level – a point to which we return below.

One other area of national transport policy which does have significant implications for regional strategies and for regional development is air transport policy. Air travel is the fastest-growing sector of transport, with the number of passengers though UK airports having grown by around 80 per cent in the period 1992–2002 and expected to grow by a further 150 per cent by 2020, on mid-point estimates, to over 400 million passengers per year. This growth places numerous pressures on the system, with capacity constraints in air traffic control, runways, airport terminals and airport access. To some extent the rise in traffic can be accommodated by a less-than-proportionate increase in aircraft movements, and this places the main pressure on terminal development and airport access. The long public inquiry into Terminal 5 at London Heathrow Airport spent considerable effort in trying to determine whether the new terminal would lead to an eventual need for new runway capacity. The government has to deal with a number of pressures here.

First, it is clear that there is a major national interest in preserving the hub capacity of the UK, and this essentially means of London, given the economic significance of connectivity into the international, particularly intercontinental, air transport system. The White Paper on air transport (DfT 2003b) refers to one-third of visible exports by value, 25 million foreign visitors and 200,000 jobs directly dependent on air transport, with one-fifth of all international travel involving trips to or through UK airports. The overall contribution of air transport to the national economy has been estimated at 1.4 per cent of GDP (Oxford Economic Forecasting 1999).

Secondly, the need to provide regional links into this system is also strong. This takes three possible forms: the development of an appropriate network of regional airports with direct flights to major destinations, the provision of feeder services to the main hubs, and the provision of improved ground transport services to the main hubs. Taking these in reverse order, the enhancement of ground transport services has been met mainly by roads, with the exception of improved rail links into the main hub airports from their main centres. Of all UK airports only Birmingham can seriously claim to be on a major intercity rail route, and this contrasts with the developments in France (Paris Charles de Gaulle and Lyon St Exupéry), Germany (Frankfurt am Main and Köln–Bonn) and the Netherlands (Amsterdam Schiphol), all major rivals to London as European hubs.

Using London as a major hub for connecting regional traffic poses a number of problems. Regional services add to congestion and may appear less valuable than international traffic. Thus an international add-on to an intercontinental fare from London may be significantly less than one from a UK regional airport.

Regional feeder flights to London as a hub also compete with regional flights to London as a destination. The latter have been subject to severe competition from the growth of low-cost carriers using airports other than Heathrow to avoid the high landing and terminal costs. The growth of low-cost carriers has also led to a very significant growth in direct traffic between regional airports in the UK and both major and regional airports in continental Europe. It is significant that the policy consultation on air transport contained very detailed separate regional papers, and the White Paper has individual regional chapters.

Thirdly, there is a strong expectation of the wider economic benefits from airport development. This, like the general problem of wider economic benefits from transport infrastructure, is not always justified and has been driven to some extent by the clustering of new business around the major hub airports. The belief is strong enough however to encourage airports, many of which are owned or managed by local authorities, to provide incentives to new carriers. This has led to concern by the European Commission that such inducements may be in contravention of EU competition law. The expectation is that direct services will both improve accessibility and hence place a city "on the map" (the same argument has been used to campaign for direct high-speed rail services) and also encourage the location of new business around the airport.

Regional and local transport planning

The development of regional and local transport strategies in the UK has been in a state of flux during the transition to a degree of devolution. Responsibility for transport in Scotland and Wales has largely been transferred to the Scottish Parliament (Stationery Office 2001) and Welsh Assembly (Welsh Assembly 2001) respectively. In England, outside London, the regional assemblies have the duty to prepare a regional transport strategy (RTS) which becomes part of the regional planning guidance (RPG). Within the framework of the RTS, local authorities have the responsibility to produce local transport plans (LTPs), which replaced the previous system of transport policies and programmes (TPPs) in 1999/2000.

The RTS for each English region has to be established within the context of the planning policy guidance for regional planning (PPS11) (DETR 2000c) and the planning policy guidance for transport (PPS13) (DETR 2000d), as well as the appropriate regional spatial strategy (RSS) for each region (see Chapter 10). This recognises the need to provide for consistency in the relationship between transport and spatial planning in the region. Subsequently the old concept of RPG is being superseded by a new concept of regional spatial strategies (RSSs) (ODPM 2003) which will be more prescriptive in determining planning applications and which will form the basis of the new RPG. This is moving closer to the system developed for London, where the Mayor has the responsibility for producing a spatial development strategy and a transport strategy, within which the individual boroughs have to produce a local implementation plan showing how they will implement the strategy within their own areas. These local implementation plans are subject to the approval of the Mayor (GOL 2000).

Taking just one regional example of an RTS to illustrate the nature of these documents, we look in more detail at that for South East England. The South

East provides an interesting case study for regional transport planning. It is, as pointed out by Thompson in Chapter 13, the largest English region in terms of population and has the fastest-growing economy and the largest economy in terms of GDP outside London. It is also a region which is strongly affected by other regions. Transport in the South East is dominated by the proximity of London and traffic to and from most other UK regions, which has to pass through at least part of the South East. Furthermore, most land traffic by road or rail between the UK (and Ireland) and continental Europe must pass through the South East to access ports or the Channel Tunnel. The region contains the UK's second-largest airport (Gatwick), and Heathrow Airport is only just across the regional boundary in London. Three major growth points of both regional and national significance are located in the region: North Kent Thames-side (part of the Thames Gateway regeneration), Milton Keynes and Ashford. Between them, these locations are being expected to share a significant part of the need for additional housing, with consequent impacts on the transport system.

The transport system of the South East cannot really be regarded as a regional transport system in the sense of a system which has a primary focus on the needs of the region. All major routes are highly subservient to the inter-regional and international location. This includes the fact that the one road route which provides some linkage between the major sub-regions within the South East is the M25 motorway, which suffers from severe congestion. Other major roads and virtually all rail routes are radial routes to and from London. Away from the major London-oriented corridors the infrastructure is generally poorly developed, and serious congestion is the principal feature. Although there are pockets of serious deprivation across the region, particularly in the coastal periphery, the region is characterised by relatively high incomes, high levels of car ownership and generally poor public transport, particularly local bus services outside the larger towns. Rail services are dominated by the need to cater for commuting flows to and from London and display many of the worst features of previous underinvestment, with slow journey times and a legacy of old rolling stock.

Economic development in the region has been characterised by the development of firms in the high-technology sector, which have tended to locate in business parks away from traditional centres, locations which are difficult to serve effectively by public transport. This has added to the congestion problems both on major inter-urban routes and in the many small to medium-size settlements which characterise the urban structure of the South East.

The current RTS was developed in a revised Chapter 9 of RPG9, the regional planning guidance for the South East (GOSE 2004). The original RPG9 (GOSE 2001) was inconsistent with the requirements of PPG11, and thus the regional assembly was asked to provide an early review of the transport chapter (SEERA 2003). The RTS is dominated by the need to deal with congestion and the region as a "gateway region". Much is therefore made of the need for transport infrastructure and the improvement of strategic links which can give a greater coherence to the region as a whole and enable it to address some of the spatial disparities within the region. Although the strategy is clearly dominated by London, there is an obvious desire to try to reduce this dominance and the dependence it implies. This strategy has been formalised into the communications and transport chapter of the draft regional plan (SEERA 2005).

The overriding strategy is one which is termed "manage and invest". Interestingly, in the SEERA draft this was termed "invest and manage", with the emphasis on the need for additional infrastructure investment to enable the region to fulfil its potential, combining this with more active management of capacity (SEERA 2003: para. 5.14). In the approved version the emphasis is very clearly first on "seeking greater utilisation of capacity on the existing transport system", "managing demand . . . particularly on the road network" and "influencing the pattern of activities and . . . new developments" (GOSE 2004: para. 9.9). Investment is clearly targeted at the international gateway and inter-regional movement functions, but also at developing regional hubs and facilitating urban renewal and renaissance for sustainable development.

Management is seen as having both "carrot and stick" components. Placing constraints on development, on mobility and on the use of congested infrastructure has to go in parallel with support to public transport, the development of multi-modal solutions for both passenger and particularly freight transport, and education through support and encouragement to travel plans for employers and for individual travel.

Priorities for investment include a large number of schemes already committed. Of the 98 investments prioritised, 33 are already committed and 50 involve road improvements, but of the committed schemes 24 are road improvements. The more innovative schemes for rail enhancement or light rail or multi-modal solutions are much less advanced. However, the regional authorities only provide the strategic framework; the actual delivery of any of these schemes depends on partnership with a large number of agencies, including those at the national level, such as the SRA (now to be replaced by a mixture of the Department for Transport and Network Rail), Network Rail and the Highways Agency, local authorities and private sector partners. Hence there has to be a two-way relationship with transport plans at the local level.

Under the previous TPP system, local authorities were required to bid annually for capital resources within a transport policy framework (see Chapter 10). Decisions on funding under the TPP system were largely taken on individual schemes rather than on the strategy as a whole. The LTP system involves the development of five-year plans, which should provide a more stable framework for funding an entire programme and integrate capital and revenue spending in the same framework. In two-tier local authorities, shire counties and their districts, the preparation of the LTP has itself to be a joint responsibility, given the division of competences.

The LTP *should* allow the local authority greater discretion in the allocation of funds to individual schemes and, although it provides a basis for a more integrated approach to all modes, which will allow for multi-modal solutions, TPP schemes, with their emphasis on capital projects, tended to favour road development. The LTP does not of course provide the finance for the larger local schemes such as light rail. These are typically the subject of some form of public–private partnership authorised by ministerial order under the Transport and Works Act 1992. By moving away from an essentially project-by-project approach to a strategic approach, it has become more important to provide a framework for monitoring and assessing progress. Hence establishing clear targets and performance indicators has become part of the system, which has to set objectives consistent with the government's transport policy, analyse local problems and opportunities and set up a long-term strategy together with a fully costed five-year programme which is likely to be affordable within the government's spending review.

Table 8.1 outlines the content of LTPs (DETR 2000a), showing how they are expected to provide a comprehensive coverage both by mode and by likely impacts on other policy areas. Schemes proposed within the LTP have to meet the government's criteria for scheme appraisal within the five objectives underlying the New Appraisal to Appraisal (DETR 1998). Appraisal has to reflect the five criteria:

Table 8.1 The coverage of local transport plans

An integrated approach	
Widening travel choices	– cars
	– buses
	– rail investment schemes
	– taxis and private hire vehicles
	– voluntary and community transport
	– cycling
	– walking and pedestrianisation
	– powered two-wheelers
	– intelligent transport systems
	– capacity reallocations
	– other measures to address congestion and pollution
Transport policy targets	– road user charging and workplace parking levy schemes
	– parking
	– road safety
	– interchange
	– travel to stations
	– park and ride
	– integration with development plans
	– regional transport strategies
	– public transport information
	– travel awareness, journeys to work and school
	– crime and fear of crime
Planning and managing the highway network	– maintenance and bridge strengthening
	– major improvement schemes
	– de-trunking
Rural transport	– rural bus services
	– community-based rural public transport
	– countryside traffic management strategies
Sustainable distribution	– freight quality partnerships
	– rail freight
	– ports
	– shipping
	– inland waterways
Integration with wider policies	– promoting social inclusion
	– integration with action on climate change, air quality and noise

Source: DETR 2000a

- *environmental impact* – to protect the built and natural environment;
- *safety* – to improve safety;
- *economy* – to support sustainable economic activity and get good value for money;
- *accessibility* – to improve access to facilities for those without a car and to reduce severance; and
- *integration* – to ensure that all decisions are taken in the context of the government's integrated transport policy.

Outside the scope of the regular LTP framework, local authorities can also bid for funds under a number of specific initiatives, particularly associated with the promotion of public transport. The urban and rural bus challenges have enabled what are essentially demonstration projects to be funded as a means of showing what can be achieved. These go beyond the endorsement of such other ideas as quality bus partnerships where local authorities agree with private sector operators of commercial bus services to make significant commitments to improved infrastructure, such as raised kerbs and priority schemes, whilst the operator makes a commitment to invest in new vehicles. Further initiatives deal with cycling, walking, the concept of home zones and the particular problem of school transport which makes such a significant contribution to urban congestion. A key initiative for LTPs is the encouragement of employers to produce travel plans which concentrate on the means of reducing the use of cars for both commuting and work journeys through the promotion of public transport and the encouragement of travel clubs and car sharing (DfT 2002).

Conclusions: consistency and conflict in strategic transport planning

The picture painted above is one of a large degree of apparent inconsistency and potential confusion in the development of transport policy and its application at national, regional and local levels. In part this has been due to the problem of understanding what transport policy is about. A large part of policy is driven by concerns over market inefficiency in the transport sector. These inefficiencies arise because of the externality problem (congestion and pollution) and the market organisation problem (the move from state-owned monopoly providers of public transport to deregulated private sector operations and the re-emergence of private monopolies). Policy confusion arises because of the way changing priorities amongst these issues conflict with one another: for example, is the attempt to achieve modal shift as a part of the battle against congestion and road traffic-based pollution consistent with the desire to introduce private sector finance and management into alternative modes? The second policy driver is the use of transport policy as one of the instruments for regional (and more general economic) development. This causes immediate conflicts, since the presumed beneficial impacts of more transport at the macroeconomic level, and especially the contribution of more transport infrastructure, often directly contradict the more microeconomic concerns of efficiency.

At a national level the government has to reconcile the pressure from regions and local authorities for capital investment, which is perceived as an aid to enhancing local competitiveness, with national constraints on public expenditure and with targets for traffic reduction on environmental and relief-of-congestion grounds. Similar concerns arise at the regional and local level in recognising that attempts to solve one problem in the transport sector (relating to one mode or one part of a given network) may have consequences elsewhere. The present government's attempts to provide an overall framework for the sector, whilst also dealing with the specific problems of individual modes, represent a worthy attempt at trying to get the right balance, but have failed to appreciate the deep-seated nature of some of the problems and show the need to try to get some quick results when the real effects will take much longer to emerge. This has led to ever changing emphases and hence difficulty in assessing the real long-term effectiveness of policies.

At the regional level, and particularly at the local level where most policy is actually delivered, the problem which emerges is one of trying to develop consistent policies within this shifting national framework. This induces a degree of competitiveness between regions and local authorities which may be useful in encouraging innovation but may also be counter-productive if it leads to mutually inconsistent policies. This is particularly clear in the moves towards user charging for roads, where a policy which shifts the burden of charging from general vehicle taxation and fuel taxes to direct charging is needed for efficiency, but individual authorities attempting to introduce charging are perceived simply as imposing yet more taxes on motorists.

There is, however, one further dimension which we have not considered. Transport policy is also a concern of the EU, since transport is one of the sectors where the treaties have made provision for a common policy. Current EU policy (EC 2001) has been based heavily around two principles: investment in trans-European networks as a means of completing the high-level EU network in the interests of promoting both competitiveness and cohesion, and improving the efficiency and sustainability of EU transport by providing for "fair and efficient" pricing of all modes. These two principles often compete with each other and are also internally inconsistent. Moreover, since the EU policy is itself only a framework within which national policies exist, and since both taxation and public expenditure on subsidies and investment are protected closely by member states under the principle of subsidiarity, it has proved difficult to produce a fully effective pan-European policy which covers all transport-related issues and all modes (Vickerman 2004b).

In some senses the emerging structure of multi-level consultation and planning is the correct one. Local policies have to be framed in the context of an overall national policy, and national policy has to be sensitive to the differing needs of regions and local areas, as well as setting a framework within which the obvious spillovers and competing interests of individual local areas can be accommodated. What is needed is a longer period of stability and consistency to enable this system to deliver. Transport remains, however, a politically sensitive subject in which both politicians and electors look for quick solutions.

References

DETR 1998. *A new deal for transport: better for everyone* (Cm 3950). Department for the Environment, Transport and the Regions. London: HMSO.

DETR 2000a. *Guidance on full local transport plans*. London: Department for the Environment, Transport and the Regions (http://www.dft.gov.uk/stellent/groups/dft_localtrans/documents/page/dft_localtrans_504005.pdf).

DETR 2000b. *Transport 2010: the 10 year plan*. Department for the Environment, Transport and the Regions. London: HMSO.

DETR 2000c. *Planning Policy Guidance 11: regional planning* (PPG11). Department for the Environment, Transport and the Regions. London: HMSO.

DETR 2000d. *Planning Policy Guidance 13: transport* (PPG13). Department for the Environment, Transport and the Regions. London: HMSO (http://www.odpm.gov.uk/stellent/groups/odpm_planning/documents/pdf/odpm_plan_pdf_606896.pdf).

DfT 2002. *Travel plans*. London: Department for Transport (http://www.dft.gov.uk/stellent/groups/dft_susttravel/documents/pdf/dft_susttravel_pdf_504128.pdf).

DfT 2003a. *Managing our roads*. London: Department for Transport (http://www.dft.gov.uk/stellent/groups/dft_roads/documents/pdf/dft_roads_pdf_022865.pdf).

DfT 2003b. *The future of air transport* (Cm 6046). Department for Transport. London: HMSO.

DfT 2004a. *The future of rail* (Cm 6233). London: HMSO.

DfT 2004b. *The future of transport: a network for 2030* (Cm 6234). Department for Transport. London: HMSO.

DfT 2004c. *Feasibility study of road pricing in the UK: report*. London: Department for Transport (http://www.dft.gov.uk/stellent/groups/dft_roads/documents/page/dft_roads_029788.hcsp).

EC 2001. *European transport policy for 2010: time to decide*. European Commission. Luxembourg: Office for Official Publications of the European Communities.

Glaister, S. 2002. UK transport policy: 1997–2001. *Oxford Review of Economic Policy* **18**, 154–86.

GOL 2000. *Strategic planning In London*. Circular 1/2000. London: Government Office for London (http://www.go-london.gov.uk/planning/downloads/splan.rtf).

GOSE 2001. *Regional policy guidance for the South East* (RPG9). Government Office for the South East (http://www.go-se.gov.uk/key per cent20business/planning/downloads/final per cent20rpg9 per cent20 report.pdf).

GOSE 2004. Regional transport strategy. Chapter 9 of *Regional policy guidance for the South East* (RPG9). Government Office for the South East (http://www.go-se.gov.uk/rpg9review/transport/downloads/RTS per cent20Panel per cent20Report/RTSfinalJuly2004.pdf).

Gourvish, T. 2002. *British Rail 1974–1997: from integration to privatisation*. Oxford: Oxford University Press.

HM Treasury, HM Customs and Excise, Department for Transport 2004. *Modernising the taxation of the haulage industry: lorry road user-charge – progress report 3*. London: HMSO.

Mackie, P. and J. Preston 1996. *The local bus market: a case study in regulatory change*. Aldershot: Avebury.

National Audit Office 2003. *Maintaining England's motorways and trunk roads*. Report by the Comptroller and Auditor General, HC 431 2002/03. London: Stationery Office.

ODPM 2003. *Regional spatial strategies*. Office of the Deputy Prime Minister. London: HMSO (http://www.odpm.gov.uk/stellent/groups/odpm_planning/documents/pdf/odpm_plan_pdf_609496.pdf).

Oxford Economic Forecasting 1999. *The contribution of the aviation industry to the UK economy*. London: DfT.

Preston, J. M. 2001. An overview of public transport reforms in Great Britain and forecasts for the future. *International Journal of Transport Economics* **26**, 23–48.

Quinet, E. and R. W. Vickerman 2004. *Principles of transport economics*. Cheltenham: Edward Elgar.

SACTRA (Standing Advisory Committee on Trunk Road Assessment) 1994. *Trunk roads and the generation of traffic*. London: HMSO.

SACTRA (Standing Advisory Committee on Trunk Road Assessment) 1999. *Transport and the economy*. London: HMSO.

SEERA 2003. *From crisis to cutting edge*. Draft regional transport strategy. Guildford: South East England Regional Assembly.

SEERA 2005. *A clear vision for the South East: the South East plan core document*. Draft for public consultation, January. Guildford: South East England Regional Assembly.

Stationery Office 2001. Transport (Scotland) Act 2001, http://www.scotland-legislation-.hmso.gov.uk/legislation/scotland/acts2001/20010002.htm.

TfL 2004. *Congestion charging Central London: impacts monitoring second annual report*, http://www.tfl.gov.uk/tfl/cclondon/cc_monitoring–2nd-report.shtml.

Vickerman, R. W. 2002. Transport and economic development. In *Transport and economic development*, Round Table 119, Economic Research Centre, European Conference of Ministers of Transport, 139–77. Paris: OECD.

Vickerman, R. W. 2004a. Private financing of transport infrastructure: some UK experience. In *Trends in infrastructure regulation and financing*, C. von Hirschhausen, T. Beckers and K. Mitusch (eds), 177–98. Cheltenham: Edward Elgar.

Vickerman, R. W. 2004b. Conflicts between transport policies and spatial development policies: perspectives on regional cohesion in the European Union. Paper to 44th European Congress of the Regional Science Association, Porto.

Vickerman, R. W., K. Spiekermann and M. Wegener 1999. Accessibility and regional development in Europe. *Regional Studies* 33, 1–15.

Welsh Assembly 2001. *The transport framework for Wales*, http://www.wales.gov.uk/subitransport/content/policy/framework/index.htm.

9 The role of planning and development in spatial labour markets

Ivan Turok

Introduction

The labour market plays a pivotal role in linking economic and social change, with far-reaching implications for the prosperity of places and people. As Roberts has indicated in Chapter 7, cyclical economic fluctuations and more enduring structural changes produce shifts in the level and nature of employment, which shape people's living standards, social status and self-esteem and the overall well-being and cohesion of the community. There, however, are growing suggestions that these relationships also work in the opposite direction, namely that the skills, attitudes and organisational capacities of the population in particular places affect the rate of economic development and employment growth. In a context of falling transport and communication costs, and heightened mobility of capital and labour, both sets of processes become more complex and less predictable.

This chapter focuses on spatial aspects of the labour market, since this is the dimension most relevant to regional planning and regional development policies. Spatial planning has limited direct purchase over qualitative features of labour supply and demand, such as workforce skills or employer recruitment practices. It also has little influence over the social and economic factors that determine inequalities in earnings or the participation rates of different population groups. However, spatial planning can affect the location of employment and access to work for residential communities through its control over land-use and housing supply, and its influence over the quality of the environment, investment in the public realm and the availability of essential infrastructure. It can also improve the functioning of the labour market, and thereby the productivity of the economy, by properly coordinating housing, transport and productive investment, even if it is not the primary driver of economic performance and employment growth. Planning has recently come under fire for allegedly constraining economic growth, through limiting the supply of land for new housing and thereby forcing up house prices, causing macroeconomic instability and hindering labour market flexibility (Barker 2004).

The chapter explores two particular, long-standing labour market issues of central importance to regional planning and development. First, it considers the *regional* dimension of labour market disparities. This is often expressed as the "North–South divide" in the UK. Apart from a concern with social justice and unemployment in the "North", this kind of regional imbalance can have wider economic costs, including congestion and inflation in the housing and labour markets of the pressurised regions of the "South" and difficulties in delivering public services because of a shortage of key workers and affordable housing. Second, it examines the *sub-regional* dimension, namely the concentration of socio-economic problems in particular cities or parts of cities. This is sometimes described as an "urban–rural" divide or a more localised problem of inner-city or neighbourhood deprivation.

In both cases the focus is on the labour market aspects, including the way people respond to urban and regional economic disparities through migration and commuting. According to orthodox economic theory, the labour market should adapt to economic changes through shifts in migration, commuting patterns, wage expectations, workforce participation or retraining and upward mobility. This is supposed to be the hallmark of a flexible labour market, which is something that governments in Britain and the United States have in particular been striving for in the belief that it is a necessary response to globalisation and increasing international competition. It is a contentious set of propositions that go to the heart of contemporary debates about the character and future of Europe (European Commission 2004a, 2004b; Gray 2004). It raises questions about who should bear the burden of economic change and to what extent governments should regulate the behaviour of business and labour, earlier discussed in Chapter 5. Mainstream labour market theory suggests that government should not intervene in these processes of market "adjustment" without clear evidence of market failure or it risks creating inefficiencies and distortions, and undermining national economic competitiveness. If some regions are prospering while others are lagging, migration *should* moderate the consequences and narrow the gap. If business activity and jobs shift from cities to surrounding towns, changes in commuting patterns *should* iron out any unemployment differences between areas. The effectiveness and wider consequences of these adjustment processes are clearly crucial in assessing the case for spatial planning and its role in relation to changes in the location of housing and economic development.

The central argument underpinning the chapter is that these adjustment mechanisms may be attractive theoretical constructs, but they do not work very well in practice. They may also have undesirable economic and social consequences that mean they should not be encouraged without reservation. Consequently, regional and urban disparities constitute important challenges for governments to address. In recent years the UK government's expectations of what the planning system can contribute to this task – through the organisation of land use and physical infrastructure – have been lowered and the role of other policies has been elevated, such as welfare-to-work, new enterprise formation and the commercialisation of university research. This is a symptom of a wider shift in emphasis in economic policy from physical resources towards intellectual resources ("science, skills and innovation"), alongside a move from public planning towards market forces. Yet there remain considerable uncertainty and debate about the appropriate solutions to urban and regional problems, bearing in mind their deep-seated, structural character. There are also important analytical and policy challenges in understanding how problems at neighbourhood, urban and regional scales relate to each other, whether their relative importance has changed over time, and how best to respond to them.

During the 1980s and 1990s there was a big shift in policy emphasis in England from regional issues to more localised problems. In recent years, these have been portrayed as isolated "pockets" of unemployment and social exclusion requiring tightly targeted interventions to build community capacity and networks ("social capital") and to raise individual skills and motivation ("human capital") (Cabinet Office 1999; HM Treasury 2000, 2001a; DfEE 2001; ODPM 2004a). The same is true in Scotland (Scottish Executive 2002). Coincidentally, there has been a shift in perspective within other parts of government back towards regions as the key spatial units for analysis and action, especially for economic rather than social development (HM Treasury 2001b; ODPM 2005a).

Meanwhile, in some departments there has been a growing perception that cities may in fact have become key engines of regional growth, driven by "soft" urban assets and knowledge resources such as universities and cultural amenities to attract and retain talent (ODPM 2003a, 2004b; Scottish Executive 2004). To observers and practitioners outside central government, the persistence of these parallel agendas is a source of confusion and frustration when "joined-up" government is supposed to be the order of the day. One of the consistent themes underlying government policy is the increasing importance attached to human and social capital (employability, skills, enterprise and networks – between individuals *and* between firms) rather than physical capital or infrastructure. The implications for the planning system are highly significant but have not yet been systematically teased out in this developing agenda.

Regional disparities

Regional economic disparities in the UK are wide-ranging and persistent, as the chapters in Part 5 illustrate. There is some debate about how best to describe and measure them. The single most important indicator of prosperity is economic output per person, measured using gross value added (GVA). Table 9.1 shows the

Table 9.1 Three indicators of regional prosperity (UK = 100)

UK nations and regions	Output levels GVA per person of working age, 2001)	Productivity levels (GDP per person employed, 2001)	Employment rate (as a proportion of working-age population, 2001)
London	127	134	95
South East	120	111	108
Eastern	111	103	106
Scotland	93	95	98
East Midlands	92	90	102
South West	92	86	107
West Midlands	91	92	100
North West	91	94	96
Yorkshire and Humberside	87	88	99
Wales	81	87	93
Northern Ireland	79	88	91
North East	77	84	92
UK	**100**	**100**	**100**

Source: Adams *et al.* 2003

level of GVA per head of working-age population for the 12 standard nations and regions of the UK as defined by the government. The North–South divide is revealed very clearly. Historical data on economic output show that the gap between the prosperous and lagging regions has been widening steadily over the last decade and more (ONS 2004a: Fig. 12.2; ODPM 2005a). Regional disparities in the UK also appear to be among the largest in Europe, although much depends on the way regions are defined and the specific indicators used (HM Treasury 2001b; European Commission 2004a).

Two of the most important drivers of regional prosperity are productivity (measured using GDP per person employed) and the employment rate (measured by the proportion of the working-age population in paid work). Table 9.1 also shows the regional disparities in these variables. Differences in productivity appear to be larger than differences in employment. There are complex reasons for this, one of which relates to the industrial and occupational structure, with low productivity sectors in the South West (such as agriculture and tourism) and high productivity sectors in London (particularly financial and business services, and professional and managerial occupations more generally). Government welfare benefits and other transfer payments tend to reduce prosperity differences and narrow the employment gap between regions. The differences between relative productivity and employment in each region suggest that the policy priorities may not be quite the same everywhere. This evidence suggests that raising productivity may be a more fundamental objective than employment in the South West, Yorkshire and Humberside and the East and West Midlands. A balanced approach may be more important elsewhere.

Compared with the other regions, London is defined more as an administrative unit and less as a functional entity or self-contained labour market. There is considerable net inward commuting from surrounding towns in the South East and East regions. This tends to inflate economic output and productivity estimates unless appropriate adjustments are made to the population denominator. An important feature of London's low employment rate is the distinctive ethnic composition of its population. The employment rates for whites and non-whites in London appear to be very similar to the employment rates for these groups across the UK as a whole – 76 per cent for whites and 58 per cent for non-whites (Adams *et al.* 2003; ONS 2004b). Consequently, the immediate reason for London's relatively low employment rate appears to be the high proportion of the working-age population from non-white backgrounds. Non-white groups face several barriers in the labour market that white people do not, including discrimination (Gordon and Turok 2005). Their skills and qualifications may also be lower on average.

Although economists usually regard productivity as the key long-term driver of prosperity, employment is typically considered the most salient issue for lagging regions because of its pervasive impact on personal income, social status, social relationships, morale, health, happiness and the quality of life. Registered unemployment was traditionally treated as the key indicator of labour market conditions, but it has become discredited over the years by successive redefinition and manipulation. Government attempts to mask the scale of unemployment during the 1980s and 1990s also contributed to a substantial growth in recorded economic inactivity at the expense of the "claimant count" because people registered for so-called "inactive benefits", such as sickness and disability (Turok and Edge 1999; Alcock *et al.* 2003).

Consequently it has become common in recent years to refer instead to the broader concepts of "non-employment", "joblessness" or "worklessness" (ODPM 2004a). This includes people of working age who are out of work but not actively looking for work, such as the 3 million UK claimants of sickness benefits. With the improvement in the UK labour market over the last decade, the government has now acknowledged the broader challenge of reducing work-lessness and not simply registered unemployment (DfEE 2001; ODPM 2004a). Some of the New Deal programmes and the recent Pathways to Work scheme are aimed at getting these groups back to work through regular work-focused interviews and advice, more stringent benefit eligibility checks, practical help with rehabilitation from adverse health conditions, and financial incentives to take low-paid jobs. There is no recognition that deficient labour demand (a shortage of relevant jobs) may be part of the problem in some regions and localities.

Table 9.2 shows that the scale and composition of worklessness varies greatly between regions. This regional dimension is surprisingly neglected in the government's main welfare-to-work programmes, which tend to be "one size fits all". They focus on personal circumstances and define the challenge essentially in terms of individual aspirations and employability. The performance of these schemes in more depressed parts of the country is inevitably undermined by their narrow scope and supply-side focus (Turok and Webster 1998; Martin *et al.* 2003). Table 9.2 also demonstrates the inadequacy of unemployment as a measure of non-employment. In August 2004, about one in eight people of working age in Wales, the North East and the North West were reliant on bene-fits related to sickness and disability. This was between four and six times higher than the proportion reliant on unemployment benefits. The proportion reliant on sickness benefits in the North and West was more than double that in the

Table 9.2 Claimants of key welfare benefits by group and region (as a percentage of the working-age population), August 2004

UK nations and regions	All	Unemployed	Sick/disabled	Lone parents	Others
North East	18.4	2.7	12.4	2.6	0.8
Wales	18.2	2.2	13.1	2.4	0.6
North West	17.0	2.3	11.6	2.5	0.6
Scotland	17.0	2.9	11.3	2.2	0.7
West Midlands	14.3	2.6	8.7	2.4	0.6
Yorkshire and Humberside	14.2	2.3	9.1	2.1	0.6
London	14.1	3.2	7.1	3.2	0.6
East Midlands	12.0	1.8	7.9	1.8	0.5
South West	10.4	1.3	7.1	1.6	0.4
East	9.7	1.5	6.1	1.7	0.4
South East	8.6	1.3	5.4	1.6	0.3
Great Britain	**13.6**	**2.2**	**8.6**	**2.2**	**0.5**

Source: DWP 2004: Table 6.2

South East. These striking differences indicate important contrasts in the life chances of people living in different parts of the country.

Regional inequalities are also apparent in household incomes, personal qualifications, the incidence of poverty, average life expectancy and a range of other indicators of personal well-being (Adams *et al.* 2003; Dorling and Thomas 2004). For instance, the gross disposable income per head in London and the South East is almost 30 per cent higher than in the North and West of Britain (ONS 2004a: Fig. 12.8). This is less than the differences in economic output and productivity, mainly because transfers through the tax and benefit system redistribute income from more prosperous people and places towards poorer groups and areas. If one takes into account differences in the cost of living between regions (especially housing costs) then the disparities in income are reduced, but they remain sizeable and are growing (ONS 2004a; ODPM 2005b).

Regional policies

An important issue for government policy and regional planning is why established market mechanisms do not reduce these imbalances. In theory, there should be at least two adjustment processes at work. First, the rising costs and congestion resulting from strong growth and tight labour and property markets in the South East should diminish the returns from investment there and provide incentives for firms to move to or expand within less prosperous regions with underused resources. The availability of surplus labour, lower housing and wage costs, spare capacity in land supply and infrastructure, less road traffic and generally lower operating costs for firms should enhance the attractiveness of lagging regions as places to invest and run businesses. Over time, economic growth, innovative ideas and new technologies should diffuse from successful to underperforming regions.

Second, the shortfall in employment opportunities in peripheral regions and the superior availability of jobs across the occupational spectrum in prosperous areas should encourage underemployed as well as unemployed workers to migrate. This should reduce the amount of surplus labour in the poorer regions and create vacancies at all levels of their labour markets. This should in turn enable upward mobility and greater satisfaction among people who were previously overqualified for their jobs in the lagging regions. At the same time migration should offset labour shortages and reduce inflationary wage pressures in the South East, thereby ensuring a more efficient allocation of resources within the overall economy.

In practice, these processes do not operate strongly and the economy is not automatically self-correcting. Market mechanisms do not necessarily reduce disparities and restore balance or equilibrium. In terms of migration, only 1 per cent of households move between regions each year (Performance Innovation Unit 2002). Large and growing regional house price differentials make it difficult for people from the North to move South, especially with a shrinking social housing sector and a small private rented sector (ODPM 2005b). Another difficulty is that potential migrants are likely to feel most pressure to move during recessions when jobs are scarce, but this is precisely the time that migration is most difficult because employers at the destination are hiring fewer new staff (Jackman and Savouri 1992). Migration is also socially selective. People in professional, managerial and technical jobs tend to be more mobile than manual workers most vulnerable to unemployment, who face bigger barriers to mobility (Champion and Fisher 2004). It appears therefore that migration is least effective where and when it is most needed and for the people for whom it is most needed. It is also likely to contribute to environmental and social problems in areas of both population decline and growth, so it is not necessarily something to be encouraged without fuller consideration of the consequences.

More generally, economic change is inherently uneven, with decisions embedded in particular social and institutional arrangements, and therefore influenced by forces that are not simply price related. Regional economic trajectories have a cumulative or "path dependent" character, that is places are held to their course of development by historical as well as contemporary factors and forces. Regions with a head start in being well endowed with particular resources, institutions or technological capabilities tend to continue growing faster than others because of self-reinforcing advantages, such as cumulative learning, innovation and economies of scale. Regions with a disadvantage in terms of peripheral location, outdated industries, redundant skills, derelict land or old building stock may continually struggle to compete. Market forces may widen disparities by skewing resources towards areas with greater confidence among investors (even if it is only in the form of herd instinct behaviour) and more immediate commercial prospects. Consequently, imbalanced and unequal patterns of regional development may continue for an extended period.

There is considerable inertia as well as positive spillovers or "externalities" keeping potentially mobile firms in the South East. Many business owners and managers, professionals and skilled technical workers perceive themselves to be locked into the buoyant housing market. If they were to sell up and move north, they might find it difficult to return. Many growth firms in technologically advanced industries (such as software, life sciences and some of the creative industries) feel tied to the "thick" labour markets of the South East with their unique reservoir of advanced skills and sophisticated suppliers to choose from. The heavy concentration of social and political power, the media and cultural organisations in London also reinforces the region's economic advantages (Amin *et al.* 2003). There are powerful cumulative forces at work that not only buttress the region's position and create a virtuous growth cycle, but also draw investment, talent and entrepreneurial skills from the rest of the country in ways that may well undermine the economic prospects of the periphery (Buck *et al.* 2002).

Historically, regional policy sought to reduce such disparities by encouraging business relocation, and expansion and new investment from the South East to the rest of the country, i.e. moving work to the workers (see Chapters 2 and 7). The policy instruments involved a combination of "sticks" (restrictions on new development) and "carrots" (financial incentives and modern infrastructure in special development areas). There was an economic as well as a social rationale for this. Imbalanced regional growth was recognised to have economic costs in congestion and other bottlenecks, inflated property prices, wage inflation and duplication of social infrastructure such as schools and hospitals. Disparities lowered the rate at which the national economy could grow without running into capacity constraints and overheating. There was a financial cost in treating the cumulative social consequences of decline and an economic gain to be had from bringing underemployed resources into productive use. However, a government U-turn in relation to this approach, based partly on a general economic slowdown and rise in unemployment across the country, means it has been progressively downgraded since the 1970s to a position where UK spending on regional grants is now less than a quarter of the EU average, despite relatively large regional disparities and the general upturn in the last decade (Wren 2003; see also European Commission 2004a: Figs 1.3 and 3.2).

The new regional policy

The new regional policy encourages greater reliance on indigenous capabilities, i.e. places making the most of their own potential and increasingly standing on their own two feet. Encouraging economic development from within by exploiting local strengths is said to be a more secure and sustainable path to success in a competitive global economy. It means creating environments where high-value, growth-oriented businesses can start up, learn from each other and succeed. It draws on *endogenous growth theory* whereby growth arises from enhanced local productivity and innovation through investment in human capital and research in leading areas of the economy. This is supported by arguments that innovation and institutional learning are most effective at the city-region level because they require face-to-face contact and therefore geographical proximity. Knowledge "spills over" between firms, which improves technical progress and efficiency across the regional economy. Key policy priorities include support for enterprise, skills and research into new technology (ODPM 2005a). Specialisation builds distinctive sector strengths through supporting institutions, suppliers, market intelligence and advanced skill-sets that can develop and sustain competitive advantage in relation to other regions.

The government describes this approach to regional development as a process of "levelling up" rather than "levelling down" (i.e. redistribution) (HM Treasury 2001b). It has been keen to avoid the possibility that regional policy might reduce output and productivity in the most prosperous areas – perhaps by diverting activity to less productive regions or abroad – and thereby depress the aggregate growth rate of the economy. It has gone further in ensuring that every region is equipped with Regional Development Agencies (RDAs) and budgets to promote growth. In many ways this is more of a national development policy than a regional one, which would prioritise growth in lagging regions. The new decentralised approach could end up legitimising uneven development through the idea of a nation of multi-speed regions, each developing at its own pace through its own institutions with no obligation of spatial equity on the centre (Amin *et al.* 2003).

One of the critical issues is the extent to which the government reinforces the growth of London and the South East through support beyond the level normally available elsewhere (see Chapter 13). Additional public investment could enable this better-endowed region to continue to pull further ahead of the North and West, and indeed draw in further skills and talent from there. The Sustainable Communities Plan for growth and regeneration is highly significant in this respect (ODPM 2003b, 2005c). Its prime objective is to accelerate house building, with an additional 200,000 houses above 2001 plans in the South East by 2016 in order to alleviate housing pressures and the shortage of affordable homes for key workers. To overcome widespread resistance to new development in this region (from NIMBY and environmental pressure groups) it proposes four major new growth areas, three of which involve some building on greenfield land (Milton Keynes, Stansted and Ashford have the potential for 300,000 new homes by 2016) and one that mostly involves brownfield land (Thames Gateway is expected to accommodate 120,000 new homes by 2016). In addition, the government says it is planning for over 300,000 jobs to be created in the Thames Gateway.

Extensive physical and social infrastructure will be required to enable this to occur, including water supply, sewerage systems, roads, schools, hospitals, primary care services, community facilities and improved transport links to London. The cost will run into many billions of pounds, which private house-builders expect the government to pay in advance. An extra £3 billion was committed for housing and transport for the first three years (ODPM 2003b), with a growing political lobby from within the South East to boost this by another £20–40 billion over the following decade to ensure the financial viability of the initiative.

Major funding is already committed or in the pipeline for improved rail services such as the Channel Tunnel railway and linked domestic services, the Crossrail project, three new universities, a new Thames Gateway bridge, preparation of strategic development sites and improvement of town centres (ODPM 2005c). These developments are very costly, particularly where reclamation of derelict and contaminated brownfield sites is involved. The key question raised is whether all this will reinforce the growth of the South East at the expense of the rest of the country, especially if the public (and consequential private) investment might otherwise have gone elsewhere. There is an assumption in the Sustainable Communities Plan that faster growth of London and the South East will spill over into other UK regions, ensuring benefits all round. However, no evidence is provided to indicate the relative strength of this effect compared with the prospect of skilled labour and other productive resources being drawn into the South East and damaging growth elsewhere.

The government clearly faces a dilemma. The more development it subsidises in the South East the more it accommodates and encourages population and employment growth. Most of this growth does not originate in, or come at the expense of, the North and West (a lot of the demand for additional housing stems from immigration from abroad or natural population growth and household formation), but some of it does. Substantial support for growth in the South East is also likely to make it more difficult to reduce regional imbalances and encourage development in the North. It is widely agreed that the government's regional policy cannot be based on squeezing development in the South and neglecting the growth pressures ("letting the South stew") in the hope of inducing firms to move north. If this was the approach, some firms might become less productive and competitive internationally, some might decide not to expand at all and a few might move abroad.

Restrictions on the supply of development land in the South also increase house prices, hitting lower-income groups and first-time buyers, and making it even more difficult for unemployed people from the North to move south. But the opposite approach of simply encouraging and indeed subsidising more and more development in the South blunts the incentives for relocation and facilitates continuing North–South migration of skills and talent, thereby sucking in important resources from the lagging regions and undermining their indigenous potential.

The government has an explicit target to narrow the gap in economic growth rates between the regions (ODPM 2005a). The phrasing of this is somewhat disingenuous since it will not reduce existing regional inequalities, merely the rate at which they are growing! This acceptance of continuing and indeed widening disparities could be said to indicate a lack of ambition and commitment to tackle the North–South divide, but it is at least consistent with the effort and investment being devoted to delivering the Sustainable Communities Plan in the South East.

For any government, there would be a difficult balance to be struck between managing and sustaining growth in the South while at the same time seeking to strengthen growth in the North. There probably needs to be stronger positive discrimination in favour of development in the North and greater encouragement of employment relocation with clear signals, policies and incentives. In doing so, there is a stronger case for emphasising positive "pull" factors (such as spare productive capacity and underused labour and land resources) rather than negative "push" factors. Potential instruments include stronger financial inducements and improved infrastructure to encourage private sector investment, more deliberate Civil Service relocation, regionally targeted research and development spending and more strategic use of prestigious science and cultural projects to act as catalysts for broad-based growth. Above all, there is an argument for some kind of national spatial development framework or planning process within which to articulate a more coherent regional strategy bringing together analysis and policy across different government departments, regions and other stakeholders. These ideas are not new, but they barely feature in government statements of regional policy, which instead emphasise local entrepreneurship, indigenous skills and measures to increase employability, i.e. regions pulling themselves up by their own bootstraps (ODPM 2005a).

Sub-regional disparities

There has been increasing concern since the 1970s with socio-economic differences *within* regions. This is partly because of evidence of growing disparities at the sub-regional level, associated with continuing net loss of jobs and population from cities to surrounding towns and rural areas ("decentralisation" or an "urban–rural" shift) (Breheny 1999; Turok and Edge 1999; DETR 2000). It is also related to evidence of increasing polarisation within cities between deprived and better-off neighbourhoods (Lupton 2003; Dorling and Rees 2003; ODPM 2005b). During the 1970s and 1980s industrial closures, rising unemployment, social malaise, occasional street disturbances, rising fear of crime and environmental degradation tarnished the image of urban areas as places to live, work, play and invest. Cities were portrayed as remnants of a bygone industrial age associated with high transport costs, physical obsolescence and low labour and capital mobility.

A more positive view of cities has emerged recently, however, within parts of the policy community. The new, optimistic urban agenda emphasises the contribution of cities to environmental sustainability (compact cities prevent suburban sprawl and high energy consumption), social cohesion (tolerant cities help to assimilate immigrants and nurture diverse communities) and economic prosperity (ODPM 2004b; Buck *et al.* 2005). At its heart is the proposition that cities can perform a vital role in reviving the economic fortunes of their wider hinterlands, especially in the lagging regions of the North and West of Britain (see Chapters 14 and 15). Great weight is now attached to the supposed competitive advantages of large cities in the contemporary economy, including business access to networks of collaborators, specialised business services, thick labour markets and modern telecommunications. "The factors of productivity in advanced knowledge based economies are concentrated in cities" (ODPM 2003a: 1). They are described as the "powerhouses" or main drivers of growth in the modern economy (ODPM 2004b). This perspective is gaining support across Europe too, where: "Urban systems are the engines of regional development" (European Commission 2004a: 28).

Evidence to support this new view of cities is limited at present. The dominant patterns and trends suggest that continuity with past trajectories is more significant than change. De-industrialisation and spatial deconcentration of jobs and population have continued to work to the advantage of towns and rural areas, especially in the southern and eastern regions of the UK (Champion and Fisher 2004; Moore and Begg 2004; ODPM 2005b). Only London has clearly experienced a turnaround in jobs and population over the last decade. Selected cities such as Leeds and Edinburgh have had slow, steady growth, but this has been a continuation on earlier trends rather than anything new. Some city centres such as Manchester, Glasgow and Birmingham have clearly enjoyed significant physical and commercial improvement since the mid-1990s, as well as an upturn in jobs, but it is far from clear whether this is mainly a cyclical phenomenon, reflecting short-term national growth in consumer spending and demand for quite traditional urban services (private and public), rather than any fundamental improvement in their economic base that is likely to be sustained (Buck *et al.* 2005).

Robust measurement of trends in sub-regional economic performance is hampered by data deficiencies. There are difficulties in using GVA per head as an indicator because the data are acknowledged to be unreliable at this scale and the figures are distorted by imbalanced commuting flows across local boundaries, particularly between cities and their suburban hinterlands. This inflates the apparent productivity of employment centres and understates that of dormitory areas. The employment rate is a more reliable measure of comparative performance, since the data are more accurate and up to date, and this indicator is more directly related to the well-being of the community.

Table 9.3 shows the employment rates for each nation and region and for the highest and lowest local authorities within them. The disparities within each region are clearly much greater than between them. The difference between the lowest and highest employment rates within each region is typically around 20 per cent (in London's case it is 30 per cent), whereas the difference between the maximum and minimum for the regions is only just over half that at 12 per cent. Table 9.3 also indicates that the areas with the lowest employment rates tend to

Table 9.3 Employment rates for nations and regions and by highest and lowest local authorities, 2003/4

Nation and region		Highest local authority		Lowest local authority	
South East	78.9	West Oxfordshire	89.3	Thanet	62.4
South West	78.6	Taunton Deane	86.8	Penwith	71.3
East	78.6	Babergh	87.9	Norwich	68.0
East Midlands	75.3	Melton	89.5	Nottingham	60.5
Yorkshire and		Craven	84.5	Kingston upon	67.2
Humberside	73.9			Hull	
West Midlands	73.4	South Shropshire	85.7	Birmingham	64.8
Scotland	73.4	Shetland Isles	84.2	Glasgow	64.3
North West	72.8	Rossendale	87.1	Manchester	59.9
Wales	70.5	Flintshire	78.2	Neath Port Talbot	62.2
London	69.3	Richmond on		Newham	52.4
		Thames	82.2		
North East	68.5	Alnwick	77.5	Easington	57.3
Northern Ireland	67.7	Castlereagh	81.9	Derry	48.9

Source: ONS 2004b

be cities, while the places with the highest tend to be rural areas, small towns or suburbs.

Unsurprisingly, the scale of non-employment or worklessness also varies more significantly within regions than between regions. Table 9.4 shows ten local authority areas in Britain with the highest proportion of their working-age population on key welfare benefits and the ten areas with the lowest. About one in four people of working age in the poorest areas were reliant on these benefits in August 2004 compared with only one in 25 people in the most prosperous areas. The areas with the highest rates of benefit dependency are all former industrial cities and towns or coalfields, with the exception of Hackney in inner London. The areas with the lowest rates of benefit dependency are all prosperous towns and rural areas in the South and East.

One of the interesting features of Table 9.4 is the apparent coincidence between the spatial distributions of different workless groups. Areas with a high incidence of unemployment tend to have high proportions of sickness claimants and lone parents. Several studies have found a similar pattern with other groups too, including unemployed youth, workless households and less-skilled workers (Green and Owen 1998; Turok and Webster 1998; Dickens *et al.* 2003). This evidence suggests that there are common factors at work irrespective of the characteristics of specific groups. The key factor appears to be the level of demand for labour in the locality. Large cities and coalfields have experienced a substantial loss of jobs, at least until fairly recently, which is why their rates of unemployment and economic inactivity are relatively high (Turok and Edge 1999; Beatty *et al.* 2002). Their labour markets are still relatively slack compared with those of smaller cities, towns and rural areas, so local people with some form of disadvantage (skill, age, disability, etc.) struggle to compete for jobs.

The urban–rural variations in worklessness are reflected in income, health, education and other socio-economic indicators. This is because unemployment,

Table 9.4 Claimants of key welfare benefits by group and local authority area (as a percentage of the working-age population), August 2004

Local authorities	All	Unemployed	Sick/ disabled	Lone parents	Others
Blaenau Gwent (W)	28.9	3.3	22.1	2.7	0.8
Merthyr Tydfil (W)	28.6	2.7	22.6	2.8	0.5
Knowsley (NW)	28.6	4.4	17.8	5.3	1.2
Easington (NE)	27.7	2.0	22.5	2.8	0.5
Glasgow (Scot)	27.6	4.2	18.1	4.0	1.2
Liverpool (NW)	27.5	4.6	17.5	4.2	1.2
Inverclyde (Scot)	25.8	5.7	15.7	3.3	1.1
Neath Port Talbot (W)	25.5	2.7	19.2	3.0	0.6
Manchester (NW)	24.2	3.5	14.8	4.9	1.0
Rhondda, Cynon, Taff (W)	24.0	2.3	18.3	2.9	0.5
Hackney (L)	23.7	5.7	10.9	5.9	1.3
Caerphilly (W)	23.6	2.9	17.4	2.7	0.6
Hart (SE)	3.7	0.7	2.2	0.5	0.3
Wokingham (SE)	3.9	0.5	2.6	0.7	0.1
Surrey Heath (SE)	4.3	0.5	2.8	0.9	0.1
Harborough (EM)	4.5	0.4	3.3	0.7	0.1
Uttlesford (E)	4.7	0.7	3.0	0.7	0.2
South Cambridgeshire (E)	4.9	0.6	3.2	0.9	0.2
South Bucks (SE)	5.1	0.9	3.2	0.9	0.1
South Northants (EM)	5.2	0.9	3.6	0.3	0.3
Mid Sussex (SE)	5.4	0.5	3.8	0.9	0.1
East Hertfordshire (E)	5.5	0.9	3.6	0.9	0.1
Waverley (SE)	5.5	0.6	4.1	0.8	0.1
West Oxfordshire (SE)	5.6	0.6	4.0	0.8	0.1

Source: DWP 2004

poverty, stress, ill-health, poor educational attainment and other dimensions of exclusion are closely connected. It is particularly apparent if one focuses on the neighbourhood scale. Figure 9.1 shows the incidence of the most deprived 10 per cent of neighbourhoods across different parts of England, based on a reworking of the Index of Multiple Deprivation (IMD) for 2004 (ODPM 2005b). The pattern is very similar if one examines particular "domains" of the IMD, including employment, income and skills/qualifications (ODPM 2005b). Cities in the North and West have more than twice as many of the poorest neighbourhoods as they would have if these neighbourhoods were evenly distributed across the country. Cities in the South and East have slightly less than one would expect, and rather more of the *least* deprived neighbourhoods in England than the average. Towns and rural areas generally have more of the *least* deprived neighbourhoods than one would expect, especially those in the South and East. They have very few of the *most* deprived areas. The clear conclusion is that both urban–rural and regional dimensions have an important bearing on the incidence of poverty and deprivation.

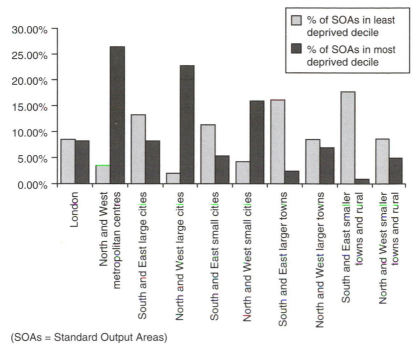

(SOAs = Standard Output Areas)

Figure 9.1 Overall incidence of deprivation 2004

Supply-side explanations and policies

The emphasis in official explanations of unemployment and worklessness is overwhelmingly on individual characteristics, including skills, aspirations, motivation, mobility, adaptability and attributes such as age and ethnicity. Much of this is encapsulated in the notion of "employability" and reflected in labour market policies such as the New Deal or other welfare-to-work measures (McQuaid and Lindsay 2005). Unemployment is said to be high in particular (urban) areas because this is where people who are not actively looking for work, or who are vulnerable to unemployment, happen to live. Concentrations of worklessness are said to exist because of the geographical sorting of different social groups through the housing system (SEU 2004). People who find it difficult to obtain or retain jobs are concentrated in run-down neighbourhoods because this is where the lowest-quality, least desirable housing is. There is rarely any hint – and often a blunt denial – in official accounts that there may not be sufficient jobs available, i.e. that labour demand may be deficient. For example, "the problem is not of an inadequate number of jobs . . . The problem is one of economic inactivity, with not enough people actively searching for work" (ODPM 2005a: 26).

The official line of argument that ends up focusing on individual attributes, or the characteristics of labour supply, runs as follows (HM Treasury 1997, 2001a; DfEE 1999, 2001). First, it is claimed that unemployment has been reduced to a localised problem confined to "pockets" at neighbourhood level and that it has little to do with slack in the wider local labour market. For example:

"unemployment is frequently a high [*sic*] localised phenomenon with high levels of vacancies co-existing with high levels of unemployment in the same travel-to-work areas" (HM Treasury 2001b: 12). "Almost without exception, areas of high unemployment lie within easy travelling distance of areas where vacancies are plentiful" (HM Treasury 2000).

Second, job opportunities are said to have increased considerably over the last decade because of economic growth and high turnover in a dynamic labour market. For instance: "even in areas where there are still pockets of high work-lessness it is often only a short travelling distance to areas where high numbers of vacancies and skill shortages can be found" (HM Treasury 2001a: para. 1.15). Moreover, there is said to a breadth of opportunities available to enable people to find a pattern of work which suits their individual circumstances: "in all parts of the UK, a wide range of different types of job are coming up all the time" (DfEE 1999: 2).

Third, residual unemployment is argued to be the result of a mismatch in skills and aptitudes between the unemployed and the needs of local employers. This is said to reflect individual failings in education, lack of self-confidence, atrophied skills and demotivation as a result of prolonged unemployment, poor interpersonal skills and unwillingness of male jobseekers to take jobs in many service industries. Local measures are required to enhance employability and reconnect disadvantaged communities to expanding employment opportunities. For instance:

> The Government does not accept that the main cause of low employment and high benefit is a lack of available jobs. Often these areas [poor neighbourhoods] are close to employment centres where jobs are appearing all the time and policy is focusing on connecting people with jobs.
>
> (Cabinet Office 2001: 69)

Fourth, jobless residents may be unable or unwilling to access employment opportunities available nearby because of barriers such as lack of information, weak personal networks, lack of affordable transport, homelessness, personal debt, drug and alcohol dependency, or financial disincentives in the welfare benefits system. People may have unrealistic wage expectations and require guidance as to what might be more appropriate, as well as practical assistance to overcome some of the specific barriers. By bringing more people into contact with the labour market it is hoped to hold down wage pressures, make labour a more attractive factor to businesses and increase the total number of jobs as a result.

Overall, the emphasis in explaining urban unemployment is placed on work-less individuals, who are said to lack aspirations or essential skills or are simply not trying hard enough to look for and hold down the available jobs. The main burden of adjustment and flexibility rests with labour rather than employers. People need to search more actively for work, to travel further afield if necessary and to be more adaptable about the kinds of work they are willing to do. Unemployment is supposed to have little or nothing to do with a local shortage of employment, i.e. deficient demand for labour.

This narrative overlooks the systematic differences in employment trends in different areas over the last three decades, resulting in the significant current labour market disparities between cities, towns and rural areas outlined above. High levels of worklessness in the former industrial cities do not exist as isolated "pockets", but rather extensive parts of each city, as the Social Exclusion Unit's study (SEU 2004) of the problem in the North and West of England discovered, but struggled to acknowledge the full implications of. These disparities are not completely unrelated to differences in skills, employability and aspirations, but such conditions are more of a *reflection* of the state of the labour market than a cause of it.

Some people got discouraged from seeking work or from investing in their education and skills because they recognised that there were not enough jobs available and their prospects of getting work were poor. This is apparent from the analysis of job vacancies and from a new indicator of labour demand – the jobs density ratio. It measures the number of jobs in each area as a proportion of the resident working-age population. The spatial units used for analysis should not be too small or the results will be distorted by imbalanced commuting flows between areas, and dormitory towns and suburbs will appear to have a problem. Used correctly, the indicator confirms that there are bigger "jobs gaps", or short-falls in employment, in some areas than in others, and that urban areas and lagging regions are worse off than the Southern and Eastern regions of England (Adams *et al.* 2003). The former industrial conurbations, coalfields and selected seaside towns clearly need more jobs.

Does the location of employment *within* urban areas matter? The official view is that it does not. Urban labour markets are considered to be relatively open, with extensive commuting across different parts of the city. The effects of job creation (or loss) in any particular location are supposed to get dissipated through a ripple effect, and unemployment gets equalised across the whole travel-to-work area as workers get displaced by other workers nearby with greater skills (Gordon 2000). There is said to be no point in trying to replace lost jobs in or near their original location because they are bound to get captured by more employable people commuting in. Employers should also not be encouraged on to brownfield sites because of the high reclamation costs compared with sites on the urban edge and beyond. The focus of urban regeneration should be on skills and employability, not spatial planning of economic development (SEU 2004).

These arguments exaggerate the openness of local labour markets, particularly for manual and low-skilled workers, who tend to have very localised commuting patterns of only a few miles (Webster 1999). The statistical travel-to-work areas tend to reflect the lengthy commutes of office workers, managers and pro-fessionals. The ability of inner-city residents to compete for jobs in the suburbs and beyond is constrained by low car ownership, poor public transport links and stiffer competition for jobs from other people the further away they go. These obstacles make it important to try to create jobs relevant to the skill-sets of people living in high-unemployment areas and in places that are accessible to them.

In cities with extensive vacant and derelict land, the best places may be the original locations from which the jobs disappeared. Such sites are likely to require improved access roads and links to regional motorways, thorough decon-tamination, reclamation and high-quality landscaping, and appropriate financial incentives to compete with greenfield sites in surrounding areas. This means that labour market policy should *not* be driven by national government departments and agencies (such as the Department for Work and Pensions) with standardised programmes insulated from the labour market realities of particular cities and neighbourhoods. Rather it should be closely coordinated with local planning policy, programmes to enhance the quantity and quality of local land supply, and measures to improve transport connectivity.

Conclusion

In an age of falling transport costs and increasing globalisation of trade and travel, it is fashionable to talk about labour market hyper-mobility and flexibility. Yet, labour markets retain significant geographical frictions and other obstacles to adjustment, including inertia and costs of change intrinsic to the physical character of the built environment. Most groups in the population also operate within local or regional rather than national labour markets. Consequently, the spatial dimension of labour markets has a profound effect on their operation and efficiency.

The consequences can be marked and persistent disparities in labour market conditions in different localities and regions. These disparities clearly matter to the communities adversely affected because of the significance of employment for personal incomes and general well-being. They are also a source of national economic inefficiency by constraining the rate at which the economy can grow without running into capacity constraints, overheated housing markets and wage inflation. Consequently, national labour market policy requires a spatial aspect in order to be effective. A standard UK- or EU-wide labour market policy patently does not fit all local circumstances. Labour market policy in Britain has always been unusually centralised and prone to the criticism of uniformity and inflexibility. This has made it difficult to link programmes such as the New Deal with local and regional economic development and planning policies.

One of the consequences of geography affecting the functioning of the labour market is that the UK economy exhibits marked regional and sub-regional inequalities in employment conditions. Government policy in recent years has tended to focus on supply-side measures aimed at increasing employability, skills and enterprise. From the evidence presented, this is more relevant to the low-unemployment areas of the South and East of England than it is elsewhere. The challenges faced in Britain's former industrial cities, towns and coalfields are different. They appear to require stronger policies to boost labour demand, particularly jobs that are relevant to the skills of workless groups and targeted towards particular cities and parts of cities, as well as regions. For this to be effective, labour market policy needs to be closely connected to spatial planning, economic development and infrastructure policy at local and regional levels, rather than pursued as a separate strand of national policy.

In some parts of the country, labour market policy needs to do much more to boost labour demand, and not restrict itself to supply-side concerns. A national spatial development framework might help different government departments, regional and local authorities, and infrastructure providers to develop a shared vision and joined-up strategy to address Britain's outstanding regional challenges. It would also help to situate initiatives such as the Sustainable Communities Plan, the Thames Gateway strategy and the Northern Way in a proper national perspective. Encouraged by wider European experience and expectations, first steps have been taken in the devolved regions of the UK, with a Wales spatial plan and a national planning framework in Scotland (see Chapter 16). These go well beyond the confines of land-use planning and management in an effort to influence other policy makers and investors. They seek to co-ordinate policies and actions in three dimensions: vertically across national, regional and local levels; horizontally across different sectors and functions; and geographically across regional and local administrative boundaries.

References

Adams, J., P. Robinson and A. Vigor 2003. *A new regional policy for the UK*. London: IPPR.

Alcock, P., C. Beatty, S. Fothergill, R. Macmillan and S. Yeandle 2003. *Work to welfare: how men become detached from the labour market*. Cambridge: Cambridge University Press.

Amin, A., D. Massey and N. Thrift 2003. *Decentering the nation: a radical approach to regional inequality*. Catalyst Paper 8. London: Catalyst.

Barker, K. 2004. *Review of housing supply: delivering stability – securing our future housing needs*. London: HM Treasury.

Beatty, C., S. Fothergill, T. Gore and A. Green 2002. *The real level of unemployment 2002*. Sheffield: Sheffield Hallam University.

Breheny, M. (ed.) 1999. *The people: where will they work?* London: Town and Country Planning Association.

Buck, N., I. Gordon, P. Hall, M. Harloe and M. Kleinman 2002. *Working capital: life and labour in contemporary London*. London: Routledge.

Buck, N., I. Gordon, A. Harding and I. Turok (eds) 2005. *Changing cities: rethinking urban competitiveness, cohesion and governance*. London: Palgrave.

Cabinet Office 1999. *Sharing the nation's prosperity: variation in economic and social conditions across the UK*. Report to the Prime Minister by the Cabinet Office. London: Cabinet Office.

Cabinet Office 2001. *A new commitment to neighbourhood renewal: national strategy action plan*. London: Social Exclusion Unit, Cabinet Office.

Champion, T. and T. Fisher 2004. Migration, residential preferences and the changing environment of cities. In *City Matters*, M. Boddy and M. Parkinson (eds). Bristol: Policy Press.

DETR 2000. *Our towns and cities: the future – delivering an urban renaissance*. White Paper (Cm. 4911). London: Stationery Office.

DfEE 1999. Employability and jobs: is there a jobs gap? Memorandum by the Department for Education and Employment to House of Commons Education and Employment Committee, Fourth report, *Employability and jobs: is there a jobs gap?*, vol. II: *Minutes of evidence and appendices*. HC60-II. London: Stationery Office.

DfEE 2001. *Towards full employment in a modern society: Norwich* (Cm 5084). Department for Education and Employment. London: HMSO.

Dickens, R., P. Gregg and J. Wadsworth (eds) 2003. *The labour market under New Labour*. Basingstoke: Palgrave.

Dorling, D. and P. Rees 2003. A nation still dividing: the British census and social polarisation 1971–2001. *Environment and Planning A* **35**, 1287–1313.

Dorling, D. and B. Thomas 2004. *People and places*. Bristol: Policy Press.

DWP 2004. *Quarterly bulletin on the population of working age on key benefits, August*. Newcastle: Department for Work and Pensions.

European Commission 2004a. *Third report on economic and social cohesion*. Luxembourg: Office for Official Publications of the European Communities.

European Commission 2004b. *Delivering Lisbon: reforms for the enlarged Union*. Luxembourg: Office for Official Publications of the European Communities.

Gordon, I. R. 2000. Targeting a leaky bucket: the case against localised employment creation. *New Economy* **6**(4), 199–203.

Gordon, I. and I. Turok 2005. How urban labour markets matter. In *Changing Cities*, N. Buck *et al*. London: Palgrave.

Gray, A. 2004. *Unsocial Europe: social protection or flexploitation?* London: Pluto Press.

Green, A. and D. Owen 1998. *Where are the jobless?* Bristol: Policy Press.

HM Treasury 1997. *The modernisation of Britain's tax and benefit system: employment opportunity for all throughout Britain*. London: HM Treasury.

HM Treasury 2000. *The goal of full employment: employment opportunity for all throughout Britain*. London: HM Treasury.

HM Treasury 2001a. *The changing welfare state: employment opportunity for all*. London: HM Treasury.

HM Treasury 2001b. *Productivity in the UK: the regional dimension*. London: HM Treasury.

Jackman, R. and S. Savouri 1992. Regional migration in Britain. *Economic Journal* **102**, 1433–50.

Lupton, R. 2003. *Poverty Street: the dynamics of neighbourhood decline and renewal*. Bristol: Policy Press.

McQuaid, R. and C. Lindsay 2005. The concept of employability. *Urban Studies* **42**(4), 197–219.

Martin, R., C. Nativel and P. Sunley 2003. The local impact of the New Deal: does geography make a difference? In *Geographies of labour market inequality*, R. Martin and P. Morrison (eds). London: Routledge.

Moore, B. and I. Begg 2004. Urban growth and competitiveness in Britain: a long run perspective. In *City Matters*, M. Boddy and M. Parkinson. Bristol: Policy Press.

ODPM 2003a. *Cities, regions and competitiveness*. Second report from the Working Group of Government Departments, the Core Cities and the Regional Development Agencies. London: Office of the Deputy Prime Minister.

ODPM 2003b. *Sustainable communities: building for the future*. London: Office of the Deputy Prime Minister.

ODPM 2004a. *Jobs and enterprise in deprived areas*. London: Office of the Deputy Prime Minister.

ODPM 2004b. *Our cities are back: competitive cities make prosperous regions and sustainable communities*. London: Office of the Deputy Prime Minister.

ODPM 2005a. *Realising the potential of all our regions: the story so far*. London: Office of the Deputy Prime Minister.

ODPM 2005b. *State of the cities: progress report to the sustainable communities summit*. London: Office of the Deputy Prime Minister.

ODPM 2005c. *Sustainable communities: homes for all – a five year plan from the ODPM*. London: Office of the Deputy Prime Minister.

ONS 2004a. *Regional Trends 38*. Available at www.statistics.gov.co.uk. London: Office for National Statistics.

ONS 2004b. *Annual local area labour force survey 2003/04*. London: Office for National Statistics.

Performance Innovation Unit 2002. *Geographic mobility: overview of the issues*. London: Cabinet Office.

Scottish Executive 2002. *Better communities in Scotland: closing the gap*. Edinburgh: Scottish Executive.

Scottish Executive 2004. *A smart, successful Scotland*. Edinburgh: Scottish Executive.

SEU 2004. *Jobs and enterprise in deprived areas*. Social Exclusion Unit. London: Office of the Deputy Prime Minister.

Turok, I. and D. Webster 1998. The New Deal: jeopardised by the geography of unemployment? *Local Economy* **12**(4), 309–28.

Turok, I. and N. Edge 1999. *The jobs gap in Britain's cities: employment loss and labour market consequences*. Bristol: Policy Press.

Webster, D. 1999. Targeted local jobs: the missing element in Labour's social inclusion policy. *New Economy* **6**(4), 193–8.

Wren, C. 2003. UK regional policy: does it measure up? (mimeo). Department of Economics, University of Newcastle upon Tyne, Newcastle upon Tyne.

Part 4

Methods and techniques of regional analysis

10 Regional transport and integrated land-use/transport planning tools

David Simmonds and David Banister

Introduction

Within the new development planning system in the UK, the regional planning authorities take on a much stronger role in determining priorities through the regional spatial strategies (RSSs), as the old structure planning system is abolished (see Chapter 7). Transport planning also takes on a much more strategic role, with the requirement for regions to produce regional transport strategies (RTSs) (DfT 2004c), as outlined in the White Paper on the future of transport (DfT 2004a). Here it is stated that transport guideline budgets for each English region will be presented in the 2005 budget to give regional stakeholders (the Highways Agency, local authorities, the railways and public transport subsidy providers) an opportunity to decide investment priorities. (It should be mentioned that transport strategies were similarly developed for Wales and Scotland.) Spending decisions on major projects will therefore continue to be taken by central government, "taking account of the regional and local stakeholder views".

The analytical context is based on "evidence based planning", but this has now been added to by the renewed interest in accessibility planning, at both the strategic and the local level (DfT 2004b), which forms part of the new policy focus on better infrastructure management. Embedded within this requirement is a move away from funding specific areas to providing a more general funding mechanism that ensures investment meets wider social, environmental and economic objectives. This reflects in part on the concern that transport decisions are related to wider regional objectives such as social cohesion, economic growth and better-quality local amenities (see Chapter 8).

In light of the above developments, the attitudes and skills base of planners need to be extended to take these new requirements on board, in particular how the more detailed quantitative analysis, which is well established within transport, can be enlarged to cover the wider regional priorities. In this chapter we outline and comment on the main practical tools used for forecasting and appraisal in regional planning and the transport dimensions of such planning exercises. To be of relevance, such plans need to be policy *and* planning sensitive, so that explicit account can be taken of the impacts of the transport change, and so that the range of impacts can be assessed by location and by social group. They should also relate to the wider economic and social context, together with an assessment of their environmental consequences (see Chapter 12). In practice, such tools are mainly quantitative models, which forecast quantities of travel and other variables, although there is also a more qualitative interpretative context, to both the analysis and the evaluation. We concentrate on transport modelling and land-use/transport interaction (LUTI) models at the regional scale, together with the appraisal of plans and policies, before ending with some comments on future developments.

Transport modelling

Transport modelling concepts

We try to give here both a brief outline of the basic concepts in transport modelling and an overview of how these are applied at the regional level. Those who wish to go into transport modelling in detail should refer to Ortúzar and Willumsen (1994).

There are two main traditions in transport modelling at national and regional levels: models which forecast total quantities of travel or transport, in terms of millions of passenger-kilometres or millions of tonne-kilometres across a whole region or economy, and those which look at the spatial pattern of transport within the area of interest, and relate to the transport network. For regional and local planning, there is usually a critical interest in where the demands for travel will arise, and the latter kinds of models are of greater importance. These divide the area of interest into zones and represent the quantities of travel in terms of either trips or tours. Trips are normally understood to mean one-way movements from place to place, which can conveniently be summarised into a matrix for each type of trip, where by convention the rows are origins and the columns are destinations. Tours mean round trips or more complicated sequences. In principle, tours can visit a number of destinations, though in practice they are most often simple out-and-back tours, which can be tabulated like trip matrices.

The practice of considering travel demand in terms of matrices is so deeply engrained that transport modellers often talk about "the matrix" to mean the matrix or matrices of trips without any further explanation. This makes it all the more important to clarify exactly what a particular "matrix" represents (and omits) when attempting to use a model or its outputs. Trip matrices can be classified into:

- *production–attraction matrices*, in which the rows are where the trip is "produced" and the columns are the places it may be "attracted" to – with "production" often corresponding to "home" in tour modelling;
- *origin–destination matrices*, which are simply trips from one place to another, irrespective of any concept of production or attraction.

Production–attraction matrices can be turned into origin–destination matrices by calculating the corresponding matrix of return trips of attractions to productions (assuming a simple mirror-image return). Origin–destination matrices cannot be converted into production–attraction matrices without additional information. The difference is important when it comes to modelling travel choices – most travel choices are made at the production (home) end. It is also important in considering travel data, as simple traffic counting exercises combined with appropriate mathematical techniques can yield origin–destination matrices, but it is *impossible* to derive production–attraction matrices without either additional data (such as census information on homes and workplaces) or interviewing travellers about the purposes for their travel (distinguishing "to work" and "from work" surveys do not necessarily do this!).

Freight movements can also be represented as matrices, either in terms of goods vehicle movements or in terms of freight units such as tonnes or container-equivalents. A major complication to freight modelling is that the size of consignment is variable: large flows are broken up (e.g. the supply of coal to a power station may be split into truckloads) and small units are aggregated (e.g. parcels in a delivery van), and goods are often moved via distribution centres where these changes and intermediate storage take place. These and logistical other complications are not often considered in practice.

The other staple ingredient of conventional transport modelling is "the network". If the term is used unadorned it generally means the highway (road) network, though public transport networks are also required. The key concept here is that of a centroid – the point from which all trips originating in a zone start, and the one at which all trips with a destination in that zone end. In the simplest case, the centroid is chosen from the nodes representing road junctions, railway stations, etc. In more complex models, each centroid is a more abstract point, linked to the "real" network by a series of dummy links or feeders. The latter may also be required to represent walking times and parking (possibly including queuing) for private car users, and walking and waiting times for public transport users.

Travel conditions as described on networks are often summarised in terms of the generalised cost of getting from one zone to another. Generalised cost measures, such as combined money costs, travel time and inconvenience or discomfort factors, can be expressed in terms of money or time. A great deal of research has been done on values of time, partly to inform generalised cost calculations but partly as a basis for assessing time savings in appraisal of transport schemes (see below).

Given the concepts of matrices and networks, the classic approach to transport modelling is the "four-stage model", which was originally developed in the 1950s (when the necessary computing power first became available) and has provided at least a key reference and point of comparison for transport planning ever since (see Dimitriou 1992 for the history and critique of this approach). The four stages are:

- trip generation;
- trip distribution;
- modal choice; and
- route assignment,

in that order. The logic is, therefore, to consider:

- how many trips will be produced in each zone;
- where they will be attracted to;
- how they will get there (by car, by public transport, etc.);
- the route they will use through the network for that mode.

In the simplest case, these four sets of calculations are carried out in a straightforward sequence. In most applications, there is some feedback between the different levels, in particular, so that the level of congestion resulting from the use of cars has some impact on choice of route and of mode. The process of forecasting routes through the network (between given origins and destinations) has been the subject of a great deal of research, and there are many methods of forecasting such choices and of calculating the resulting levels of congestion. Mode choice has also been extensively researched, trip generation and distribution rather less so. This is partly because, in many applications, trip generation and distribution are assumed to change in fairly simple ways as a result of land-use changes (e.g. doubling the population will double the number of trips). Within this broad approach, we identify below a number of different applications:

- *Conventional regional models:* These have been developed mainly for planning inter-urban (road) investments, though recent examples are more likely to be multi-modal. They typically have hundreds of zones, correspondingly detailed road networks, and relatively little if any detail of different types of trips or travellers except to distinguish in-work (business) travel from the other movements. They typically ignore walking and cycling, ignore intra-zonal (within-zone) movements (which by definition do not use the longer-distance network) and take a very simple view of parking. They are usually implemented either to represent average traffic over a 12- or 16-hour day, or possibly to represent the morning peak period (e.g. 07h30 to 09h30). An example of such a model is the Central Scotland Transport Model (CSTM3 – www.tmfs.org.uk/CSTM3/index.html).
- *Corridor models:* These look only at trips along particular corridors, so they cannot be full four-stage models (because by definition they cannot consider destinations outside these corridors). Typically they deal only with mode and route choice.
- *Disaggregate models:* There has been much discussion about the possible use of disaggregate modelling, in which for some stages of the four-stage process the conventional matrices are replaced with samples of individual travellers and their trips. This approach allows more detail about traveller characteristics (e.g. income, car ownership, age, size of group travelling together) to be taken into account in ways that are computationally impractical with the standard matrix approach (simply because the matrices become too large to process). Typically the disaggregate approach is applied to trip generation, distribution (often in terms of tours rather than trips) and (possibly) mode choice, with a more conventional matrix-based assignment process to allocate trips to routes. This approach has been used in a number of important national and regional models in continental Europe, in particular the Netherlands (see Bakker *et al.* 2000), but also in Alsace (Girard *et al.* 1995) and Norway (Hamre *et al.* 2002). The first such model in the UK – the PRISM model of the West Midlands conurbation – has been completed fairly recently (see Van Vuren *et al.* 2004).
- *Strategic regional models:* These models typically follow the same general structure as the four-stage model, often with the addition of a time-of-day choice. They disaggregate travel into a greater number of purposes than the

typical four-stage model, in order to reflect the different characteristics of (say) shopping trips compared with commuting trips, give more attention to ensuring that the costs of travel (including congestion) affect all of the choices modelled, including trip frequency and trip distribution, and seek to find the equilibrium between all these choices and the resulting congestion, on roads and (in some cases) of parking and of public transport. All these refinements add greatly to the computing time required and, as a result, these models typically work with coarser zones and correspondingly simpler networks. This line of modelling (reviewed in Roberts and Simmonds 1997) began with the London Area Model developed by TRRL in the 1980s (reported in Oldfield 1993); recent examples include an extensive model of South East England. In recent years a number of strategic regional models have been linked to land-use/economic models such as SEATPC and SWYMMS.

It must be kept in mind that even strictly conventional four-stage modelling is the exception rather than the rule in transport planning. A great deal of modelling is done, and a great many decisions are made, on the basis of more restrictive analyses, e.g. looking only at drivers' choice of route for road schemes, or applying simple fare or time elasticities for public transport proposals, without considering impacts on choice of mode or destination. It is also the case that all types of transport models (except possibly corridor models) have been more extensively used at urban levels rather than for regional planning.

Land-use/transport interaction models

The term "land use" is used throughout to cover a range of human activities, particularly residence and employment, the state of the built environment, and some aspects of the natural environment. "Land use" so defined is of relevance to "transport" for at least three reasons:

- Activities and the interactions between them generate the demands for transport.
- Those activities and interactions are to a greater or lesser extent influenced by the availability of transport.
- The linkages between transport and activities may be important to the appraisal of transport strategies, especially when trying to consider whether the transport system is providing the kinds of accessibilities that activities (i.e. people and businesses) require, rather than simply providing mobility.

It is helpful to understand land-use/transport interaction in terms of the decisions made by different categories of economic "actors", within the different markets in which they interact. Figure 10.1 illustrates the role of transport in relation to the different groups of people and organisations that are influenced by transport. It identifies the main categories of actors:

- the population, both as individuals and as households;
- firms, with a special category for property developers; and

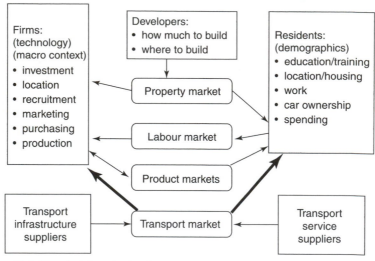

Figure 10.1 Key decisions by land-use actors

- providers of transport infrastructure and services, which may of course be firms or the government.

Government is not explicitly shown as an actor, but can of course influence many of the actors' decisions directly or indirectly, and most of the use of models is devoted to forecasting the impacts of possible government interventions. Residents and firms interact with each other through a number of markets, mainly:

- in property;
- labour; and
- goods and services.

Through these interactions, changes in transport may have indirect impacts on people or businesses that have no direct interest in the transport change at all. It therefore is necessary to consider not only predicting the land-use consequences of transport change, but also the implications for appraisal of the way in which the influence of transport is passed on through the interactions of different actors.

It is important to recognise that the "land-use" system is *never* static, and that "transport" is only one of the factors that influence how it changes. The treatments of all the other factors – such as demographics, the workings of the development process, etc. – are among the things which distinguish the different approaches to land-use modelling.

The influence of transport on land use

Transport influences the decisions of residents and firms in a number of ways which are considered in more detail below. These influences can be clarified by considering the key decisions made by different categories of land-use actors, also shown in Figure 10.1.

All of the different kinds of decisions listed for firms and residents are likely to be influenced, in most cases and to some degree, by the transport system. One of the features of these decisions is the range of frequencies with which different kinds of decisions are made and for how long these decisions commit the actors. For example, households make decisions about shopping weekly or daily, and can go shopping in different locations every week or every day if they wish. The cumulative effects of households' shopping decisions will influence the decisions of developers and retailers about where to provide shops. These decisions are less frequent and will typically commit retailers for years and the use of the land possibly for decades.

Other points to note are that:

- The land-use impacts of a transport change may extend far beyond the spatial scope of the transport proposal itself – they can extend at least as far as the area in which the transport change affects accessibility, and secondary effects may extend further.
- A great deal of locational change takes place through the changing occupation of existing buildings – with changes in either the density or the nature of the occupation (for example, one type of business replacing another, or retired persons occupying housing previously occupied by families with children), and new building accounts for only a minority of the supply available to potential occupiers.
- The value of property is an important influence – if improvements in transport increase the demand for space in a particular location, the resulting increases in rents may affect households or businesses which have no direct interest in the transport change itself.

It follows from the above points that:

- In many cases changes in composition are likely to be more significant than changes in totals. For example, changes in provision for commuter travel may have a significant impact on where the working population and its dependants live, but a much smaller impact on the distribution of the total population (as households without workers move into the areas that the workers are leaving).
- Significant land-use effects may occur within the market for existing property, with no new development and no formal change of use, and therefore beyond the control of the planning system.

It should also be noted that "regeneration", "economic impacts" and so on are all particular aspects of what are here referred to as land-use effects.

Approaches to LUTI modelling

The state of play in LUTI modelling, as it relates to present or immediate future UK practice, can be summed up by identifying two approaches:

- *Numerous applications of aggregate models.* These are models which work in terms of variables that measure the number of households of each kind in each zone, etc.
- *Research into applications of microsimulation modelling.* These are models which work in terms of lists of households, with details of their characteristics, including their zone, etc.

The aggregate models are represented mainly by the MEPLAN, TRANUS and DELTA packages, plus the MENTOR system, which is a subset of MEPLAN adapted to work with different transport models, all explained below.

The MEPLAN and TRANUS models

From the mid-1960s to the late 1970s, research in the Martin Centre at Cambridge University developed a family of interactive land-use and transportation models collectively known as the Martin Centre Model (Simmonds 1994). These models are now represented mainly by the MEPLAN and TRANUS packages (de la Barra 1989; Hunt and Simmonds 1993; Williams 1994).

The central feature of this approach is the use of a spatial input–output model as the means of generating both the location of activities (mainly households and jobs) and the interactions between them (e.g. travel to work). In this model, employment generates the demand for labour, and acts as a control on where households locate in order to supply labour; households in turn demand certain forms of employment and act as a control on where that is located. It is assumed that activities simultaneously compete for space, resulting in equilibrium prices. It is further assumed that the location of activities is influenced by the generalised costs of supplying labour to employers and services to residents; these generalised costs are generated by the transport system. Outside this equilibrium system, a supply model is used to simulate the expected behaviour of developers over time, and another model is used to simulate the location of activities which are not demanded within the input–output system (that is, the employment activities which constitute the economic base of the system modelled – from which the spatial input–output process starts, and households which do not supply labour).

The transport models in MEPLAN and TRANUS predict modal split and assignment, with adjustment for times for capacity constraints, given transport demand by type and flow. Again, random utility concepts are used in the transport model. Information about costs, travel times due to congestion, etc. are fed back into the land-use economic model to provide time-lagged measures of accessibility between zone pairs. This feedback, however, does not occur instantly in the same time period, but is time-lagged. The distribution of activities is directly influenced by the transport outputs from the previous modelled year – nearly always five years earlier. The indirect effects of changes in transport on floor-space supply (which also influences activities) may take several periods to consolidate.

The results of the MEPLAN and TRANUS models include sets of flow matrices, in labour, services, etc., from the results of the spatial input–output model, and the final characteristics of each sector: production, consumption and prices. Households are treated very much as economic entities, namely that they consume housing and other inputs and produce labour. The most established application of MEPLAN in the UK is the LASER model (Williams 1994; Jin and Williams 2002), though this has been considerably simplified from the above description. TRANUS has been applied to Swindon (de la Barra 2001) and to Inverness.

The DELTA package

This model was developed by David Simmonds Consultancy. In contrast with the MEPLAN/TRANUS tradition, it does not have a central mechanism equivalent to their spatial input–output model, but involves a number of distinct models of different processes of change by different actors. Ideally, these would correspond directly to the different decisions of different actors (and the associated market interactions) illustrated earlier in this chapter. DELTA itself does not incorporate transport modelling capabilities but has to be linked to an appropriate transport model, usually of the strategic regional transport type (or an urban equivalent). For discussion of the DELTA design, see Simmonds (1999,[1] 2001) and Simmonds and Feldman (2005).

The full form of DELTA consists of six urban and three regional sub-models. The urban-level models (working at the zone level) forecast changes in:

- households and population;
- car ownership;
- location (of households and of jobs);
- employment and commuting;
- physical development; and
- housing area quality.

The regional sub-models work at a broader spatial level (travel-to-work areas) and forecast:

- investment;
- production and trade; and
- migration of households between these areas.

These sub-models are applied in a fixed sequence for each one-year period. The location or relocation model is the main focus of interactions both between activities and space and between land use and transport. Its main function is to predict the location of those activities that are mobile in this period, taking accounts of changes in accessibility, transport-related changes in local environment, area quality and the rent of space.

There are complex time lags between years, so that the impacts of a significant transport change take a number of years to emerge (typically five to seven years for direct impacts on households, and ten years or more for impacts on employment). In addition to location, transport or accessibility conditions also impact directly on car ownership, employment/commuting, investment and production/trade; the other sub-models are only indirectly affected by transport. A key distinction from the MEPLAN/TRANUS approach is that, whilst household location is influenced by accessibility to work opportunities, the impact of employment on household numbers and distribution is much less direct.

The DELTA package was first applied to Edinburgh (Simmonds and Still 1999), and has since been used to develop the Greater Manchester Strategy Planning Model (Copley *et al.* 2000), the Trans-Pennine Corridor Model (Coombe *et al.* 2001; Simmonds and Skinner 2001) and the South and West Yorkshire Strategic Model (Simmonds and Skinner 2004), as well as for several other studies in Scotland and England.

Microsimulation models

Microsimulation models start with a sample of individual units (e.g. households and their members, jobs or dwellings) and work by forecasting the choices or changes affecting each individual unit. They do not of course claim to be able to forecast exactly what will happen to any identifiable individual, or what he or she will choose to do, but aim to represent the range of changes and responses that will arise within any group of individuals. One key advantage of microsimulation is that the modeller can work with a wide range of data about the individual or the household, and is not required, as is the case with all the aggregate models, to force all individuals or households into a limited set of categories. Income, for example, can be treated as a continuous variable rather than being banded, and it is possible to take account of which member of the household is receiving the income (this is why, for example, microsimulation has been quite extensively used in analysing the incidence of alternative tax and benefit regimes on households).

A second key advantage is that microsimulation allows much more flexibility in how decisions are represented. Most aggregate models (of transport and of land use) effectively assume that households or individuals making decisions have perfect information about all the alternatives available to them, and are willing to trade off any combination of characteristics (e.g. they will accept any quality of housing if it is made cheap enough). Microsimulation can make it possible to consider the impact of imperfect information, the ways in which actors may seek information before making decisions, and the consequences of decisions involving "rules" (e.g. "I wouldn't live there if you paid me . . ."). However, the complexities of introducing these refinements and of applying microsimulation-based models should not be underestimated.

A number of land-use/transport models using microsimulation for at least some processes (usually those to do with households and population) have been built in Germany (Wegener 1982) and North America (Waddell 2001; Hunt and Abraham 2004). Two such models using a software package called MASTER were built in the UK by Mackett (1990) in the 1980s. The latter stream of work is now being revived in research for the Department of Transport (see Ballas *et al.* 2005).

Comments on LUTI models

In this section, we have concentrated on the principles behind LUTI models, illustrating these with examples of operational models in current use in the UK. There are other packages available; for example, ITLUP (also known as DRAM and EMPAL)[2] is the most widely used urban modelling package in the US (Putman 1996). MUSSA[3] (Martínez 2000), NYMTC-LUM[4] (Anas 1998) and UrbanSim[5] (Waddell *et al.* 1998) are three other operational models, all of which treat the land market through changes in prices in land use and development. Space constraints have not permitted any discussion of more traditional travel demand forecasting models such as EMME/2, TRANPLAN and UTPS, reviewed in Miller *et al.* (1998).

As noted above, there is a renewed interest in microsimulation models, particularly at the city and regional scales. It is unlikely that microsimulation-based land-use/transport models will become common, certainly in the short term, but some of the results from this stream of work may well start to influence other aspects of modelling and analysis for regional planning. Microsimulation modelling should also facilitate further moves towards dynamic modelling based on a better understanding of how households and individuals adapt to changing circumstances over time. At present the land-use components of the models mentioned do (to varying degrees) incorporate such dynamics, whilst the transport models do not (i.e. they are cross-sectional). For the given pattern of land uses, the choices forecast in the transport model (e.g. mode choice and time of travel) reflect only the transport conditions at that point in time, rather than reflecting a gradual process of adjustment to previous conditions. Calibration of models on genuinely dynamic data (in particular, on panel data containing information about the same sample of individuals over a substantial period of time) is as yet the exception rather than the rule, but more such analysis is essential if the processes of land-use/transport change are to be fully understood.

Appraisal of plans and policies

From COBA to NATA

As with all decisions, choices have to be made about which particular investments give the best value for money, taking account of the wider social and environmental constraints. Transport appraisal has a long history from the first use of cost benefit analysis on the London-to-Birmingham motorway (Coburn *et al.* 1960). The classic COBA cost benefit analysis method of appraisal (DoE 1972) calculated costs and benefits of a new road in terms of the travel time savings, accidents cost savings and savings in vehicle operating costs, which were then discounted over a period of 30 years to give a net present value and a net present value over cost ratio. Over time this method was extended to social cost benefit analysis, where a wider range of costs and benefits was included in the appraisal, but the thinking was much the same, with each project being evaluated in fairly narrow economic terms and in isolation from the wider context.

More recently, there has been a fundamental switch in project appraisal away from the sole concern with value for money in a narrow economic sense to a much broader concern over the social and environmental costs, together with a greater awareness of the range of transport modes available, and the indirect or non-transport effects of major transport investments. The new approach to transport appraisal (NATA) was introduced as a means to broaden transport appraisal, so that trunk road investment proposals could be prioritised. It was also intended to counter some of the criticisms that had been raised by SACTRA and others (DETR 1998a; ACTRA 1978; SACTRA 1986). In the NATA process, there were certain steps that needed to be taken prior to the formal appraisal process, which were defined as a "transport study" (see Table 10.1, column 1).

This part of the process is reasonably well established, but there were five underlying objectives for transport that were outlined in the 1998 White Paper (DETR 1998b). These covered the environmental impacts (direct and indirect on users and non-users), safety (accidents and security), economy (efficiency, reliability, value for money), accessibility (ability to reach different locations and facilities by different modes) and integration (how policies work together). In many ways these broad objectives marked a major switch in policy priorities away from a primarily economic focus towards a much wider range of concerns. In turn, this makes it even more difficult for planners to come up with clear recommendations from their analysis. In terms of evaluation, the key document becomes the appraisal summary table (AST), the one-page statement of the impacts of the transport investment proposal (see Table 10.2, column 1). It sets out the consequences of each alternative using the five objectives above,

Table 10.1 Summary of the five main steps in NATA and SEA

Road – new approaches to transport appraisal (NATA)	*Environmental – strategic environmental assessment (SEA)*
1 Agreement on a set of project-specific objectives, which the solutions should seek to satisfy – these would reflect government and regional priorities.	1 Baseline environmental information and problem identification.
2 Analysis of the present and future problems of the transport system – this involves modelling activity as outlined earlier in this chapter.	2 Prediction of strategic environmental effects of the plan.
3 Exploration of potential solutions for solving the problems and of meeting the objectives – again this involves modelling and discussions with the stakeholders.	3 Identification of strategic alternatives and their effects and consultation with stakeholders and the general public.
4 Appraisal of potential solutions, seeking combinations which perform better as a whole – this is the *ex ante* appraisal stage.	4 Reporting how the results of the SEA and consultation responses have been taken into account in the adopted plan.
5 Selection and phasing of the preferred solution – this is again based on analysis and consultation with the public and with transport providers. Alternatively, the phasing could take place over the short, medium and longer term, with the same objectives but different constraints.	5 Provision of a non-technical summary of the SEA and the monitoring of the actual effects of the plan during implementation.

Table 10.2 NATA criteria and OPRAF checklist of impacts

Road – new approaches to appraisal (NATA) criteria	*Rail – Office of Passenger Rail Franchising (OPRAF) checklist of impacts*
1 Environmental impact: – noise – local air quality – landscape – biodiversity – heritage – water	1 Impacts on operators and providers: – financial costs and revenues
2 Safety	2 Rail user impacts – fares – journey time and frequency – reliability and punctuality – interchange requirements – crowding – station and information facilities – ticketing facilities – times of first and last trains – passenger security – disabled access – on-train cycle facilities – safety
3 Economy: – journey times – vehicle operating costs – journey time reliability – scheme costs	3 Impacts on travellers by other modes: – congestion – crowding, safety and local impacts
4 Accessibility: – access to public transport – community severance – pedestrians and others	4 Environment: – local and regional
5 Integration	5 Other impacts – option values – transitional costs of change – preference for the status quo – accessibility

Based on Vickerman (2000), Tables 1 and 2

reflecting the wide variety of impacts arising from transport projects. Accompanying the AST is a set of comments on whether the scheme meets regional and local objectives, and to what extent the problems identified would be resolved by the solutions being proposed. There would have to be some criteria against which such a judgement could be made, and the use of visual techniques (such as mapping) is one means by which the impacts can be demonstrated.

In addition to the NATA summary table (the AST), and the comments on whether regional and local objectives have been effectively achieved, the appraisal needs to take account of distributional and equity impacts, the affordability and financial sustainability of the solution (including both public and private financing inputs), and its practicability and public acceptability through the use of checklists. These checklists measure the feasibility, the complexity, the timescale, the phasing and the political consequences of making a decision. There is no doubt that the appraisal process has become more transparent and comprehensive, but one now wonders how any major decision can actually ever be taken, as there are so many elements within the process. We now have a truly expansionist approach rather than the narrow reductionist approach typified by COBA.

Rail evaluation has been viewed differently to road evaluation, as financial appraisal has been central, with time savings on railways resulting from investment leading to increases in demand and higher fares. Elasticities are used to generate the expected increases in revenues. In addition to financial appraisal, the Office of Passenger Rail Franchising (OPRAF) has prepared a checklist to take account of the wider costs and benefits of railways, and to move some way to ensuring compatibility with the NATA approach (Table 2, column 2). The economic and regeneration benefits are excluded, owing to estimation problems and the possibility of double counting, but there is allowance made for additionality (Banister and Berechman 2000).

Strategic environmental assessment (SEA)

SEA covers environmental assessment carried out at the broader level than the individual project, and it has been extensively used within the EU to evaluate the Trans-European Transport Networks (TEN-T). Its scope is broad, as it is intended to be strategic in its scale and thus more appropriate to regional analysis, but it also includes all modes of transport and a much wider range of impacts, including both economic and environmental effects (SACTRA 1999).

The SEA Directive came into force in the UK on 21 July 2004 (EU 1999), and it is now a requirement to prepare an SEA, including an environmental report and a non-technical summary, for all major plans or strategies, including national transport investment programmes, regional transport strategies and even the local transport plans (LTPs) (see Chapter 12). The GOMMMS (Guidance on the Methodology for Multi-Modal Studies) has moved part-way towards SEA, as there is a switch to a mixture of measures to address multi-modal transport problems, rather than the more traditional single solution to a problem for a particular mode of transport. In the GOMMMS, there was also an explicit statement on objectives and the definition of the transport problem, together with an integrated appraisal, where the five objectives of transport policy were addressed, as outlined in the previous section. But further developments are necessary in the methods used to fully embrace the principles of SEA, namely its strategic scale, its concern with meeting objectives (rather than impacts), and its environmental focus, in particular how policies, programmes and plans can lead to sustainable development (Therivel 2004).

As noted in Table 10.1 (column 2), there is a clear correspondence in the five stages between NATA and SEA, but with a more central focus in the environmental effects. But to take full account of the SEA directive requires coverage of both the natural environment and some of the human effects, such as effects (positive and negative) on health and material assets, and the secondary or cumulative effects. Appraisal really needs to be turned around so that it is led by the SEA, rather than trying to fit SEA to existing appraisal methods. In this way it can become central to all applications of NATA, and the preparation of the LTPs and the regional transport strategies.

The SEA objectives need to be stated in terms of desired direction of environmental change, with measurement being summarised as a set of indicators. The purpose of this data collection and the development of indicators is to help with understanding and predicting the effects of changes brought about in environmental quality resulting from the implementation of a particular plan, and to monitor that change over time. This means that a continuous process is set up with key time horizons taken at 5, 10 and 15 years into the future, and the impacts need to be compared to the environmental situation if no plan was implemented. However, there is a potential discontinuity here, as the environmental effects are often long-term and permanent (e.g. on global warming), whilst many of the transport investments have short-term and immediate effects (e.g. in terms of accident reductions).

Three key issues need to be addressed if the requirements of the SEA Directive are to be fully embraced in UK appraisal practice. Firstly, the analysis of risks and uncertainties seems to be an important element in all evaluation, yet it does not feature in the requirements for SEA (Flyvbjerg *et al.* 2003). There has been an increasing concern over the accuracy of both the demand forecasts and the cost estimates for new transport projects. Although there is no systematic bias in the analysis, it has caused increased uncertainty over the quality of the assumptions used in the demand forecasts and the cost estimates, and its usefulness in the planning process. It has also made it increasingly difficult to engage the private sector in financing transport projects, as these are seen to be high-risk, with their long time horizons from planning to opening, and their complex interfaces between the different political interests and stakeholders. Recent research for the UK Department for Transport has attempted to quantify this optimism bias in the cost estimates for transport projects (Flyvbjerg 2004), which is summarised in Table 10.3.

Table 10.3 Optimism bias in cost estimates for transport projects

1 Experience from some 250 transport projects has been used to calculate the probability of cost overruns. These projects relate to road and rail investments, and to fixed links (bridges and tunnels), in the UK and elsewhere.

2 The empirical analysis suggests that, if the risk for a road project is to be under 20 per cent, then there should be an uplift of 32 per cent on the estimated capital expenditure.

3 If a 50 per cent risk level is appropriate, then the uplift can be reduced to 15 per cent.

4 For rail and fixed link projects, the corresponding figures for the 20 per cent risk level are 57 per cent and 55 per cent respectively, and for a 50 per cent risk level they are 40 per cent and 23 per cent respectively.

5 It should be noted that all these values are obtained from the database of the 250 projects, and that a distribution has been derived for each type of investment, with the risk levels being calculated from those distributions.

Secondly, the SEA Directive also takes a much wider perspective on appraisal than is current in the UK, and it is difficult to see how the two approaches to transport assessment can be made compatible. For example, Table 10.4 summarises the criteria for determining the likely significance in terms of the characteristics of the plan, their effects and the area affected. Rather than trying to fit the SEA Directive into current appraisal practice, perhaps we should take SEA and then try to make NATA and the other methods fit into it.

Thirdly, there is the problem of how to bring the diverse range of effects together into a simplified form that makes sense to decision makers, as they are the individuals who are ultimately responsible and accountable. They need advice that is both clear and consistent, in terms of what is being said, and in terms of what the consequences might be of following particular courses of action (including the do-nothing option). Multi-criteria evaluation is one such approach, which tries to maintain transparency through weighting the different criteria used in the evaluation. Preferences are elicited from the key stakeholders through the quantification of upper or lower bounds or through inequalities that reflect the importance, the values and the uncertainties that they attach to the different components of the SEA. Criterion weights are calculated to minimise discrimination between options consistent with the preferences expressed, so that potential bias risks are reduced. This allows both flexibility

Table 10.4 Criteria for determining the significant effects

1 The characteristics of the plan or programme, including:
   – the degree to which it sets a framework for projects and other activities, either with regard to the location, nature, size and operating conditions or by allocating resources;
   – the degree to which it influences other plans and programmes, including those in a hierarchy (e.g. local development frameworks, community strategies, air quality management areas);
   – its relevance for the integration of environmental considerations, in particular with a view to promoting sustainable development;
   – relevant environmental problems;
   – its relevance for the implementation of Community legislation on the environment (e.g. air quality standards).
2 Characteristics of the effects and of the area likely to be affected, having regard to:
   – the probability, duration, frequency and reversibility of the effects;
   – the cumulative nature of the effects;
   – the trans-boundary nature of the effects;
   – the risks to human health or the environment (e.g. due to accidents);
   – the magnitude and spatial extent of the effects (including the geographical area and size of the population likely to be affected);
   – the value and vulnerability of the area likely to be affected, owing to: a) special natural characteristics or cultural heritage (e.g. whether it affects designated areas or other sensitive areas such as wildlife corridors), b) exceeded environmental quality standards or limit values (e.g. how close the baseline – current and likely future – is to exceeding any relevant standards), c) intensive land use (e.g. whether the plan facilitates new areas of development), d) the effects on areas or landscapes which have a recognised national, Community or international protection status.

Source: EU 1999: Annex II

and transparency in the derivation of the weights, as the stakeholders are involved throughout in the process, and the degrees of discretion are controlled so that individual results do not influence the overall weights in a disproportionate manner (Sayers *et al.* 2003).

Comments on appraisal

The requirements for transport appraisal have moved beyond a narrow evaluation of the individual project, towards a much broader-based appraisal of plans, programmes and policies. This is well illustrated by the recent SEA Directive and the requirement to take account of a much wider range of environmental and social objectives. This does not mean that the economic objectives and value for money are less important, but it reflects the realisation that investment decisions have a much wider range of costs and benefits. It also means that it becomes easier to include both transport and land-use factors in appraisal, with the use of planning principles and criteria against which judgements can be made.

In some ways, the NATA framework has anticipated the SEA Directive, but in others it leaves difficult questions to be resolved. We have identified three key issues here, namely the treatment of risk and uncertainty (optimism bias may help to address the cost overrun problem, which is part of this problem), the inclusion of a much wider range of criteria in the SEA than have traditionally been covered in COBA or NATA, and the means by which variables that are measured in different metrics can be brought together (weightings derived from multi-criteria analysis can help in this respect).

Future developments

Transport and integrated land use and planning have changed substantially over the last 50 years. It has remained as a robust methodology for the analysis of the transport impacts, and more recently it has become more explicit in the investigation of the land-use interactions. Models are now more flexible and less data intensive, allowing for the particular interests of decision makers to be included. Yet the demands of those same decision makers are becoming more difficult to accommodate, as there is an increasing interest in economic development effects arising from transport investments, the land value capture issue, and the impacts of road pricing and congestion charging on urban areas, including the effects on house prices and retail turnover.

In addition to well-established and evolving approaches to transport and land-use modelling and appraisal, there is also a new emphasis on accessibility planning, where the focus of analysis becomes activities that businesses and people need to take part in, rather than mobility. Accessibility is important at both local and regional scales, as it is now seen that transport has both local costs and benefits and regional impacts through the wider network effects. Modelling approaches have adapted to this change through coarser-zoned strategic approaches that explicitly tackle these interactions, and through a new generation of microsimulation models. Both of these approaches are being linked in new ways to present the information visually. In some cases, user-friendly modelling and mapping techniques can allow planners and transport modellers to test the outcomes of different strategies interactively, though as yet this is only possible with relatively simple analyses or where the modelling proper has been carried out in advance.

Modelling also needs to take a longer-term perspective – to look at the next 25 or even 50 years, so that transport can be linked to sustainable development and technological change more effectively. The increasing use of exploratory and backcasting scenario methods is one way to understand the transport and development impacts of trend-breaking futures, rather than relying mainly on trend-based approaches (Banister *et al.* 2000). Moreover, as mentioned earlier, there is a need for modelling to get closer to understanding and representing the dynamics of change at the individual level.

There is also a need to raise awareness of modelling and enhance the skills base so that planners and transport practitioners can communicate more effectively with each other and broaden the narrow base of traditional analysis, so that sustainability, regeneration and social inclusion can all be encompassed (see Chapter 8). The processes must have wide stakeholder involvement and clear objectives, with transparency in the tools used. In this way, trust and respect between all parties can be built up. This issue is particularly important at the regional level where there is a lack of democratic accountability and the technical capacity to support integrated policy analysis (DfT 2004c). This limitation, together with the differing requirements of the key government departments (Department for Transport, the Office of the Deputy Prime Minister, and the Department of Trade and Industry), means that it is even more important now to use a systematic and transparent process to analyse and evaluate transport alternatives within the widest possible range of land-use and development contexts.

Notes

1. Note that this article is still of relevance for its description of the initial thinking behind the design of DELTA, but is very much out of date as regards the detailed content and scope of the package; these are better outlined in Simmonds (2001) or in Simmonds and Feldman (2005).
2. Integrated Transportation and Land Use Package, Disaggregate Residential Allocation Model and Employment Allocation Model – note that the DRAM and EMPAL land-use elements can be used with other transport models.
3. Modelo de Uso de Suelo de Santiago.
4. New York Metropolitan Transit Commission Land Use Model.
5. Urban land and floor-space markets.

References

ACTRA 1978. *Trunk road assessment*. Report of Advisory Committee on Trunk Road Assessment, Leitch Committee. London: HMSO.
Anas, A. 1998. *NYMTC transportation models and data initiative: the NYMTC Land Use Model*. Williamsville, NY: Alex Anas and Associates.
Bakker, D., A. Daly and P. Mijjer 2000. Updating the Netherlands national model. European Transport Conference 2000. *Proceedings of PTRC Seminar K, Transport Modelling*. London: PTRC.

Ballas, D., G. Clarke, O. Feldman, P. Gibson, J. Jin, D. C. Simmonds and J. Stillwell 2005. A spatial microsimulation approach to land-use modelling. Paper prepared for the CUPUM conference, London.

Banister, D. and J. Berechman 2000. *Transport investment and economic development.* London: UCL Press.

Banister, D., D. Stead, P. Steen, J. Akerman, K. Dreborg, P. Nijkamp and R. Schleicher-Tappeser 2000. *European transport policy and sustainable mobility.* London: Spon.

Barra, T. de la 1989. *Integrated land-use and transport modelling.* Cambridge: Cambridge University Press.

Barra, T. de la 2001. integrated land use and transport modeling: the TRANUS experience. In *Planning support systems*, R. K. Brail and R. E. Klosterman (eds). Redlands, CA: ESIR.

Coburn, T. M., M. E. Beesley and D. J. Reynolds 1960. *The London–Birmingham motorway: traffic and economics.* Road Research Laboratory, Department of Scientific and Industrial Research, Technical Paper 46. London: HMSO.

Coombe, D., A. Skinner, D. Simmonds and B. Davidson 2001. Strategic environmental assessment in the Trans-Pennine Corridor. *Proceedings of the Institution of Civil Engineers: Transport* **147**, London.

Copley, G., A. Skinner, D. Simmonds and J. Laidler 2000. Development and application of the Greater Manchester Strategy Planning Model. Paper presented to European Transport Conference 2000. *Proceedings of PTRC Seminar K, Transport Modelling.* London: PTRC.

DETR 1998a. *A new deal for trunk roads in England: understanding the NATA.* London: Department of the Environment, Transport and the Regions.

DETR 1998b. *A new deal for transport: better for everyone.* July. London: Department of the Environment, Transport and the Regions.

DfT 2004a. *The future of transport: a network for 2030.* July. Department for Transport. London: HMSO.

DfT 2004b. *Guidance on accessibility planning in local transport plans and other supporting documentation.* London: Department for Transport.

DfT 2004c. *The integration of regional transport strategies with spatial planning policies.* March. London: Department for Transport.

Dimitriou, H. T. 1992. *Urban transport planning: a developmental approach.* London: Routledge.

DoE 1972. *Getting the best roads for our money: the COBA method of appraisal.* Department of the Environment. London: HMSO.

EU 1999. Assessment of the effects of certain plans and programmes on the environment. European Union. Draft Strategic Environmental Assessment Directive COM(99)073, published in its final form in June 2001 (ED/2001/42/EC).

Flyvbjerg, B. 2004. Procedures for dealing with optimism bias and transport planning. Guidance document written for the Department for Transport in association with COWI Consultants, DfT, June, London.

Flyvbjerg, B., Bruzelius, N. and Rottengatter, W. 2003. *Megaprojects and risk: an anatomy of ambition.* Cambridge: Cambridge University Press.

Girard, T., H. Gunn, D. C. Simmonds, P. Thirion and C. Weiss 1995. A regional model of Alsace. *Proceedings of the PTRC 23rd European Transport Forum: seminar on models and applications.* London: PTRC.

Hamre, T. N., A. Daly, J. Fox and C. Rohr 2002. Advanced modelling to overcome data limitations in the Norwegian national transport model. *Proceedings of European Transport Conference*, 9–11 September 2002, Homerton College, Cambridge. London: PTRC.

Hunt, J. D. and D. C. Simmonds 1993. Theory and application of an integrated land-use and transport modelling framework. *Environment and Planning B* **20**(2), 221–44.

Hunt, J. D. and J. E. Abraham 2004. Household allocation module of Oregon 2. Paper presented to the Transportation Research Board annual conference, January, Washington, DC.

Jin, Y. and I. N. Williams 2002. A new land use and transport interaction model for London and its surrounding regions. *Proceedings European Transport Conference: applied transport methods*, 9–11 September 2002, Homerton College, Cambridge. London: PTRC.

Mackett, R. L. 1990. The MASTER model. TRRL Contract Report 237, Transport Road Research Laboratory, Crowthorne.

Martínez, F. J. 2000. Towards a land use and transport interaction framework. In *Handbooks in transport*, Handbook 1: *Transport modelling*, D. Hensher and K. Button (eds). The Hague: Elsevier.

Miller, E. J., D. S. Kriger and J. D. Hunt 1998. Integrated urban models for simulation in land use policies. Final report, Transit Cooperative Research Project H–12, University of Toronto Joint Programme in Transportation, September, Toronto, www.nas.edu/trb/crp.nsf.

Oldfield, R. H. 1993. A strategic transport model for the London area. TRRL Research Report 376, Transport Road Research Laboratory, Crowthorne.

Ortúzar, J. de D. and L. G. Willumsen 1994. *Modelling transport*, 2nd edn. Chichester: Wiley.

Putman, S. H. 1996. Extending DRAM model: theory practice nexus. *Transportation Research Record* **1552**, 112–19.

Roberts, M. and D. Simmonds 1997. A strategic modelling approach for urban transport policy development. *Traffic Engineering and Control* **38**, 377–84.

SACTRA 1986. *Urban roads appraisal*. London: HMSO.

SACTRA 1999. *Transport and the economy*. Report of the Standing Advisory Committee on Trunk Road Assessment. London: HMSO.

Sayers, T. M., A. T. Jessop and P. J. Hills 2003. Multi-criteria evaluation of transport options: flexible, transparent and user-friendly? *Transport Policy* **10**(2), 95–105.

Simmonds, D. C. 1994. The Martin Centre Model in practice: strengths and weaknesses. *Environment and Planning B* **21**(5), 619–28.

Simmonds, D. C. 1999. The design of the DELTA land-use modelling package. *Environment and Planning B* **26**(6), 665–84.

Simmonds, D. C. 2001. The objectives and design of a new land-use modelling package: DELTA. In *Regional science in business*, G. Clarke and M. Madden (eds). Berlin: Springer.

Simmonds, D. C. and B. G. Still 1999. DELTA/START: adding land-use analysis to integrated transport models. Paper presented to the World Conference on Transport Research, Antwerp, 1998. Published in *Transport policy*, H. Meersman, E. van de Voorde and W. Winkelmans (eds). Amsterdam: Elsevier.

Simmonds, D. C. and A. J. Skinner 2001. Modelling land-use/transport interaction on a regional scale: the Trans-Pennine Corridor model. *Proceedings of the European Transport Conference 2001: applied transport methods*. London: PTRC.

Simmonds, D. C. and A. J. Skinner 2004. The South and West Yorkshire Strategic Model. In *Applied GIS and spatial analysis*, J. Stillwell and G. Clarke (eds). Chichester: Wiley.

Simmonds, D. C. and O. Feldman 2005. Land-use modelling with DELTA: update and experience. Paper prepared for the CUPUM conference, London.

Therivel, R. 2004. *Strategic environmental assessment in action*. London: Earthscan.

Van Vuren, T., A. Gordon, A. Taly, J. Fox and C. Rohr 2004. PRISM: modelling 21st century transport policies in the West Midlands. *Proceedings of European Transport Conference*, Strasbourg, Seminar on applied transport methods. London: PTRC.

Vickerman, R. 2000. Evaluation methodologies for transport projects in the United Kingdom. *Transport Policy* **7**(1), 7–16.

Waddell, P. 2001. Between politics and planning: UrbanSim as a decision-support system for metropolitan planning. In *Planning support systems*, R. K. Brail and R. E. Klosterman (eds). Redlands, CA: ESIR.

Waddell, P., T. Moore and S. Edwards 1998. Exploring parcel-level GIS for land use modelling. *Proceedings of the ASCE Conference on Transportation, Land Use and Air Quality: Making the Connection*, May, Portland, OR.

Wegener, M. 1982. Modelling urban decline: a multilevel economic-demographic model for the Dortmund region. *International Regional Science Review* **7**(2), 217–41.

Williams, I. N. 1994. A model of London and the South-East. *Environment and Planning B* **21**(5), 535–53.

Further reading

This chapter has concentrated primarily on the regional transport planning issues in the UK. There are many informative and complementary texts that outline similar thinking on transport analysis and appraisal in other countries that are listed below:

Bristow, A. and J. Nellthorp 2000. Transport project appraisal in the European Union. *Transport Policy* **7**(1), 51–60.

ECMT 2000. *Strategic environmental assessment for transport*. Paris: OECD.

Fischer, T. B. 2002. *Strategic environmental assessment in transport and land use planning*. London: Earthscan.

Nijkamp, P. and E. Blaas 1994. *Impact assessment and evaluation in transportation planning*. Dordrecht: Kluwer Academic Press.

The UK government has a web-based transport analysis guidance (TAG) site called WebTag, www.webtag.org.uk.

11 Regional household projections and strategic housing allocations

Nick Gallent

Introduction

This chapter provides a review and critique of the way in which the planning process deals with future housing requirements, mainly in terms of the number of homes needed in England over the current projection period to 2021. It considers how national calculations of population change and household formation are translated into regional housing figures, and into housing land allocations for the purposes of forward planning (eventually for inclusion in the new local development frameworks – LDFs), and how national and more local considerations are combined to shape outcomes on the ground.

The chapter begins by setting out the objectives of the planning system in relation to future housing provision, discussing the balance between housing quantity, quality, sustainability (economic, social and environmental) and related policy areas. It asks why we plan for housing in the way that we do, and what the current (based on regional planning guidance targets) system – and the post-2004 system – hopes to achieve in terms of broad national outcomes and local results. This is followed – in the remainder of the first half of this chapter – by a review of the current approach to demand forecasting, noting the roots of modern population projection techniques (1920s), their use in household projections (1950s) and the gradual refinement of techniques over the last half-century. In recent times, the way we forecast housing need and plan for residential development has perhaps been characterised by greater reliance on local intelligence – at least in the rhetoric of central policy – with some allowance made for a broader range of social issues affecting population and household trends: it has also been marked by government's call for a move away from prediction and corresponding provision to a greater concern for demand management (the so-called "plan, monitor and manage" approach). The review consists of an examination of each of the key steps taken to reach broad regional targets for housing provision and looks at:

- the use of national data to calculate population change (*in situ* and migration driven) from which household change (nationally) is projected; and
- the cascade-down of national figures to regions and counties (or unitary authorities) based on assumptions of capacity, growth potential and policy objectives (e.g. achieving recycling targets).

The second half of the chapter considers how broad housing targets are translated into appropriate housing land allocations by regional bodies in partnership with counties and district authorities. Household projections – at least at the national level – offer a (largely) objective measure of housing requirements within a highly subjective and political context. Calculated building rates are rarely achieved, and all eventual decisions are politically driven. Therefore, to what extent does the current process contribute to the "right" decisions being reached? Does the cascade through the different planning tiers mean that figures are subjected to too much political modification? Is the role of the Secretary of State the right one? Is too much housing opposed by a well-housed majority, represented by local political interests? And are low rates of current building a result of government's obsession with its brownfield target? These are some of the broader questions that are addressed in the second half and towards the end of this chapter. The overall aim is to set out the current challenges facing planning for housing in England, including issues of quantity, quality, sustainability and method.

Planning for housing: the objectives of the system

In 1984, DoE circular 15/84, *Land for housing*, established that the role of the planning system in relation to housing was largely about allocating sufficient land for house building. Indeed, Wenban-Smith (2002) has noted that, in the 1980s:

> the public focus of central government policy was on ensuring that the land provided for in Development Plans was genuinely available for use, and that there was at least a 5-year supply of such land in locations attractive to the house building industry.
>
> (2002: 35)

Emphasis was placed on predicting demand, and guaranteeing appropriate supply through planning.

Much has changed over the last two decades. The first Planning Policy Guidance Note 3 (PPG3), *Housing* (issued in 1988, the year that William Waldegrave, then Secretary of State, expressed concern over the level of guidance given to planning authorities in respect of local planning policy), retained this narrow focus on "sufficiency" of supply and prediction of demand. But within a year, a new version of PPG3 was issued, and this time with a far broader take on planning's role. No longer was the sole focus to be on land release, but planning authorities were also to look at issues of affordability (the meaning of which is constantly challenged) and at the role planning might play in ensuring that future development would satisfy a spectrum of needs. The planning system's role in procuring affordable housing was emphasised in DoE circular 7/91, *Planning and affordable housing*. Its broader remit was confirmed in a new PPG3 in the following year, which also drew attention to issues of design, density, and links to other areas of policy. The most recent version of planning guidance for housing (at the time of writing) was published in 2000 (PPG3), and this is likely to be reviewed again shortly[1] as the government moves towards shorter, more aspirational, "planning policy statements" as part of its wider reform agenda.

However, the central objective of the planning system in relation to housing is still ensuring "sufficiency of supply" and meeting housing requirements, though this is now tempered by concerns over the quality of new homes and ensuring that house building occurs within a framework of sustainable development. Hence, the system is called upon to influence development density (aimed at achieving more sustainable urban form and thereby supporting viable public transport infrastructure), enhance the ecological aspects of design and promote choice. Paragraph 2 of PPG3 (DETR 2000a) sets out eight tasks for planning authorities, which also provide the underlying concepts guiding planning for housing:

- Plan to meet the *housing requirements* of the whole community, including those in need of affordable and special needs housing.
- Provide wider housing opportunity and choice and a better mix in the size, type and location of housing than is currently available, and seek to *create mixed communities*.
- Provide sufficient housing land but give priority to *reusing previously developed land* within urban areas, bringing empty homes back into use and converting existing buildings, in preference to the development of greenfield sites.
- Create more *sustainable patterns of development* by building in ways which exploit and deliver accessibility by public transport to jobs, education and health facilities, shopping, and leisure and local services.
- Make more *efficient use of land* by reviewing planning policies and standards.
- Place the needs of people before ease of traffic movement in designing the layout of residential developments.
- Seek to reduce *car dependence* by facilitating more walking and cycling, by improving linkages by public transport between housing, jobs, local services and local amenities, and by planning for mixed use.
- Promote *good design* in new housing developments in order to create attractive, high-quality living environments in which people will choose to live.

The system of planning for housing in the UK has always concerned itself with the *quantity, quality* and *location* of new homes (Carmona *et al.* 2003). However, these concerns have been repackaged over the last 20 years, and particularly since the arrival of a Labour government in 1997. The 1984 circular mentioned above set out the primary function of planning, though it did not reflect the factors taken into account by local authorities when deciding where to allocate land for housing, or how authorities might work with development interests to ensure that housing provided fits the market and reflects what people actually want and need. Today, these issues are given more explicit treatment. Arguably, planning in the mid–1980s was located in a broadly "developmental" paradigm (Murdoch and Abram 2002), which was gradually diluted during the 1990s by an environmental agenda. Later in the 1990s, the priority of policy was to balance these sometimes conflicting agendas whilst introducing a new emphasis on the efficient use of resources, on place making, on social balance and inclusion, and on lightening the ecological footprint of new development. These issues have been sown together into an official view of "sustainable development", articulated in the government's consultation draft of Planning Policy Statement

(PSS) 1 (ODPM 2004). The objectives of planning, in both a strategic (national) and a developmental (local) sense, are of course the same, or rather the former provides a framework for the latter, and the latter should comply with the former: to provide enough new homes, of the right quality, in the most appropriate locations. In the next part of this chapter, I trace government's changing strategy – and its methodologies – for trying to guarantee this outcome. The key question throughout is whether historical and current approaches to calculating housing demand play a useful role in the achievement of this outcome.

Calculating housing need: underlying methods

Government has engaged in the business of forecasting population change since the 1920s, when it first became concerned with social security payments; indeed, "one of the main uses of these earlier projections [produced by the Government Actuary's Department] was in connection with the long-term financial estimates under the Contributory Pensions Acts and other schemes of social insurance" (ONS 1999: 3). In the 1950s, the procedures for forecasting became more formalised as government came to recognise the importance of translating population change into household change and hence setting a target for future housing provision (ONS 1999). Population projections were made each year between 1955 and 1979, and then every second year until 1991. Since then, projections have been calculated using 1992-based, 1994-based and 1996-based mid-year estimates. In recent times, population and subsequent housing demand predictions have become more "scientific" (or at least more technically involved and refined) and now define a "formal set of relations between the various tiers of government – central, regional, county and district – and were used to ensure that local government [housing] designations meshed with national requirements" (Murdoch and Abram 2002: 67). As noted in the last section, providing for future household growth is one of the most fundamental planning activities of government and involves the translation of population projections (derived by taking base population cohorts, calculating birth rate additions and death rate subtractions, and taking into account the effects of migration) into household projections. Murdoch and Abram provide an overview of how this is achieved (2002: 66–9), and an official summary is set out in Table 11.1.

The two key methodological elements of this process occur at Stages 1 and 5 in Table 11.1: the first involves the use of a "growth composition" approach to project changes in the base population; the second involves the calculation of the proportion of household "representatives" within the base population as a means of transforming population projections into household projections and thereby arriving at base figures that can be cascaded to the regions, the counties (where appropriate) and ultimately local planning authorities. These two techniques are now briefly explained.

Growth composition

Population projections are calculated using a growth composition – sometimes referred to as "cohort survival" – approach. This involves making projections

Table 11.1 From population to household projections

Stage 1: The Government Actuary's Department (GAD) projects the resident population at the national level, on the basis of assumptions regarding mortality, fertility and international migration. This is then broken down for sub-national areas by the Office for National Statistics (ONS).

Stage 2: The marital status of the population is projected by GAD. This is an assessment of legal (*de jure*) marriages cross-analysed against whether or not couples are cohabiting. The proportions cohabiting in 1991 and 1992 were estimated by OPCS and projected for future years by GAD.

Stage 3: The institutional population is projected by the DETR. This is the population resident in residential care homes, nursing homes and long-stay hospitals.

Stage 4: The institutional population is subtracted from the total resident population to leave the private household population.

Stage 5: Within each age/gender/marital-cum-cohabitational status category, household membership rates are projected from historical data derived from censuses and (at national level) Labour Force Survey (LFS) data. These rates are then multiplied by the appropriate private household population projection.

Source: Murdoch and Abram 2002

for successive years running from one mid-year to the next. The approach is described in the National Population Projections (ONS 1999: 42):[2]

> For each age, the starting population plus net inward migrants less the number of deaths produces the number in the population, one year older, at the end of the year. To this are added survivors of those born during the year.

In practice, the base population of the United Kingdom (and its constituent parts) is divided by gender and into age cohorts (0 to 4, 5 to 9, 10 to 14 and so forth). Changes within each cohort are projected as the cohort ages, e.g. the cohort "female 25 to 29" will have p members in year x, but in year $x+1$, p will have changed as a result of migration and deaths; furthermore, this cohort will have produced a number of infants aged 0 for the year $x+1$. Therefore the growth composition model assumes that migration, deaths and births will effect change in the population profile (comprising age cohorts split by gender) that can be projected into the future, giving an overall picture of population change whilst also revealing the shifting age structure of the population.

With regard to migration, a known number of migrants is added to the total population to obtain the population aged $x+1$. Migration is assumed to occur evenly throughout a given year, and therefore half join the population at age x and half at $x+1$ (this distinction is made as base population shifts are calculated on a mid-year to mid-year basis, whilst fertility and mortality rates are produced for calendar years: therefore, this assumption regarding migration becomes important in relation to deaths in a given year – see below). The accuracy of any projection is dependent on the robustness of underlying assumptions. At this level and in relation to migration, I do not wish to enter into great detail regarding these assumptions other than to note that international migration figures draw on the International Passenger Survey (IPS), conducted since the

1960s; this is also used to project the age and sex distribution of future migrants, extrapolated from historic figures. A key problem with these data (which is becoming increasingly important) is that they do not address the issue of asylum or "visitor switches" (short-term visitors who extend their stay): I return to this issue below. Further data on migrations between the countries of the UK are derived from the National Health Service Central Register (NHSCR).

I noted above that migration is assumed to occur evenly from mid-year to mid-year; the number of deaths (expressed as the mortality rate q_x), however, is calculated for calendar years. Hence, "the number of deaths in a year is obtained by adding half of the net inward migrants at each age to the number in the population at the beginning of the year and applying the mortality rate" (ONS 1999: 42). The q_x mortality rate is a derivative of a "central death rate" (m_x) for the entire population: q_x rates represent the probability of dying at a particular age, linked to the central rate (and changes in the rate extrapolated from historic data). Finally, births during each year are calculated by "multiplying the average number of women at each single year of age during the year . . . by the fertility rate applicable to them during that year" (1999: 42). Cohort (or "age specific") fertility rates have been calculated since the 1960s; recent trends suggest a fall in fertility rates amongst "women in their twenties, but a continuing increase at older ages" (1999: 26). However, additions to the population through natural increase are complicated by both migration and infant mortality: the number of infants aged 0 at the end of the year (i.e. those joining the pyramid) is the number of survivors plus "half the number of net migrants aged 0 last birthday".

A key point to take from this brief description of the growth composition approach to projecting changes in the base population is that any projection is only as robust as the assumptions that underpin it. Arguably, the great unknown in the above approach is migration. Estimates of death and birth rates draw on well-established sources, and changes in these rates will be determined, for the most part, by discernible advances in medical science (reducing the probability of non-accidental death) and by fairly clear socio-cultural shifts resulting in reduced fertility rates amongst younger women. I am not suggesting that the assumptions are entirely safe, but, barring the sudden onset of war, famine or pestilence or, indeed, generous benefit allowances and tax breaks for younger mothers and larger families, it is likely that wild fluctuations in these rates will be avoided. Migration, on the other hand, is less controllable through domestic policy or spending: instability in the Balkans, the expansion of the European Union, war in the Middle East, and the vagaries of the global economy are just a few of the factors that may drive sudden surges in economic migration, applications for permanent residence, and asylum claims. This is important in housing terms because projections of change in the base population provide the starting point (Stage 1 in Table 11.1) for government's calculation of household change, and ultimately influence the amount of land allocated by local authorities for new development.

Household representatives

In the household projections for England (DETR 1999), it is explained that: "projections are compiled by applying household membership rates to a projection of the private household population disaggregated by age, sex and marital/cohabitational status and summing the resulting projections of house-hold representatives" (1999: 53).

The critical term here is "household representatives". The extraction of *representatives* from the base population (see the last sub-section) enables the projections of population change to be translated into projections of household change. In recent UK censuses, households have been defined as "one person living alone or a group of people [who may or may not be related, and therefore may or may not constitute 'families'] living or staying temporarily at the same address with common housekeeping". Projections are made for five separate household types: married-couple households, cohabiting-couple households, lone-parent households, other multi-person households, and one-person house-holds. It would of course be possible to simply project changes in mean house-hold size on the basis of historical data from the censuses; future population projections could then be divided by this figure to give projections of the *total* number of households. However, such an approach would tell us nothing about the changing balance of different household types over time. It certainly would not alert policy makers to the fact that future household growth is likely to be dominated by a proportional rise in the number of one-person households. For this reason, a household representative approach to projecting changes is used.

This approach involves placing all individuals in the population into one of 11 distinct household member categories. These categories are listed in Table 11.2. The relative proportions of people in each category are referred to as "household membership rates", and these rates are derived from "a special analysis of a 10 per cent sample of the 1991 Census; the ONS Longitudinal Study samples from the 1971 and 1981 Censuses and the Labour Force Survey (LFS) from 1992 to 1997" (DETR 1999: 54). The first five household members listed in Table 11.2 (which also serves as a worked example) are in fact "household representatives": the proportion of representatives amongst the total number of members is pro-jected into the future using census data and LFS figures and assumes that "life cycle" changes will cause some members to become representatives at some

Table 11.2 Household members/representatives

Category	No.
Married-couple household representative	82
Cohabiting-couple household representative	80
Lone-parent household representative	32
Other multi-person household representative	70
One-person household representative	105
Husband in a concealed married-couple family	21
Male cohabiter in a concealed cohabiting family	16
Parent in a concealed lone-parent family	32
Wife in a married-couple family	82
Female cohabiter	80
Other individual	64
TOTAL	**664**

point in the future. The various assumptions concerning household representative are set out by the DETR in each of their published household projections (see DETR 1999: 54–5); these are not repeated, though it is perhaps worth explaining the process through a worked example.

In a population of 1,000 persons, 336 are "dependent children"; that is, dependants aged 0 to 15, or aged 16 to 18, never married and in full-time education. This leaves 664 non-dependants, who each need to be categorised into the 11 household member types given in Table 11.2.

Of this total, 369 are "household representatives" (in the first five categories): therefore the population of 1,000 (including dependent children) forms 369 households, or an average household size of just over 2.7 persons (total population divided by representatives). The logic here is that all non-representatives (the last six categories) reside in households "headed" or "represented" by persons classified as being in one of the first five categories (as do dependent children). Hence, husbands in a concealed married-couple family, male cohabiters in a concealed cohabiting family, parents in a concealed lone-parent family, and other individuals are all household members of the "other multi-person household representatives". Likewise, wives in a married-couple family and female cohabiters are household members of the married-couple household representatives and cohabiting couple representatives respectively. This means that of the total 369 households in our worked example, 22.2 per cent are married couples; 21.6 per cent are cohabiting couples; 8.6 per cent are lone parents; 18.9 per cent are multi-person households; and 28.4 per cent are one-person households.

The obvious advantage of this approach is that, when applied to the underlying projections of population change, it enables government to forecast the shifting balance of household types, e.g. more people living alone, fewer legally married couples or a greater number of large multi-person households. Such information is clearly useful on a number of fronts, not least when policy makers concern themselves with future demand for housing. It is certainly far more meaningful than simply calculating changes in average household size. The 1996-based projections suggest that the total number of households in England will rise by 19 per cent to 2021; the number of one-person households is projected to grow by 2.7 million and account for 71 per cent of the total increase in the number of households in England (DETR 1999: 5). This forecast increase in people living alone has become a headline message in recent housing debate, with many analysts questioning the implications of a larger number of smaller households for future house building.

But before turning to issues of housing and housing supply, further reflection is needed on the assumptions and methods behind the translation of population change into household projections. Firstly, I noted in the last sub-section that any projection is only as robust as its underlying assumptions; the assumptions concerning population change impact directly on calculations of household formation. This is an obvious point. Secondly, additional assumptions are introduced during the process of moving from population to household shifts. A key assumption here concerns "concealed families": three types of concealed family are listed in Table 11.2. Because the terms "household" and "family" are not synonymous (DETR 1999: 49) and only the total numbers of households forming are projected, there is an assumption that concealed families will remain concealed or rather that concealment of some families is simply a feature of household growth and development. However, if we analyse this feature of household development more closely then a different interpretation is possible. The official line is that some "families" (e.g. lone parents or young couples) *choose* to remain within a larger multi-family household, perhaps to benefit from the support of parents in looking after children. This is a plausible explanation. However, it is equally plausible to suggest that concealment is indicative of housing under-supply. Exclusion of concealed families from total household numbers eventually results in projections of housing demand and need that ignore the needs of these families: less housing land is allocated, fewer homes are built and therefore concealment becomes a symptom of the housing shortage. The argument then follows that if government treated these as *potentially* separate households, concealed because of an inability to secure accommodation of their own, then projections would be larger and land allocations more realistic (all historic projections have underestimated actual household growth).

Similarly, a feature of some overheating housing markets is the tendency for people to group together to buy homes; hence partnerships form between London-based "young professionals" who enter into formal contracts for shared mortgages. This may result in a surge in multi-person households in some sub-regions and, eventually, to further concealment of essentially separate families within larger households. It is sometimes argued that the exclusion of concealed families from projected household totals lessens the risk of eventual housing over-supply. However, the evidence (see, for example, Barker 2004) is that under-supply poses an immediate and longer-term threat to local communities and the national economy. There are many factors resulting in under-supply, some of which will be considered later in this chapter: amongst these factors, the statistical containment of concealed families within the current approach to projecting changes in household numbers is clearly problematic.

Housing requirements

Separate household projections are made independently for individual projection areas (DETR 1999: 55), which enables estimates to be converted into housing requirements (Adams and Watkins 2002: 99) expressed as regional and county figures. This is an issue not touched upon in the last two sections, but which is explained diagrammatically by Breheny (1999) (see Figure 11.1). Stages 1 and 4 in Figure 11.1 have already been discussed at length; the procedures for arriving at population and household figures for individual regions and counties are part of the same approach. The national projections (on the underlying 1996 population-based) suggest that the total number of households in England will rise from 20.2 million in 1996 to 24.0 million by 2021: a rate of about 150,000 households per year. This is the "trend figure" for household growth.

Corresponding trend figures are produced for the regions. For example, DETR figures suggest that the number of households in the North West will increase from 2,812 million in 1996 to 3,016 million in 2016: an increase of 249,000 households (DETR 1999: 40). This is converted into a trend figure for the region: in this case, a formation rate of 12,450 households per year. In *Regional planning guidance for the North West* (RPG13) (GONW 2003), this regional control figure is not set out explicitly. However, it is stated that the "Guidance takes a realistic and responsible view of future housing requirements, within the context of an

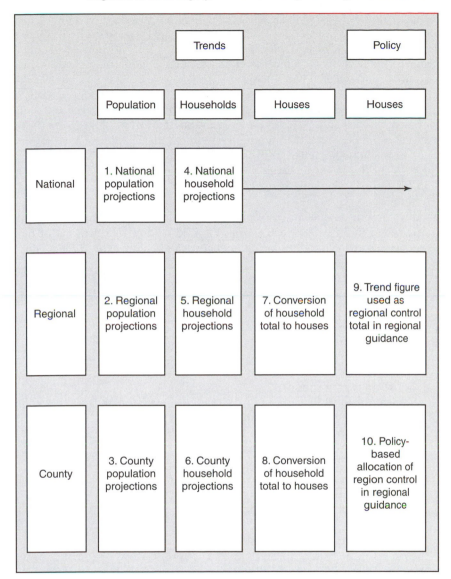

Figure 11.1 Local housing allocations in regional guidance
Source: Breheny 1999

up-to-date projection of household growth" (2003: 68). What this means in reality is that the "Guidance puts forward a level of housing provision slightly higher than that given by the projections [i.e. 12,790 compared with 12,450 projections]" (2003: 68). Hence we move from a trend-based figure (Stage 9 in Figure 11.1) to a policy-based allocation of regional control within regional guidance (Stage 10), allowing for economic growth rates, household formation and migration rates slightly in excess of those incorporated, which takes account of regional capacity (infrastructural capacity including transport and waste) and the opportunities to extend that capacity (adding to infrastructure, building new schools, providing new services, managing waste and so forth). In RPG13, a broad regional policy-based allocation is stipulated (12,790 units per annum) together with policy-based allocations for each of the region's unitary authorities and shire counties (GONW 2003: 69).

Adams and Watkins (2002: 102) explain that the "primary aim of the RPGs is to provide a framework for development plans, which must be taken into consideration by local authorities in the preparation and review of structure plans, or in metropolitan areas, the unitary development plans". Housing allocations are an important component of this framework. In the case of the North West region, the policy-based allocation to the counties and unitary authorities (Stage 10 in Figure 11.1) takes into account (after GONW 2003: 70):

- the core development principles and spatial development framework (included in RPG13), which establish a need to direct 25 per cent of new housing provision to the conurbation cores and 60 per cent to the region's metropolitan area;
- the government's 1996-based population and housing projections;
- the findings of the North West regional housing need and demand study;
- the anticipated level of economic growth in the region indicated in the North West Development Agency's regional (economic) strategy;
- the way in which households occupy dwellings, including the demand for and location of different types, size and tenure and the age and condition of the existing housing stock;
- means of making the best use of the existing housing stock and the need to reduce the present level of vacancy;
- the potential for new housing to be accommodated on previously developed land or by reuse of existing buildings;
- the results of urban potential studies undertaken in the North West;
- the housing land supply and development plan allocations already committed within the region;
- the risk of exacerbating the potential scale of abandonment of older housing stock; and
- environmental and other policy considerations.

On this basis, policy-based allocations are cascaded down the planning hierarchy. For example, Manchester ends up with an annual average rate of housing provision net of clearance of 1,350 units; the figure for Bolton (unitary authority) is 450, and for the Wirral 160 per annum. Regional planning guidance notes that these allocations should be kept under constant review in line with government's call for a "plan, monitor and manage" approach to housing provision. However, the journey from national projections of population change to housing allocations within structure and unitary development plans is almost complete. The final complicating factor is that "many authorities make their own forecasts" (Adams and Watkins 2002: 102), leading them to question the figures set out in regional guidance. The questions asked may be grounded in analyses of local market conditions or the extent to which land is really available for development, or they may be motivated by political considerations. The

Secretary of State has the power to call in structure plans (etc.) that duck beneath regional control figures, though this is often a last resort, as great emphasis is placed on "local negotiation [which] seeks to improve the local ownership of the numbers" (2002: 102).

From household formation to strategic housing allocations

Towards the end of the last section, it became clear that housing figures are increasingly "spatialized" (Murdoch and Abram 2002: 72) as they cascade down the planning hierarchy with counties (where they exist) retaining the power to make "strategic" housing allocations on particular sites (Stevenage West in Hertfordshire is an example of such an allocation, set out in the 1998 structure plan), though a principal function of the counties and of structure planning is to divide regional control figures (or agreed revisions of these figures) between local planning authorities based on capacity and local assessments of need, alongside many of the same considerations that guide regional to county allocations (see above). A more detailed discussion of this process is presented by Murdoch and Abram (2002).

In recent years, the current system of planning for new housing has been subject to fierce criticism: the failure to deliver enough homes may have severe economic knock-on effects (Barker 2004), while delivering too many brings an environmental cost (DEFRA 2004). The wrong types of homes in the wrong locations may amplify existing social problems or create new ones. All in all, getting the right number of homes of the right type in the most appropriate locations is one of the biggest challenges the planning system faces in the new millennium. A failure to deliver will result in a high price being paid by individual communities, by society at large and by the environment (see Carmona *et al.* 2003: 6–15). In 2002, the Joseph Rowntree Foundation's inquiry into land for housing concluded that there must be (adapted from Barlow *et al.* 2002: 25):

- A much fuller debate on how housing growth will be accommodated, and acceptance that avoiding the growth agenda will result in the biggest housing crisis that England and Britain more generally has ever faced.
- Recognition that, although the "efficient use of land" is important, of greater importance is the need to ensure sufficient housing to meet demand. The current debate on brownfield and greenfield development can obscure the wider question and divert attention away from the need for immediate action. Figures presented by Alan Holmans to the inquiry revealed that the housing crisis is snowballing as building rates fall consistently below what is required. There is urgent need for action.
- Higher densities must be coupled with good design, innovation and management. But again, the density debate should not be used as an excuse to delay on supplying additional homes.
- Reform of planning practice to ensure the sufficient release of housing land and to ease development through the planning process. The culture of planning must also be changed, delivering positive outcomes rather than merely reacting (often negatively) to development pressure.

These conclusions clearly set out an order of priority for the new-house-building debate, one in which the absolute supply issue takes precedence. The aim here is to consider how the mechanisms of forecasting housing demand (and thereby making development plan land allocations) can contribute to under-supply. I have already noted at several points that the assumptions that underpin projections may themselves weaken the reliability of official figures. In the same vein, Adams and Watkins (2002: 103–9) note a number of methodological concerns relating to the broad projection process, described in the last part of this chapter:

- Firstly, there are inherent shortcomings of an approach that is "backward looking" and trend based. Trends – including the propensity of more people to live alone – often decelerate, but the rate of deceleration may not be reflected in periodic social statistics. Some commentators have argued that this can imply that projections tend to overestimate future growth. Holmans (2001), however, suggests that recent projections have *underestimated* the importance of reductions in household size and contends that more house-holds will form in the period ending 2021 than official figures suggest.
- Secondly, the projections are blind to economic realities. Changes in the economy may influence the rate of household formation and consequent levels of housing demand. There is a case, therefore, for factoring economic indicators (including unemployment levels or interest rate forecasts) into the household projections.
- Thirdly, there is a suggestion that the projections themselves are "self-fulfilling": "the provision of housing to meet expected demand ensures that further demand occurs, and this in turn leads to increased future pro-jections" (Adams and Watkins 2002: 104). This suggests that either house-holds form more rapidly where housing is readily availability (i.e. availability drives formation) or households migrate to those areas to which housing is being directed (i.e. availability provides an impetus for migration, especially when coupled with greater job opportunities).
- Fourthly, serious doubts have been raised over the reliability of data per-taining to both domestic and international migration flows. For domestic flows, greater accuracy can be achieved for those years immediately pre-ceding a census; at other times, figures are less reliable. For international flows, there are considerable discrepancies between census estimates and estimates derived from the IPS (see above), which reduces confidence in the reliability of both these potential sources.
- Generally, there is a view that the limitations noted above all result from too great an emphasis being placed on the national perspective; more robust data are needed on local market conditions, migration patterns, housing needs and existing building stock. The systematic collection of these types of data locally would, it is suggested, provide a firmer foundation for forward planning.

The "crudeness" of national projections is a recurring criticism, and there is a widespread belief that a failure to take account of spatial economic con-siderations or the realities of local housing markets reduces the chances of the system "delivering dwellings of the required type and size or in the appropriate locations" (Adams and Watkins 2002: 106). Indeed, the Barker Review concluded that planning needs to make "better use of information about prices and preferences" (Barker 2004: 6) to ensure a quicker and more flexible response to changing market conditions. At this point, I wish to return to the questions raised at the beginning of this chapter: these largely related to the use of the projections when trickled down to the counties and local authorities, to political interventions (local and national), to the use of local intelligence and, of course, to outcomes on the ground.

Baker and Wong (1997) have suggested that the relationship between policy and political considerations – including the priority to be given to "re-using previously-developed land within urban areas, bringing empty homes back into use and converting existing buildings, in preference to the development of greenfield sites" (DETR 2000b) – and technical calculations is often a difficult one. Uncertainties surrounding some technical assumptions, together with the power of specific political priorities (see King 1999: 11), influence projections as they cascade down to the planning stage. A number of technical shortcomings have already been noted; the intention now is to focus on policy and political influences. Debates in the North West of England (leading up to the publication of RPG13 in March 2003) and in the East of England (in preparation for the new RPG14 in 2004) can be used to illustrate the various entanglements, debates and compromises which regularly accompany the issuing of regional housing figures. I have already noted that regional trend figures are frequently questioned during the preparation of regional planning guidance: the standing committees of local authority representatives together with the regional assemblies and development agencies introduce broad assumptions regarding economic growth and regional capacity to arrive at a policy-based allocation. During the examination in public (EIP) of draft RPG13 (in spring 2001), considerable debate focused not on the guidance's core strategy, but on the housing figures. Draft regional planning guidance had been published in July 2000 by the North West Regional Assembly (NWRA 2000) in which it was argued that "a higher level of growth than that which underpin[ned] the government's figures" was anticipated, resulting in faster rates of household formation and migration. Hence, the draft RPG made provision for 343,000 additional households (357,400 after adjustments for vacancy rates, or 17,150 units per annum) (NWRA 2000: 30).

Following the EIP, a panel report, and a number of required changes from the Secretary of State, a revised public consultation draft of RPG13 was issued in March 2002 (GONW 2002a). Planned housing provision for the region had now fallen to a policy-based allocation of 12,790 units: the level set in the final RPG published exactly one year later. The debates that shaped this revision pre-dated the 2000 draft of the guidance and can be traced back to the Regional Housing Forum with its membership comprising representatives from the House Builders Federation (HBF) and a number of environmental interests including the Campaign to Protect Rural England (CPRE), the Royal Society for the Protection of Birds (RSPB) and local groups such as Friends of the Lake District. Consensus amongst the environmental lobby was that the economic growth card was being overplayed, backed by the house-builders and accepted by some local councils whose interests lay in projecting an image of healthy growth rather than conceding the likelihood of economic uncertainties ahead.

Arguably, the arrival of a new PPG3 in 2000 gave environmental interests the upper hand. King (1999) has suggested that:

> while in the 1950s and 1960s the balance between providing homes and protecting the environment appears to have been tilted in favour of homes, from the 1980s onwards the balance has tended to tilt more in favour of protecting the environment.
>
> (1999: 10)

With the environment in the ascendancy, groups opposed to control figures higher than the trend-based allocation were able to use national planning guidance to portray draft RPG figures as being out of step with government thinking (particularly in respect of land recycling and building reuse). Inevitably, both the economic arguments and the environmental concerns were overstated, and it was left to the EIP panel to force a compromise. A key problem here is that, through the process of regional brokering, an "objective" calculation of household formation can quickly become a highly subjective housing allocation, determined not by real demand or need but by the agendas of competing political groups. Environmental pressures are likely to have greatest impact in those areas and sub-regions viewed as more "sensitive"; hence shire counties may end up with smaller allocations than metropolitan boroughs, whereas the original trend-based figures pointed to the need for a more even spread of new homes. However, there was little evidence of this occurring in the North West: between 2000 and 2003, the *relative* allocation to the Mersey Belt and to the rest of the conurbations fell by two percentage points, whilst the relative allocation to the shire counties rose by the same amount (NWRA 2000: 30; GONW 2003: 69). The *absolute* downsizing across the region was fairly evenly distributed.

A schedule of the amendments to the original draft of RPG13 was published by GONW in May 2002. This shows that the EIP panel broadly agreed with the housing provision figures set out in the draft RPG13 (GONW 2002b: 120), but that the Secretary of State took a very different view. Indeed, the Secretary overruled the panel's broad agreement with the original policy-based allocation and annualised figures, stipulating a "reduction of 15% on the draft RPG figure" (2002b: 121). The need for the reduction was attributed to lower economic growth rates than anticipated two years earlier, a high reported incidence of low demand in the region and a need to promote "more sustainable patterns of provision". The detailed explanation given was as follows:

> The draft RPG level of housing provision significantly exceeds the 1996-based household projections. It has as its economic basis a "high (maximum) growth" scenario, which utilises the 1996-based household projections and applies to them a high (2.5% annual growth in GDP) growth rate and a reduced rate of unemployment. Actual growth to date is nearer to the draft RPG's "moderate growth" scenario, suggesting necessary housing provision would accord with the 1996-based household projections (249,000 dwellings by 2016). In the Secretary of State's view, the draft RPG level of housing provision also pays insufficient regard to vacancy rates and the incidence of low demand. Accordingly, the Secretary of State proposes the annual average rate of provision to be based upon a total provision of 256,000

dwellings over the period 1996–2016. Whilst this is a reduction of 15% on the draft RPG provision, it is still in excess of that implied by the "moderate growth" scenario.

(GONW 2002b: 125)

The growth scenarios referred to by the Secretary of State derived from work undertaken for GONW by Manchester and Liverpool Universities in 1999/2000 (DETR 2000b). Three scenarios were devised, relating migration and household formation to low, moderate and high economic growth forecasts. GONW and its regional partners chose to select the high-growth scenario to guide the policy-based allocation; the justification for this decision could of course be questioned, especially in light of the low-demand issues referred to by the Secretary of State. However, central government's own preference for the moderate-growth scenario was based on economic performance figures for only 24 months of the full projection period, another questionable justification. The choices made are of course politically motivated: the regional assembly's draft figures reflected the preferences of the house-building lobby and local councils. The Secretary of State's objective was to secure the government's target for reusing previous development land; in the same year, John Prescott was able to tell the Commons – whilst making his planning policy statement and paving the way for the Planning and Compulsory Purchase Bill – that government had exceeded its 60 per cent brownfield benchmark by one percentage point. However, Shadow Planning Minister Eric Pickles was quick to rebuff the boast, pointing out that new house building had fallen to an all-time low and therefore "60% of not very much is not very much" (*Hansard* 2002). Indeed, there has been much recent criticism of government's emphasis on target setting, which may become the primary measure of success, overriding all other considerations.

The particular narrative behind the eventual "adoption" of a policy-based allocation in the final version of RPG13 (GONW 2003) is not dissimilar to the story behind all nine sets of regional planning guidance in England. Central government pays lip-service to the need for local ownership of the figures (Adams and Watkins 2002: 102), but eventually these are issued by government itself, which will naturally demand that the level and proposed distribution of provision accord with its own policy aims. In the case of regional guidance in North West England, this meant a net figure that was extremely close to official (trend-based) projections of household growth.

Arguably, the close relationship between the Secretary of State, the Government Office and the regional assembly acts to limit potential discord surrounding the regional control figures. There is scope for far greater disagreement between the counties and local planning authorities, on the one hand, and the regional assembly (which has the task of preparing draft RPG), on the other. This has certainly been the case during the ongoing preparation of regional guidance for the East of England. A draft of RPG14 was scheduled for publication in October 2004 (and a final version of RPG14 was due to appear in 2006, but effort subsequently switched to the production of the region's RSS). The context for regional planning guidance in the East of England is very different from the context in the North West. Government is extremely keen that housing provision figures set in RPG14 (and RPG11 – South East England) should accord with its sustainable communities plan (ODPM 2003): this means setting policy-based figures in excess of the 1996-based projections. In a letter to the East of England Regional Assembly, Lord Rooker, Minister for Regeneration and Regional Development, set out the government's position:

> You [referring to the chairman of the East of England regional planning panel] asked me for an indication of what level of growth should be considered for the LSC [London–Stansted–Cambridge] Growth Area and I indicated that I would be looking for your assessment of what would be required to get to 40,000 above current RPG levels by 2016 – with 35,000 as a minimum, compared with a base of around 90,000 in existing RPG (for the LSC area including Peterborough and the Cambridge sub-region). This is consistent with the scale of potential we referred to in the Sustainable Communities Plan. For comparison, the Milton Keynes/South Midlands Growth Area has submitted growth proposals for 44,300 on a base of 89,000 in existing RPG.
>
> (Rooker 2004)

The government's agenda across the South East and East of England is to push up planned allocations, thereby attempting to stave off a future crisis in housing provision. This has led to unease amongst the regional bodies and local authorities, who firstly share concerns over how infrastructure can be provided to sustain such growth and secondly are worried that many communities will vociferously reject the inflated allocations. Indeed, the chairman of the regional planning panel has called the "step change" in the allocations "ambitious" and has pointed out that it is "one which has not been universally welcomed throughout all parts of the region" (Reynolds 2004). Acknowledging the importance of infrastructure in securing a settlement, the chairman also conveyed his hope that regional technical studies would assist Lord Rooker in securing the "best possible infrastructure settlement for the East of England in the forthcoming 2004 Spending Review". Making sure the necessary infrastructure accompanies the revised allocations is described as crucial to obtaining *local political support*; the regional assembly expressed doubts as to whether headway could be made on the preparation of regional guidance without this support.

In the months leading up to this exchange between Lord Rooker and the regional assembly, a number of East of England authorities voiced concerns over potentially inflated allocations. The banked draft of RPG14 sets a regional target of 478,000 additional dwellings between 2001 and 2021 (EERA 2004: 109): in Hertfordshire (the eastern parts of which fall into the London–Stansted–Cambridge growth area), an interim target of 72,000 units (3,600 annualised) has been set. This is "interim" partly because the figure is likely to be affected by technical studies of additional capacity in the London–Stansted–Cambridge–Peterborough corridor, and partly because:

> In Hertfordshire, the dwelling figures reflect an initial view of distribution in the county. . . pending an assessment of urban capacity, options for greenfield development, principally urban extensions, and appropriate density assumptions for use in assessing potential housing supply. A further study is to be undertaken to investigate the appropriate scale and density of

potential housing supply from previously developed land, sustainable development options for possible greenfield development (including possible Green Belt releases), and mechanisms for ensuring that a sequential test can be applied to prioritise the supply from previously developed sources versus greenfield development.

(EERA 2004: 112)

This and earlier statements from EERA prompted a joint response from the county and district councils in Hertfordshire. Late in 2003, and prior to the issuing of a first draft of RPG14, Hertfordshire's local authorities were aware that the regional assembly was likely to call upon them to allocate land for an additional 20,000 homes across the county above a 66,000 allocation already proposed by EERA. Under the direction of the regional assembly, the authorities were asked to look at five growth scenarios (A to E), the highest of which would lead to 86,000 extra homes in the county during the projection period to 2021 (HertsDirect 2003a). The initial reaction of the county was to point out the potentially negative impact of this additional allocation, in terms of both the loss of greenfield sites and the repercussions for local communities. By November, the county's executive member for environment was calling on the regional assembly to give greater consideration to infrastructure needs, and the potential loss of both greenfield sites and green belt land. Criticisms of the regional assembly's approach, and its lack of realism, became more defined, with the county and districts raising the following concerns (after HertsDirect 2003b):

- Even with the lowest-growth scenario (A, with 66,000 additional households), there will be a need to build on significant areas of green belt and on greenfield sites.
- The "particular pressures on Hertfordshire" have not been recognised.
- The timescale given for the submission of district-level figures proved to be inadequate and did not allow "for the proper development of robust figures" which can stand up to sustainability appraisal and public examination.
- Some districts do not have the capacity to meet their own housing needs.
- There is a need to ensure that consistent methodology (for arriving at district figures) is followed across the region.
- The figures (i.e. the regional policy-based allocations) vary greatly depending on what assumptions are made (e.g. the amount of people expected to move into the county over the next 20 years).

The local perspective differs greatly from the regional and the national one. For the county and districts, the "pressures on Hertfordshire" relate to the loss of greenfield sites and, given the priority to defend such sites, the inability of some districts to find enough land to meet the housing needs of local people. The timescale for feeding into RPG is held to be particularly problematic, as is the lack of consistency in arriving at district figures (there is at least a suggestion that districts in different counties deal with capacity issues in different ways). Key amongst the criticisms contained in the joint response is that, although Hertfordshire's authorities have been obliged to submit local figures, the rush to get these out and lack of a consensual strategy has meant that "they have not agreed their own preferred locations for new housing and numbers have there-fore been estimated". Crucially, "The figures are not a true representation of where houses can be accommodated, but are the result of a mathematical exercise in order to respond to pressure from the Regional Assembly" (Herts-Direct 2003b).

The national perspective is somewhat different. In a joint response from the National Housing Federation and Chartered Institute of Housing to the 2003 consultation exercise leading up to the banked draft of RPG14, it is argued that "many parts of the East of England, particularly those influenced by the growing London Travel to Work Area, are subject to severe housing pressures" (NHF/CIH 2003: 1). The biggest pressure facing the East of England – and Hertford-shire – results from "migration from equity rich or income rich Londoners" moving into the region and fuelling house price rises (2003: 3). Because of this, local household formation is suppressed and past housing allocations have been inadequate to accommodate growth or meet needs. Hence, the key pressure facing Hertfordshire is not RPG14's inflated allocations, but past historic short-falls in housing supply, which, it might be argued, have prompted the response outlined in the sustainable communities plan. The county and the districts view a recent slowing of household formation in Hertfordshire as licence to resist higher control figures in RPG14; however, the NHF and CIH argue that:

> the slowdown in household formation [is] symptomatic of current market pressures and not a long term fundamental change. We therefore think Scenario C is unlikely to be correct and RPG14 must plan for a higher dwelling provision than the current RPG, as indicated by the other three scenarios. Our best estimate would be that the annual dwelling requirement is likely to be somewhere between scenarios B and D.
>
> (NHF/CIH 2003: 4)

With Scenario A representing the base level of growth and E representing an 86,000 dwelling target, the first draft of RPG14 has, as I noted earlier, set an interim policy-based allocation of 72,000 units. This is below the recommenda-tion of the NHF and CIH, but is likely to be subject to later revision. Debates over the level of growth throughout the East of England are unlikely to subside. Local resistance to higher allocations have shaped political debate in Hertford-shire at least since the publication of the county's structure plan in 1998, and the strategic allocation at Stevenage West prompting the Campaign against Stevenage Expansion (CASE). In the context of these local and regional concerns, it is easy to lose sight of the household projections as they become obscured by, and frequently relegated behind, the local controversies that embroil new housing provision. Within Hertfordshire, there is a belief that an emphasis on the mathematics of provision has resulted in too little attention being given to local outcomes and to questions of infrastructure, affordability, local need, environmental capacity, and the actual types of homes that should be built. However, preparations for a new RPG14 (or for a revised regional spatial strategy for the East of England) were at an early stage at the time of writing and, although debates were centred on housing numbers, much was going on behind the scenes to address these concerns.

Conclusions

The controversies that regularly accompany the publication of regional control figures in RPG tend to obscure the fact that the household projections are only one factor amongst many used to guide county and local housing allocations. The methods for arriving at these projections are far from perfect, as noted earlier in this chapter. Problems begin at the population projection phase and are carried forward into predictions of household formation (Adams and Watkins 2002: 103–9). These then become an imperfect starting point for calculating policy-based regional allocations.

In this chapter, I have shown how regional bodies, central government and local authorities respond to the household projections in different ways. Regionally, there is perhaps a greater sense of "ownership" in the figures, which are eventually adopted by the Government Office, the representative of the Secretary of State in the regions. Locally, it is often the case that both counties and districts believe that government places too much weight on broad trends and ignores local concerns; such a view is inevitable given the political pressures on local representatives, and the strategic priorities of regional planning. However, there are legitimate concerns over the pressure placed on districts to respond quickly and positively to RPG consultations. Government is keen to ensure "local ownership" of figures and targets, but often this ownership is foisted on unwilling local partners. Arguably, central government is the real champion of the household projections, though that is not to say that these are accepted in their undiluted form. A substantial part of this chapter examined how two regions have dealt with issues of household growth; in both cases, the figures (draft in the case of RPG14 and final within RPG13) owe more to central government intervention than local or regional negotiations. Both sets of figures have emerged in the context of government's communities plan, which aims to stave off housing under-supply in the South of England and resist over-supply in the North. In the North West, four years of debate over economic growth and household formation ended in 2003 with the publication of an RPG13 containing a policy-based housing target only marginally above the 1996-based projection figure. In the East of England, central government is already playing a central role in ensuring that the region accepts the need for growth well in excess of its own projections. The level of intervention in both cases is striking; in the North West, the Secretary of State sliced 100,000 units from the draft allocation; in the East of England, Lord Rooker has set out government's "requirement" for tens of thousands of additional homes in each of the sub-regions, concentrated in its planned growth areas (defined in the communities plan).

Planning for housing in England is an overtly political process; many of the assumptions that underpin the projections themselves are politically motivated, including the containment of concealed households and the treatment of different forms of international migration. But the clearest political interventions occur when trend-based targets are translated into allocations; each tier of planning and government has its own agenda and its own motivation. This might suggest that the projections themselves lose much of their initial potency as they become just one factor amongst many "framing" the debate. Indeed, the first draft of RPG14 neglects to even mention the projections when setting out the factors that need to be taken into account when planning future housing provision in the region: PPG3 priorities, the sustainable communities plan, and the region's own economic strategy and spatial development framework are all key considerations, but the projections are not listed as a guiding concern (EERA 2004: 108).

The Secretary of State is the most powerful player in this political wrangle. The regions and local authorities have been called upon to manage demand, to feed local intelligence into regional housing debates and to avoid the "predict and provide" mentality of the past. Recent events in the East of England have suggested that authorities are keen to engage with government on housing provision issues, but many feel that Whitehall continues to railroad them along a preordained path: government has *predicted* growth and it remains their responsibility to simply *provide* for it. Government has staked its political future on the success of the communities plan, and this plan will need driving from the centre, perhaps rendering its own "plan, monitor and manage" approach to housing provision increasingly meaningless.

Notes

1. PPS3, *Housing* was published in December 2006.
2. The approach is now described on the Government Actuary's website (http://www.gad.gov.uk/).

References

Adams, D. and C. Watkins 2002. *Greenfields, brownfields and housing development*. London: Blackwell.

Baker, M. and C. Wong 1997. Planning for housing land in the English regions: a critique of the housing projection and regional planning guidance mechanisms. *Environment and Planning C* **15**, 73–87.

Barker, K. 2004. *Review of housing supply: delivering stability – securing our future housing needs*. London: HM Treasury.

Barlow, J., K. Bartlett, A. Hooper and C. Whitehead 2002. *Land for housing: current practice and future options*. York: Joseph Rowntree Foundation.

Breheny, M. 1999. People, households and houses: the basis to the "great housing debate" in England. *Town Planning Review* **70**, 275–93.

Carmona, M., S. Carmona and N. Gallent 2003. *Delivering new homes: processes, planners and providers*. London: Routledge.

DEFRA 2004. *Study into the environmental impacts of increasing the supply of housing in the UK*. London: Department for Environment, Food and Rural Affairs.

DETR 1999. *Projections of households in England to 2021*. London: Department of the Environment, Transport and the Regions.

DETR 2000a. *Planning policy guidance note 3: housing*. London: Department of the Environment, Transport and the Regions.

DETR 2000b. *North West housing demand and need research*. London: Department of the Environment, Transport and the Regions.

DoE 1984. *Land for housing*. Circular 15/84. London: Department of the Environment.

DoE 1991. *Planning and affordable housing*. Circular 7/91. London: Department of the Environment.

EERA 2004. *Regional planning guidance for the East of England draft strategy*. RPG14. Bury St Edmunds: East of England Regional Assembly.

GONW 2002a. *Draft regional planning guidance for the North West incorporating the Secretary of State's proposed changes*. RPG13. Manchester: Government Office for the North West.

GONW 2002b. *Draft regional planning guidance for the North West: schedule of the Secretary of State's proposed changes and statement of reasons for changes*. RPG13. Manchester: Government Office for the North West.

GONW 2003. *Regional planning guidance for the North West*. RPG13. Manchester: Government Office for the North West.

Hansard 2002. Record of Parliamentary debate, 18 July, column 443.

HertsDirect 2003a. Hertfordshire under pressure to find space for extra homes, http://www.hertsdirect.org/environment/plan/extrahousing (accessed 30 March 2004).

HertsDirect 2003b. Hertfordshire authorities respond to East of England Regional Assembly, http://www.hertsdirect.org/environment/plan/eoferesponse (accessed 30 March 2004).

Holmans, A. 2001. *Housing demand and need in England 1996–2016*. London: Town and Country Planning Association.

King, D. 1999. Official household projections in England: methodology, usage and sensitivity tests. Working Paper 47. Joint ECE-EUROSTAT work session on demographic projections, Perugia, 3–7 May.

Murdoch, J. and Abram, S. 2002. *Rationalities of planning: development versus environment in planning for housing*. Aldershot: Ashgate.

NHF/CIH 2003. *Draft joint response from the National Housing Federation and the Chartered Institute of Housing to the consultation leading to regional planning guidance (RPG14) for the East of England*. Wellingborough: National Housing Federation Midlands.

NWRA 2000. *People, places and prosperity: draft regional planning guidance for the North West*. Wigan: North West Regional Assembly.

ODPM 2003. *Sustainable communities: building for the future*. London: Office of the Deputy Prime Minister.

ODPM 2004. *Consultation on Planning Policy Statement 1: creating sustainable communities*. London: Office of the Deputy Prime Minister.

ONS 1999. *National population projections 1996-based*. Series PP2 no. 21. Office for National Statistics. London: Stationery Office.

Reynolds, John (EERA) 2004. Letter to Lord Rooker, http://www.eelgc.gov.uk/eelgcDocs/Agenda%20item%204%20annex%20B.doc (accessed 30 March 2004).

Rooker, Lord 2004. Letter to John Reynolds (EERA), http://www.eelgc.gov.uk/eelgcDocs/scannedlordrooker.doc (accessed 30 March 2004).

Wenban-Smith, A. 2002. A better future for development plans: making "plan, monitor and manage" work. *Planning Theory and Practice* **3**(1), 33–51.

12 Regional planning and sustainability assessment

John Glasson

Introduction

A key premise of this chapter is that the regional level of planning is a particularly appropriate level of planning for the integration of bio-physical and socio-economic development issues, and for the delivery of sustainable development. Yet such delivery has often foundered on the twin rocks of institutional and methodological constraints. This chapter focuses on the positive approaches to overcome such constraints over the last two decades, with a particular focus on what can be summed up under the generic heading of sustainability assessment. The chapter outlines the evolution, with particular reference to the UK, in its EU context, of approaches to such assessment via environmental impact assessment (EIA) for major and strategic projects, and strategic environmental assessment (SEA) and sustainability appraisal (SA) for plans and programmes. It includes examples of innovative applications of EIA, SEA and SA, in relation to UK major projects, multi-modal transport corridor studies, EU Structural Funds, and the new generation of English regional spatial strategies. It concludes with an assessment of progress to date towards the goal of a more integrated approach to sustainable development.

Sustainable regional planning and development

Socio-economic development and a high-quality natural and built environment can be uncomfortable, and often incompatible, partners. The resultant impacts of development on the environment are recognised by governments at all levels, from international to local, but the causal downward spiral can be difficult to reverse. In the European Union, several decades of environmental action plans have had mixed impacts on various environmental indicators. Whilst we can point to some successes, for example reduction in the impact on ecosystems of "acid rain", and improvement of the quality of water at designated bathing beaches in the EU, an assessment of the state of Europe's environment (EEA 2003) highlights some powerful and problematic drivers of change, and serious trends in many environmental indicators. For example, road freight traffic increased by 44 per cent in Western Europe in the 1990s. Almost 400 million foreign tourists visited Europe in 2000, 56 per cent of the world's international tourist market; numbers are expected to grow by 50 per cent by 2020, with a doubling of air traffic in Europe. Almost half of Europe's domestic animal breed diversity is categorised as being at risk of extinction, and the trends are negative. There is also the overriding issue of climate change. Over the past 100 years, the mean temperature in Europe has increased by about 1.2 °C; it is projected to increase by another 1.4 to 5.8 °C between 1990 and 2100.

Yet for over two decades the concept of sustainable development has offered a way forward which is potentially more positive. The International Union for the Conservation of Nature (IUCN) highlighted sustainable development as the link between economic development and the natural environment. The oft-quoted reminder from the IUCN (1980) that "we have not inherited the earth from our parents; we have borrowed it from our children" was taken a step further in the Brundtland Report (UN World Commission on Environment and Development 1987). Brundtland rejected the argument that economic growth and good environmental quality were mutually exclusive. But can the good intentions be converted into good practice? Debate on the "ends" and "means" of sustainable development has continued apace, including, *inter alia*, arguments about the relative merits of "weak sustainability" and "strong sustainability"; "social justice" and "environmental justice"; and "inter-generational" and "intra-generational equity". Major international conferences (Rio in 1992, and Johannesburg ten years later) have made some progress and introduced some innovations (for example, Agenda 21), but more than anything have highlighted the immensity of the world's environmental issues. Wang *et al.*'s (1993) observation of over a decade ago that sustainable development is "a challenge that remains to be confronted" still rings true. The observation also noted that this was an issue particularly at the regional level.

However, potentially the regional level may have a central role to play as the focus for "territorial integration" – between the natural and socio-economic systems within a territory. Friedmann and Weaver (1979) have reminded us that in the evolution of regional planning in the USA there were some innovative, although not always successful, experiments at such integration, exemplified by comprehensive river-based regional development schemes such as that for the Tennessee Valley. The subsequent integrated regional development planning approach adopted by the Organization of American States in the 1980s (OAS 1984) incorporated a regional diagnosis of economic, social and environmental issues in order to develop strategies that dealt with them in an integrated way. The revival of regional planning in the 1990s, coupled with the growth of decentralisation/devolution movements, has refuelled the interest in the regional level as an appropriate level for delivering sustainable development (see Campbell 1991; Roberts 1994; Hardy and Lloyd 1994; Glasson 1995; Clement and Hansen 2001; Benneworth *et al.* 2002). The regional level may, for example, demonstrate some contiguity of socio-economic systems, such as commuting zones, and natural systems, such as river basin catchment areas. Much of this interest has been EU based, but there is also interest worldwide. Jenkins *et al.* (2003) from Australia, drawing on recent US activity (US National Research Council 2002), note that:

> After a decade of trying to implement Agenda 21 at a national level, a number of recent reviews of how to progress sustainability are concluding that the appropriate scale to address the concept is at the regional or

sub-national level. These reviews suggest that regions are an appropriate basis for considering sustainability.

Todes (2004) notes that there are also examples of initiatives in sustainable regional planning and development in several developing countries' contexts. Her discussion of the evolution of South Africa's integrated development plans as potential frameworks for achieving sustainable regional development focuses particularly on integration and a multi-sector approach.

Sustainability principles and practice

An overview of principles

The concept of sustainable development, and its manifestations in terms of process and practice, have generated considerable debate and have continued to evolve over time (Pezzoli 1996). Globally the term "sustainability" has become increasingly preferred, as it emphasises the stance that is required to enable "sustainable development"; but the terms are often used interchangeably. Some of the characteristics of sustainability – the three key dimensions, the holistic approach, the importance of integration and the movement towards sustainable outcomes – are now briefly discussed, prior to an examination of the problems of implementation in practice, and an outline of some of the key tools of assessment, with particular reference to regional planning and development.

A much used contemporary definition refers to the "triple bottom line" (TBL), seeking to achieve outcomes through an integration of environmental protection, social advancement and economic prosperity. Figure 12.1 shows how the three dimensions are separate, but there are important areas of overlap that need to be found and explored. The aim is to minimise trade-offs (for example, not sacrificing an important wetland for a marina development) by seeking to

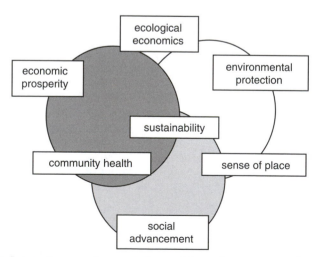

Figure 12.1 Integrating environmental, social and economic dimensions of sustainability

increase synergies providing mutually reinforcing solutions. It is useful and interesting to note different perspectives on, or at least modifications of, the traditional three overlapping circles approach. For example, in Figure 12.2, the triangular diagram stresses the holistic nature of sustainability within the borders of the triangle and the need to advance on several fronts to achieve the green, just and growing region. Of course the relative pace of advance will vary between the fronts and this is one of the challenges of a sustainability strategy. The concentric circle diagram in Figure 12.2 seeks to emphasise that, within the three-part definition of sustainability, there is an implicit hierarchy. The environment is the foundation to any concept of sustainability. We cannot

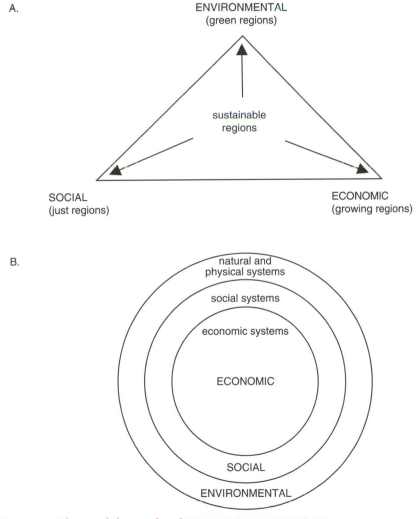

Figure 12.2 Sustainability – other diagrammatic representations

A. Source: Adapted from Campbell 2003
B. Source: Adapted from MacNaughton *et al.* 1997; Pope *et al.* 2004

survive without the "goods and services" provided by the earth's natural and physical systems. Without a decent environment there is probably nothing, as reflected in the rise on the international agenda of climate change issues. Living on the earth we have many social systems, and each has some type of economic system. Without a well-functioning social system, an economic system cannot be productive.

The holistic approach to sustainability is now generally accepted, and built into policy in many countries. Indeed, in some countries, the three elements have been developed further. The "strategy for sustainable development in the UK" (DETR 1999) was seen as meeting four key objectives at the same time in the UK and the world as a whole:

- social progress which recognises the needs of everyone;
- effective protection of the environment;
- prudent use of natural resources;
- maintenance of high and stable levels of economic growth and employment.

The definition thus differentiates between two types of physical environment, and makes explicit reference to global responsibility. A subsequent major update, *Securing the future: delivering the UK sustainable development strategy* (DEFRA 2005), introduced a revised set of guiding principles:

- living within environmental limits;
- ensuring a strong, healthy and just society;
- achieving a sustainable economy;
- promoting good governance; and
- using sound science responsibly.

The holistic approach also implies more integration, which, besides bringing synergies, can also reduce duplication and waste and lead to a more efficient use of scarce resources. There can be several dimensions to integration. These can include integration of policy areas, for example the often contested land-use and transport integration. There can be an integration of institutions and agencies of government and others, which can be horizontal across a particular level of policy/action, for example for a particular region, or vertical, for example seeking better linkages between local, regional and national in a particular policy area. Following from institutional integration, there can be movements towards plan integration, for example via an "integrated regional development framework" for a particular location. There can be integrated approaches in terms of methodologies, particularly for sustainability assessment of the four Ps (policies, plans, programmes and projects). But above all there is integration of vision, principles, objectives, outcomes and targets in relation to sustainability.

Some constraints on practice

However, it is important to recognise the major constraints on the achievement of sustainability in practice. At a general level, Trudgill (1990), in *Barriers to a better environment*, reminds us via the "AKSTEP" acronym of the potential constraints of lack of **A**wareness, **K**nowledge, **S**ocial concern, appropriate

Technology, Economic resources and Political will, all of which can provide effective barriers. In particular, in advanced economies, key factors tend to focus on political/institutional willingness or otherwise to act, and on technical/methodological difficulties.

Institutionally, regional planning is often seen as the "cuckoo in the nest", between local and national levels. It may lack the power base and legitimacy of other levels of government and planning (Harvie 1991), and can be viewed with mistrust from both above and below, for "empowered" regions can be a significant force in the country. It can be a contested area between many stakeholders with their varying interpretations of regional planning objectives – physical/land-use planning, economic development or wider intra-regional planning or inter-regional planning? Yet, as noted throughout this book, there has been a renewed interest in regional planning and regionalism in many countries in the European Union, and especially in the UK.

Yet even if the institutional context is improved, can we overcome the methodological constraints involved in socio-economic and bio-physical issues/policy/integration? What are appropriate environmental, social and economic targets and indicators for a sustainability strategy? Do we have appropriate baseline data for all the dimensions of sustainability? What should be the nature of assessment procedures for projects, policies, etc.? The focus of the remainder of this chapter is on the evolution of such assessment procedures, their application in the regional context, and their strengths and weaknesses. It builds in particular on the emergence over the last 20–25 years of a range of approaches to assess the impacts of "development actions" on the "environment". Reflecting international developments (see Glasson *et al.* 2005), these approaches include environmental impact assessment (EIA), strategic environmental assessment (SEA) and sustainability appraisal (SA). In Europe, the introduction of EIA and SEA directives from the European Commission (CEC 1985, 1997, 2001) has been an important driver. The emerging approaches demonstrate a number of trends, including from the narrow project focus of EIA to the wider strategic plan and programme, higher-tier, focus of SEA; and from the bio-physical focus of early EIA activity, and to some extent current SEA activity, to the more holistic SA approach including physical, social and economic dimensions. This evolution of assessment approaches is now discussed, with particular reference to strategic issues and regional development and planning.

Major projects and environmental impact assessment

Major projects and their impacts

Regional development and planning invariably involve major projects, including economic infrastructure (such as roads, railway lines, energy projects and water and waste management facilities) and social infrastructure (such as hospitals and universities), in addition to manufacturing and service industry activities (ranging from petro-chemical plants to shopping centres to leisure theme parks). The problems of infrastructure provision can provide serious constraints on effective regional planning, and this is a contemporary issue in the UK. Major projects often involve substantial expenditure (for example, £500 million for a conventional gas-fired power station), cover large areas, employ many people and have wide-ranging and significant impacts. Like a large stone thrown into a pond, a major project can create ripples with impacts spreading over a region and beyond. The environmental impacts may be of several types: physical and socio-economic; direct and indirect; short-run and long-run; local and strategic; adverse and beneficial; and reversible and irreversible (Glasson *et al.* 2005). The latter distinction is a particularly important one because environmental resources cannot always be replaced; once destroyed, some may be lost for ever.

Major projects also have a planning and development life cycle, including a variety of stages, as outlined in Figure 12.3. The impacts of a project change over

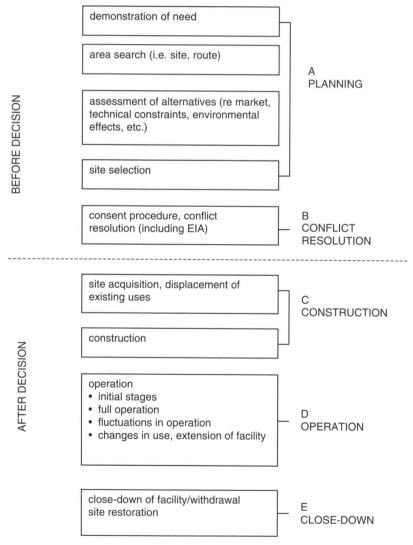

Figure 12.3 Generalised planning and development life cycle for major projects (with particular reference to impact assessment on the host area)

Source: Glasson *et al.* 2005

the life cycle. They are normally most marked during the project construction and operational stages. The construction stage can be particularly disruptive and may run for many years, as exemplified by the construction of London Heathrow Terminal 5 and its impacts on the surrounding road system. But impacts vary between project types. Utilities (such as a reservoir, or a power station) may have their most marked socio-economic and bio-physical impacts during construction; in contrast, the impact of service activities (such as a shopping centre or a theme park) may be more prominent in their operational stage. Nor should we forget about the other stages in the life cycle. Project planning, even at the very initial stage, can also have significant impacts. For example, a consultation exercise on alternative locations for an international airport in a region can lead (and has led) to property blight and serious resident concern in targeted locations. At the other end of the life cycle the closedown or decommissioning of a project can also have important effects, and the decommissioning of nuclear power stations provides a topical and long-running example for the UK, as for several other countries.

The role and nature of EIA

Environmental impact assessment (EIA) in a process for assessing the impacts of major projects in advance; as such, it provides a good example of the precautionary principle. The aim is to provide the decision maker with a systematic examination of the environmental implications of a proposed action, and alternatives, before a decision is taken. If any identified serious adverse impacts cannot be mitigated, it can provide evidence for the refusal of development permission. EIA can also provide a process under which developers can formulate more environmentally sensitive developments to avoid such an outcome. Overall, EIA can be an important force for more sustainable development.

The origins of EIA date back to the US National Environmental Policy Act of 1969, known as NEPA, but it was the European Commission EIA Directive of 1985 (CEC 1985) which provided the major impetus for action in the UK, and in several other EU Member States. The directive, to be implemented by 1988, distinguished between a set of projects for which EIA is mandatory (Annex I) and those for which EIA is discretionary (Annex II), depending on the characteristics of the projects, and the host environment. Annex III provides an outline of the information required in an EIA (see Table 12.1). Figure 12.4 amplifies Annex III to highlight the important steps in the EIA process, leading to the production of an environmental impact statement (EIS) for use in decision making. EC Directive 85/337 included a requirement for a five-year review. A report published in 1993 (CEC 1993) showed general satisfaction that the "basics of EIA are mostly in place", but expressed concern about several aspects, including insufficient consultation and public participation, lack of information about project alternatives, weak monitoring and inconsistent implementation of the directive across member states.

An amended Directive 97/11, to be implemented by 1999, was agreed in 1997 (CEC 1997). This included additional Annex I and Annex II projects (see Table 12.1), plus other important procedural changes, including the need for a developer to provide an outline of the main alternatives studied, and an obligation on a competent authority (primarily the local planning authority in the UK)

Table 12.1 Key elements in EC EIA Directive 85/337 (as amended)

Projects requiring EIA under EC Directive 85/337 *(as amended)*

Annex I (mandatory)
 1 Crude oil refineries, coal/shale gasification and liquefaction
 2 Thermal power stations and other combustion installations; nuclear power stations and other nuclear reactors
 3 Radioactive waste processing and/or storage installations
 4 Cast-iron and steel smelting works
 5 Asbestos extraction, processing, or transformation
 6 Integrated chemical installations
 7 Construction of motorways, express roads, other large roads, railways, airports
 8 Trading ports and inland waterways
 9 Installations for incinerating, treating, or disposing of toxic and dangerous wastes
10 *Large-scale installation for incinerating or treating non-hazardous waste*
11 *Large-scale groundwater abstraction or recharge schemes*
12 *Large-scale transfer of water resources*
13 *Large-scale waste water treatment plants*
14 *Large-scale extraction of petroleum and natural gas*
15 *Large* dams *and reservoirs*
16 *Long pipelines for gas, oil or chemicals*
17 *Large-scale poultry or pig rearing installations*
18 *Pulp, timber or board manufacture*
19 *Large-scale quarries or open-cast mines*
20 *Long overhead electrical power lines*
21 *Large-scale installations for petroleum, petrochemical or chemical products.*

Annex II (discretionary)
 1 Agriculture, silviculture and aquaculture
 2 Extractive industry
 3 Energy industry
 4 Production and processing of metals
 5 *Minerals industry* (projects not included in Annex I)
 6 Chemical industry
 7 Food industry
 8 Textile, leather, wood and paper industries
 9 Rubber industry
10 *Infrastructure projects*
11 *Other projects*
12 *Tourism and leisure*
13 Modification, extension or temporary testing of Annex I projects

Information required in an EIA under EC Directive 85/337 *(as amended)*

Annex III (IV)
 1 Description of the project
 2 Where appropriate (*an outline of main alternatives studied and an indication of the main reasons for the final choice*)
 3 Aspects of the environment likely to be significantly affected by the proposed project, including population, fauna, flora, soil, water, air climatic factors, material assets, architectural and archaeological heritage, landscape, and the interrelationship between them
 4 Likely significant effects of the proposed project on the environment
 5 Measures to prevent, reduce and, where possible, offset any significant adverse environmental effects
 6 Non-technical summary
 7 Any difficulties encountered in compiling the required information

Note: 1997 amendments are shown in italics.

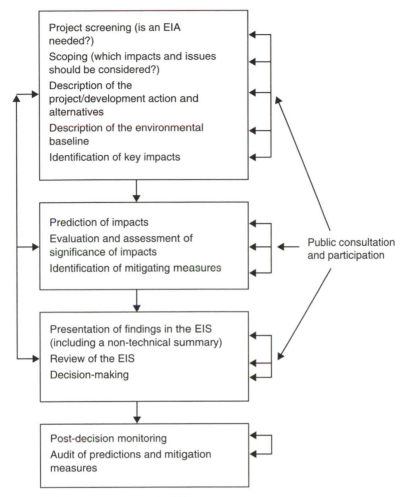

Figure 12.4 Important steps in the EIA process

Note: EIA should be a cyclical process with considerable interaction between the various steps.

Source: Glasson *et al.* 2005

to provide an opinion to a developer about the information to be supplied in an EIS, if requested by the developer.

EIA evolving practice

The EIA Directive is only one of over 200 European directives in the environmental policy field. There has been some concern about what is seen as an "implementation deficit" in the field – with more policy than action (Lowe and Ward 1998). However, this has proved to be less of a problem with regard to EIA, especially in the case of its application in the UK, although various reviews at the EU and at the UK level have raised a number of issues.

A third review of the original directive, as amended by Directive 97/11/EC (CEC 2003), undertaken for the Commission by the Impacts Assessment Unit at

Oxford Brookes University (UK), provided a detailed overview of implementation in practice, and highlighted some key implementation issues. These include considerable variations in thresholds used to specify EIA for Annex II projects; for example, three turbines would trigger mandatory EIA for a wind farm in Sweden, compared with 50 in Spain. There are also considerable variations in the number of EIAs being carried out in member states, varying from a post-1999 annual average of over 7,000 in France to about 70 in the Netherlands. There are also variations in public consultation, and in the key elements included in EIA. A lack of systematic monitoring of a project's actual impacts by the competent authority is a weakness in many countries. Overall, EIA systems in the EU provide an example of divergent practice in a converging system (Glasson *et al.* 2005; Glasson and Bellanger 2003).

In the UK, approximately 700 EISs are produced per annum (post-1999 directive amendments), dominated by the five key categories of waste, extraction, roads, urban/retail and energy projects. The location of such projects provides an interesting barometer of development activity. Up to 2000, the county of Kent had the most EISs, reflecting the impact of the Channel Tunnel and associated projects. Various reviews of EIA/EIS quality, and the costs and benefits of the process, show an increasing acceptance of and valuing of the process by the stakeholders involved – competent authorities, developers, consultants and affected parties/pressure groups (DoE 1996; Glasson *et al.* 1999; Wood 2003; Glasson *et al.* 2005). There has been considerable capacity building, with the production of an array of guidance documents and training programmes, and a gradual improvement in the quality and utility of EIA activity. Some high-profile projects, including ports and power stations, have been substantially changed or even abandoned, at least partly because of impacts revealed by EIA.

Yet EIA practice has also revealed some systemic weaknesses in the process. Practice has tended to be primarily bio-physical in focus, with only limited consideration of socio-economic impacts. However, most development decisions involve trade-offs between bio-physical and socio-economic impacts. Chadwick (2002) and Vanclay (2003) highlight the importance of socio-economic impacts assessment (SIA), and Glasson (2005) provides an example of the utility of such assessment for the management of the construction-stage impacts of Britain's last (to date) nuclear power station project, Sizewell B in East Anglia. There can be an important symbiotic relationship between developing public participation approaches and the fuller inclusion of socio-economic impacts. SIA can establish the baseline of groups, which can provide the framework for public participation to further identify issues associated with a development proposal.

Other EIA weaknesses, now responded to in the Amended EIA Directive, include the limited consideration of cumulative impacts, and project alternatives. Impacts associated with individual projects can be minor, but cumulatively the impacts of multiple projects can impose a significant impact on the environment in what Odum (1982) refers to as "the tyranny of small decisions". Piper (2000) provides valuable evidence on the state of UK practice on cumulative effects assessment (CEA), drawing on research on a number of case studies, including the ubiquitous wind farms, and the accumulation of projects in estuary sub-regions.

A recent methodological innovation, which can be seen to address alternatives and to provide a link to a more strategic level of assessment, is a multi-modal appraisal of transport options. These studies draw on a revised government appraisal framework for major road projects (DETR 1998), and normally relate to attempts to improve transport along congested corridors. In South East England they include, for example, the A34 Corridor, the South Coast and others (see SEERA 2003). However, one of the pioneers of such studies was the 1998–99 common appraisal framework study for part of the M4 Corridor in South Wales undertaken by Ove Arup consultants for the Welsh Office (subsequently Welsh Assembly) (Ove Arup 1999). The aim was to consider options to resolve traffic congestion on the M4 around Newport, east of Cardiff. Options appraised, on the basis of environmental, financial, economic and safety criteria, included: do minimum, M4 relief road, enhanced public transport, traffic management demand, and a hybrid approach. The appraisal methodology involved assessment of scenarios against performance indicators for particular objectives. For example, the objective of "emissions from transport affecting local air quality are minimised" was assessed by an indicator "length of highway experiencing a change in NO_x emissions". An array of findings was brought together in a Common Appraisal Summary Table (Table 12.2). Perhaps predictably it was the hybrid scenario which came through the best, and the Welsh Assembly felt unable to support the package of measures – which it saw as bad for the competitive position of Wales!

Policies, plans, programmes and strategic environmental assessment

From EIA to SEA

The recent and rapid rise of strategic environmental assessment (SEA) is, in many respects, a response to the problems with the existing system of project EIA. Project EIAs tend to be reactive to development proposals rather than being proactive in steering development away from environmentally sensitive sites. As already noted, EIAs have not adequately considered cumulative impacts and have been problematic in addressing alternatives – partly because in many cases such alternatives will be limited by choices made at a more strategic level. SEA can be defined as:

> A systematic process for evaluating the environmental consequences of proposed policy, plan or programme initiatives in order to ensure they are fully included and appropriately addressed at the earliest appropriate stage of decision making on par with economic and social considerations.
>
> (Sadler and Verheem 1996)

This definition involves SEA as a process in parallel with the plan-making process, rather than an add-on at the end of the process. Glasson and Gosling (2001) provide a taxonomy of recent SEA practice from low integration to full integration with plan making – typified as from a "stapled-on" model to a "holistic" model.

SEA relates to policies, plans and programmes – generally summarised as PPPs. A policy is defined as an inspiration and guidance to action (e.g. to provide housing for those currently not able to access the UK housing market); a plan is a set of coordinated and timed objectives for the implementation of the policy

Table 12.2 M4 (South Wales) common appraisal framework study

Indicator	Objective	Road building scenario	Enhance public transport scenario	Traffic/demand management scenario	Hybrid scenario
Transport: Local issues I.e. Relief to M4, avoid adverse impact on Newport	Optimise local impact (e.g. J25–26, 2007)	M4 objective achieved – 43% reduction. Minimal impact on Newport.	M4 objective not achieved – 6% reduction. Small beneficial impact on Newport.	M4 objective achieved – 77% reduction. Increase in traffic in Newport (11% by 2007).	M4 objective achieved – 58% reduction. Increase in traffic in Newport (24% by 2007).
Transport: Strategic issues I.e. Accessibility, integration, freight	Assist national transport objectives	Does not assist these objectives.	Assists these objectives.	Neutral to these objectives (owing to lack of facilities for suppressed highway trips).	Assists these objectives.
Environmental: Local issues I.e. Noise, NO_x emissions	Minimise adverse local impact	Local benefits to existing M4 corridor. Local adverse effects on the levels.	Improvement in local conditions, but some areas deteriorate.	Complex effects on local conditions, some improvements but adverse effects from traffic diversion.	Complex effects on local conditions, some improvements but adverse effects from traffic diversion although less than T/DM.

Environmental: Strategic issues E.g. greenhouse gas emissions, designated sites of national importance.	Minimise adverse strategic impact	Increase in CO_2 emissions (2% peak hour). Loss of 73ha from SSSI.	Reduced CO_2 emissions (4% peak hour). Loss of 22ha from SSSI.	Large reduction in CO_2 emissions (16% peak hour). No landtake from SSSI.	Reduced CO_2 emissions (8% peak hour). Loss of 1.2ha from SSSI.
Economic: Local issues	Maximise traveller benefits Maximise accident savings	Traveller benefits: £440m Accident cost savings: £56m	Traveller benefits: £1,038m Accident cost savings: £83m	Traveller benefits: £3,556m Accident cost savings: £241m	Traveller benefits: £464m Accident cost savings: £74m
Economic: Strategic issues Capital cost of scenarios (undiscounted)	Maximise economic value	Net present value of: £273m	Net present value of: £1,103m	Net present value of: £549m	Net present value of: £1,332m
Total		£340m	£930m	£176m	£653m
Attributed		£340m	£255m	£176m	£129m

Source: Ove Arup (1999)

(e.g. the UK Sustainable Communities Plan); and a programme is a set of projects in a particular area (e.g. housing projects in the Milton Keynes sub-region). In theory PPPs are tiered, as illustrated in Figure 12.5, with, for example, the UK government's road policies, set out in its White Paper on roads, giving rise to suggested road schemes, which are then incorporated in a national roads programme, which in turn provides a basis for specific routes, for which project EIAs are prepared (Glasson *et al*. 1999). In practice, the boundaries between tiers are often unclear and, as will be noted later, there has been a marked reluctance by governments to engage in SEA at the policy level.

The EU SEA directive and its precursors

As for NEPA in the USA, it was the initial EC intention that one European directive would cover projects *and* PPPs, but member states' agreement was only possible with a directive restricted to projects only. Ever since, the EC/EU has been seeking to bring in the more strategic level of assessment, and Directive 2001/42/EC "on the assessment of the effects of certain plans and programmes on the environment" (CEC 2001) was finally passed on 21 July 2001, to become fully operational three years later. However, over the 20-year period the EC/EU has sought to advance SEA in various ways. The EC's Environment Directorate General (DGXI) established internal procedures for the Commission whereby (a) all DGs must examine their PPPs' environmental repercussions at the time when the PPPs are first conceived and (b) any proposed PPP which is likely to have a significant environmental impact is marked with a "green star", and the impact discussed and justified in the accompanying documentation. However, not much information exists about the "green star" system. Rather more transparent is the

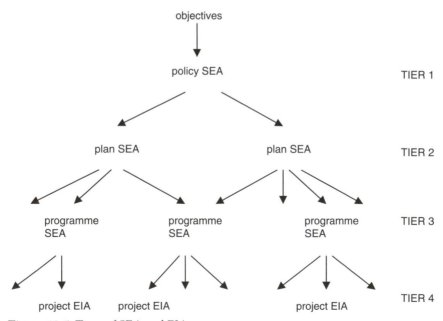

Figure 12.5 Tiers of SEA and EIA
Source: Glasson *et al*. 2005, after Wood 1991

operation of the procedure required by DGXI that Structural Fund applications should be accompanied by an "environmental profile".

The EU is on an "integration path", moving from a free trade area to various degrees of economic and monetary, and to some extent political, union. It is also growing in terms of member states and population, with an increase to 27 members and a population of almost 500 million with the addition of the accession states in 2004 and 2007. But the removal of barriers to trade and factor movements, and the addition of member states with low GDP, can also emphasise the "centre–periphery" model of differential prosperity. The EU must be fair as well as free, and over time a counterbalancing regional policy has developed to aid the problem regions in member states. EU regional policy uses a variety of mechanisms known collectively as the Structural Funds – the European Regional Development Fund (ERDF), the European Social Fund (ESF), the Cohesion Fund and others – to support investment in infrastructure in the regions. The funding is now immense – almost half of the EU budget – and is targeted at the most disadvantaged (Objective 1) regions. But the resultant infra-structure – high-speed rail systems, major roads, energy facilities and the like – can have serious environmental impacts. Because of this, since 1995 member states have had to produce an "environmental profile" to accompany the regional development plans which pull together investment requirements for problem regions/sub-regions, and which are required in order to access Struc-tural Funds. The profile requires a description and discussion of: (i) key environmental issues (e.g. designated environmental areas); (ii) the environmental impact of the regional development plan; and (iii) the relevant legal and adminis-trative framework for environmental policy and regional planning.

The SEA Directive, which became operational from July 2004, applies to plans and programmes in member states, including regional plans, but agreement could not be reached on the inclusion of policies. The directive relates to plans and programmes for agriculture, forestry, fisheries, energy, industry, transport, waste management, telecommunications, tourism, town and country planning or land use. Just what is included in this list will vary between member states, probably only becoming clear over time through precedent and lawsuit. The directive's requirements are summarised in Table 12.3. Draft plans and pro-grammes must be accompanied by an "environmental report" that discusses the baseline, the likely effects of the plans and programmes, and alternative options, mitigation measures and monitoring arrangements.

SEA implementation in the UK

The SEA Directive is being implemented through different regulations in each devolved administration (England, Scotland, Wales and Northern Ireland), and through additional guidance documents prepared by different government agencies for their specific plans and programmes (Therivel 2004). Guidance for land-use plans in England, including the new generation of local development frameworks (LDFs) and regional spatial strategies (RSSs) required under the Planning and Compulsory Purchase Act, has been provided by the Office of the Deputy Prime Minister (ODPM 2003). Other guidance has been prepared for Scottish development plans (Scottish Executive 2003), and for local transport plans (DfT 2004), and more is being developed. Table 12.4 summarises the

Table 12.3 Requirements of the EU SEA Directive

Preparing an environmental report in which the likely significant effects on the environment of implementing the plan, and reasonable alternatives taking into account the objectives and geographical scope of the plan, are identified, described and evaluated. The information to be given is (Article 5 and Annex I):

a. an outline of the contents, main objectives of the plan, and relationship with other relevant plans and programmes;
b. the relevant aspects of the current state of the environment and the likely evolution thereof without implementation of the plan;
c. the environment characteristics of areas likely to be significantly affected;
d. any existing environmental problems which are relevant to the plan including, in particular, those relating to any areas of a particular environmental importance, such as areas designated pursuant to Directives 79/409/EEC and 92/43 EEC;
e. the environmental protection objectives, established at international, Community or national level, which are relevant to the plan and the way those objectives and any environmental considerations have been taken into account during its preparation;
f. the likely significant effect on the environment, including on issues such as biodiversity, population, human health, fauna, flora, soil, water, air, climatic factors, material assets, cultural heritage including architectural and archaeological heritage, landscape and the interrelationship between the above factors (these effects should include secondary, cumulative, synergistic and short-, medium- and long-term permanent and temporary, positive and negative effects);
g. the measures envisaged to prevent, reduce and as fully as possible offset any significant adverse effects on the environment of implementing the plan;
h. an outline of the reasons for selecting the alternatives dealt with, and a description of how the assessment was undertaken, including any difficulties (such as technical deficiencies or lack of know-how) encountered in compiling the required information;
i. a description of measures envisaged concerning monitoring in accordance with Article 10;
j. a non-technical summary of the information provided under the above heading.

The report shall include the information that may reasonably be required taking into account current knowledge and methods of assessment, the contents and level of detail in the plan, its stage in the decision-making process and the extent to which certain matters are more appropriately assessed at different levels in that process to avoid duplication of the assessment (Article 5.2).

Consultation:
– Authorities with environmental responsibilities, when deciding on the scope and level of detail of the information which must be included in the environmental report (Article 5.4).
– Authorities with environmental responsibilities and the public shall be given an early and effective opportunity within appropriate time frames to express their opinion on the draft plan or programme and the accompanying environmental report before the adoption of the plan or programme (Article 6.1, 6.2).
– Other EU member states, where the implementation of the plan or programme is likely to have significant effects on the environment in that countries (Article 7).

Taking the environmental report and the results of the consultations into account in decision making (Article 8).

Provision of information on the decisions
When the plan or programme is adopted, the public and any countries consulted shall be informed and the following made available to those so informed:

– the plan or programme as adopted;
– a statement summarising how environmental considerations have been integrated into the plan or programme and how the environmental report pursuant to Article 5, the opinions expressed pursuant to Article 6 and the results of consultations entered into pursuant to Article 7 have been taken into account in accordance with Article 8, and the reasons for choosing the plan as adopted, in the light of the other reasonable alternatives dealt with; and
– the measures decided concerning monitoring (Articles 9 and 10).

Monitoring the significant environmental effects of the plan's or programme's implementation (Article 10).

Quality assurance: environmental reports should be of a sufficient standard to meet the requirements of the SEA Directive (Article 12).

Source: ODPM 2005a

Table 12.4 Contents of the guidance on SEA of English land-use plans

1 *Introduction*
   Purpose of the practical guide
   Other guidance on SEA
   Acknowledgements
2 *Background and context*
   Objectives and requirements
   The directive's field of application
   Provisions on screening and exemptions
   The directive and SEA practice
   Who should do SEA?
   The level of detail in SEA
   SEA and other forms of assessment
   The regulatory impact of the directive
3 *SEA and consultation*
   Requirements for consultation
   The consultation bodies
   Consulting the public
   Practical aspects of consultation
   Transboundary consultation with EU member states
4 *SEA and sustainable development*
5 *Stages of SEA*
   Introduction
   Stage A: Setting the context and objectives, establishing the baseline and deciding
           on the scope
   Stage B: Developing and refining alternatives and assessing effects
   Stage C: Preparing the environmental report
   Stage D: Consultation and decision making
   Stage E: Monitoring implementation of the plan or programme
EC directives and other international instruments related to the SEA Directive
Glossary
Appendices
   1 Indicative list of plans and programmes subject to the SEA Directive
   2 Other relevant plans, programmes and environmental protection objectives
   3 Collecting and presenting baseline information
   4 Sources of baseline information
   5 Developing SEA objectives, indicators and targets

Table 12.4 – *continued*

---

6 Developing and assessing alternatives
7 Prediction and evaluation of effects
8 Assessing secondary, cumulative and synergistic effects
9 Quality assurance checklist
10 Monitoring
Frequently asked questions on the SEA Directive
References and further information
The SEA Directive

Source: ODPM 2005a

contents of the ODPM (2005a) guidance. The guidance provides stage-by-stage advice, supplemented by very useful information on techniques, methods and sources in the appendices. Table 12.5 outlines the five key stages.

At the time of writing, only one year after the implementation of the directive, there is only limited documentation of SEAs of land-use plans. Aided by a growing cohort of environmental consultancies with appropriate expertise, some local and regional planning authorities are beginning to come to terms with the directive's requirements. There are reasons to be hopeful that SEA can help to make a more rigorous environmental case, to consider real alternatives, to be open and consultative, and to become a more efficient process as experience develops (Levett 2005).

Table 12.5 Stages in the SEA process

A. *Setting the context and objectives, establishing the baseline and deciding on the scope*
   Identifying other relevant plans, programmes and environmental protection
      objectives
   Collecting baseline information
   Identifying environmental problems
   Developing SEA objectives
   Consulting on the scope of SEA
B. *Developing and refining alternatives and assessing effects*
   Testing the plan or programme objectives against the SEA objectives
   Developing strategic alternatives
   Predicting the effects of the plan or programme, including alternatives
   Evaluating the effects of the plan or programme, including alternatives
   Mitigating adverse effects
   Proposing measures to monitor the environmental effects of the plan or
      programme implementation
C. *Preparing the environmental report*
   Preparing the environmental report
D. *Consultation on the draft plan or programme and the environmental report*
   Consulting the public and consultation bodies on the draft plan or programme
      and the environmental report
   Assessing significant changes
   Making decisions and providing information
E. *Monitoring the significant effects of implementing the plan or programme on the
      environment*
   Developing aims and methods for monitoring
   Responding to adverse effects

Source: ODPM 2005a

However, SEA does pose a number of challenges to practice. In particular, the ODPM guidance stresses the importance of integrating SEA fully into the plan-making process – making inputs at each stage where decisions are taken. It should also be integrated with sustainability appraisal (SA) to provide an integrated treatment of environmental issues, together with economic and social issues. The chapter now considers this very important SA approach, and its relationship with SEA.

Sustainability appraisal: widening the scope of assessment

Towards sustainability appraisal

During the 1990s there was an evolution of UK government guidance on the "environmental appraisal" of development plans, prior to the introduction of the requirements of the SEA Directive. The evolution was begun with PPG12: *Development plans and regional planning guidance* (DoE 1992), which required authorities to carry out such appraisal. It was followed by *Environmental appraisal of development plans: a good practice guide* (DoE 1993), which outlined the nature of such appraisal – including identification of a wide range of environmental components (e.g. air quality, urban "liveability") and various matrix approaches to assess plan policies/objectives against the components, and against each other. In 1999, PPG12 was revised; it advised authorities to consider a range of social, economic and environmental effects in a broader "sustainability appraisal". This harmonised with the objectives of the "strategy for sustainable development in the UK" (DETR 1999) noted earlier. By the end of 2001 most local authorities in England and Wales and all regional authorities had had some experience with appraisal (Therivel and Minas 2002).

Guidance on sustainability appraisal

Under the Planning and Compulsory Purchase Act 2004, SA is mandatory for RSSs, development plan documents (DPDs) and supplementary planning documents (SPDs). Final guidance (ODPM 2005b) sets out the nature of such appraisal, which has been designed to satisfy the requirements of both SA and SEA (as required under the SEA Directive) in a single process. As such, the SA guidance incorporates the SEA guidance noted earlier (ODPM 2005a).

The SA guidance stresses that SA is an integral part of good plan making and should not be seen as a separate activity. Figure 12.6 provides an overview of the SA process. SA is seen as taking a long-term view of the development of the area covered by a plan, taking into account the social, economic and environmental effects of the proposed plan. As with plan making, to be most effective SA should be (after ODPM 2004):

- *objectives-led:* so that the direction of desired change is made explicit and targets may be set;
- *iterative:* a process through which successive stages and drafts of the plan can be appraised with the aim of producing more sustainable outcomes;

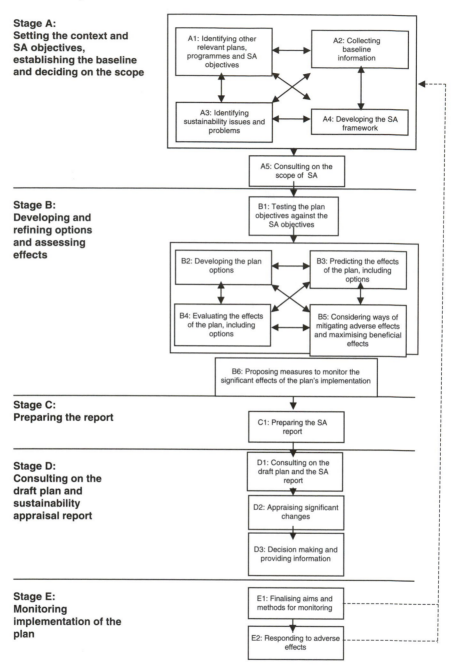

Stage A:
Setting the context and
SA objectives,
establishing the baseline
and deciding on the scope

A1: Identifying other relevant plans, programmes and SA objectives

A2: Collecting baseline information

A3: Identifying sustainability issues and problems

A4: Developing the SA framework

A5: Consulting on the scope of SA

Stage B:
Developing and
refining options
and assessing
effects

B1: Testing the plan objectives against the SA objectives

B2: Developing the plan options

B3: Predicting the effects of the plan, including options

B4: Evaluating the effects of the plan, including options

B5: Considering ways of mitigating adverse effects and maximising beneficial effects

B6: Proposing measures to monitor the significant effects of the plan's implementation

Stage C:
Preparing the report

C1: Preparing the SA report

Stage D:
Consulting on the
draft plan and
sustainability
appraisal report

D1: Consulting on the draft plan and the SA report

D2: Appraising significant changes

D3: Decision making and providing information

Stage E:
Monitoring
implementation of the
plan

E1: Finalising aims and methods for monitoring

E2: Responding to adverse effects

Figure 12.6 The sustainability appraisal process – stages and tasks
Source: ODPM 2005b

- *evidence-based*: including relevant baseline information against which the potential effects of the plan and plan options can be measured and assessed;

- *inclusive*: including early and ongoing involvement of the public, statutory authorities and other relevant stakeholders at appropriate stages;
- *timely*: programmed alongside the whole of the plan preparation process so that the results are taken into account;
- *transparent*: based on tools and methods that can be easily understood, and that meet the requirements of the SEA Directive;
- *independent*: involving an objective and balanced consideration of the issues and the plan; and
- *useful*: providing clear conclusions and recommendations on how the plan can be altered to increase sustainability, and on future monitoring.

The implementation of the guidance is in its early stages. The establishment of the baseline of relevant data and indicators can be a substantial exercise, especially for the pioneering studies, although the array of information sources is improving rapidly. The later stages of the process raise important issues of weight given to different objectives of sustainable development. There can be a fear from "environmental stakeholders" that environmental objectives may be squeezed out by what are seen as more pressing and immediate social and economic objectives. The guidance stresses that "no one of these objectives is more important than the other. Although there can be tensions between them, in the long term success in one is dependent on the others" (ODPM 2004).

Current practice of SA for RSSs

The East of England Plan (EERA 2004a) has provided an early example of the SA approach. The Plan is for a region under continuing and heavy growth pressure. The East of England includes elements of some of the major growth areas in the Sustainable Communities Plan (ODPM 2003), especially at Thames Gateway and Milton Keynes/South Midlands, plus the likely impacts of airport growth at Stansted. The Plan envisages 476,000 new houses and 421,000 new jobs over the 20-year plan period. The SA of the Plan started in 2002, and a sustainability appraisal report was completed in late 2004 (EERA 2004b). The long process has produced a long SA report – 800 pages, with 138 sustainability indicators and 124 policies assessed. The overall assessment had quite an impact in the media. Whilst the majority of the policy impacts were assessed as positive – for example, "aiming to bring employment, housing, amenities and services into better balance with each other in each part of the region" and "support for key sustainability principles of reducing the need to travel, conservation of important environmental assets, and preparing for climate change" – there were some issues. Identified serious problems included: water resources, flood risks, quantity of movement to be accommodated, urbanisation and competition for land. Overall the SA identified well some of the major impacts of the Plan and the vital importance of appropriate infrastructure investment, particularly in public transport. It also pioneered the SA approach, but hopefully it will not set a precedent for 800-page documents!

The RSS for the South East of England, known as the South East Plan, was issued as a consultation draft in early 2005 (SEERA 2005). The task of the Plan was to provide a framework for the development of this most dynamic region for the period to 2026. The region has been typified as the "locomotive" of the UK economy; it has a population of over 8,000,000 people, and includes all or parts of the major growth areas identified in the Sustainable Communities Plan (ODPM 2003), at Ashford, Milton Keynes/South Midlands and especially Thames Gateway. Projected population increase between 2001/2 and 2026/7 could be of the order of 1,000,000, with the increase in number of households not much less, at about 800,000. The affordable housing of the current population plus anticipated growth is a major issue for this congested region.

The SA for the South East used an integrated approach which not only brought together SA and SEA, but also included health impact assessment (HIA) – to consider the potential impacts of policies on people's health and well-being and on health inequalities (Figure 12.7). The aim was to provide an efficient and clear process, with an evidence base that covered a wide number of areas and which ensured equal attention for the different aspects of sustainability. The SA considered a range of policy options derived from three different annual rates of housing growth and two spatial options – continuation of existing policies, and a sharper focus on sub-regions with particular economic potential and/or regeneration needs. The assessment framework considered the options against a list of regional sustainability objectives (see Table 12.6). These were derived from earlier work in the region – the regional sustainable development framework (SEERA 2001) and the integrated regional framework (IRF) (SEERA 2004a) – which translated the national Sustainable Development Strategy into a set of 25 objectives, indicators and targets for the region. The analysis to date shows the inherent tensions between the Plan's objectives of promoting economic growth and improving social conditions – which rely on the development of housing and other infrastructure – and the objectives to protect environmental assets and promote environmental sustainability. The SA has also been conducted for the sub-regional strategies in the Plan. Overall, the Plan is proving even more controversial than that for the East of England, with the levels of housing growth and the infrastructure deficit at the forefront of the debate.

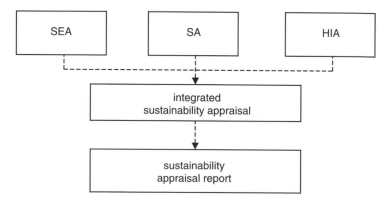

Figure 12.7 South East Plan – structure of sustainability appraisal process
Source: SEERA 2005

Table 12.6 Extracts from regional options and policy assessment framework in SE Plan

	Does the plan . . .?		*Comments*
1	ensure that everyone has the opportunity to live in a decent, sustainably constructed and affordable home?	?	Housing policies are generally supportive of this objective, although it is recommended that the Vision aspire to achieving decent housing for all. However, options based on the lower growth levels (e.g. 25,500 per year) will not be sufficient to meet housing needs across the region, and affordable housing shortages will worsen.
4	reduce poverty and social exclusion and close the gap between the most deprived areas in the South East and the rest of the region?	✗	Although the Plan recognises the importance of the issue, there is little emphasis on this in the economic development policies, and none of the spatial options seek to focus development in such a way that deprived communities within the region would particularly benefit. In broad terms, the Plan appears to be based on an assumption that, by supporting economic growth across the South East as a whole, deprived communities within the region will naturally also benefit. This assumption is not necessarily true and, moreover, a continuation of current economic growth patterns within the region will exacerbate, rather than reduce, inequalities in health.
10	improve efficiency in land use through the reuse of previously developed land and existing buildings, including reuse of materials from buildings, and encourage urban renaissance?	✓	The policy framework covers many key issues, including urban renaissance, reuse of land and the quality of the built environment. However, many of the policies are recommendations rather than requirements.
12	address the causes of climate change through reducing emissions of greenhouse gases and ensure that the South East is prepared for its impacts?	✗	The policy framework sets out policies to reduce greenhouse gas emissions and to adapt to climate change. However, even if these policies are implemented, continued development within the region will inevitably lead to increased CO_2 emissions through domestic energy use, transport, etc. The Plan does not provide any answers to how economic development and greenhouse gas emissions might be "decoupled". Climate change adaptation issues have been addressed more effectively, and are discussed under questions 2 and 18.

Table 12.6 – *continued*

Does the plan . . .?		Comments
20 ensure high and stable levels of employment so everyone can benefit from the economic growth of the region?	✓	The Plan is clearly designed to deliver a regional GVA growth rate of 3% p.a. and to improve the region's competitiveness, which if achieved is likely to produce more employment opportunities and encourage in-migration within the region as a whole. Policies are in place to support access to the labour market, and the spatial options provide housing growth to support labour market expansion, although the lower growth rates are unlikely to meet all the housing requirements of the region's economy
21 sustain economic growth and competitive-ness across the region?		if higher economic growth rates were expected. It is less clear whether all communities within the South East will benefit from employment and economic growth, as the Plan does not have a strong focus on those parts of the region which suffer from deprivation.

Key:
✓ overall impact likely to be positive
? overall impact neutral, mixed or unclear
✗ overall impact likely to be negative
Source: SEERA 2004b

Conclusions: summary and future

The regional and sub-regional levels of planning can be particularly appropriate levels of planning for the delivery of sustainable development. Institutional innovations, for example the introduction of regional assemblies and the production of statutory regional spatial strategies in England, can provide vehicles for the pursuit of a more holistic approach with more integration of the environmental, social and economic dimensions of development. The procedures, methods and techniques of sustainability assessment can provide the means to integrate the consideration of sustainable development into the planning process.

The progress to date shows a widening both in activity scope from the narrow project focus of EIA to the wider strategic plan and programme, higher-tier focus of SEA/SA, and in content scope from the primarily bio-physical focus of early EIA activity to more holistic approaches – for EIA, to some extent for SEA, and for SA. EIA now has considerable support from the range of stakeholders involved, and major projects of strategic significance can be substantially modified through the process to improve their sustainability. However, EIA does have some limitations, as noted in this chapter. SEA/SA can provide a more proactive strategic approach. Practice is much more limited than for EIA, but the SEA Directive and the introduction of UK SEA and SA guidance should accelerate good practice. Hopefully such practice will be well integrated with the planning process to deliver innovative and sustainable regional development and planning. SEA/SA can help to make a better plan to achieve better quality of life and environmental outcomes, but such plans need stakeholder commitment and implementation. Much depends on national policy responses to the constraints on sustainable development, including the vital issue of infrastructure funding.

References

Benneworth, P., L. Conroy and P. Roberts 2002. Strategic connectivity, sustainability development and the new English regional governance. *Journal of Environmental Planning and Management* **45**(2), 199–217.

Campbell, S. 1991. Integrating economic and environmental planning: the regional perspective. Paper presented to the Joint ACSP and AESOP Congress, Oxford.

Campbell, S. 2003. Green cities, growing cities, just cities? Urban planning and the contradictions of sustainable development, in *Readings in planning theory*, 2nd edn, S. Campbell and S. Fainstein (eds). Oxford: Blackwell.

CEC 1985. On the assessment of the effects of certain public and private projects on the environment. *Official Journal*, L175. 5 June. Brussels: Commission of the European Communities.

CEC 1993. *Report from the Commission of the Implementation of Directive 85/3373/EEC on the assessment of the effects of certain public and private projects on the environment.* COM (93), 28 Final. Brussels: Commission of the European Communities.

CEC 1997. Council Directive 97/11/EC of 3 March 1997 amending Directive 85/337/EEC on the assessment of certain public and private projects on the environment. *Official Journal*, L73/5. 3 March. Brussels: Commission of the European Communities.

CEC 2001. *Directive 2001/42/EC on the assessment of the effects of certain plans and programmes on the environment.* Brussels: Commission of the European Communities.

CEC 2003. (Impacts Assessment Unit, Oxford Brookes University). *Five years report to the European Parliament and the Council on the application and effectiveness of the EIA Directive* (http://europa.eu.int/comm/environment/eia/home.htm).

Chadwick, A. 2002. Socio-economic impacts: are they still the poor relations in UK environmental statements? *Journal of Environmental Planning and Management* **45**(1), 3–24.

Clement, K. and M. Hansen 2001. *Sustainable regional development in Nordic countries.* Nordregio Report 8. Stockholm: Nordregio.

DEFRA 2005. *Securing the future: delivering the UK sustainable development strategy.* London: Department of Environment, Food and Rural Affairs.

DETR 1998. *New appraisal framework.* London: Department of Environment, Transport and the Regions.

DETR 1999. *A better quality of life: a strategy for sustainable development in the UK.* London: Department of Environment, Transport and the Regions.

DfT 2004. *SEA guidance for transport plans and programmes.* London: Department for Transport.

DoE 1992. *Development plans and regional planning guidance.* PPG12. Department of the Environment. London: HMSO.

DoE 1993. *Environmental appraisal of development plans: a good practice guide.* London: Department of the Environment.

DoE 1996. *Changes in the quality of environmental impact statements.* Department of the Environment. London: HMSO.

EEA 2003. *Europe's environment: the third assessment.* Copenhagen: European Environment Agency.

EERA 2004a. *East of England Plan.* Norwich: East of England Regional Assembly.

EERA 2004b. *East of England Plan: sustainability appraisal report.* Norwich: East of England Regional Assembly.

Friedmann, J. and C. Weaver 1979. *Territory and function: the evolution of regional planning*. London: Arnold.

Glasson, J. 1995. Regional planning and the environment: time for a SEA change. *Urban Studies* **32**(4–5), 713–31.

Glasson, J. 2005. Better monitoring for better impact management: the local socio-economic aspects of constructing Sizewell B nuclear power station. *Impact Assessment and Project Appraisal* **23**(3), 215–26.

Glasson, J. and J. Gosling 2001. SEA and regional planning: overcoming the institutional constraints – some lessons from the EU. *Journal of European Environmental Policy* **11**(2), 89–102.

Glasson, J. and C. Bellanger 2003. Divergent practice in a converging system? The case of EIA in France and the UK. *EIA Review* **23**, 605–24.

Glasson, J., R. Therivel and A. Chadwick 1999. *An introduction to environmental impact assessment*, 2nd edn. London: ECL Press.

Glasson, J., R. Therivel and A. Chadwick 2005. *An introduction to environmental impact assessment*, 3rd edn. London: Spon Press.

Hardy, S. and G. Lloyd 1994. An impossible dream? Sustainable regional economic and environmental development. *Regional Studies* **28**(8), 773–80.

Harvie, C. 1991. English regionalism: the dog that never barked. In *National identities: the constitution of the UK*, B. Crick (ed.). Oxford: Blackwell.

IUCN 1980. *World Conservation Strategy*. Geneva: International Union for the Conservation of Nature.

Jenkins, B., D. Annandale and A. Morrison-Saunders 2003. The evolution of a sustainability assessment strategy for Western Australia. *Australian Environmental Planning Law Journal* **20**, 56–65.

Levett, R. 2005. Making SEA worth the effort. Paper presented at Conference on SEA: The First 6 Months, Oxford Brookes University, Oxford.

Lowe, P. and S. Ward 1998. *British environmental policy and Europe*. London: Routledge.

MacNaughton, P., R. Grove-White, M. Jacobs and B. Wynne 1997. Sustainability and indicators. Chapter 8 in *Green management: a reader*, P. McDonagh and A. Prothero (eds). London: Dryden Press.

OAS 1984. *Integrated regional development planning: guidelines and case studies from OAS experience*. Washington, DC: Organization of American States.

ODPM 2003. *Sustainable communities: building for the future*. London: Office of the Deputy Prime Minister.

ODPM 2004. *Sustainability appraisal of regional spatial strategies and local development frameworks: consultation paper*. London: Office of the Deputy Prime Minister.

ODPM 2005a. *A practical guide to the Strategic Environmental Assessment Directive*. London: Office of the Deputy Prime Minister.

ODPM 2005b. *Sustainability appraisal of regional spatial strategies and local development documents*. London: Office of the Deputy Prime Minister.

Odum, W. 1982. Environmental degradation and the tyranny of small decisions. *Bio Science* **32**, 728–9.

Ove Arup 1999. *M4 motorway between Magor and Castleton: common appraisal framework study – summary report*. Cardiff: Welsh Office.

Pezzoli, K. 1996. Sustainable development: a transdisciplinary overview of the literature. Paper presented to the Joint ACSP and AESOP Congress, Toronto.

Piper, J. 2000. Cumulative effects assessment on the Middle Humber: barriers overcome, benefits derived. *Journal of Environmental Planning and Management* **43**(3), 369–87.

Pope, J., D. Annandale and A. Morrison-Saunders 2004. Conceptualising sustainability assessment, *EIA Review* **24**, 596–616.

Roberts, P. 1994. Sustainable regional planning. *Regional Studies* **28**(8), 781–7.

Sadler, B. and R. Verheem 1996. *SEA: status, challenges and future directions*. Report 53. The Hague: Ministry of Housing, Spatial Planning and Environment.

Scottish Executive 2003. *Environmental assessment of development plans: interim planning advice*. Edinburgh: Scottish Executive.

SEERA 2001. *A better quality of life in the South East*. Guildford: South East England Regional Assembly.

SEERA 2003. *From crisis to cutting edge*. Guildford: South East England Regional Assembly.

SEERA 2004a. *Integrated regional framework (IRF)*. Guildford: South East England Regional Assembly.

SEERA 2004b. *Sustainability appraisal of the consultation draft South East Plan: non-technical summary*. Guildford: South East England Regional Assembly.

SEERA 2005. *The South East Plan: consultation draft*. Guildford: South East England Regional Assembly.

Therivel, R. 2004. *Strategic environmental assessment in action*. London: Earthscan.

Therivel, R. and P. Minas 2002. Ensuring effective sustainability appraisal. *Impact Assessment and Project Appraisal* **19**(2), 81–91.

Todes, A., 2004. Regional planning and sustainability: limits and potentials of South Africa's integrated development plans. *Journal of Environmental Planning and Management* **47**(6), 843–61.

Trudgill, R. 1990. *Barriers to a better environment: what stops us solving environmental problems?* London: Belhaven Press.

UN World Commission on Environment and Development 1987. *Our common future* (Brundtland Report). Oxford: Oxford University Press.

US National Research Council 2002. *Our common journey: transition towards sustainability*. Washington, DC: National Academy Press.

Vanclay, F. 2003. International principles for social impact assessment. *Impact Assessment and Project Appraisal* **21**(1), 5–12.

Wang, Y., J. Byrne and S. Wagle 1993. Towards a politics of sustainability: the responsibilities of industrialised countries. *Regions* **183**, 4–7.

Wood, C. 1991. EIA of policies, plans and programmes. *EIA Newsletter* **5**, 2–3. Manchester: University of Manchester.

Wood, C. 2003. *Environmental impact assessment: a comparative review*, 2nd edn. Harlow: Prentice Hall.

Part 5

Strategic and regional planning in practice

13 Strategic and regional planning in the Greater South East

Robin Thompson

Introduction

The wider South East comprises London and the metropolitan region (see Figure 13.1). It is an exceptionally large and unusually diverse region. Its population of 18.5 million is larger than that of many nation states. The different parts of the region exhibit a wide range of social, geographical and economic characteristics. These vary, for example, from the wealthy and economically dynamic areas of Central and West London and the Thames Valley to the relatively deprived and economically depressed parts of the Thames Gateway and of the Isle of Thanet to the east.

Strategic planning at the regional level seeks to identify a clear long-term spatial strategy for a defined territory. It has to address issues of complexity, uncertainty and ambiguity, yet achieve a sufficiently simple and clear direction,

Figure 13.1 Regions of the Greater (or wider) South East.
Source: Prepared by GLA DMAG

so that stakeholders can understand and support it in the use of their own powers and resources. One definition of regional planning is "an exercise in persuasion, seeking to encourage those agencies with the power to act and manage regional development to adopt and use agreed strategies and to follow particular guidance" (Glasson 2002: 247).

Strategic planning for the wider South East has to meet some particularly complex challenges. The boundaries of the region have been continuously disputed and no single institution is currently charged with responsibility for it. The region itself has pronounced differences in economic performance, social composition and environment, for example between the east and west. Moreover there is fierce dispute over the dominant policy issue of how to accommodate housing growth. The phenomenon of growth is itself complex, with high rates of in-migration, especially from overseas, and out-migration.

For most of the last century, geographers and planners worked on the basis that there was a mono-centric city region with London as its core city and with a hinterland that expanded as London suburbanised and deurbanised into its surrounding areas. More recently, this model has been replaced with the concept of a single "mega city region" (Hall and Pain 2006) within which rapid communications, economic liberalisation and technical advances have generated dense flows of people, goods and information. In this model, the settlements of the region are seen as tightly interconnected. Indeed, the wider South East has also been characterised as a "polycentric urban region", in which London continues to occupy the core city role above a hierarchy of other cities and towns, all of which interact with each other (Davoudi 2003).

The region is too large and too central to the national economy for government to permit it substantial autonomy. Moreover, London's world city role means that vast numbers of its transactions are made across the globe with no regard for regional boundaries. London increasingly performs the role of a world city (Sassen 2001). Central London has become one of a small number of focal points for global business. Its ability to provide highly developed specialist support systems for international finance and business has generated growth that is of critical importance to the national economy as a whole.

Roberts in Chapter 7 distinguishes between a national/regional preoccupation with economic planning at the regional level and a regional/local concern with physical planning. This has certainly been true in the Greater South East, with national government making regular interventions, primarily to promote economic competitiveness. London's role as the capital city and national centre for government, business and finance, arts and culture, tourism and education has reinforced Whitehall's wish to see London and its hinterland perform its national functions effectively. Conversely local government has tended to be preoccupied with physical containment of growth.

Indeed, Newman and Thornley (2005) suggest there is a "global/local" tension in London with pressures from international business and finance interests that seek ever-stronger economic competitiveness. The "new regionalism", discussed in Chapter 5, sees leading agencies in the market sector participating increasingly in regional matters. It follows that, in the Greater South East, regional planning policy has to engage with large, powerful and international private sector agencies. So, for example, any attempt to constrain economic growth through regional planning instruments would need to demonstrate extraordinary persuasiveness if it is to satisfy this set of private sector stakeholders that market interests would not be threatened.

This chapter looks at the strategic planning of the wider South East and at the ways in which this has sought to address the region's complexities and to reconcile the powerful differences between stakeholders about key objectives of regional policy. The daunting task of "persuading" the region's multitudinous agencies is made still more demanding by a central and enduring policy issue upon which there are powerful divisions. The persistent growth of the population and economy of the region, especially of London, has always generated arguments between the advocates of continued growth and the proponents of constraint and environmental protection (Wannop 1995). These arguments tend to be persistent and often bitter. Finding a regional planning direction that can successfully negotiate between these two standpoints has proved to be extraordinarily difficult (see Chapter 12).

This discussion also examines attempts to manage the central issue of growth in the London city region: the containment of that growth through spatial strategies that include protection through the green belt and rural conservation and the accommodation of growth through planned dispersal across the wider region. It examines alternative strategic techniques of, on the one hand, imposition of a clear regional policy through a top-down approach using strong and deterministic plans and, on the other hand, attempts to find a bottom-up consensual approach. The chapter also discusses the search for a regional planning mechanism that is powerful enough to set a clear agenda but that is not so powerful that it threatens other major stakeholders at both national and local level. The chapter particularly focuses on recent and current regional policy and mechanisms and assesses their effectiveness.

The evolution of regional planning in the Greater South East

Much of the time, there has been denial of the need for strategic planning for the South East. The struggle to gain acceptance of the need for a plan for the wider London region has a long history. For much of the last century the concept of a comprehensive plan for the wider metropolitan area failed to take hold, despite the expansion of London. After the formation of the London County Council (LCC) in 1889, London's physical area continued to grow. However, proposals to extend the LCC area in line with that growth were resisted, most especially in the suburban areas beyond the LCC boundary that had no desire to be swallowed up into a metropolitan authority.

The most powerful exercise in strategic regional planning over the early decades of the last century was that of Ebenezer Howard, rather than that of any regional planning institution. His vision of planned development of garden cities offered a clear and simple strategy as a means of management of London's decentralisation (Howard 1902). Indeed it provided an enduring "metaphor" for urban management. However, there was no authoritative body with the power to take forward Howard's vision in a comprehensive way over a sustained period of time.

It was the need for strategic and regional planning generated by the Second World War that stimulated the first effective efforts at a formal regional plan for the Greater South East. It was central government rather than the regional planning committee that gave the impetus for the preparation of a Greater London Plan by Patrick Abercrombie. Abercrombie's celebrated plan of 1944 articulated a strong regional policy. It envisaged a strategy of decentralisation into satellite towns. A green belt would restrain tendencies towards the further outward sprawl of London. These central themes were adopted by central government. In particular it drove the implementation forward through the new town development corporations.

Despite its almost mythological status amongst planners and despite the vigour of the subsequent new towns programme, the spatial concepts of the Abercrombie Plan were to a significant extent frustrated by two factors. Firstly, Abercrombie made little attempt to engage the local planning authorities in the formation of his plan and instead proposed a regional planning board, which would be charged with its implementation. This proposal was thwarted by the LCC and by other entrenched local authority interests. These local constituencies were unwilling to cede powers to a regional authority. The complexity of the operational context for the plan was not appreciated. Secondly, Abercrombie's plan was technically deterministic – i.e. a regional "design" imposed upon the existing fabric. In practice, the world did not behave as the master-planner's vision suggested it should. For example, demographic change and the market economy actually generated a much faster rate of decentralisation than his plan had envisaged. The exercise did not allow for future uncertainty. Despite the erosion of some of its provisions, however, the Abercrombie Plan provided an extremely potent set of concepts about the accommodation of growth. It can be argued that the South East has been "living off the capacity created by the Abercrombie Plan" ever since (Williams 2002: 226).

As already pointed out in earlier chapters of this book, the Conservative governments of the 1950s had a strong aversion to regional planning. Nevertheless, the problems created by London's growth were increasingly difficult to ignore. They included matters of sensitivity to the government such as protection of the green belt. Eventually, the Standing Conference on London Regional Planning was created in 1961. It was to prove an enduring body, albeit one whose nature changed.

Finally, the government bowed to the logic that London had entirely outgrown the boundary of the LCC. The 1964 South East Study revealed that only 3 million of the "London region's" 18 million population lived inside the LCC boundary. However, the Conservative government's creation of the new Greater London Council in 1965 was less motivated by regional planning considerations than by political influences. The exodus of affluent voters out of the LCC area and into the hinterland was progressively reducing the prospects of a Conservative majority on the LCC. The new Greater London boundary captured many of these voters, but was more tightly drawn than one that would have reflected a coherent metropolitan authority. The Greater London Council was given relatively modest planning powers, with key statutory functions of development control and local planning resting with the boroughs.

The Labour government's attempt to wrestle with the scale and location of growth came with the Strategic Plan for the South East in 1970, which covered a significantly wider area than Abercrombie's had done. Across the wider region, it envisaged that half of future regional growth would be accommodated in a set of growth and expansion areas. The plan represented a serious attempt to impose a strong spatial framework. Like the Abercrombie Plan, it employed techniques based upon a relatively simple and clear strategic allocation of growth. Again, however, strategic planning failed to consider future uncertainties and to explore alternative scenarios: for example, the Strategic Plan failed to anticipate the dramatic reduction in household size that was to greatly increase the demand for housing (see Chapter 11).

The Thatcher government was deeply antipathetic to strategic and regional planning, preferring to rely on the "instincts of the market" (Thornley 1993). The GLC was abolished. Strategic planning for the South East rested now firmly with central government with the advice of the South East Regional Planning Conference (SERPLAN). Its membership comprised the county councils and representatives of the district councils and London boroughs. SERPLAN's main role was to advise on regional planning guidance, although the powers of final approval rested firmly in Whitehall. SERPLAN was a voluntary, subscriber organisation, which therefore had to achieve consensus, or at least a minimal level of acceptance of policy, by all its members. It maintained a secretariat, which developed a reputation for high-quality research and information.

For 20 years, SERPLAN did a creditable job in drawing together the interests of a large and politically and geographically diverse set of local authorities (Wannop 1995). In particular, it was more successful than its predecessors in reconciling the ambitions of London and the rest of the South East. This in part reflected a growing consensus that London's decentralisation was both debilitating for the capital and irritating for the surrounding areas that were expected to accommodate much of the development. There was a growing recognition that urban regeneration was a more sustainable solution than de-urbanisation (see Chapter 2). This meant that, before the end of the century, London's position had become one of seeking the retention of population and economic growth within its boundary.

SERPLAN's strategic approach was inevitably one of seeking consensus on objectives. By adopting this approach at a time when central government was unwilling to take regional planning seriously, SERPLAN was able to promote the general interests of the Greater South East and to influence the strategic agenda in a number of areas. On some of the most contentious issues, it proved enormously difficult to reach agreement. Even on a critical matter such as airport expansion, SERPLAN found itself unable to take up a clear and incisive position. As a result it sometimes failed to provide the decisive advice that would shift government thinking. SERPLAN identified the need to address the issue of imbalance between the prosperous west and depressed east in its New Strategy of 1990. However, county councils and the private sector proved unwilling to conform to the proposal.

The struggle to produce regional planning guidance

In 1995, SERPLAN began to prepare draft regional planning guidance (RPG) for submission to an examination in public (EIP) and for ultimate government decision. SERPLAN also made its draft regional planning guidance an instrument for the promotion of sustainable development. In these and other fields,

SERPLAN was at the leading edge of ideas that later became standard. Not surprisingly, the issue that caused SERPLAN the greatest trouble, and which eventually contributed heavily to its demise, was that of housing growth. Throughout the RPG process, the conference struggled to deliver the housing numbers that government household projections had suggested would be needed to accommodate continuing growth. This issue exposed again the intra-regional divisions along the spectrum from support of growth to support of protectionism. The political sensitivities of growth created a regional debate that was obsessive about housing figures to the neglect of other very important elements of the SERPLAN proposals. The politicians on the conference repeatedly rejected alternatives that included higher housing figures and proposals for new settlements.

In its search for consensus, SERPLAN adopted a "plan, monitor and manage" approach. It argued that there were numerous uncertainties about future levels of housing need and that a more flexible approach would allow decisions on housing quantities to be made in the light of future experience. A baseline figure was to be agreed. Thereafter, individual planning authorities would identify specific housing numbers in their development plans, based upon urban capacity studies. Responsibility for delivery of this central element of regional planning policy would therefore be at the local level in a bottom-up process.

At the examination in public in 1999, SERPLAN's officers argued that this approach would allow the region to manage uncertainty about the future. However, in a scathing report, the Panel dismissed this argument as deliberate obfuscation and a denial of SERPLAN's obligation to offer a clear strategic direction. Instead the Panel took a top-down approach: RPG should, in its opinion, set out targets for housing that would then become the obligation of local authorities to deliver. It claimed:

> A set of anodyne policies is not, in our understanding, what is now required of RPG by Government . . . Uncertainty and perhaps lack of confidence on the part of planners does not justify the planning system leaving all other stakeholders in a state of continuing uncertainty.
>
> (GOSE 1999: 5)

The Panel's report was harsh. The government took a middle line between SERPLAN's draft guidance and the recommendations proposed by the Panel when it published its own draft revised RPG in 2000. Although government supported most of SERPLAN's planning principles, it was clearly unwilling to entrust local planning authorities with the ultimate specification of housing figures. Not surprisingly, it was sceptical about the willingness and ability of a large number of councils to produce new development plans in short order and to face up to delivery of housing in sufficient quantities. On the fundamental policy issue of housing growth, the regional planning body sought to persuade the local planning agencies by giving them ownership of detailed delivery. However, the regional body failed to persuade the national planning agency, which intervened because it did not trust the local level to produce the regional planning goods.

In strategic planning terms, SERPLAN was right to acknowledge the need to manage high levels of uncertainty and sought to achieve "legitimacy through consensus" (Newman and Thornley 2005). However, it appeared to delegate much of the decision making and implementation to a lower-tier set of agencies that manifestly did not fully subscribe to the regional planning goals.

A major part of the national government's concern was that a shortfall in housing provision would not only fail to meet demand, but would also undermine the capacity of the region to support continuing economic growth. An insufficient delivery of new homes would constrain labour supply and drive up house prices. This concern manifested itself not only around the debate on housing numbers, but also around the question of the location and nature of economic development. Although SERPLAN's draft RPG clearly supported the continued economic expansion of the region, and especially of London's world city role, it introduced some qualification. Growth was to be steered towards priority areas of economic regeneration and most notably Thames Gateway. In order to assist this process and to prevent overheating in the areas that were experiencing high levels of market-driven growth, SERPLAN proposed that further economic development in these growth areas should only be allowed where it was clearly essential to the wider regional economy. These areas were mainly to the west of London and were to be designated as "areas for economic consolidation". SERPLAN argued that this calming of economic growth areas was necessary to achieve more balanced regional development and to promote sustainable development in which economic growth did not threaten to exceed environmental capacity.

This strategy attracted the wrath of the Panel, which argued that RPG had a duty to promote economic development in the national interest. It argued that the principle of sustainable development lacked rigour and was being deployed to exercise inappropriate restraint on successful local economies. In the final RPG, government watered down SERPLAN's constrained approach to economic development in the west.

Once again, the agency of national planning had intervened to establish the primacy of the national interest in economic development. This intervention also reflected the interests of the private development sector and was mirrored by the Regional Development Agency. Although government accepted the value of sustainable development in principle, in practice it came down on the side of market-led economic growth.

At the end of the tortuous process of producing RPG for the Greater South East, a regional strategy did emerge, which endorsed much of SERPLAN's work. However, the adopted RPG lacked a coherent and incisive regional vision. It contained limited new ideas about where and how development should be concentrated and left too much to be fought over at the local level in inquiries on local plans and planning applications. As a result the delivery of growth, and especially of housing growth, has proved to be contentious in many parts of the region, with consequential delays and failures to deliver housing targets.

The process also illustrated the complexity of the regional planning task of balancing a number of strategic elements. The multiple goals of regional planning were in distinct contrast to the single goal of economic competitiveness of the regional economic development bodies. Despite their support for policies such as sustainable development, all three Regional Development Agencies in the Greater South East were able to pursue a single fundamental objective of

economic growth and to enlist the support of both government and the private
sector in pursuit of that prime objective.

The publication of the government's draft revised regional planning guidance
in December 2000 effectively marked the end of regional planning in the Greater
South East facilitated by a single planning agency representing the whole region.
SERPLAN was wound up and regional planning for the Greater South East
passed to the three new bodies: the Greater London Authority, the South East
England Regional Assembly (SEERA) and the East of England Local Govern-
ment Conference (later to become the East of England Regional Assembly –
EERA).

The restructuring of regional planning mechanisms

The government's decision to give responsibility for regional planning to three
different bodies perhaps illustrated its disillusionment with the ability of a single
regional body to deliver regional strategy. The entirely arbitrary nature of the
boundaries of the South East and East of England regions reflected government
contempt for coherent regional planning in the Greater South East. The new
regional planning powers were devolved to bodies that inherited the purely
administrative boundaries used to set up the three Government Offices in 1994.
The London boundary re-instituted the earlier GLC boundary. However,
the South East region formed an "L" shape stretching from Oxford to Dover (see
Figure 13.1) without any geographical, historical, cultural, social, economic or
demographic coherence or identity. The East of England boundary threw
together East Anglia and an arbitrary quadrant of the SERPLAN region. The
lack of serious challenge to this utterly unsatisfactory arrangement for regional
planning purposes was perhaps a reflection of the general exhaustion created by
the RPG process and of the low priority that regional planning assumed in the
Greater South East in the devolution agenda.

Apart from London itself, the new South East and East regions had no concrete basis for the development of their own regional identity. Their single most
significant characteristic is that all parts of these two new regions are significantly
under the influence of London, which acts as a centre of employment, consumption and entertainment. Neither new region has a clear primary city. No one in
the South East would regard Guildford as anything other than an administrative
centre of convenience. Any claim by Cambridge to be the primary city of the
East of England is disputed elsewhere in the region.

This presents SEERA and EERA with a serious problem. In the new regionalism, a strong identity for the region is seen as essential. In an era of global
competition, successful regions are supposed to be those that offer a clear image
and identity around which marketing can evolve and investment can be attracted.
Both regions have in fact devoted substantial efforts and resources to the creation
of a form of identity, with the Regional Development Agencies to the fore.
In both cases, this identity revolves around the concept of an economically
successful, competitive region rather than a collaborative region.

In order to be seen as legitimate new entities, the South East and East have to
minimise the significance of London as a separate region. In this scenario, any
form of vigorous cooperation on strategic planning across the three new regions

is regarded as inimical to the development of the identity of the individual region. At the same time, the London region, always liable to introversion, has been preoccupied with the establishment of its own new regional planning machinery and policy. The Mayor of London was given responsibility in the London Government Act of 2000 for the production of a new spatial develop-ment strategy (SDS). Ken Livingstone, the first Mayor, gave high priority to the publication of the SDS in his first four-year term. The Greater London Authority (GLA) became preoccupied with the challenge of producing a new form of regional plan using new legislation and an entirely new organisation.

It is not, therefore, surprising that collaboration on regional planning issues across the three new regions received low priority. A Pan-Regional Forum on Planning was established in 2001. The Forum consists of representatives from the two regional assemblies and from the GLA and boroughs. It has no executive powers, no budget and no staff. The Forum meets three times a year and offers advice, principally to government and to the three regional planning authorities.

The fragmentation of regional planning in the Greater South East has been furthered by the presence of two other sets of agencies with some significant regional planning power and influence. The three Government Offices for London, the South East and the East have substantial powers of influence and intervention and, in the case of the latter two regions, of managing statutory regional strategies through their final approval stages. The three Regional Development Agencies are charged with operating within regional planning guidance: indeed the regional assemblies and the Mayor have powers of super-vision of RDA policy in order, in part, to ensure compliance. However, in practice, the RDAs are powerful influences upon regional planning because of their promotion of economic development.

Across the wider South East, therefore, there are no fewer than *nine* powerful regional agencies with important powers and influence upon regional planning. The Government Offices represent central government within the region, and the RDA boards are appointed by central government. In the regional assemblies, local authorities share responsibility with representatives of the private and voluntary sectors. National and local interests are powerful in both the South East and the East of England regions.

SEERA and EERA are at an advanced stage in the process of producing what will become regional spatial strategies. The effectiveness of regional planning under the new arrangements in these two regions cannot yet be readily assessed. However, regional planning in London has made an extremely powerful start with the publication in 2004 of the London Plan, the Mayor's name for the spatial development strategy.

Regional planning in London: the London Plan

Over the second half of the last century, efforts to produce a strong strategic plan for London were spasmodic. Only one statutory plan was approved in the whole of the GLC's existence. Attempts to produce a subsequent plan were thwarted by the abolition of the GLC at a late stage in the process of statutory approval. Thereafter, direct responsibility for strategic planning in London rested squarely with central government. The boroughs formed a voluntary body called the London Planning Advisory Committee (LPAC) to coordinate planning between the boroughs. LPAC offered a source of sound advice on policy and research. However, LPAC remained advisory and was unable to require reluctant boroughs to toe a collective line on either plans or strategic development control decisions.

After the abolition of the GLC, London did gain some benefits from the fact that central government carried responsibility for its strategic planning. For example, there was a greater propensity for large-scale transport infrastructure projects to be approved during the period in which there was no elected strategic body for London than there has subsequently been under the mayoral system. Despite its general antipathy to strategic planning, the government had assumed full direct statutory power for London and felt some responsibility for the role. Nevertheless, the absence of a strategic planning and development control authority contributed to problems such as growing inequalities between rich and poor parts of London, increased traffic congestion and inter-borough conflicts and competition (see Chapter 5).

In contrast, the London Plan introduced an incisive and ambitious planning vision for the city's future (Mayor of London 2004). It enthusiastically embraced continuing population and economic growth in London and promised to accommodate this within its own boundaries in the interests of sustainable development. The Plan set targets for this growth, with an expectation that these should if possible be exceeded. It founded its strategy on London's world city role, and growth in Central London and more high-rise buildings were proposed in support of this. The East of London was given first priority as an area with both the need and the capacity for large-scale regeneration. A large programme of public transport improvements was included to support the Plan's spatial strategy (see Figure 13.2). As a spatial development strategy, the London Plan included a wide spectrum of spatial policy for key sectors such as housing, health, education and training.

At the examination in public, held in 2003, there was remarkably little challenge to the Mayor's central strategy of accommodating growth. The arguments centred instead around firstly the location of that growth and secondly the capacity of the supply side to support it. Whilst the boroughs generally accepted the priority afforded to East London, many of them contested the level of growth proposed for Central London, which was to absorb 40 per cent of housing and economic growth. This reflected the different emphasis between the Mayor's strategic vision of London as a world city and the desire of the local planning agencies to capture growth for their local economies. The EIP Panel recommended a more explicitly polycentric policy in which Central London's role was clearly balanced by an assertive role for the metropolitan and district centres. However, it did not suggest any alteration in the distribution of growth set out in the draft Plan.

The key agencies at national and local level did express concern that the delivery of growth rested substantially upon the supply of infrastructure and resources that were not within the Mayor's direct control. This was especially true of the public transport schemes that the Mayor promoted as essential to the spatial distribution of growth in the key areas of East and Central London. In fact, most of the schemes had been identified in RPG3. However, the power of decision on projects as large and significant as Crossrail rested with the Treasury.

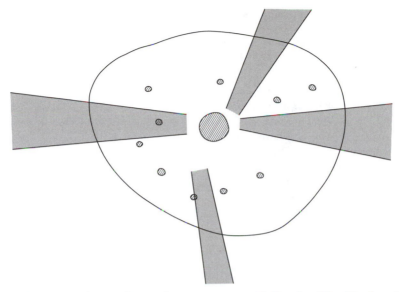

Figure 13.2 Growth corridors and town centres in the London Plan (the four "sets of lines" are the main growth corridors and the dots are the Central Activity Zone and metropolitan town centres)

Source: Mayor of London 2004

It would be for Whitehall to decide whether they were sufficiently central to the national interest to justify their costs.

The Mayor was relatively successful in persuading the various agencies to support his Plan. Central government did not use its ultimate power of intervention. The Mayor was able to argue that his policies were entirely in line with national guidance: he skilfully took some of this guidance to its extreme edge without actually contravening it. Private sector interests were largely supportive of the Mayor's strategy. His strategy focused on the global business and finance role and the delivery of the supply side needed to promote international and domestic business. Professor David Lock, representing a business interest at the EIP, commented that the provision of clear targets for housing and employment was extremely helpful for the development industry, which liked to know where it was and what it could and couldn't do.

Local planning authorities and representatives of local voluntary and community groups found it impossible to articulate any coherent objection to the Plan strategy. They focused on their local and sectoral interests. It was as if, after two decades without a strategic authority in London, the local agencies were scarcely able to engage at the strategic level.

The effectiveness of the London Plan will be judged over coming years. However, it is clearly an unusually cogent expression of regional planning policy. It is instructive to examine why the Mayor was able to construct such a relatively strong regional strategy and why he was relatively successful in persuading the national and business agencies and the key local agencies of the desirability of that regional policy.

The Mayor's Plan has multiple objectives, like any other regional plan. However, one individual has executive responsibility for the Plan. The Mayor does *not* need to take policy through a committee system or to negotiate around Plan objectives with representatives of a range of interest groups. Ken Livingstone was able to assert his strong personal vision and to take a robust approach to strategy making. It can be argued that the Plan makes rather cursory efforts to examine alternative scenarios as advocated in Chapter 4. However, the clarity of decision making has produced some very assertive strategic elements such as the congestion charge, the emphasis upon intensification and the policy supporting affordable housing of 50 per cent in all new developments.

The Mayor is the elected leader of the London community and has substantial powers of delivery through policy, development control, funding and advocacy. His role in preparing a spatial development strategy for London gives the Mayor the obligation to work with a wide range of other strategic agencies. The London Plan has a strong technical basis in its identification of "drivers". These are forces such as economic, technological, social, environmental and demographic change that are deemed to be far too powerful and deep-rooted to be changed by plans or planners. The London Plan, instead, seeks to exercise spatial management and influence over these forces and in this respect it is seen by its advocates to be more securely founded on reality than earlier regional strategies in the wider South East.

Regional planning in the new South East and East of England regions

The two regional assemblies face a more challenging process than the Mayor. They are required to produce regional spatial strategies, which have a very similar "policy stretch" to the London spatial development strategy. However, their remit is only to prepare strategies. Thereafter, it is the Government Office in the region that takes the draft strategy through the examination in public and on to adoption of the final strategy. At all stages, therefore, the regional planners are operating under the threat of national intervention – and Whitehall has demonstrated that it is willing to make such interventions.

The national agency therefore holds ultimate power in the process. Beneath the regional planning agency, the local agencies are numerous and also have significant power. The assemblies themselves contain an indirectly elected or nominated set of representatives from the local authority and the private and voluntary sectors. In the South East assembly, for example, this totals 111 representatives. Some agencies below the regional level are especially weighty players. The county councils are the traditional seat of strategic planning. They have been especially active in the past decade in seeking to contain housing growth. The withdrawal of structure plans has deprived them of one of their most significant responsibilities. The counties in the two regions have thus been prominent in their efforts to limit the regional planning powers of the RDAs and RAs and to maintain a strategic planning role for counties in the Planning and Compensation Act. Indeed they have been able to retain significant responsibilities for sub-regional planning.

It is difficult, therefore, for SEERA and EERA to formulate policy without substantial "buy-in" from the counties. District councils are also active on the regional stage and tend to be protective of their local interests. Whereas the Mayor has clear executive power to make the London Plan, the local planning authorities in these two regions have a higher court to which they can appeal in the form of central government, both at the examination in public and through-out the strategy-making process.

SEERA and EERA have wisely placed strong emphasis upon the sub-regional dimension. Their spatial strategies are being developed to a significant extent by the accumulation and integration of sub-regional studies. The local planning authorities are able to exercise substantial power in the formulation of these sub-regional policies. The regional planning agency is then left with the challenge of integrating them and achieving an overarching strategy. SEERA and EERA are demonstrating an impressive technical approach. Their initial policy formulation has been well grounded in the global, European, national and regional spatial dimensions. Both are taking innovative approaches to public engagement in an effort to overcome the lack of public interest in regional planning. SEERA for example has made extensive use of MORI polling and IT techniques and has held a vigorous series of "topic debates" with stakeholders.

Nevertheless, both regional planning exercises were at risk of foundering over the perennial issue of housing growth. In the South East, the assembly opted for the lowest range of the modest alternative housing targets it was invited to consider. In the East of England, the assembly chose to ignore the government's request for it to increase its housing target and said that its own lower figure is only deliverable if substantial investment is made in infrastructure.

Sub-regional planning

One mechanism for bridging the gap between regional growth aspirations and local desire for containment has been the use of sub-regions as a mechanism for mediation between the wider metropolitan region and the local interest. All three regional planning bodies have placed heavy emphasis upon sub-regional planning. Sub-regional activity has operated in a number of situations:

- *Trans-regional planning*. There are a number of development corridors that cross regional boundaries. The most important is the Thames Gateway, which includes parts of all three regions. It is significant that the government has chosen to award planning of the Gateway to a dedicated team working in its own office. The London–Stansted–Cambridge–Peterborough corridor studies have been managed at a more regional level, but government has shown its willingness to engage by disputing the housing figures. There are also lower-key inter-regional collaborations for the Western Wedge between West London and the Thames Valley and for the corridor from South London through Gatwick/Crawley to the South Coast.
- *In the South East and East regions*. A number of sub-regions have been identi-fied for special policy development. These include city regions such as Oxford and corridors such as that along the South Coast.
- *In the London sub-regions*. The London Plan places strong emphasis upon sub-regional development frameworks as the vehicle for implementation of the Plan and mediation between London-wide policy and local policy.

- *Transport studies.* A number of sub-regional transport studies have been initiated to look at strategic transport proposals, including the multi-modal studies which are elaborated upon in Chapter 10.

The sub-regional approach has a number of attractions in the wider South East. It offers a vehicle for mediation between the regional and local interests. Sub-regional boundaries can be defined in a flexible way because there is no institutional ownership of the territory. They are also a neutral ground because no single planning agency has statutory powers for the sub-region. However, it follows that most sub-regional planning does not have statutory force until it is reflected in regional and local plans, so that buy-in from the relevant authorities is essential.

Sub-regional planning also offers a means of shifting policy away from the mono-centric pattern that has been so much a preoccupation because of the dominance of London. There are important connections between other parts of the Greater South East that can be developed through this mechanism. The challenge for the new regional planning authorities will be to ensure that the outcomes of these sub-regional activities are compatible both with each other and with the overall regional interest.

National government has itself used the sub-regional mechanism to promote its strategic objectives, notably through the Sustainable Communities Plan, which proposed that 200,000 additional households should be planned for in four growth areas. The principal area was the Thames Gateway. In addition, areas around Stansted Airport, Ashford and Milton Keynes were nominated (see Figure 13.3). These areas were to receive financial and other inducements to

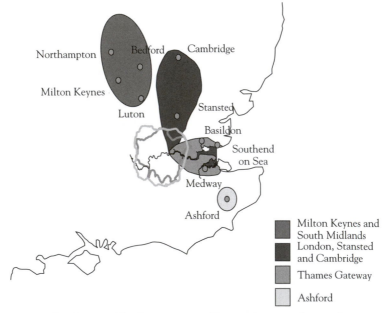

Figure 13.3 The Sustainable Communities Plan and national growth areas in the wider South East

Source: Prepared by GLA DMAG. Maps based on OS boundaries © Crown Copyright (GLA) (LA100032379)(2004)

accept extra housing growth, including investment in infrastructure. The Sustainable Communities Plan effectively pre-empted a significant element of regional planning in the three regions.

The growth areas do represent a quite rational and decisive approach to the perennial problem of accommodating housing growth in the Greater South East. The regeneration of the Thames Gateway and its reservoir of development land has been an uncontested national planning priority. Ashford and Stansted are international gateways. Milton Keynes has the infrastructure and impetus to support continued growth.

Nevertheless, there remains something deterministic in the approach of the national planning agency to the growth areas. The pattern of top-down strategy making has been continued. For example, the figure of 200,000 extra homes was educated guesswork in which the regional and local planning agencies were offered little ownership. The government did not reach specific agreement on the housing target for Thames Gateway with the regional and local planning stakeholders until well after the announcement of its own target of 120,000 homes in the Sustainable Communities Plan.

Maintaining inter-regional coordination

The Pan-Regional Forum has in the meantime sought to coordinate the work of the three regional agencies. One of its first main tasks was to try to mediate on the inter-regional impacts of the London Plan. The Plan attempted to set the Mayor's strategy in the context of the wider South East region. It asserted the Mayor's eagerness to work with the other two regional authorities on matters such as inter-regional transport and on waste disposal. However, the Plan's enthusiastic embrace of London's expansion as a world city created a dilemma for the other two regions. They shared a palpable relief that London was accepting its full responsibility to contain its own growth and the consequences of that growth, such as greater self-sufficiency in waste disposal.

Nevertheless, SEERA and EERA were discomforted by the implications of the London Plan's growth strategy. They are particularly worried by the fact that economic growth in London is predicted to increase commuting into London. The London Plan contained a potential shortfall of around 120,000 resident workers to fill the projected increase in employment. The two regions believed that this could reduce labour supply in their own areas and would exacerbate the pressures on commuting transport services. They also feared that the capital might be unable to house its growing population.

The EIP Panel supported the notion that the final London Plan should say more about its wider regional context and recommended that more should be done to achieve higher levels of housing within London. However, it shied away from any recommendation that growth in London should somehow be constrained in order to limit its impacts on the two surrounding regions. The concerns of SEERA and EERA were rooted in the long history of London's decentralisation and were put forward in a responsible way. However, they were also effectively suggesting that the three regions in the wider South East should pursue a strategy of self-sufficiency. The logic of their argument would lead to the situation in which each of the regions planned for balance in its own housing and employment growth. In theory, this is an attractive proposition which supports a more sustainable community approach and reduces the need for inter-regional commuting. In practice, however, it is wholly impracticable in a "mega city region" in which settlements, people and economies throughout the region are intertwined and interactive.

The South East and East of England regions were also in effect seeking to protect their own competitive position by searching for a means to constrain the economic performance of London. This is entirely understandable in terms of the agenda of regional competition and identity that they have set themselves, but London's world city role remains the fundamental driver for economic performance across *all three* regions.

Nevertheless, the three new regional planning authorities have a substantial degree of consensus on inter-regional policy. There is agreement on the importance of sustainable development and urban regeneration, and upon the need to relate strategic public transport investment to priority areas for development. The Pan-Regional Advisory Forum has been able to take a united line upon matters such as the Thames Gateway development and even on airport expansion policy. It has also been able to mount a joint lobby of central government for extra resources to support an increase in affordable housing.

The Forum has instituted a joint information, research and monitoring programme. This has particularly focused upon the contentious issues of labour market balance sheet, employment growth and community flows in a joint effort to "manage" this issue. The greater willingness of London to absorb the impacts of its growth, including its housing, waste and environmental impacts, has undoubtedly contributed to the cordial atmosphere between the three new agencies.

However, the current arrangements remain inadequate. Each region is developing its formal strategy on a different timescale. Each of the three strategies has a different end date. So policy coordination is extraordinarily difficult. The absence of permanent dedicated staff and a secretariat severely inhibits the Forum's effectiveness. The Greater London Assembly felt sufficiently uneasy about inter-regional arrangements, and about the extent to which the draft London Plan located itself in an inter-regional context, to set up a scrutiny review (London Assembly 2004). The review concluded that the London Plan should say much more about the inter-regional dimension – as indeed the final Plan does. It went on to conclude:

> the weight of evidence presented to us suggests that, from a London perspective, this re-organisation has not been helpful to the planning of the wider metropolitan London region, with its hinterland split between two surrounding regions and no over-arching planning mechanism.

Despite this conclusion, the scrutiny committee fell short of recommending an overarching strategy for the Greater South East or of proposing that the Forum should have power to take executive decisions. Instead it suggested a stronger mediation role and an acceptance that "the Advisory Forum should provide the wider regional context within which the strategic planning partnership in the Greater South East should operate". To this end, it recommended that the Forum should have a modest permanent secretariat.

Fragmentation of regional policy

The fragmentation of planning policy is exacerbated by the complexity of the new institutional arrangements. In addition to the nine primary agencies, there are other key actors such as the housing authorities, which contribute to the regional housing strategy. Indeed the move towards regional spatial strategies will draw in a wide range of other regional and local agencies in sectors such as health, education, transport and the environment.

There is, then, a weak institutional capacity for trans-regional policy and collaboration across the wider South East, despite the growing interdependence of the activities that take place within it. The problem remains, as it has always done, the unwillingness of both the national and the local planning agencies to contemplate a strong regional planning agency for an area as large, populous and economically powerful as the Greater South East. The sheer size and complexity of the wider South East mean that it is also perceived by local agencies as too large a unit to be sufficiently sensitive to the particular needs of its many and various parts.

The fragmentation of planning in the wider South East carries a number of risks. These include:

- *negative competition between the three regions*, especially in the field of economic development;
- *failure to agree on trans-regional capital investment*, including resourcing of transport investment: individual regions may be unwilling to support investments that they perceive will bring bigger benefits to neighbouring regions;
- *lack of coordinated approaches* to the achievement of social cohesion and especially to attacking imbalances between the east and west of the wider region;
- *weakness in dealing with cross-border matters*, such as retail development, transport and waste disposal;
- *inability to mount sufficiently strong lobbying in the wider regional interest*. The three regions contribute more than they receive from the national economy and have lower levels of public investment per capita than other UK regions so that lobbying for more resources should be an inter-regional priority.

One means of reducing the risks of fragmentation would be to create financial incentives for greater inter-regional planning incentives. Another suggestion, made by Ian Gordon, is that there might be a single Government Office for the whole Greater South East (Gordon 2003). This might help to remove the ambiguities around the role of the Government Offices, which have been part supporter and part regulator (with a distinct taste for the latter). However, there is a risk that a single Government Office might increase even further the dominance of central government in regional planning.

Conclusions

Taking a long-term perspective on the performance of regional planning in the wider South East over the past century, a number of conclusions can be drawn.

The principal planning concept has been the management and containment of development. There have been loud assertions from bodies such as the Campaign to Protect Rural England that planning policy has failed in this effort and the result is excessive sprawl and environmental destruction. An alternative view is that regional planning has maintained a coherent polycentric spatial pattern of development.

An aerial photograph would show that there is a clear distribution of settlements that are separated by substantial swathes of undeveloped land. However weak the local quality of development may be and however poor the "edge" of development often is, the Greater South East remains preponderantly free of built development. The green belt has been a crude instrument, but it has been successful in the strategic purpose of preventing the sprawl of the built-up area of London. Only about 14 per cent of land in the wider South East is developed.

There remain concerns about the supply side of regional planning. In some places, especially in the South East region, district councils have failed to meet regional housing targets and failed to address the need for higher densities. This has contributed to a situation in which house prices have risen faster than incomes, and in which the supply of affordable housing is grossly inadequate, leading to social and labour supply problems. The Greater South East has to meet demand from some 1.5 million new households over the period 1996–2016. There remain doubts about the will and powers of the regional and local planning and housing and construction agencies to meet this demand. The focus on urban regeneration and upon the growth areas will assist in this effort, but regional policy needs to be identifying the sources of accommodation of growth beyond 2020.

The economic performance of the Greater South East has been strong in UK terms: the three regions have had the three fastest rates of economic growth over the past decade. However, London and the South East have the two largest intraregional variations in levels of GDP in the UK. There remain serious problems of poverty in inner-city areas and on the coastal periphery of the Greater South East. The east/west imbalance has also not been addressed. There are exceptional points of growth such as the City of London and Cambridge and exceptional areas of economic and social depression such as East London and Thanet.

The sheer density of transport infrastructure in the wider region has provided some degree of elasticity in supporting continued growth. However, radial routes into London are under increasing pressure. Transport infrastructure across the wider region on an east–west axis is poor and orbital movement is difficult, especially around London. Attempts to create new patterns of movement and settlement are inhibited by inadequate transport support. Congestion is already severe in several areas, but there is no central government commitment to the levels of transport infrastructure improvement needed.

There is a growing awareness of the need to manage the environmental consequences of continued growth. As income levels rise, the regional authorities face the challenge of finding forms of development and encouraging kinds of behaviour that will result in genuinely sustainable patterns of development.

The future of regional planning in the Greater South East remains uncertain. The London Plan has entered its implementation stage, and the final spatial strategies for the other two regions have yet to be published at the time of writing this chapter. The emergence of spatial strategies does offer the prospect that the planning debate may be able to shift from the obsession with housing numbers. The London Plan and the evolving strategies in the other two regions could become powerful mechanisms for the coordination of sectoral policy.

It is perhaps not surprising that regional planning across the wider South East has been more successful at containment of development than it has been at achieving forms of development that encourage more equitable and sustainable communities. For the most part, regional planning has operated through consensus and advisory mechanisms and has relied upon implementation through the planning powers of the local agencies. This has inevitably resulted in conservative and parochial approaches to meeting development needs.

On a few occasions, central government has sought to stimulate a more radical approach by introducing executive agencies with a mandate to deliver growth, such as the New Town Development Corporation and the London Docklands Development Corporation. However, Whitehall has generally been unwilling either to devolve real planning power to the regional level or to enforce its desire for a more visionary and strategic approach to regional needs through the imposition of executive agencies.

Different approaches have been taken towards managing the complexity and uncertainties of the strategic planning process. The early deterministic plans, such as that of Abercrombie, lacked the flexibility to handle unanticipated change. Although they offered clarity of purpose, this was not sufficiently shared with stakeholders, so that ownership was weak. Conversely, the SERPLAN consensus model took pains to engage stakeholders, and especially the local authorities. It sought flexibility through the "predict and provide" mechanism. However, it failed to offer the degree of relative certainty of direction, which strategic planning needs if it is to manage rather than react to market forces.

Much of the difficulty rests with the lack of a clear identity, "organising concept" or metaphor for the region and the absence of sufficient champions to mobilise support for a regional strategy in the way Healey regards as essential for effective planning (Healey 1997). For example, there has been quite limited opportunity to bid for European funding in the way that has helped to galvanise regional cooperation in other UK regions with greater potential to access external funding.

The size and complexity of the regional planning constituency are such that it has proved hard to achieve the "institutional thickness" of a successful collaborative region. The Greater South East has been trapped between a national government unwilling to delegate sufficient powers and responsibility for resource distribution and a multitudinous and divided set of local constituencies unwilling to come together for the common good. Perhaps it is not surprising in these circumstances that strategic planning in the wider South East has essentially been a story of "muddling through".

References

Davoudi, S. 2003. Polycentricity in European spatial planning. *European Planning Studies* **11**, December.

Glasson, J. 2002. Regional guidance and governance. In *Contemporary issues in regional planning*, T. Marshall, J. Glasson and P. Headicar (eds). Aldershot: Ashgate.

Gordon, I. 2003. Joining up the Greater South East. Conference papers on "The new regionalism", Barbican, July.

GOSE 1999. *Report of the Panel*. Examination in public on RPG for South East England. Guildford: Government Office for the South East.

Hall, P. and K. Pain 2006. *Learning from mega city regions in Europe*. London: Earthscan.

Healey, P. 1997. *Collaborative planning*. London: Macmillan.

Howard, E. 1902. *Garden cities of tomorrow*. London: Swan Sonnenschein.

London Assembly 2004. *London in its regional setting*. London: Greater London Authority.

Mayor of London 2004. *The London Plan*. London: Greater London Authority.

Newman, P. and A. Thornley 2005. *Planning world cities*. London: Palgrave.

Sassen, S. 2001. *The global city*. Princeton, NJ: Princeton University Press.

Thornley, A. 1993. *Urban planning under Thatcherism*. London: Routledge.

Wannop, U. 1995. *The regional imperative*. London: Regional Studies Association.

Williams, C. 2002. Regional planning in South East England. In *Contemporary issues in regional planning*, T. Marshall, J. Glassen and P. Headicar (eds). Aldershot: Ashgate.

14 Strategic and regional planning in the North East

Paul S. Benneworth and Geoff Vigar

Introduction

Planning systems are often portrayed as having two interrelated functions. First, they aim to resolve conflicts between neighbours over the use of land; second, they aim to assert and promote particular place qualities to improve quality of life, economic competitiveness or environmental conditions (Vigar *et al.* 2000). These purposes come together in strategic plans to set out principles which can shape polices and practices in specified territories to produce a set of outcomes which meet particular goals. However, the functions which the plans articulate need not necessarily be limited to the scale at which the plans are drawn up. The second purpose of planning in practice inevitably involves horizontal co-ordination of policies and practices across policy sectors within specified territorial limits and also a vertical dimension in bringing together actors from various spatial scales.

Indeed, plans in practice are regularly drawn up within hierarchies, with smaller-scale plans reflecting purposes and qualities assigned to them by higher-level plans. A range of EU countries for example have national spatial strategies which assign particular roles to particular places, and the negotiations at a national level are arguably more important in determining the spatial planning framework covering local and regional scales than local planning activities. Indeed, one consequence of the introduction of a European scale to spatial planning, the so-called European Spatial Development Planning (ESDP) Framework, is potentially to take away further from local planning the key decisions which determine the types of activities which governments will promote in particular places (Jensen and Richardson 2003).

In this way, in seeking to shape policy domains of other actors, and in uniting actors both within and across policy themes, planning can be engaged in processes of meta-governance (Jessop 2002). Such a role has been given greater currency through New Labour's emphasis on policy integration, often termed "joined-up governance" as shorthand. However, our argument in this chapter is that, while territory could be providing a useful focus for such integrating activity, the problems faced by territorial integration have yet to be fully addressed.

Regional spatial planning has risen in importance in England in the last 15 years, as other contributors to this volume have already observed, but still lacks mechanisms to shape the actions of national policy communities. Failure to address this problem is undermining the value that spatial planning can provide through offering a meta-governance system (see Chapter 3). Our argument is that the specific problem the North East faces is that it has been assigned an inappropriate role by national spatial planning. UK, and particularly English, policy making is dominated by the "sectoral principle", i.e. Parliament allocates funds to functional ministries, which spend those funds achieving their goals, encouraging national policy makers to develop isolated policies targeted upon particular problems, thereby reducing complex problems which vary between places to simplistic diagnoses.

As a consequence of this sectoral principle, English spatial planning is focused on dealing with the problems of the South East, although, as the previous chapter shows, its determination to do that through national planning policy means that the Greater South East is only "plannable" through integration of a wide range of regional actors. In the North East, we note that the RSS/RPG has difficulty in playing a dispute resolution role, because its focus on solving South Eastern problems gives it little relevance to the North East of England. Our contention is that the North East also has problems of plannability; we as a result draw on a number of sub-regional vignettes to highlight the importance of system discretion in making the North East "plannable". In the final section, we discuss how regional planning might be reformed at a national level in ways that would improve local decision making.

The resurgence of English regional planning

The introduction of regional planning guidance in the 1990s was part of an attempt to give coherence to a public sector which had become increasingly fragmented in the 1980s. The choice of the "region" as a coordinating scale was given further impetus after 1997 with the imposition of extra duties for regional planning, and with a gradual evolution of regional institutions. There were two main strands in post-1997 regionalisation. Firstly, Regional Development Agencies (RDAs) were created in 1999, with a responsibility to draw up regional economic strategies (RESs) for their regions. Their success led to further powers from Whitehall with the introduction of a single integrated budget in 2002. The second strand was in creating a regional political tier, mobilising existing local political actors, creating so-called regional chambers, combining local authorities and social/economic partners, with a statutory responsibility to scrutinise the RES. As these chambers had a strong common membership with the local authority regional planning conferences responsible for the regional planning guidance, in many cases, the two organisations merged.

However, these changes were largely to improve regional input to regional economic strategies; planning changes were driven elsewhere, most significantly in the wake of the 2002 regional devolution White Paper (DTLR 2002). Mainly proposing arrangements for elected regional assemblies, Chapter 2 of this White Paper set out a set of technical changes to be implemented immediately, including passing regional planning responsibility to the regional chambers. This chapter therefore implemented much of the 2001 planning Green Paper, creating regional spatial strategies (RSSs) as the dominant document in the local planning process, with the chambers also being given responsibility for integrating the various regional strategies, including RES and RSS, and a range of other fields.

It is then seemingly strange to argue that regional planning in England still lacks a strong territorial dimension; our critique is not of direction of travel but of substantive process. Land-use planning in the UK reached a nadir in the 1980s, pared back to its regulatory core, following assaults from right-wing governments of the day (see Chapter 2). For a variety of reasons, the regionalisation process has not led to planning principles being promulgated in which particular regions' plans reflect the specific planning needs of those regions. Indeed, as Vigar *et al.* (2000) have demonstrated, regionalisation has been dominated by Whitehall control and so the new meta-governance is dominated by sectoral requirements, including departmental funding arrangements *rather than* territorial needs. It will take time for the new principles of spatial planning to give rise to territorial planning that can perform the meta-governance role of joining up strategies at the regional scale as envisaged by central government (Hammond 2003). Such territoriality is weak not just in regional planning documentation but also in regional economic strategies and regional sustainable development frameworks (Benneworth *et al.* 2002; Counsell *et al.* 2006). We now turn to look at how the dominance of the political centre over the English system has undermined the role of the territorial dimension as a coordinating device for spatial planning.

Planning territories or managing departments?

There are two problems with the territorial integration of planning in England. The first is the aforementioned lack of national pressure to join up policies regionally. The other element undermining territoriality in England is the continued absence of a strong set of national spatial priorities. Although the Sustainable Communities Plan (ODPM 2003a) attempts to set some such priorities, it focused heavily on "end of pipe solutions" to low housing demand, doing little to affect the economic drivers that might address North–South imbalances. Indeed, the policy focus for the first year was entirely on creating new growth communities in the South East and South Midlands without attempting to create similar growth poles outside that "core" economic region (ODPM 2003a, 2003b).

This does not mean that there are not territorial priorities embedded in the planning framework; since the late 1970s, the planning system has focused on dealing with the problems undermining growth in more successful regions, in particular London and the Greater South East regions. Their economic success has created a particular set of problems, such as congestion and overheating, to which the planning system has addressed itself, thereby neglecting the planning issues facing less successful regions. Transport planning, in particular, contains an implicit bias towards the South East because of its focus on using passenger journeys as the benchmark for cost benefit analyses. Without transport policy makers at a national level recognising the role that large infrastructure investment plays in the economic development of the northern and western regions, regional planners have no scope to draw up plans in which their visions for new infrastructure are realised (Rice and Venables 2003).

Such spatial biases as do exist in the English planning system are much less explicit, which in turn makes them much harder to address systematically and rationally through national planning policy. The lack of explicit spatial policies which embed hidden spatialities also makes it very difficult to assert, and hence control, the territorial implications of sectoral policies to ensure that national policy makers recognise the territorial impacts of supposedly spatially insensitive policies (Gillespie and Benneworth 2002; Amin *et al.* 2003). This problem can be divided into two elements: the dominance of policies which deal with core problems, and the fact that problems that peripheral regions face are not just more severe versions of core problems.

The set of national (i.e. South East focused) priorities in English planning undermines government efforts to narrow the growth disparities between the economic core and the peripheral areas of England and the UK. A good example can be seen in the case of the policy pertaining to new towns; the impact of the policy is very different in booming and declining places, but new towns were introduced across Britain with a limited regard to the particular contextual situations in which they were created. It is then unsurprising that the single policy has had very different results. New towns in the South East have a very different character from those in the North East; Stevenage and Harlow have become overspill housing and commuter villages for London workers, while Cramlington, through the judicious attraction of inward investment, has become something of a sub-regional, rather than regional, growth pole (Benneworth 2004). This of course has the unwelcome side effect of reinforcing the economic status quo, rather than using the planning system as a means of remediating the economic effects of the domination over the UK urban system by London.

The second element of the problem is not just that policies play out differently in different places, but that the needs and problems of less successful places, to which they might look to the planning system to provide a solution, are systemically different from those of the more successful places in whose interest the planning system is designed. This is illustrated clearly with the case of housing policy, where there is a clear North/South divide in the way the market operates, the North facing growing dereliction and the South massive under-supply. Until very recently there has been only a single policy framework to deal with a complex issue in which there are systemic territorial differences.

It is necessary to stress that there is a strong national planning framework within which regional plans are drawn up. Alden (2002) highlights 14 areas where effective spatial planning at any scale requires such strong national powers, including the harmonisation of local practices around national concepts but also ensuring that the spatial allocation of activity meets the needs of the UK economy and is complementary to the social policy goals of the government. In Chapter 13, Thompson has in some sense considered the fit between national and regional planning principles in the South East, a region where there at least should be some commonalities between these two scales. In this chapter, we now turn to ask how regional planning operates within a framework not immediately relevant to the region being planned. Using a number of vignettes of particular issues which arose in preparing regional planning guidance for the North East, we note how this lack of ideas about what territory might mean produces a sometimes confused and incoherent system, unsuitable for making the hard decisions necessary to deliver regeneration and renewal in a less successful region. In some instances, this is due to a lack of capacity to think about space, place and territory; in others the problems are more systemic, with the regional actors' infrastructure powerless in the face of long-established sectoral power. In this chapter, we explore the emergence of a regional planning framework for the North East, particularly in the context of the issue of economic competitiveness. We begin by looking at the problems the region faces.

Planning and the economic problems of the North East

The North East of England is a region with strong identity, in part fostered by a sense of isolation from London and central government, but also through its early experiences of industrialisation, depression and de-industrialisation. In comparison with other UK regions it is small in population terms (2.5 million in 2001) but covers a large surface area (850,000 hectares). It consists of three major conurbations: Tyneside, centred on Newcastle; Wearside, centred on Sunderland; and Teesside, centred on the city of Middlesbrough (see Figure 14.1). To the north and south of Tyneside are two rural former coalfield areas where urban problems are exacerbated by their remoteness from urban service provision. The remainder of the region is also rural with varying degrees of remoteness and a number of market towns. The region contains two national parks and two areas of outstanding natural beauty.

Its strong sense of regional identity contributes to an unusually large commitment from elite groups to regional devolution, although in 2004 a referendum rejected an elected regional assembly to have had powers over transport/spatial planning. In addition, regional cohesion belies the strong allegiances government and citizens often hold to individual settlements. There is a great deal of rivalry between these places, which has consequences for the making of a joint strategy, especially where local politicians (and other stakeholders) engage in essentially parochial and clientelist practices, undermining cooperation and collaboration between places above a lowest common denominator. This parochialism is at odds with the generally held external perception of the North East as a region with a great deal of political coherence.

The key policy issue facing the North East is its long-term economic decline. Although the region was an early industrialiser in the late eighteenth century, by the end of the nineteenth century increased competition from the newly industrialising Germany and United States had toppled it from its dominant position. From that time onward, the forces which had driven economic development in the North East declined. After the Second World War, the region's economy remained dominated by weakly competitive coal, steel and shipbuilding industries, and the post-war economic history is dominated by their decline and almost total disappearance, and the failure of national policies to progress beyond managing that decline.

This long-term economic decline manifested itself through an attendant set of problems to which the English planning system lacks relevance, driven by the retreat of English planning to its regulatory core in the 1980s. Even to this day, planning remains heavily influenced by New Right ideologies in which the role of planning is seen in terms of reducing congestion costs, and so-called diseconomies of agglomeration in core regions. This approach dominates thinking within central government; even after 1997, White Papers across Whitehall have affirmed a focus on "place competitiveness" over a more redistributive approach (DTI 1998, 2000; DTI and DfEE 2001; HM Treasury 2001). The closest

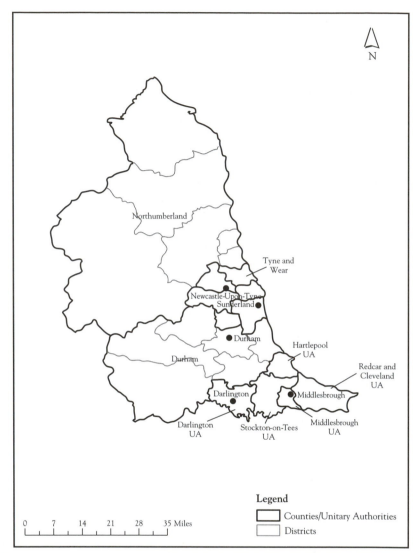

Figure 14.1 The North East region and its conurbations
Source: Benneworth *et al*. 2006

that government has come to recognising the spatial imbalances implicit within this approach was the commitment in the 2001 innovation White Paper to "widening the circle of winners".

A key problem facing the North East is the lack of a regional decision mechanism which can integrate the different national priorities into a cohesive planning framework for the region. Consequently, we argue that the main challenge for national planning policy makers in helping the North East of England to address its deep-seated economic, social and environmental challenges is providing mechanisms to directly address regional problems with national policies. The North East has deep internal divisions; Northumberland,

South Teesside and Durham have GVA levels 15 per cent *below* the (already low) regional average, whilst Tyneside and Darlington have GVA levels over 15 per cent *above* the regional level. Even within sub-regional areas, wealth exists as pockets of affluence next to pockets of poverty; the risk with a focus on competitiveness is promoting increased connectivity between these wealthy islands, bypassing their impoverished neighbours, and foregoing the constructive capacity of spatial planning to balance economic development within a territory.

Regional planning in the North East to the 1990s

As already explained by a number of earlier contributors to this book, the origins of regional planning in England date back to the 1920s. The 1940 Barlow Report represented the first clear attempt to decentralise and deconcentrate the UK economy through regulatory mechanisms. The post-war planning framework had a series of provisions to ensure what Cullingworth refers to as the "proper distribution of industry" (1982: 16), most notably the introduction of Industrial Development Control Certificates (IDCs). There was a clear role for the North East in this arrangement, as a centre of manufacturing activity. The IDC regime was used to ensure that manufacturing activity went to such "manufacturing regions", discouraging the emergence of alternative industries which could draw workers away from the task of driving the post-war national reconstruction effort (Hudson 1989).

This was consolidated in the 1960s with two reports which highlighted the specific regional challenges facing the North East. The Hailsham Report (1962) and the Challenge of the Changing North (1966) were developed at a time when regional planning was coming for the first time into vogue and the decline of North Eastern industry had not played through to its climax. However, the creation of the regional economic planning councils (REPCs) in 1965 politicised both this regional planning process and, more critically, the tools by which it was implemented. When the REPCs were abolished by the incoming Thatcher government, the national planning framework lost its capacity to spatially allocate economic activities between regions, capacity further undermined by the growing hegemony of neo-classical thinking in Whitehall. The acceptance by neo-classicists of uneven development as a fair market outcome has been highlighted by Lloyd (2002) as inimical to the practice and philosophy of planning. Alongside the philosophical and ideological dimension to these changes, the practical difficulties the central government had in dealing with the practicalities of coordinating physical and economic planning also drove a wedge between spatial and economic planning.

A number of changes in the North East during the 1980s further contributed to this erosion of regional planning capacity. Firstly, the Tyne and Wear County Council (TWCC) was abolished in 1986; it coordinated action across the main metropolitan area in the North East, the cities of Newcastle and Sunderland, the new town of Washington, and the industrial areas along the Tyne between Newcastle and the North Sea. The county council had been a place in which the balanced development of the sub-region was arranged, in particular in dealing with the urban flight from inner Newcastle and Sunderland to their neighbouring and greener authorities. The removal of TWCC meant that there was no common metropolitan interest in supporting and regenerating inner-city areas, and the late 1980s and early 1990s saw the rise of many low-density, car-dependent and service-barren detached housing estates in North and South Tyneside contemporaneously with the collapse of established housing estates in the West End of Newcastle and the Sunderland Hendon Docks area.

Secondly, a very strong economic development coalition emerged, driving the planning process. Unlike elsewhere in the country, low land and property prices meant that there was not a strong development industry of realtors and developers; even to this day, the skyline of the city centres of Sunderland and Newcastle is remarkably low in comparison with the office towers dominating Manchester, Birmingham and Leeds. Development in the region was strongly shaped by the availability of subsidies, and the Government Office, English Estates and other public sector actors assumed a strong role in organising access to such subsidies. This encouraged office development away from city centre sites where land prices were relatively high, and subsidies absent, to out-of-town greenfield locations (cf. "Newcastle Great Park").

An interrelated third problem was that development in the North East was dominated by a series of exceptional planning instruments outside the traditional planning system. Local authorities were keen on enterprise zones, but their effects were largely on the intra-regional distribution of jobs, as opposed to overall job creation. Similarly, two urban development corporations (UDCs) in the region were given sweeping powers to physically regenerate riverside areas of Teesside, Tyneside and Wearside. Their territorial remit was very narrowly defined, in each case covering small packages of land next to the rivers, the site of former industrial activities, with the UDCs getting sweeping planning powers over those sites. UDCs focused strongly on flagship regeneration schemes, often with little connection to their local surroundings. Tyne and Wear Development Corporation (TWDC) was criticised particularly strongly by Robinson (1993) for this inability or unwillingness to engage locally, something that was partly addressed in the later years of its operation.

Thus, by the time that regional planning was introduced in England, capacity to deliver effective solutions to regional problems was undermined, at a national scale by a focus on regulating congestion problems, and regionally by focusing on regenerating discrete land packages with a series of exceptional instruments. Mechanisms for collaboration between places had been undermined, and local authorities focused on how the regional plan could benefit them rather than using it to shape a balanced and well-connected regional economy.

In addition, there was not a strong market demand push, but there was an active coalition of stakeholders with an interest in having land released to develop using subsidies. The overwhelming discourse of economic decline and the need for regeneration tended to be narrowly constituted and drove out attendant discourses of environmental quality, social equity and quality of life.

There was also a tacit acceptance that the planning system could not deliver solutions to North Eastern problems, undermining local authorities' commitment to regional planning. The provision of discretionary powers in planning policy guidance (PPG), the so-called exceptional circumstances clause, was always there for the region should it need a legitimate means of fulfilling aspirations, a provision frequently mobilised in the 1990s to accommodate development which promoted "regional competitiveness" but lay in conflict with established spatial policies.

Together, these three factors undermined regional pressure to produce a regional plan that represented much more than a lowest common denominator. When RPG1 (the North East) was published in 1993, it was indeed widely criticised for its lack of coherence, and underwent continual revision and redrafting throughout the 1990s. In many cases, the impetus for this was national; the original RPG promoted out-of-town shopping as a means of regenerating derelict industrial land. However, the Department of the Environment placed a moratorium on such projects as a direct response to the creation of the White Rose Centre in West Yorkshire and as a general shift in policy occurred.

This national policy shift overrode the supposedly broad-based regional strategy, and the ease with which this happened reflected both a lack of regional commitment to RPG and the centralisation of the planning system at that time. The problems inherent in RPG did not augur entirely well for the revision of the RPG in the late 1990s. Indeed, the revised RPG was severely criticised by the planning inspector for its lack of priorities and inability to broker agreements on key issues such as strategic economic sites. In the next section, we look at the revised RPG process, and the planning framework it produced, before looking at specific planning case studies where the deficiencies we have already highlighted rendered the RSS incapable of producing a sensible solution.

Contemporary regional planning in the North East

The first version of the RPG for the Northern region (the North East and Cumbria) was issued in 1993. However, this excluded Tyne and Wear, which was subject to its own PPG, issued in 1989 (DoE 1989). The separation of these two areas had the effect of undermining the links between planning in the main conurbation and planning in its hinterland. Arguably this could have accelerated population drift from the principal regional conurbation to its hinterland and undermined regeneration in the conurbation, not least because of the extremely brief nature of the guidance relating to the conurbation and the lack of importance attributed to regional spatial planning at the time. These problems were acknowledged in the decision to introduce an RPG covering the entire North East; the shift in focus to the North East from the North reflects the creation of the Government Offices for the Regions. Although for planning purposes Cumbria was included at that time with the four North Eastern counties, Government Offices used DTI regional office boundaries as their foundation, and the DTI included Cumbria in their North West region (although bizarrely not Merseyside, an anomaly that began with Heseltine's interest in Merseyside from 1981, and which was not rectified until the late 1990s).

A revision of RPG began in 1995, covering the North East region. Following the development of an issues paper in 1996 and a consultative draft, a final draft was submitted to central government in 1999. Through all the various revisions the main aim of the RPG was to achieve "regeneration" within the conurbations, rural and coalfield areas. The final RPG was published in November 2002. It was almost immediately set into a review process to turn it into a regional spatial strategy under the new spatial planning system. A draft version of RSS emerged in November 2004 (NEA 2004). It was engagingly structured around key themes and sought to set a development framework to 2021.

In contrast to the South East region, it is worth briefly stating how the substantive issues for the North East vary from those of a core region such as the South East. In national housing policy, where the key issue is producing sufficient units in serviced communities, outside the South East continued population decline in the metropolitan areas has contributed to processes of abandonment and issues of low demand in former local authority estates. This has taken place in parallel with large-scale land release for housing to provide executive homes, rationalised in terms of its contribution to economic development. While such measures are resisted by environmental groups across England, that resistance is felt much less keenly in the North East where environmentalists are excluded from the mainstream development discourse which defines which issues can be debated in North East strategy forums (Haughton and Counsell 2004). As Chatterton (2002) indicates, this discourse defines economic competitiveness very narrowly, focusing on social inclusion and environmental protection only inasmuch as they contribute to the attractiveness of the region to firms as a place to do business.

Where the planning system would habitually be expected to make an impact, the RPG fails to operate successfully as a mediating and decision-making tool. The consequence of this is that, when such controversial decisions have to be taken, RPG does not provide a procedure which leads rationally to the best decision and a legitimate mandate to proceed. Instead, regional actors appeal to the Secretary of State, to form an extra-planning vehicle, or an otherwise ad hoc agreement. Planning documents always include a caveat that exempts them from covering exceptional circumstances, and this discretion is regularly invoked in taking such controversial decisions in the region. We now use a small number of vignettes that highlight in more depth how regional planning in the North East has been shaped in recent times, and the role played by this "system discretion" in making the North East "plannable" given the identified failings of the RPG process.

Transport issues

Transport issues are typically and potentially one of the most significant topic areas for regional guidance (see Chapters 8 and 10). In recognition of this they are given greater weight under the new RSS system. This requires the regional planning boards (the regional chambers) to prepare a regional transport strategy (RTS) as part of RSS. In the North East, the timing of RPG preparation was such that the requirement to prepare an RTS emerged quite late in the process. In addition, transport policies in RPG were dependent on a number of studies that were under way and had not then reported.

That said, while RPG set out a number of important policy statements, concern had already been expressed over the somewhat "woolly" nature of some of the transport policies in it, particularly arising from an almost total lack of prioritisation of schemes. The absence of firm detail often arose from incomplete studies of sub-regional corridors, strategic rail services, ports and airports, much of which depended on national agencies, often themselves in a period of extreme institutional change. The transport chapter of the RPG continued into the final version of RPG as an "interim statement" of strategic transport objectives (GONE 2001). However, the fundamental point was that RPG was unable to make any firm prioritisation of the transport needs of the region, and effectively abdicated its responsibility to the regional transport strategy.

At this time, a process of preparing a separate regional transport strategy (RTS) was begun, with the RTS designed to be absorbed into the new RSS. However, many of the problems that beset the transport policies of RPG were also apparent in the draft RTS (Vigar and Porter 2005). Chief among these were: the dependence on agencies with their own agenda to implement much of the public transport policy; the difficulties in getting agreement on measures relating to demand management across the region; and a focus on schemes and capital funding rather than quality-of-life issues and measures dependent on revenue funding. That said, the process was able to secure agreement on some issues such as region-wide parking standards and on priorities such as the East Coast Main Line.

However, even given this focus on "schemes", arguably the most significant infrastructure proposal in the region at this time, the Second Tyne Crossing, was not debated in any depth through either RPG or RTS. This project was being promoted under the Transport and Works Act legislation in Parliament, and neither RPG nor RTS provided significant arenas within which to debate its merits. The promoter of the project, Nexus, acting in its role as passenger transport authority, saw it as an economic development project as well as an attempt to reduce congestion on a strategic transport link. It made some very strong claims, most notably that it would create 50,000 jobs in North Tyneside, which flew in the face of much evidence on the relationship between infrastructure investment and economic development. The project, furthermore, seemed likely to induce a great deal of (longer) commuting journeys, increasing the overall stress within the transport network whilst undermining efforts at demand management and the promotion of public transport. It thus seemed a rather curious position for an organisation promoting public transport to be in, given the inevitable increase in car mobility it would promote. That said, as the new crossing would have to pay for itself there were few options in relation to using it as a way of improving public transport options. Such issues were left to the inquiry, though, and the regional planning arenas had little role in debating them.

One area completely missing from regional debate was the potential for new rail and light rail systems to increase the functional linkages between outlying communities dependent on the Tyne and Wear conurbation, and the Tyneside city-region. This arose because the Strategic Rail Authority (SRA) assigned a priority to a number of those schemes, and then, as its available funding declined owing to increased spending on rail maintenance nationally, North Eastern schemes fell outside the scope of what could be funded. Thus, national factors made *impossible* the reopening of the Blyth–Ashington and Sunderland–Durham lines, potentially of regional importance by increased accessibility from deprived rural coalfields to new urban employment opportunities.

Newcastle Great Park

Newcastle Great Park (NGP) is a special development of sub-regional significance, in which green belt land was used out of the urgent need to prevent urban flight from the city of Newcastle (see Figure 14.2). The project rationale was to provide attractive housing and employment facilities near to Newcastle Airport. The land was allocated in the Newcastle Plan of 1993 and in subsequent unitary development plan (UDP) drafts.

In housing terms the proposal was also aimed at broadening the portfolio within the city's housing stock, providing the types of housing sought after by those perceived to be leaving the Newcastle local authority, namely executive housing in an "urban village" setting. The monocultural nature of the stock provided, which contravened central government advice on mixing tenures and housing types, was offset against an innovative deal that sought to provide social housing elsewhere in the city in return for land allocations at NGP itself.

The scale of this proposal, and its provision for a large portion of a particular type of housing, makes it of regional significance, but RPG had little to say about this allocation. It was left largely to the individual local authority to promote the idea and then arrange its passage through the call-in process by the Secretary of State, whose imprimatur, rather than that of RPG1, clearly lies on Newcastle

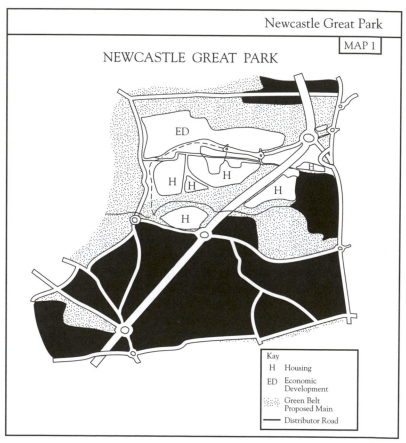

Figure 14.2 Newcastle Great Park: a special development of sub-regional significance

Source: NCC 2006

Great Park. RPG housing debates at the time were more focused on general numbers, with the regional authorities over-providing relative to central government guidance. Indeed, housing numbers were eventually reduced by the Secretary of State to ameliorate the environmental impact and prevent an undermining of efforts at promoting housing markets in the inner city (Haughton and Counsell 2004).

The real planning issue for the North East raised by NGP was managing economic boom in particular locales to stimulate housing renewal elsewhere. Newcastle faced a small version of the housing dilemma facing the whole region, namely the juxtaposition of market hot-spots next to blighted estates. The NGP plans argued for a rebalancing of housing to ensure that people wished to remain in the local authority area. However, there was no attempt to use the growth of the most successful areas to "drag up" less successful areas. The net effect, even within Newcastle, was to promote disconnected pockets of privilege connected by the road network rather than producing a more integrated and balanced urban hierarchy.

RPG has shown not only that it was incapable of producing an alternative vision to an "archipelago knowledge economy" spatial structure within Newcastle, but also that it was incapable of bringing local authorities together to promote balanced urban development and regeneration. RPG seemed to accept that these new estates were necessary to meet the expressed needs of knowledge workers, whose presence was vital for "regional competitiveness", a need stressed in many regional strategies. By separating the two problems of overheating and dereliction, and implicitly ignoring potential combined solutions, RPG failed to add any kind of strategic regional value.

Strategic employment sites

The third area where RPG has failed to move beyond a lowest common denominator is in its designation of so-called strategic employment sites (SESs) in the region. The very phrase "strategic sites" suggests a very limited number of flagship locations where planners seek to cluster industrial and service activities, create knowledge overspill, limit negative externalities and generate wealth for the region. However, looking more closely at the RPG, there are 35 strategic sites for a population of 2.4 million, indeed more than one site per unitary or district authority. A closer look at their location shows they are not as widely distributed as this number suggests, with the majority in Sunderland, Stockton and Middlesbrough. However, whatever this pattern of sites is, it is *not* strategic.

We argue that this reflects three issues in the region, none of which was ever properly dealt with in RPG. The first is that the location of the SESs is led by the availability of land in places where there are public incentives to develop it. A number of the sites in the south of the region are locations remediated by the former Teesside Development Corporation and for which no long-term purpose has been found. Only three of them are really strategic in the sense of being sites where property development could stimulate and reinforce economic development by encouraging the clustering of knowledge-intensive businesses, in Great North Park, around the Gateshead riverside, and amid the chemicals cluster on Teesside. The remainder are merely packages of land, near to good transport links and deprived communities for which it is easy to acquire development subsidies.

The second is that the region's discourse of competitiveness is still strongly shaped by a desire to attract inward investment; many of the high-profile investors in the North East – Nissan, Siemens, Fujitsu and Samsung – moved into "clean", out-of-town sites developed specifically for their needs. Although a number of high-profile closures in the 1990s have reduced the once-mesmeric hold that inward investment had over regional planners, there is still a residual belief that the availability of good, greenfield sites is important for regional competitiveness. It could be argued that the presence of 35 strategic sites is more about providing a real estate catalogue for inward investors than any attempt to use spatial concepts such as "growth poles" or "clusters" to use strategic sites to drive forward regional economic development.

The third issue is that there is clearly an element of the lowest common denominator in identifying such sites. Agreement on strategic sites was difficult in RPG, reflecting difficulties of brokerage between local authorities accountable to local constituencies interacting in the voluntary regional chambers. The absence of a body, such as an elected assembly, empowered to make difficult decisions makes the continuation of this highly likely. At present, with the regional chamber dominated by individual local authority representatives, such decisions have proved impossible (Haughton and Counsell 2004). Over-supply of sites was thus undermining strategic efforts to support regeneration in the coalfields and the urban core where social, economic and environmental reasons favoured their development.

Critically assessing the new regionalism in the North East

A number of issues flow from a consideration of RPG for the North East, but running throughout the vignettes is the dominance of the economic regeneration agenda in the media and the minds of stakeholders. This is reflected in the consensus view of strategy in the region, and has a number of significant consequences. Firstly, the RPG/RSS tends *not* to be taken as seriously as it might. The "strategic exceptions" clause facilitates this, and there is no strong environmental lobby to dispute its dominance. The RDA is a very strong voice in the region, and the RES appears to draw few principles from the spatial strategy. The RSS is, therefore, not shaping development and investment, and in the minds of a powerful economic development community it does not occupy a position of parity, as is the system intention, with the RES (Haughton and Counsell 2004).

As the RPG and RSS are not seen as highly significant, there are questions concerning the purpose of the strategy and the significance of the process by which it is drawn up. If you regard one important role of planning, as we do, as its being an integrating force, then *ownership* and *process* are central to the capacity planning has to effect real change. This has particular resonance with an opening theme in this chapter, namely whether planning was an integrating force.

It is our view that the opportunities presented by meta-governance are being lost and, more importantly, are unlikely to be better developed in the immediate future. There is a clear issue of "plannability" here: developments of strategic significance are taking place. Great North Park is a good example of such a development, which has largely emerged within a national framework, through the authority of the Deputy Prime Minister. The key issue here is that this has happened *despite* the planning system. To produce the projects the North East needs to solve its economic problems, i.e. to render the North East "plannable", regional actors are forced to rely on system discretion, which in turn means that system integration lacks any kind of purchase to shape proposed regional projects. Although integration and steering of strategies are not themselves significant without delivering results on the ground, failure to deliver strategic integration inhibits any attempts to promote balanced territorial development.

The problem seems to be that there is not a real focus for economic develop-ment in the region. Although the RES sets out a set of priorities, they remain, even in latest versions, generic attempts to address piecemeal problems rather than an overarching new vision of the region (Benneworth and Roberts 2002). Our critique of the RSS then is of a failure to capture the nature of strategic spatial development which can lodge in the minds of key policy makers and, moreover, do so in ways that convince them to develop policies suitable for the North East. Although there is a strong knowledge base, especially around planning, the poor fit of things like strategic sites to transport planning means that this knowledge base is undercapitalised.

Earlier in this chapter we have argued that strategic planning could potentially solve the regional problems of the North East. On the basis of this analysis, it appears as if shaping national policy priorities is first necessary to build capacity to address the region's economic development problems. In our concluding discussion which follows, we explore whether a national spatial strategy, and in particular the Sustainable Communities Plan, could begin to build some of this capacity for action in such demand from the region.

Might a national spatial strategy be the answer? Lessons from Holland

A national spatial strategy is a mechanism through which particular local and regional demands can be met and problems can be solved, providing different tools, instruments and arrangements to reflect very different local conditions. There is a range of governments in Europe that use national spatial strategies as a means of coordinating spatial development; such strategies are not dependent on particular regional–national relationships. Belgium, Ireland and the Netherlands each have very different forms of regional governance and centre–regional relations, but each country uses a national spatial strategy to coordinate develop-ment planning. Indeed Wales, Scotland and Northern Ireland all now have national planning frameworks. In this section, we look briefly at the case of the Dutch national spatial planning to demonstrate how, in a situation comparable to England, national-scale planning helps to facilitate more effective, and more territorially nuanced, regional planning.

The Dutch spatial strategy is promulgated by the Ministry for Housing, Spatial Planning and Environment (VROM), created in 1982 to integrate the needs of the various sectors. Planning was dominated until the 1960s to address post-war concerns, at which point housing was brought within the planning ministry. The responsibility of the new ministry was further expanded in 1982 to cover the environment in response to contemporaneous environmental protection laws, thereby creating VROM. The basis document for the national spatial plan is the *Nota Ruimte*, which uses a number of spatial concepts to explain how the plan intends to achieve its aims of a better-planned Dutch spatial system. These spatial concepts, which could apply anywhere, are then grounded into particular places; this grounding process ensures that particular places are allocated roles in the Dutch space economy.

The Dutch national spatial strategy uses the concept of "network cities" as the organisational principle for its urban structure. However, this is grounded into six concrete named network cities, including the Randstad, Groningen–Assen and Twente (Enschede–Hengelo–Almelo) (2005). The overall planning aim is to allocate land to create opportunities for the development of diverse economic and social activities to strengthen the overall position of the Dutch economy. The role of the network cities within this is to allow for the concentration of scarce economic resources into dense investment foci to maximise their urban competitiveness, which in turn allows other places to concentrate on providing leisure opportunities and maintaining landscapes of national importance (VROM 2004: 3).

Although a strict territorial demarcation has recently been somewhat diluted in the latest *Nota Ruimte*, the clear articulation of both sectoral and territorial principles means that it is clear that, in planning terms, urbanised areas such as Apeldoorn–Deventer–Zutphen are not to be treated as such "network cities". Consequently, there is a presumption against targeted urban expansion in these areas, so the concept provides the urban structure for the economic organisation of the country, with the majority of the economic core zones falling in and around these six network cities. Consequently, the Apeldoorn–Deventer–Zutphen triangle is explicitly not part of a Dutch economic core zone.

These core economic zones have in turn been adopted by the Ministry of Economic Affairs as the basis for its strategic planning. The national economic strategy for the Netherlands, *Pieken in de Delta* (Peaks in the Delta), strongly reflects those positions set out in the spatial plan. Indeed, the national economic strategy contains a map in which the different zones of the country, made up of two or three similar regions, are each given a "brand" or place in the national economy. Each network city corresponds to one of these zones, so Groningen is styled as the gateway from the Randstad to North East Europe, and Limburg is styled as the technological leading region, reflecting the presence of the Eindhoven research and development complex. Thus regional innovation policy from the Ministry of Economic Affairs has concentrated on investing in the South East and Eastern regions, which are both designated as the leading sites for Dutch technological innovation.

One issue which is clear in planning systems with strong and well-articulated national spatial strategies, such as this Dutch case, is that there are clear winning and losing territories within this system. With the *Nota Ruimte*, some provinces, notably Friesland, have no such economic core zones, whilst other provinces (such as Flevoland or Drenthe) are only included in those zones in a very limited form because of their functional linkages to the network cities, casting them as residential rather than industrial areas. There is no implication from this that there is no concern for balanced territorial justice within the Dutch planning system, just that development in the peripheral north is to be concentrated in an effort to create a growth pole around the Groningen network city.

The Dutch case is presented because of the lessons which it gives in demonstrating the value of national joining up as a mean of integrating regional planning. We have already noted that, in the course of the regionalisation project in the UK after 1997, the government has consistently emphasised the role of regional bodies in joining up strategies at a local scale. What the Dutch system demonstrates is the importance of a national strategy in producing joined-up thinking about the economic role of particular places. In the final section, we turn to look once more at the Sustainable Communities Plan, to ask whether, in light of this Dutch experience, it is sufficient to create a planning framework that meets the deep-seated economic needs of the region. The key question for assessing the importance of the Sustainable Communities Plan is to ask what role does it see for less successful regions, and how does it bend other policy domains to support remaking those places into that role?

Conclusions: the Sustainable Communities Plan as a "national spatial strategy" for the North?

The Sustainable Communities Plan is a flagship policy of the government, and was an attempt to produce a coherent approach to urban policy. The Communities Plan itself has five themes which constitute the sectoral organising logic for RPG, namely affordable housing, housing abandonment, decent homes, liveability and countryside protection. Two of these have clear spatialities, affordable housing for the South and East of England, and housing abandonment for the North and Midlands. It is interesting that very different levels of resources have been committed to these two themes: £5 billion was allocated for the provision of affordable housing whilst only £500 million was made available for the market pathfinders (admittedly a pilot project). Thus although the Communities Plan seems to offer tools for all regions, it favours certain activities that are more prevalent in some regions than others.

The main weakness of the Communities Plan is its failure to offer a strong territorial organisational principle for the North East and its failure to set out a positive vision for the place of the North East in the UK economy. Although documents have been published for each English region setting out how the Communities Plan applies to them, there is no formal and explicit prioritisation between different regions for economic development and regeneration. There is one such explicit spatial/territorial provision, for four "key growth areas" around the South East, but these are a reflection of existing demand for housing rather than an attempt to create new regional growth poles. By contrast, there is no provision for creating any such propulsive location outside the orbit of London.

There is a weak territorial dimension to the plan, a recognition that the main focus of the policy did relate to dealing with the problems of overheating in the South East and ameliorating housing market collapse outside this core region. This recognition led the ODPM to launch the "Northern Way" in February 2004, nine months after the main plan was launched. The Northern Way is a strategy for the three Northern regions, namely the North East, North West and Yorkshire and the Humber (see Figure 14.3). The approach appears eminently sensible because all three regions face similar sets of problems, although they are

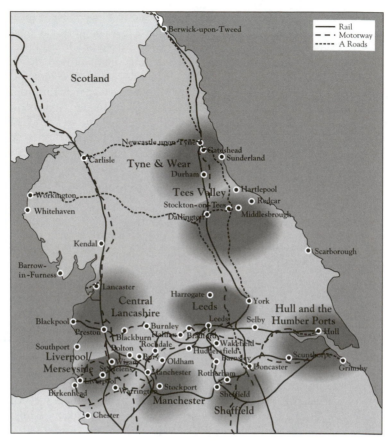

Figure 14.3 City regions and the Northern Way

Source: Northern Way 2005

themselves a very diverse set of regions, and these problems are different to those faced by the core regions.

However, more problematic is the fact that government considers "joining up" to be a process that takes place at regional level. There is no commitment within government to ensuring that those national policies which shape public investment flows also support regional renaissances across the nine English regions. In short, the territorial implications of mainstream sectoral programmes are not "region-proofed".

Although there is an inter-regional dimension to the Northern Way, there are two flaws in its presentation. The first is that the report only considers the three Northern regions, despite an acceptance that balanced regional growth in the UK requires balancing between the North and South. The second is that it appears to accept the need to consolidate strengths, and Manchester appears in the report as the dominant city-region. We would point out here the limitations to inter-regional planning and strategies that exclude certain regions.

If the Sustainable Communities Plan seems disadvantageous to the North East of England, then it is worth rearticulating that it is, nevertheless, an improvement on the prior situation. Although the Communities Plan does not offer specific territorial growth policies for peripheral regions, the recently announced Science City programme under the aegis of the Northern Way strategy allocates £100 million to three northern cities, York, Newcastle and Manchester, to invest in science and technology to promote economic development. Prior to 1997, it is certainly true to say that the North East mainly attempted to use policy instruments designed to manage housing expansion and to promote economic development and regeneration, and this created a set of problems which the available instruments were unable to address.

Finally, what is less clear is whether, and to what extent, the Northern Way will be able to give the North East an improved role in the UK economy. The real fault line for regional planning in England is, as we have seen, that policies for the South East are largely inapplicable to the North East, highlighting once again the importance of context, as emphasised in Chapter 5. This fault line cannot be addressed by the Northern Way as it stands, and seems to require a national-level framework in which planning and economic policy decisions are taken with a transparent regional dimension. This would permit the "losers" as well as the "winners" from particular policy decisions to be clear. In this chapter, we argue that regional planning has been a significant *lost opportunity* for the region, although through no fault of the regional participants. If the North East is to harness the potential benefits of regional planning that other authors have made clear, this demands a national planning statement with a clear set of territorial visions for all the English regions.

References

Alden, J. 2002. Scenarios for the future of regional planning within UK/EU spatial planning. Ch. 3 in *Contemporary issues in regional planning*, T. Marshall, J. Glasson and P. Headicar (eds). Aldershot: Ashgate.

Amin, A., D. Massey and N. Thrift 2003. *Decentering the nation: a radical approach to regional inequality*. London: Catalyst.

Benneworth, P. S. 2004. In what sense "regional development"? Entrepreneurship, underdevelopment and strong tradition in the periphery. *Entrepreneurship and Regional Development* **16**(6), 437–58.

Benneworth, P. S. and P. Roberts 2002. Devolution, sustainability and local economic development: impacts on local autonomy, policy-making and economic development outcomes. *Local Economy* **17**(3), 239–52.

Benneworth, P. S., P. Roberts and L. Conroy 2002. Strategic connectivity, sustainable development and the new English regional governance. *Journal of Environmental Planning and Management* **45**(2), 199–218.

Benneworth, P. S., J. Tomaney, S. Gonzalez, M. Coombes, L. Humphreys and A. Pike 2006. Memorandum of evidence on "What future is there for regional government?". In *What future is there for regional government?* Office of the Deputy Prime Minister: Housing, Planning, Local Government and the Regions Inquiry. London: Stationery Office.

Chatterton, P. 2002. Be realistic: demand the impossible – moving towards "strong" sustainable development in an old industrial region? *Regional Studies* **35**(5), 552–61.

Counsell, D., G. F. Haughton, P. Allmendinger and G. Vigar 2006. "Integrated" spatial planning: is it living up to expectations? *Town and Country Planning*, September.

Cullingworth, J. B. 1982. *Town and country planning in Britain*. London: George Allen & Unwin.

DoE 1989. *Strategic guidance for Tyne and Wear*. Regional Planning Guidance Note 1. Department of the Environment. London: HMSO.

DoE 1998. *Our competitive future: building the knowledge-driven economy*. Department of Trade and Industry. London: HMSO.

DTI 2000. *Excellence and opportunity: a science and technology policy for the 21st century*. Department of Trade and Industry. London: HMSO.

DTI and DfEE 2001. *Opportunity for all in a world of change: a White Paper on enterprise, skills and innovation*. Department of Trade and Industry and Department for Education and Employment. London: HMSO.

DTLR 2002. *Your region, your choice: a White Paper on regional government*. Department for Transport, Local Government and the Regions. London: HMSO.

Gillespie, A. and P. Benneworth 2002. Industrial and regional policy in a devolved United Kingdom. In *Devolution in practice: public policy differences within the UK*, J. Adams and P. Robinson (eds). London: Institute for Public Policy Research.

GONE 2001. *Regional planning guidance for North East England*. Newcastle: Government Office for the North East.

Hammond, C. 2003. Joining up policy in the English regions. Unpublished Ph.D. thesis, University of Newcastle upon Tyne, Newcastle.

Haughton, G. and D. Counsell 2004. *Regions, spatial strategies and sustainable development*. London: Routledge.

HM Treasury 2001. *Productivity, 3: The regional dimension*. London: HMSO.

Hudson, R. 1989. *Wrecking a region: state policies, party politics and regional change in north east England*. London: Pion.

Jensen, O. B. and T. Richardson 2003. *Making European space*. London: Routledge.

Jessop, B. 2002. *The future of the capitalist state*. Cambridge: Polity.

Lloyd, G. 2002. Urban regeneration and community development in Scotland: converging agendas for action. *Sustainable Development* **10**, 147–54.

NEA 2004. *VIEW: shaping the North East – the regional spatial strategy for the North East consultation draft*. Newcastle: North East Assembly.

NCC 2006. *Revised master plan and supplementary planning document and the sustainability appraisal for Newcastle Great Park*. Newcastle: Newcastle City Council.

Northern Way 2005. *Moving forward*. Newcastle: Northern Way.

ODPM 2003a. *Sustainable communities: building for the future*. Office of the Deputy Prime Minister. London: HMSO.

ODPM 2003b. *Making it happen: the Thames Gateway and the growth areas*. London: Office of the Deputy Prime Minister.

ODPM 2004. *Making it happen: the Northern Way*. London: Office of the Deputy Prime Minister.

Rice, P. and A. J. Venables 2003. Equilibrium regional disparities: theory and British evidence. *Regional Studies* **37**, 675–86.

Robinson, F. 1993. More than bricks and mortar? A new report on urban development corporations, University of Durham.

Vigar, G. and G. Porter 2005. Regional governance and strategic transport policy: a case study of North East England. *European Spatial Research and Policy* **12**(1), 89–108.

Vigar, G., P. Healey, A. D. Hull and S. Davoudi 2000. *Planning, governance and spatial strategy in Britain: an institutionalist analysis*. London: Macmillan.

VROM 2004. *De vijfde nota ruimte: ruimte voor ontwikkeling* [The fifth national spatial plan for the Netherlands: space for development]. The Hague: Ministerie voor Volkshuisvesting, Ruimtelijke Ordening en Milieu.

15 Strategic and regional planning in the North West

Gwyndaf Williams and Mark Baker

Introduction

The commitment to regional planning activities within the UK has, as pointed out elsewhere in this book, waxed and waned over time, with a mixture of political will, professional commitment, legislative backing and organisational structure, highlighting what has essentially been a frustrating story. The 1980s in particular was marked by a downgrading of government concern for strategic planning in the face of a commitment to market-led development and to project realisation; "the capacity of the strategic planning system seemed to be weaker than at any time since 1945, with the range of strategic issues to be confronted being greater than ever" (Breheny 1991: 235).

The last decade, however, has marked a significant watershed in the re-emergence of interest in strategic matters, and this chapter explores the degree to which the emergence of regional institutional frameworks has built up a regional consciousness (Mawson 1997). It also considers whether this offers the prospect of providing links between strategic spatial planning and regional development more widely, and is evidence of a political commitment to accountability at the regional level. It focuses in particular on inter-agency involvement in the development of a strategic planning framework for North West England, and considers the development of a regionally coherent strategy in what has historically been one of the UK's most fragmented regions.

Such concerns have been set within the wider context of increasing professional and academic interest in the organisation of the state as a territorial entity, and the multifaceted process of re-territorialisation that has gained in currency over the past decade. It is clear that this has involved commitments to break down historic preoccupations with a single national policy framework, as indicated in the preceding chapter, in order to deal with complex issues that involve systematic territorial differences. Part of the received wisdom stemming from such "new regionalist" perspectives as outlined in Chapter 5 centres on the widely held notion that regions such as the North West need to acquire a clear and coherent institutional identity if they are to induce improved economic performance.

Deas (2006) notes that such arguments have been given added salience by three factors of particular relevance for North West England. Firstly, the region has a history of fragmentation and evidence of the limited effectiveness of previous efforts to develop regionally based institutions, being continually frustrated by potent inter-jurisdictional tensions and city-based identities that have limited the development of a popular regional consciousness. Secondly, the region's historical experience of economic sluggishness and lack of competitive dynamism relative to South East England has fuelled long-standing concerns over intractable, structurally embedded and politically sanctioned inter-regional inequalities. Finally, there have been reservations as to the region's ability to exploit emerging EU funding regime developments that focus on regional coherence and institutional architecture evident elsewhere in the EU, which could be holding back the region's potential.

The regional context of the North East

Bristow (1987) viewed the North West as one of Britain's most fragmented regions, with imprecise boundaries compounded by the diversity of its economy and the fragmentation of its polity, and with little experience of political responses at the regional level to the challenges posed by recession and decline. Strong traditions of political and economic rivalry have been particularly noticeable between Manchester and Liverpool, where "the culture of parochialism has tended to predominate, with local interests determining outcomes, and with areas often in conflict over resources" (Wong and Howe 1995: 2). Others have noted that the very looseness of possible regional coalitions – unable to confront crucial issues likely to affect development – has historically made the region unable to set any sort of strategic priorities.

The region extends over 14,140 square kilometres and has a population of 6.9 million and a labour force of 2.6 million (see Figure 15.1), making it the second-largest region in Britain. Three-fifths of its population live in the major conurbations of Greater Manchester (2.6 million) and Merseyside (1.4 million) – both with population densities of over 2,000 persons per square kilometre – with further concentrations in the largely Victorian industrial towns of Central and East Lancashire and North Cheshire. One of the world's first industrial regions, and still one of the country's leading manufacturing locations, it has been particularly badly hit by the process of de-industrialisation. It has a poor reinvestment record, the lowest rate of new firm formation in Britain, and poor regional performance in terms of inward investment (Tickell *et al.* 1995). The region is peripheral to existing and emerging European markets, and has been hit hard by contemporary changes in defence-related industries.

The North West, however, has a large market with good access to both domestic and other markets, and production costs are low. Manchester is England's most sophisticated financial centre outside London, and Manchester Airport is by far the largest provider of international services outside the South East. Its transport infrastructure is good but needs upgrading, whilst its environmental settings are diverse. Intra-regionally, the impact of economic change has been uneven and fragmented, with Merseyside perceived as being in a state of continual crisis from which it is only now beginning to emerge. Greater Manchester has attempted to overcome structural decline through vigorous image building, whilst the less urban parts of Cheshire, Lancashire and Cumbria have demonstrated relative success.

In terms of public administration, the region has lacked coherence, with no regional administrative focus, possessing two regional offices of government

Figure 15.1 The North West region

throughout the 1980s and 1990s, and with 46 local authorities (3 counties, 25 shire districts, 3 unitary authorities and 15 metropolitan districts). This has been compounded by institutional variety involving both the public and the private sector, with such fragmentation within the region being considered to be high in comparison with other British regions.

During the early 1990s, however, the North West saw the gradual emergence of a regional consciousness, involving the modifying of local governance, pragmatic public–private cooperation, and the fledgling promotion of business leadership at the regional level (Burch and Holliday 1993). In the context of modifying local governance, this involved both the restructuring of government administration within the region and the initial establishment of a regional association of local authorities in order to provide a more coherent regional message and image.

Following a manifesto commitment, the Conservative government established Government Offices for the Regions (GORs) in the early 1990s in order to decentralise strategic policy making to the regions, and to coordinate government activity (Mawson and Spencer 1997). In the North West, however, in order to coincide with the "realpolitik" of the region, this new "coordinated approach" did not go so far as to centralise such coordination in one regional office, and the North West (alone amongst British regions) sustained its existing dual presence until 1998, with the Government Office for Merseyside (GOM) and the Government Office for the North West (GONW). Whilst this may have ensured that the region received more public investment overall, it clearly did *nothing* for the regional coordination of investment and development activity.

Of greater significance was the establishment of the North West Regional Association (NWRAss) as a consortium of all local authorities, with the aim of promoting the image and influencing the future prosperity of the region, as well as acting as a regional voice in lobbying the UK government and European institutions (NWRAss 1993). This was clearly encouraged (by both the European Commission (EC) and the North West Business Leadership Team) to enable the region to reflect structural realities facing development opportunities, and in order to facilitate local cooperation for leveraging in additional investment. It was also established as an essentially defensive attempt to ensure that the North West remained competitive in gaining European Structural Funds. It was clearly an attempt to overcome perceived deficiencies in Britain's territorial distribution of power, improve working relationships between public administration and business leaders, and raise regional awareness and a forum for debate. The driving force was clearly the gradual emergence of a regional elite within the region, consisting of leading politicians and senior officers from county councils and the large metropolitan districts, and regional business and employment interests.

This institutional development did not, however, simply depend on local perceptions of a need to develop a unified and coherent approach, but was also in relation to the undertaking of a number of specific tasks. Chief amongst these was the preparation of the first North West regional economic strategy, some years before the creation of the North West Development Agency (NWDA) (PIEDA 1993). From an EU perspective, significant rule changes governing the distribution of Structural Funds focused increasingly on indications of political coherence within constituent regions, and a move towards medium-term programme strategies, and this undoubtedly stimulated the development of such an initiative.

Following the publication of the regional economic strategy, NWRAss established two parallel but interrelated structures: firstly, a Strategy Secretariat to move the strategy forward, to monitor its application, and to develop cooperation and collaboration across the region; and, secondly, a committee coordinating the distribution of Structural Funds and other funds from the European Community. These wider aims were subsequently accommodated through the establishment of the North West Partnership in December 1994.

A parallel development also saw the emergence of the initial regional planning guidance (RPG) for the region (NWRAss 1993) as a framework for moving forward the focus of local development plans. These first-generation strategies undoubtedly put to the test the depth of political and institutional commitment to collaboration that existed within the region, with these initial frameworks being subsequently strengthened and enhanced with the production of new economic development and planning guidance at the regional level, reinforced by the emergence of initial regional housing and of infrastructural statements.

The early years

The emergence of a spatial development strategy

Over the past three decades the region's broad spatial development thrust has focused on the major conurbations, with the Strategic Plan for the North West (North West Joint Planning Team 1974) stressing the need to concentrate development and renewal investment in the Mersey Basin, and with additional investment proposed in a series of surrounding new towns. Within this context, land-use policy in the 1980s – expressed through metropolitan structure plans and specific subject plans – was focused on the core of the conurbations, this being reinforced by a commitment to retain a tight green belt. Such an approach was underpinned by the surrounding county structure plans of Lancashire and Cheshire, which additionally focused on regenerating medium-sized towns that had developed rapidly in the nineteenth century, often around single industries. With the abolition of metropolitan authorities in 1986 this focus on conurbation cores remained evident in the subsequent strategic guidance prepared for metropolitan areas (Merseyside: DoE 1988; and Greater Manchester: DoE 1989) and the initial RPG for the North West (GONW and GOM 1996).

If the metropolitan areas are taken as exemplars of such policy expression then Greater Manchester benefited from an existing conurbation-wide framework set by its structure plan, with the thematic focus of draft strategic advice being concerned with urban regeneration and economic revitalisation. Environmental enhancement and the use of green belt policy to reinforce this focus were complementary thrusts. Whilst, in general, agreement was quickly reached between districts on the proposed advice, a number of divergent views did appear, owing to the resurgence of old rivalries and district aspirations. This was particularly illustrated with reference to housing land allocations figures, out-of-centre retail development, and "adjustments" to green belt boundaries. On Merseyside, political dissonance between the respective authorities was even more obvious, which undoubtedly disadvantaged guidance preparation, with the conurbation lacking an overarching framework for undertaking more detailed work. At officer level, strenuous efforts were made to produce a coherent view, with the main thrust of guidance being remarkably similar to that found in Greater Manchester. Thereafter, the process of unitary development plan (UDP) preparation could begin at the metropolitan district level, a process that was not to be fully completed for a decade (Williams 1999; Batey 1999).

Local authority reflection on the process of preparing metropolitan strategic guidance in the late 1980s noted, however, that a "lowest common denominator" policy document had emerged in both cases as a result of attempting to accommodate policy and political differences between individual districts. Resulting policy guidance was thus non-controversial, but provided little in the way of a metropolitan-level vision, or a consideration of the relationship between the future of metropolitan sub-regions within the North West and an emerging regional strategy. Whilst the planning framework set the context for the strategic content of individual development plans, its influence declined as the UDP process progressed in the 1990s. Indeed, there is little feeling that the summation of UDP strategies at individual local authority level, when combined at conurbation level, provided a strategic metropolitan vision. Moves during the rest of the 1990s to focus on the strategic planning debate at the regional level were to devalue further specifically metropolitan-area concerns (Deas and Ward 2000).

The increasing significance given to a development plan-led system in the early 1990s (DoE 1992) was accompanied by a commitment to enhancing the strategic dimension. This took the form of government advice that each English region should produce regional planning guidance that would provide the framework for development plans and the basis for regional cooperation and advocacy. This had long been felt to be a weakness within the region, with the initial Strategic Plan for the North West not having been subject to monitoring and review procedures to prepare the region for the dramatically changed circumstances of the 1990s:

> The North West is unique amongst the major regions of the United Kingdom in emerging into the 1990s with no coherent statement of priorities and opportunities . . . [This] weakens the region's case in seeking new infrastructural investment, and hampers the co-ordination of transport and development . . . [It] undermines the confidence of developers and financial institutions, and the scope for attracting new private investment.
>
> (RTPI North West 1990: 32)

The impetus for strategy formation often arises from a particular institutional setting, with key stakeholders initiating concern and attempting to mobilise interest. Indeed, several months prior to the establishment of NWRAss's officer working groups, GONW had already begun to initiate the regional strategy-making process by producing a putative guidance note at the end of 1991, the content of which was to influence significantly the later *Greener growth* document (NWRAss 1993). Even at this stage, however, sub-regional representations were made, with Lancashire criticising GONW's efforts as paying insufficient attention to sustainable development, and Cumbria noting that the document was weak on sub-regional issues and ignored the county's peripherality. Merseyside authorities noted the lack of reference to the resources needed to fulfil the objectives, and the absence of any real analysis of the region's capacities and weaknesses, a view similarly held by Cheshire.

It was thus not until autumn 1992 that a region-wide meeting of strategic planning officers took place to decide upon the strategy-making process, and to begin to address the issue of stakeholder involvement. This meeting set the context for RPG preparation, establishing a working group and agreeing that the output of such deliberations would be a fairly low-key document. It was concluded that no additional staff resources were available to undertake such work, with the central input into the eventual RPG13 having to be fitted around existing commitments. Concern was expressed over the timetable proposed for consultation with outside agencies and agreement to focus on a few selected key stakeholders. The output from this work – *Greener growth* – marked the beginning of institutional collaboration at a strategic level (NWRAss 1993). However, the issues identified in the document largely mirrored topics noted for consideration in official guidance on the process, reflected the content of other regions' draft RPGs and revealed no real sense of regional distinctiveness.

The document sets out local authority views on: regional planning needs in relation to the provision of a strategic development framework; economic development, housing and environmental concerns; transport and traffic issues; and the need for a closer working relationship at regional level to further European opportunities and competitiveness. The primary focus of the development framework was to continue to press for regeneration to concentrate on the conurbations and older urban areas, together with a balanced portfolio of development sites outside such areas. A complementary dimension to this perspective was an argument for modest growth of towns along the west coast transport spine, and the need to consider future green belt boundaries.

The subsequent formal draft of RPG for the North West was issued by GONW and GOM, and broadly reflected earlier advice (GONW and GOM 1996). It was intended to guide the preparation of strategic land-use plans in Cheshire, Cumbria and Lancashire, and to take over from metropolitan strategic guidance for Greater Manchester and Merseyside. The draft recognised the continuing centrality of the Mersey Belt as a focus for investment, but with scope for a modest shift in emphasis towards a "North–South spine" (focused on the M6 corridor) as development plans rolled forward. It noted that the aim was to give a regional dimension to national planning policies and other government policies and statements, and urged that a regional perspective be adopted for prioritising land-use development opportunities. The document noted that development plans in preparation across the region had varying time horizons, and asked NWRAss to urgently consider options for standardising such time frames in order to facilitate monitoring and review. More prophetically, it maintained that such guidance would be used strategically by the government's regional offices to assess grant-related submissions and to set priorities for the public expenditure they managed.

Two major points of contention between the draft RPG and the earlier *Greener growth* document however emerged. Firstly, it was noted that there was no evidence to indicate an overall shortage of land and buildings in urban areas to accommodate the region's development needs to 2011, and that established green belts would therefore be maintained. In contrast, *Greener growth* had actively supported the need to review green belt boundaries if it could be proved that not releasing such land would prejudice the revitalisation of the region. Secondly, the housing figures submitted in *Greener growth* were based on the 1989-based Office of Population Censuses and Surveys (OPCS) household projections. A requirement of draft RPG was for the NWRAss to review these figures in the light of 1993-based OPCS population and household projections, which suggested that housing figures should be considerably higher (particularly in Greater Manchester), with concurrent impacts on the continuation of established boundaries. More worryingly, evidence was already emerging of the lack of ownership of the eventual guidance by the region's main stakeholders, this being expressed subsequently at the Cheshire Structure Plan EIP.

The final regional planning guidance (RPG13) was adopted in May 1996, completing nationwide coverage of such guidance (Baker 1998). It was locally accepted that, whilst it encompassed much of the policy concerns of earlier documents, a significant additional workload would be generated for NWRAss, particularly in actively monitoring its implementation, requiring the full support of its constituent authorities and access to available resources for this purpose. In particular, it was expected that early work would focus on a review of housing needs and urban potential, prioritised locations and categorisation of strategic employment sites, facilities for the regional disposal and management of waste, and strategic options for accommodating the region's development needs up to and beyond 2011.

Following the publication of the RPG, the region's local authorities began to pressurise NWRAss to pursue such work, in order that it would link with reviews of UDPs and structure plans. However, it was clear to NWRAss from the outset that such commitment would require external financial and institutional support, facilitating further development of partnership building and stakeholder involvement within the region. The first outcome of such a concern was the commissioning of an urban capacity study to develop a practical and robust methodology for estimating the potential of urban areas to absorb future growth (Llewellyn Davies 1997). The requirement to review the sustainable management of waste also facilitated closer institutional collaboration in the region, with growing links emerging between NWRAss and the Environment Agency.

Progress on other areas of monitoring, though, was slow, this being highlighted by a lack of institutional coordination in compiling a unified regional strategic employment sites portfolio. A number of such lists had been prepared – an input into the RPG exercise, a NWRA/INWARD portfolio inputted into the regional economic strategy, and a separate study commissioned by English Partnerships – each with differing rationales that had proved difficult to harmonise. A sub-group of the North West Partnership was thus established to explore the scope for a more coordinated approach. In a wider context, GONW was keen to push forward RPG monitoring on a number of fronts, particularly in the light of the timetable for reviewing development plans in the region and in the context of strengthening RPG13. It accepted that this might require outside institutional assistance and the building of stronger links with other agencies within the region.

The promotion of an economic development strategy

From the early 1970s the North West had become progressively less successful in attracting direct foreign investment, with the North West Industrial Development Association (NORWIDA), established in 1931, increasingly lacking credibility as an effective promoter (Dicken and Tickell 1992). It was replaced by the North West Agency for Regional Development (INWARD) in 1985, funded by the Department of Trade and Industry (DTI) but with membership subscription support from both business interests and local authorities. Its close relationship with the DTI's Invest in Britain Bureau and its quasi-statutory function meant that it was precluded from discriminating solely in favour of areas where the local authority was a member, and this resulted in some local authorities refusing to join (e.g. Manchester). Similarly some business interests felt that their networking benefits were best met by Chambers of Commerce, with INWARD's remit being too closely tied to the DTI's. This created problems for the organisation's funding base, its legitimacy to speak as a regional voice, and its effectiveness operationally, all signs of the problems of strategic fragmentation inherent in the region (Tickell *et al.* 1995).

The commitment to provide a regional voice to take forward the regional economic strategy (RES) led to the launch of North West Partnership, bringing together key decision makers from the public, private and voluntary sectors, the labour movement and higher education. Its aim was to provide a consultative framework, leading to greater understanding between partners and agreement on how to meet the challenges facing the region. It aimed to focus action on a key set of priority areas (e.g. linking the regional economic strategy with the transport strategy and environmental action plans, exploring further EU funding opportunities and contributing to the work of its Committee of the Regions), but it rapidly became evident that to be effective it would need to be properly resourced and staffed. Whilst public sector bodies attempted to co-opt private sector interests, business people also began to pursue their own strategic agendas, the key group being the North West Business Leadership Team (NWBLT 1999). Chaired by the Duke of Westminster, with membership restricted to 30 business leaders with corporate strength in the region, it acted most effectively as a political lobby, exploiting extensive individual contacts and the collective weight of its membership. The achievement of the NWBLT is difficult to quantify, but it undoubtedly promoted a sense of "North West" amongst the region's major executives during the early 1990s, and broadened the region's lobby in Westminster. However, a degree of competition for credibility between INWARD and the NWBLT remained throughout the remainder of their lives, with the NWBLT continuing to exercise its reactive lobbying influence, and with INWARD perceiving its focus as being in the inward investment field.

Any attempt at regional strategy building had, in the past, produced fragile coalitions, not durable partnerships, with the whole aim being not to step on toes or to focus on potentially divisive issues. Thus a number of studies had concentrated on supply-side concerns dealing with promotional and infrastructural issues, and had couched aims and objectives in the vaguest and most general terms. An initial Civic Trust for the North West (1986) study outlining development opportunities within the region was reviewed, updated and presented as a regional promotional strategy, being a joint initiative by the Civic Trust for the North West, INWARD, the North West Business Leadership Team and the North West Region Group of Eight (Civic Trust for the North West 1991). As well as regional promotion, it aimed to develop a strategic vision of the North West based on a series of proposals concerning the stimulation of entrepreneurship, new planning guidelines for the location of "prestige companies", enhancement of communication infrastructure, and the promotion of new residential and service industry initiatives in the major urban centres. Its shortcomings as a "strategic vision" have been noted, particularly its naive belief in the strength of a "vision" and a "will", rather than the realities of the global economy and the region's pre-existing infrastructural deficiencies.

A separate study commissioned by private sector construction interests set out a development agenda based on a twin strategy combining a "worst first" with an "invest in success" strategy (North West Group of Eight 1989). This report promoted a vigorous regeneration policy, combined with the pursuit of "strategic assets". These were conceived as small to medium-sized towns with a high quality of life and offering a positive magnet for investment, perceived as being particularly well represented in North West England. This was again essentially a symbolic promotional and marketing study which did not have any direct involvement from either local authorities or the business community, and was in no way an executive plan with agreed delivery mechanisms.

The region thus entered the 1990s still without a development strategy, with any attempts to suggest the setting of priorities or to handle distributional issues by supposedly "strategic" organisations seen to be too fragile and divisive. However, following the revision of the EC's approach to the allocation of Structural Funds, the NWRAss/NWBLT commissioned an independent economic strategy for North West England (PIEDA 1993). This was an overdue attempt to demonstrate, at sub-regional level, a collective "North West interest" rather than nascent parochialism, with the focusing of minds based on the common objective of leveraging money from Europe. "There is absolutely no doubt about it that if it hadn't been for that private–public sector involvement, the regional strategy would never have been agreed, and the benefits that will flow from it would never have been here" (Peck and Tickell 1994: 256).

Drafting the strategy and the consultation process was centred on NWRAss's working groups, a NWBLT monitoring group and a number of presentations made to North West Business Forum, and regular consultation with the EC's DGXVI and the regional offices of the Department of the Environment (DoE) and the DTI. The main components of the study were to focus on economy, environment and infrastructure, with the crucial issues facing the region perceived to be the availability of resources and the efficiency with which they were used.

The initial intention was that the strategy be fully ratified by the end of 1992, but its launch was delayed by disputes over the expansion of airport capacity at Manchester rather than a supplemental role for Liverpool (a similar conflict to that which arose in regional planning guidance over strategic development sites) and dissonance over whether the region needed a regional development company, with a wider remit and broader powers than INWARD. Heads were "knocked together" and final ratification took place in May 1993. The strategy put together a vision which would initially stabilise the region's relative decline and would thereafter promote economic convergence that facilitated moving closer to European averages in terms of economic performance. Both the Partnership and NWRAss decided to review the regional economic strategy in 1996, to move the focus forward to 2004. This was brought together by the North West Partnership Task Group in summer 1996, chaired by the NW Confederation of British Industry (CBI), and had local authority and other representation (CBI, BLT, Chambers, TECs, private sector and higher education institutions). At this stage it was noted that since the original RES considerable regional changes had taken place that had to be accommodated in order to reflect economic and institutional realities beyond the millennium. These influences – the establishment of integrated regional offices of government, the restructuring of higher education, amendments to Structural Fund financing arrangements, and the launch of challenge funding arrangements in relation to regeneration – were also to be set within the context of emergent views on the preparation of regional transport strategies and regional planning guidance, and statements on regional sustainability concerns.

The main conclusion of the 1996 RES review was that the region was still declining relative to the UK average, but that the rate of decline was decreasing, and that there was a need to concentrate on developing the "modern parts of its economy". A strong proactive role was required in building links with other regions, and in developing a long term lobbying strategy for Europe, whilst at the same time benchmarking itself against best global practice. It was clear that the region had to foster an innovation culture, promote connectivity between the workforce and education, and develop a strong human resources strategy. The small and medium enterprise (SME) sector remained weak and in need of support; a broadly based portfolio of strategic employment sites was required; and the swathe of sub-standard housing required strong action if both sustainable economic development and inward investment were to be facilitated. In addition, major advances were required in IT and telematics, and the need for a strong coordinated transport strategy was considered particularly urgent.

Establishing contemporary structures for regional development

Institutional development

The return of a Labour government in 1997, with a commitment to push forward the regional agenda, saw the launch of two separate but fundamentally interacting institutional structures, namely the North West Development Agency (NWDA) and the North West Regional Assembly (NWRA). It was clear though from the outset that a tripartite regional framework would emerge between NWDA, NWRA and the existing regional office of government (GONW) (Baker 2002; Baker *et al.* 2000).

Approved in November 1998, the Board of the NWDA (consisting of a chair and 12 members – four local authority, six private sector and two others) was formed to manage and oversee the Agency's work. In the run-up to its formal launch, its main work was to integrate the four different elements of the organisation within the region – Single Regeneration Budget, English Partnerships, Rural Development Commission and INWARD. From the beginning there was a feeling that the relationship between the NWDA and sub-regional bodies (e.g. MIDAS, Mersey Partnership, West Cumbrian Development Agency) needed further clarification if political difficulties were to be avoided, and an "interim secretariat" undertook considerable activity at this stage to ensure that such agencies were fully on board for the launch of the new body. Following its launch in April 1999, with staffing largely transferred from incorporated agencies, and an annual budget of £250 million (only around 1 per cent of public spending within the region), it was clear that it had little scope for initial flexibility. To deliver its policies, however, the new agency intended to set up a series of area offices and specialist teams to enable it both to focus on project delivery sub-regionally (e.g. Greater Manchester) and to reflect regional diversity (e.g. coastal towns and rural areas). Its most pressing first task was to produce a new RES, which was expected to be approved by government by the end of 1999.

The challenges for NWDA from the outset were: to ensure that it could influence the policies of the agencies and programmes that it did *not* control; the issue of regional accountability and its working relationships with NWRA and GONW; its relationship with central government and its reporting role to ministers, whilst at the same time retaining the support of sub-regional bodies; and the need to ensure the cohesiveness of regional strategic objectives prepared by differing bodies. It was, therefore, to take considerable time in "bedding down" to its new relationships and responsibilities, to ascertain the significance or permanence of such a body and its contribution to ensuring the increasing competitiveness and cohesion of the region.

A key component of emerging legislation was to be the establishment of a parallel regional Chamber organisation to represent local authorities and other major stakeholders within the region, which became known as the North West Regional Assembly (NWRA). The activities of the existing North West Partnership and the North West Regional Association were subsumed within its operation, but the regional association of local authorities was still expected to meet as a formally separate body when specific local government responsibilities were involved (e.g. preparation of RPG and the regional planning conference). The Assembly has a membership of 80, being dominated by local authority representation. Representatives were nominated by each local authority within the region, plus additional representatives for Cheshire and Lancashire county councils to reflect population numbers and minority political party balances, together with a number of co-opted members. The non-local authority sector membership represents business, education, the labour movement and the voluntary sector, with the aim of ensuring adequate and effective representation of the main regional economic development stakeholders.

The Assembly's annual budget is largely funded from its membership, pro rata based on population. It meets quarterly, and is committed to arranging an annual regional conference to provide a forum for regional stakeholders and politicians to review the state of the region and the NWDA's activities and progress (NWRA 1998). Its Policy Committee coordinates policies and takes decisions on matters as delegated/authorised by the Assembly. It oversees the work of a series of key priority groups originally established by the North West Partnership and the North West Regional Association, but now incorporated into the work of the Assembly. For regional planning work, the key priority group that has been responsible for preparing a framework for reviewing and reformulating RPG has been the Environment, Transport and Planning Group. Accountable to this group is a small strategic policy unit that houses a regional planning team.

The economic development agenda

Following the passing of the legislation for the RDAs, draft guidance was given to each "shadow" secretariat on the proposed content of regional development strategies, with the NWDA producing a draft strategy in the summer of 1999, and organising a series of Panel meetings on specific themes seen as critical for the region's future. The difficulty of getting private sector involvement necessitated a "key sector" approach being adopted in their case, around an action plan targeted on integrated themes (see Table 15.1). The main vision of the final RES, published in December 1999, was to facilitate the creation of a region

Table 15.1 Regional economic strategy proposals

Investing in business and ideas:
– encourage investment in targeted high-growth sectors on a world stage;
– enhance the region's ability to create and develop knowledge and to translate knowledge into high-value products, applications and services;
– invest in entrepreneurship and accelerate business start-ups;
– raise the productivity and competitive performance of the region's existing business by pursuing business excellence;
– improve and simplify business support.

Investing in the environment:
– restore and manage the region's highest-quality environmental assets;
– regenerate areas of dereliction and poor environment;
– project a positive image through coordinated marketing and tourism promotion;
– promote new sources of renewable energy;
– promote high standards of design and energy conservation in new developments.

Investing in infrastructure:
– help to provide a strategic planning framework which encourages high levels of private investment in commerce and housing;
– develop the region's strategic communications links by ICT and rail/sea/air/road;
– provide a first-class portfolio of sites and properties for inward investment and other business investment;
– support the provision of regional infrastructure for sport, leisure, the arts, culture and conferences.

Investing in people and communities:
– place communities at the heart of the region's growth;
– bring economic and social conditions in the poorest neighbourhoods to an agreed benchmark in terms of the region as a whole;
– attract and develop major arts, cultural and sports events;
– support regeneration in housing, especially in key regeneration areas;
– raise the demand of employers for skilled people and increase their skills investment;
– raise individual demand;
– invest in equality of opportunity for learning and in an efficient labour and learning market;
– recognise the national and international remit of HEIs.

Source: Authors (adapted from NWDA 1999)

that attracts and retains the skilled and talented; brings everyone into the mainstream of community life; nurtures its environment, heritage and culture; kindles creativity, innovation and competitiveness; transforms its image; and strengthens its infrastructure. The thrust of such proposals focused on four existing themes, namely: investing in business and ideas; investing in the environment; investing in infrastructure; and investing in people and communities (NWDA 1999).

Once this broad strategy had been adopted, the key intention was to develop a series of action plans to take forward the main areas of activity, with the NWDA attempting to work closely with NWRA and GONW to integrate policy and programme delivery within the region. It was intended that the regional strategy be reviewed every three years, and that NWDA would produce an annual report and corporate plan setting out its progress in meeting performance targets and in refining its objectives within a wider context.

The RES was reviewed in September 2002 in an attempt both to update it in terms of changes in national and regional policy and to take stock of the previous three years' experience. Whilst the main vision was not significantly amended, it was seen to offer an opportunity to provide a clearer, more focused approach to the region's economic development priorities. Bilateral meetings were held with key partners, and the revised document was launched in spring 2003, with the action plan setting out the detail of RES implementation up to 2006. This incorporated and expanded on the actions contained in various complementary documents (e.g. the rural recovery plan and the North West ICT strategy) and, like its predecessor, was subject to sustainable development appraisal. The challenges facing the region in the early twenty-first century were seen to need concerted action on five key priorities (NWDA 2003):

- improving the transport and communications infrastructure and its image;
- addressing the skills deficit and weakness in the education and learning infrastructure;
- improving the quality and delivery of business support services, and the provision of quality business sites and accommodation;
- securing significant increases in levels of public and private sector R & D; and
- enhancing the image of the region both nationally and internationally, taking advantage of the region's diverse strengths.

These priorities were to be underpinned by the delivery of ten strategic objectives, and influenced by a series of issues seen to impact on the key priorities:

- the need to coordinate effort to ensure maximum benefits from the EU, particularly with regard to enlargement issues and the post–2006 funding agenda;
- the confirmation of the central role of public services to the regional economy, and the importance of health as a major issue affecting regional competitiveness;
- an acceptance that the region's natural resources are a major but undervalued contribution to both the quality of life and the economy of the region;
- a recognition that the region's universities are an important economic driver and are developing proposals that will contribute to the region's economic and social regeneration; and
- the centrality of the RDA working alongside others in the region to respond to and to influence government policy proposals.

In terms of delivering the 2003/06 action plan, the RDA is committed to producing annual progress reports and the development of suitable performance indicators to monitor performance.

Regional planning guidance and the spatial planning agenda

Following the issuance of RPG within the North West (RPG13, 1996), a working group of officers within the region – the RPG steering group – continued to monitor its implementation. It was this group that, in early 1998, published a "stock-taking report" that identified the need to review such guidance arising from changing regional circumstances and national policy development consequent on the return of the Labour government.

Institutional reorganisation, consequent on the establishment of the NWDA and the NWRA, meant that the regional planning conference responsible for reviewing RPG was not transferred to the regional assembly directly (owing to the conflict of interest perceived to exist amongst its minority non-local authority membership). Instead, it would be exercised through the assembly's elected local authority membership – the North West Local Government Association (NWLGA) – thereby ensuring the reorganisation of both the regional planning process and the working arrangements needed to carry out the review of RPG13.

From the outset, however, the new framework was intended to be far more inclusive than the system it replaced, allowing for a significant number of stakeholders to get involved at a variety of levels. Internally, its remit was also perceived to have a mandate that was wider than a strictly land-use planning document, and it was expected to take the form of a fully fledged regional strategy on a par with NWDA's RES. The key stakeholders responsible for preparing the draft RPG were NWRA and GONW, the focus of the region's commitment to demonstrate institutional collaboration. This growing confidence in the relationship was exemplified by the commissioning of a joint programme of research and a series of liaison meetings outside the new regional planning structure. Concern was however raised at this stage as to the hierarchy of regional strategies and the interdependence of the RES and the RPG and, consequently, the potential for conflict between them.

Many of the institutions associated with the preparation of the initial RPG in the early 1990s were accommodated within the four working task groups – environment, transport, economy, housing – established to influence centrally the content of the emerging review. With the emergence of the NWRA, the Environment, Transport and Planning Key Priority Group became the significant member-level group to oversee this work, this being subsequently taken forward by an RPG steering group (consisting of local authority officers and GONW and Environment Agency representation) and the RPG team within the assembly. It was not formally part of the assembly or regional planning team's chain of accountability, but rather a sounding board for the ongoing review. The RPG's team was itself supported by task groups (housing and population, environment resources, transport and communications, and economy), established to ensure participation from as wide a range of groups and individuals as possible.

Whilst membership of the task groups was based on professional expertise, in practice members often seemed reluctant to freely offer technical advice, mindful of their employers' perspective and representative role. In an attempt to identify the universe of possible stakeholders beyond membership of the task groups, the NWRA identified other stakeholders through the various sub-regional databases that had been gathered for structure plan and UDP review purposes. Around a thousand regional consultees were contained in this database, with these institutions organised into a series of "non-core groups", the focus of formal public consultation on the draft RPG when issued.

The aim of the review was to produce a "new style RPG, based on a robust vision of the future, and to deliver a sustainable strategy for spatial development in the region" (NWRA 2000: 1). The preparation process was expected to go through a series of stages, the first of which was to establish the key issues that needed to be addressed, and particularly to overcome criticism of the original RPG as a document possessing only limited regional distinctiveness. Inevitably at this stage questions were also asked as to the extent to which the existing RPG (1996) and *Greener growth* (1993) documents should be considered and possibly updated (accommodating 1996-based population/household projections), prior to the full launch of the RPG review process. Additionally, the parallel development of a regional transport strategy, the regional economic strategy and regional housing statement, and a regional sustainable development framework document was bound to influence early discussions.

The first stage of this process involved the identification of themes and key issues expected to provide a set of strategic goals for the review of RPG, with the various task groups holding "brainstorming" sessions to identify core themes. These sessions involved discussion of a broad framework for issue categorisation, the identification of the key questions that RPG should address, and a crude prioritisation of the main issues. This exercise helped provide a creative input for the RPG team, contrasting markedly with earlier attempts which for the most part had involved reiterating national guidance and "borrowing" issues from other regions. It undoubtedly helped explore from the outset varying perspectives amongst task group members on specific issues, and helped focus on how each other's concerns could be accommodated. The issues paper, *RPG: listening to the North West* (NWRA 1999c), was published for public consultation, focusing on six themes seen as being critical for sustainable regional planning within the region, namely:

- prudent management of environmental and cultural assets;
- the promotion of economic growth with social progress;
- urban renaissance;
- sustaining rural, peripheral and coastal communities;
- physical regeneration and environmental improvement; and
- regional accessibility, both intra- and inter-regional.

To focus on such concerns more specifically, the paper identified a series of key themes affecting the region that the emerging RPG would have to deal with. These targeted aspects of housing, population and community development concerns; economic and environmental resource issues; and transport and communication considerations. In addition, given the region's traditional lack of cohesion, particular attention was felt to be needed for issues of sub-regionalisation, sustainability appraisal, and the coordination of timetables of both investment strategies and development plans. It was inevitable that the initial output from this process did not provide a particularly coherent or tangible vision of the region's difficulties and opportunities, acknowledging that it would be challenging to translate the "wish list" into pragmatic and implementable policies capable of being developed on the ground. The production of the issues paper was, however, a definite attempt to promote an inclusionary strategy amongst both the core membership, represented by the various task groups, and "non-core stakeholders", who were more numerous but had few points of access to the decision-making process.

Following on from initial consultation over the key issues, the RPG team approached the preparation of strategic options for the region, aiming to combine a thematic strategy with a spatial focus. An initial scoping exercise was undertaken to evaluate the framework provided by existing national and regional policy guidance, this being combined with the output from initial consultation. A parallel process was undertaken in relation to identifying sub-regional and coherent geographic areas within the region, with the RPG team working closely with individual officers from the task groups in articulating and refining such work. The RPG team was thus able, by summer 1999, to set out a work programme for developing an option strategy, with public consultation on RPG strategic options to follow later in the year.

The emerging options paper was to be set within the context of the six key themes already identified, with successive iterations of the emerging "Choices for the North West" document being circulated between the RPG team, the task groups, the RPG steering group and GONW, with the content being substantially redrafted as a result of the process (NWRA 1999b). The resulting document envisaged a choice of six options for the overall scale and nature of change to be accommodated within the region in the period to 2021, and five possible foci covering the broad location and physical form of associated development. The six visions covered themes of environmental priority, green communities, equitable growth, green growth, economic priority and balanced growth (the latter undoubtedly a contrived focus for the preferred strategy). The spatial foci considered decision factors affecting the broad distribution of change, and presented a rationale focused on:

- metropolitan concentration achieved through urban regeneration;
- metropolitan concentration achieved through urban regeneration and urban expansion;
- Mersey Belt and North–South spine achieved through urban regeneration and urban expansion;
- key transport corridors achieved through urban regeneration, urban expansion and some smaller towns expansion; and
- dispersed development achieved through urban expansion, smaller towns expansion and possible new settlements.

The document recognised that the spatial development options were more complex to consider than the strategic vision, and accepted that further work would be required to quantify and assess them in detail. Such work was expected to be undertaken as part of the combined NWRA and GONW sponsored research studies, and also the parallel commissioning of a study by the NWDA into the spatial implications of the RES. In addition, consultants were approached at this stage to undertake a sustainability appraisal of both the RES and the emerging RPG.

In relation to the consultation responses to the strategic options paper, whilst only a minority of total responses favoured the "balanced growth" vision, the vast majority of statutory bodies were strongly supportive of this option, with most of the opposition to this approach (private individuals and pressure groups) advocating a commitment to the "green communities" vision. In spatial terms, a commitment to "metropolitan concentration through urban regeneration" was strongly articulated, this being reinforced by support for "some urban expansion". As a secondary consideration, there was also strong backing for the option dealing with "transport corridors achieved through urban concentration and some smaller towns expansion". In an attempt to further increase the transparency of the process, a "Choices for the North West" conference was organised in November 1999 which fleshed out the local ramifications of the various visions and spatial options.

The first few months of 2000 were occupied with the initial drafting process for the final RPG document to be submitted to GONW, the eventual submission being followed by a formal public consultation exercise and a Panel being appointed to hold the subsequent public examination. The draft RPG was eventually published in July 2000 and was intended as a spatial strategy which would establish "a broad framework for the preparation of development plans by the North West's local authorities up to 2021" (NWRA 2000: 1). The document was claimed by NWRA to take account of the emerging sustainability framework for the region, and to support the vision set out in the NWDA's RES. Its overriding aim was to promote sustainable patterns of development and physical change, and the guidance was therefore built around six objectives which, it was noted, cut across traditional planning objectives and had been the subject of wide consultation and broad support (NWRA 2000: 5):

- to achieve greater economic competitiveness and growth and associated social progress;
- to secure an urban renaissance in the cities and towns of the North West;
- to sustain the region's smaller rural and coastal communities;
- to create an accessible region;
- to ensure the prudent management of the region's environmental and cultural assets; and
- to secure environmental quality.

An important aspect of the strategy to achieve these broad aims was a spatial development framework that emphasised the concentration of development and urban renaissance resources on the conurbations of Greater Manchester and Merseyside. Resulting from the earlier consultation processes, this was something of a shift from the established focus on two corridors (the Mersey Belt and the North–South spine) and represented more of a "polycentric" approach that was justified by NWRA in sustainable development terms: "the most effective way of developing sustainable settlements is to focus on the use of existing housing stock and improve access to services" (NWRA 1999c: 10).

Outside the Mersey Belt, development was to be concentrated in the larger regional towns and cities within Lancashire and Cheshire, and in the priority regeneration areas of East Lancashire, Lancashire's coastal towns, and West Cumbria and Furness. Although the document itself was somewhat unconventional in terms of its layout – traditional topic-based chapters being eschewed for a thematic structure based around the six core objectives set out above – the content generally reflected continuity with earlier approaches to strategic and regional planning in the North West. As well as the general spatial strategy already referred to, some of the more significant policy stances included a commitment to existing green belt boundaries, except on Merseyside, where the need for a strategic review of boundaries was identified to meet potential development needs beyond 2021.

Regional housing provision requirements of 357,000 dwellings were set out in the draft RPG, of which some 65 per cent overall were expected to be met on brownfield sites (rising to 85 per cent in the conurbations). The implications of these, including the distribution of housing provision requirements within the region at the sub-regional level, were that only local housing and employment needs would be met in the more affluent rural areas such as Cheshire and that, consequently, wider development pressures would not be met in such areas. Thus, for example, there would be no planning for higher growth rates and/or the easing of green belt restrictions. This was articulated despite the references in the NWDA's RES to an area running from South Manchester and Northern Cheshire through to Chester and Ellesmere Port termed the "Southern Crescent", identified as an area of economic opportunity and hence a potential engine for wider regional growth. Unlike the NWDA, which saw potential in allowing further economic expansion in this area as a catalyst for enhanced regional development more generally, the NWRA clearly took the position which considered that letting development pressures rip here would, as well as having potentially serious adverse environmental impacts locally, seriously detract from the more pressing aims of renewal in the conurbations and metropolitan core.

These strategic issues supplied much of the ammunition for the subsequent discussion of the draft RPG at the public examination (March 2001) and the subsequent Panel report (July 2001). Although this stretched to some 180-odd pages and contained 104 detailed recommendations, compared with the controversies surrounding equivalent Panel recommendations in other regions [most notably that of the South East], the Panel report for the North West contained few significant changes and did not call into question the general approach or strategy set out by NWRA (Acton *et al.* 2001). The Panel also resisted requests to alter the basic format of the draft document. However, they did make some recommendations on its content with a view to giving even greater prominence to principles of sustainable development and to clarifying the relationship between the core strategy and the six objectives.

On housing numbers, the Panel endorsed the NWRA's plan for some 357,000 new dwellings, despite the fact that this was higher than the need suggested by the latest national household projections, and was derived from challenging assumptions on future improvements in the region's GDP growth rates and unemployment rates. On the issue of the Southern Crescent, they unequivocally supported the NWRA's stance, stating that this concept should "not take a bite out" of the Mersey Belt, and that there would be no useful purpose in identifying such an area. They also concurred with the NWRA's approach to the region's existing green belts and, despite calls for reconfigured sub-regions by GONW in particular, advised strongly against any unnecessary partitioning of the region in case it should weaken the all-encompassing strategy for the region as a whole. They did, however, call for greater emphasis on the promotion of cross-boundary working, including the production of related sub-regional strategies where appropriate. Overall then, despite the wait, when it arrived the Panel report could be described as something of an anti-climax, especially for those organisations advocating change. In its response, the NWRA offered full support for the recommendations within it.

If, however, the NWRA had envisaged that this marked the end of the RPG process as far as substantive content was concerned, and that the policies set out in the draft RPG would all now be confirmed by the publication of the Secretary of State's final RPG, they were somewhat mistaken. The subsequent consultation on the Secretary of State's proposed changes to the draft RPG (GONW 2002) and the final publication of RPG13 in April 2003 (GONW 2003) did generally endorse the NWRA's overall strategy, albeit effectively burying any vestiges of the North–South spine concept and introducing a new title for the Mersey Belt – henceforth to be termed the North West Metropolitan Area (NWMA). There was also a reluctant acceptance of the Panel's recommendation not to introduce any other formal sub-regional divisions. However, unlike the Panel, the Secretary of State effectively endorsed concerns expressed at the public examination that the draft RPG's housing requirements were based on unrealistic estimates of future economic growth by suggesting a significant reduction of 15 per cent in the overall annual rate of provision of new housing to 2016 (representing a change from 300,900 new dwellings required to 256,000) and an increase in the proportion of new housing to be built on previously used land from 65 to 70 per cent (rising to 90 per cent in the metropolitan cores, now termed regional poles).

Although the related internal distribution of new housing land was left broadly the same across the different sub-areas, this decision has subsequently had significant repercussions on new housing land allocations in virtually all areas of the region outside the conurbation cores and renewal areas. The result has been that a significant number of authorities, predominantly shire districts, have found that they have more than enough existing commitments and/or allocations to meet future regional requirements, and have subsequently restrained almost all new housing development for the foreseeable future. Indeed, by the end of 2003, some local authorities were reporting that they already had over ten years' supply of housing land already committed. The resulting so-called "moratorium" on new housing development has subsequently been applied to an increasing number of local authorities within the region, causing much controversy with the house-building industry and raising further questions in terms of the ability of such areas even to meet indigenous needs for affordable housing against a backdrop of rapidly rising house prices (HBF 2005).

In contrast to the debate over RPG housing figures, and once again highlighting the extreme spatial diversity within the North West region, at around the same time the government launched the Sustainable Communities Plan (ODPM 2003b), as part of which Housing Market Renewal Pathfinders were established to tackle problems resulting from housing market failure (see Chapter 11). Four of these nine Pathfinder areas were to be located in the North West and, as a result, amendments were also made to the final RPG13 to reflect this initiative. Equally significant, from a contemporary viewpoint of regional development prospects for the region, was the promotion of a growth strategy dimension for England's northern cities, labelled the Northern Way initiative (ODPM 2003a, 2004a) (see Chapter 14). This has provided a core theme for current activities in connection with the preparation of the regional spatial strategy (Williams 2005).

In summary, then, the final RPG13 reinforced the concentration of development in the North West Metropolitan Area (NWMA), with particular emphasis placed upon the two regional poles and their surrounding areas (the Liverpool and Greater Manchester conurbations). In doing so, the NWMA was redefined to include south Warrington and east Ellesmere Port and Neston, and strengthened policies were added for the regeneration of all the regeneration priority areas that had earlier been identified by the NWDA. This concentration of development, and its associated severe restrictions in terms of housing requirements outside the conurbations, was further underpinned by the insertion of new reasoning into Policy SD5, which stated that "the discouragement of urban sprawl therefore becomes, for a variety of reasons including economic competitiveness and housing markets in the conurbation cores, a crucial element of the spatial development framework" (GONW 2003: 56).

Current regional spatial strategy development

Although a partial review of RPG13 was initiated in 2003, the subject of a short public examination (November 2004), this mainly focused on a limited range of topics such as minerals and energy policy and was essentially seen as a tidying-up exercise. Work of a more strategic nature, in terms of the development framework for the region as a whole and its sub-regions, has subsequently moved on to the process of developing the regional spatial strategy (RSS) in line with the major reforms to the planning system set out by the Planning and Compulsory Purchase Act 2004. As far as the RSS process is concerned, the new requirements are spelt out in detail in PPS11 (ODPM 2004b), which has become the focus of current assembly thinking. The proposed timetable for this is also affected by the government's wish that the RSS for all three Northern regions should be available in 2006 as part of the wider Northern Way initiative. An initial issues paper for the proposed RSS was thus published for public consultation, and an associated workshop, bringing together stakeholders from across the region, was held in November 2004 (NWRA 2004).

The issues document is quite sketchy on what the RSS will contain and what approach it will take. However, unlike its neighbour in Yorkshire and the Humber, which states quite openly that its RSS has opened up the possibility of beginning afresh (YHRA 2004), the North West adopts a tone in its issues paper that seems more focused on carrying forward existing work, rather than more explicitly taking on the new spatial planning approaches advocated in PPS1 (ODPM 2005). Given the emphasis on sub-regional integrated studies, championed earlier by GONW, it is not surprising that the potential identification of sub-regions was one of the major topics discussed at the workshop, with such areas being identified functionally, with somewhat "fuzzy" boundaries. Discussions took place in early 2005 with the strategic planning authorities in the regions as to how these matters should be addressed in the RSS and, as part of this exercise, briefs for the preparation of sub-regional strategies were drafted by NWRA for: Liverpool/Merseyside city region; Central Lancashire city region; Greater Manchester city region; Carlisle and North Cumbria; West Cumbria and Furness; and the Lake District. This has been complemented by work already undertaken on a West Cheshire/North East Wales sub-regional study (GVA Grimley 2004).

Thus, in terms of the latest RSS preparation exercise, many of the old issues which contributed to the RPG process can be expected to resurface. These will certainly include: the spatial distribution of development and associated sub-regional and local housing requirements and brownfield land targets; the provision of affordable housing, especially in the shires; and the overriding emphasis on regeneration and renewal in the region's urban core areas. Indeed, a general focus on the conurbations has been a long-standing feature of regional strategy building over the past three decades, despite some changes in terminology (Mersey Belt, North West Metropolitan Area, regional poles, etc.). These long-established issues may well be joined by some newer issues, for example those linked to education and health, and initiatives, such as the Manchester knowledge capital initiative centred on the area's universities, as well as enhanced emphasis on cross-regional challenges arising out of the government's Northern Way initiative (ODPM 2004a).

The North West Plan, the draft regional spatial strategy, was published and submitted to government in early 2006, with public consultation until June, and with the examination in public held at the end of 2006 and early 2007. Final RSS for the North West is expected to be approved by government at the end of 2007 (NWRA 2006). The draft spatial strategy aims to stimulate growth opportunities of the region's three city regions, promote the regeneration and growth in key regional towns and cities complementary to the regional centres, underpin the potential of key service centres and enable rural areas to gain better access to such services, and promote integrated coastal zone management concepts, whilst maintaining the general extent of green belt provision.

Conclusions

Whatever the detailed issues that might emerge over the next few years, there remains a clear need to develop a robust long-term vision for the region, now linked to the government's broader Northern Way agenda, and where RSS becomes a significant delivery mechanism. In doing so, it is essential that greater integration between the key players in terms of regional strategy making and, particularly, between the RSS and RES is achieved, thus avoiding some of the arguments and fragmentation that have traditionally plagued earlier regional strategy formulation processes. It *must* do this within an institutional context that is likely to remain as complex and fragmented as at any time over the years covered by this chapter. The resounding defeat of the proposals for a directly elected regional government in November 2004 effectively killed off any possibility of a similar institutional solution in the North West. Instead there is the prospect of a continuing tripartite arrangement of NWRA, NWDA and GONW and the consequent emphasis on partnership, collaboration and shared ownership if any future strategic vision for the region is to stand any chance of implementation, as opposed to just gathering dust on a shelf. To this end, the establishment of a joint senior officer group to coordinate the respective strategy-making exercises appears a step in the right direction.

Nor is it certain that the failure of the devolution agenda will simply imply a continuation of the status quo. Instead, one potential consequence could well be a reduction in the support for, and importance of, the regional scale as a level of strategy making more generally, with the NWRA in particular in a battle to maintain its legitimacy into the future. Such a decline in the role of the region as a scale of strategy making is already apparent in the Northern Way agenda, which emphasises an inter-regional vision on the one hand (embracing all three Northern regions) but based around a sub-regional "city region" agenda. This concept is not alien to the North West, as the focus on the Mersey Belt conurbations over the years has shown, but inherent in such an approach lies the danger of increased rural–urban tensions in a region which, geographically, is predominantly rural in character.

The recent reforms to the planning system that remove the direct strategic planning responsibilities of the counties reinforce the fear of some rural communities that they will be even more marginalised. The Northern Way influence also suggests an increasing top-down, rather than bottom-up influence on regional policy, as the government increasingly realises it needs to be more proactive if its national Sustainable Communities Plan is to be operationalised. Finally, there is also the need to embrace a wider range of stakeholders than just those in the governmental arena at whatever scale. Though crucial, the support of the private sector is not, however, assured, as the increasing tensions between calls for housing restraint from the public sector agencies involved in the housing market renewal initiatives and the house-building industry's development aspirations amply demonstrate.

In conclusion, the region has certainly moved a long way from the fragmentation and rivalry between institutions and geographical areas that characterised earlier attempts at strategic planning and economic development at the regional scale, but the challenges ahead for the region and all those involved in strategic policy making are still considerable.

References

Acton, J., J. Mattocks and D. Robins 2001. *Draft regional planning guidance for the North West: public examination 13 February–2 March 2001 – report of the Panel*. Manchester: Government Office for the North West.

Baker, M. 1998. Planning for the English regions: a review of the Secretary of State's regional planning guidance. *Planning Practice and Research* **13**, 153–69.

Baker, M. 2002. Government Offices for the Regions and regional planning. In *Contemporary issues in regional planning*, T. Marshall, J. Glasson and E. Wilson (eds), 61–78. Basingstoke: Ashgate.

Baker, M., I. Deas and C. Wong 2000. Obscure ritual or administrative luxury? Integrating strategic planning and regional development. *Environment and Planning B* **26**, 763–82.

Batey, P. 1999. Merseyside. In *Metropolitan planning in Britain: a comparative study*, P. Roberts, K. Thomas and G. Williams (eds), 97–111. London: Jessica Kingsley.

Breheny, M. 1991. The renaissance of strategic planning? *Environment and Planning B* **18**, 233–49.

Bristow, R. 1987. The North West. In *Regional problems, problem regions and public policy in the UK*, P. J. Damesick and P. Woods (eds). Oxford: Clarendon Press.

Burch, M. and I. Holliday 1993. Institutional emergence: the case of North West England. *Regional Politics and Policy* **3**, 29–50.

Civic Trust for the North West 1986. *Renaissance North West: a plan for regional revival*. Manchester: Civic Trust.

Civic Trust for the North West 1991. *England's North West: a strategic vision for a European region*. Manchester: Civic Trust.

Deas, I. 2006. The contested creation of new state spaces: contrasting conceptions of regional strategy building and land use planning in North West England. In *Territory, identity and space: spatial governance in a fragmented nation*, M. Tewdwr-Jones and P. Allmendinger (eds), 83–105. London: Routledge.

Deas, I. and K. Ward 2000. From the "new localism" to the "new regionalism"? Interpreting Regional Development Agencies. *Political Geography* **19**, 273–92.

Dicken, P. and A. Tickell 1992. Competitors or collaborators? The structure and relationships of inward investment in Northern England. *Regional Studies* **26**, 99–106.

DoE 1988. *PPG11: strategic planning guidance for Merseyside*. Department of the Environment. London: HMSO.

DoE 1989. *RPG4: strategic planning guidance for Greater Manchester*. Department of the Environment. London: HMSO.

DoE 1992. *PPG12: development plans and regional planning guidance*. Department of the Environment. London: HMSO.

GONW 2002. *Regional planning guidance for North West England (RPG13): draft for consultation*. Manchester: Government Office for the North West.

GONW 2003. *RPG13: regional planning guidance for North West England*. Manchester: Government Office for the North West.

GONW and GOM 1996. *Regional planning guidance for North West England*. RPG13. Government Office for the North West and Government Office for Merseyside, Manchester and Liverpool.

GVA Grimley 2004. *Sub-regional study of West Cheshire and North East Wales*. Manchester: GVA Grimley.

HBF 2005. The economic importance of house building in the North West. Report for House Builders Federation by Nathaniel Lichfield and Partners, London.

Llewellyn Davis 1997. *Measuring urban potential for housing*. Wigan: North West Regional Assembly.

Mawson, J. 1997. The English regional debate: towards regional governance or government. In *British regionalism and devolution*, J. Bradbury and J. Mawson (eds). London: Jessica Kingsley.

Mawson, J. and K. Spencer 1997. Origins and operation of the Government Offices for the English Regions. In *British regionalism and devolution*, J. Bradbury and J. Mawson (eds). London: Jessica Kingsley.

North West Group of Eight 1989. *Northern nights: a development agenda for the North in the 1990s*. Manchester: North West Group of Eight.

North West Joint Planning Team 1974. *Strategic Plan for the North West*. London: HMSO.

NWBLT 1999. *Social responsibility report: investing in our community*. Manchester: North West Business Leadership Team.

NWDA 1999. *Regional economic strategy for North West England*. Warrington: North West Development Agency.

NWDA 2003. *Regional economic strategy*. Warrington: North West Development Agency.

NWRA 1998. *Constitution, priorities and structures*. Wigan: North West Regional Assembly.

NWRA 1999a. *Regional planning guidance review: views from the North West – the issues*. Wigan: North West Regional Assembly.

NWRA 1999b. *Regional planning guidance review: choices for the North West – consultation on strategic options for the region*. Wigan: North West Regional Assembly.

NWRA 1999c. *Regional planning guidance: listening to the North West*. Wigan: North West Regional Assembly.

NWRA 2000. *People, places and prosperity: the draft RPG for the North West*. Wigan: North West Regional Assembly.

NWRA 2004. *Regional spatial strategies: issues paper*. Wigan: North West Regional Assembly.

NWRA 2006. *The North West Plan: draft regional spatial strategy.* Wigan: North West Regional Assembly.

NWRAss 1993. *Greener growth: regional planning guidance for North West England.* Manchester: North West Regional Association.

ODPM 2003a. *Making it happen: the Northern Way.* London: Office of the Deputy Prime Minister.

ODPM 2003b. *Sustainable communities: building for the future.* London: Office of the Deputy Prime Minister.

ODPM 2004a. *Northern Way: moving forward.* Office of the Deputy Prime Minister. London: HMSO.

ODPM 2004b. *PPS11: regional spatial strategies.* London: Office of the Deputy Prime Minister.

ODPM 2005. *PPS1: delivering sustainable communities.* Office of the Deputy Prime Minister. London: HMSO.

Peck, J. and A. Tickell 1994. Too many partners? The future of regeneration partnerships. *Local Economy* 9(3), 251–65.

PIEDA 1993. *Regional economic strategy for North West England.* Manchester: NWRA/NWBLT.

RTPI North West 1990. *North West 2010: the pressing case for strategic planning.* Bolton: RTPI, North West Branch.

Tickell, A., J. Peck and P. Dicken 1995. The fragmented region: business, the state and economic development in North West England. In *The regions and the New Europe*, M. Rhodes (ed.), 247–72. Manchester: Manchester University Press.

Williams, G. 1999. Greater Manchester. In *Metropolitan planning in Britain: a comparative study*, P. Roberts, K. Thomas and G. Williams (eds), 112–30. London: Jessica Kingsley.

Williams, G. 2005. *The spatial implications of the North West's Housing Market Renewal Pathfinder programmes.* Wigan: North West Regional Assembly.

Wong, C. and J. Howe 1995. Destined for rivalry? The case of two city regions in North West England. Paper presented at RSA international conference, Gothenburg.

YHRA 2004. *PLANet Yorkshire and Humber: developing the regional spatial strategy – draft spatial vision and strategic approach.* Leeds: Yorkshire and Humber Regional Assembly.

16 Strategic planning in the Glasgow metropolitan region

Vincent Goodstadt

Introduction

Strategic decisions of their very nature are long-term, directional and integrative. In the context of spatial planning they are also about the geographic scale at which decisions need to be taken (see Chapter 4). Planning can only be effective if the right decisions are taken at the right level of government. This is critical to provide the proper context for decisions to be taken and for appropriate alternatives to be considered. It also ensures that the true community of interest is properly defined.

Discussions about the levels of decision making, however, tend to be dominated in European Commission parlance by reference to "the principle of subsidiarity". There is subsequent pressure for decision making to be taken at the lowest possible level. This emphasis, however laudable, often tends to reinforce parochialism and fails to take account of two factors. The first is that the concept that there is a uniquely appropriate level for decision making is an illusion. Decisions which need to be taken at different levels apply to the same region or locality. The second and related issue is that this emphasis on localism has led to a "democratic deficit" in society whereby those who are affected by decisions are excluded by administrative geography from those decisions.

These problems are most evident at the national level, where projects and policies which affect all the community are handled through "local" procedures, and third-party rights are not properly dealt with since they are too complicated or dispersed. For example, what was the scope for Scottish communities to have a say on London Heathrow Airport's Terminal 5 project or the Yorkshire Dibden Bay port proposals? Yet these communities have as much interest as the "local" community in "the infrastructure of the nation".

At present local interests often prevail or at the very least frustrate decisions that should be taken in the wider community, for example in terms of the provision of new infrastructure or meeting housing needs. It is this tension between local and (national) strategic interests and the failure to address them that undermines the effectiveness of the planning system. These threats are witnessed in a variety of ways as: institutionalised NIMBY ("not in my back yard") or CONU ("control others not us") attitudes, a dumbing down of public debate, or a gap between the rhetoric of plans and sectoral or silo approaches to strategic decision making (Goodstadt 2001).

As discussed and illustrated elsewhere in this book there are in general four levels of decisions that dominate planning discussions depending on the terminology and definitions used – local, regional, national and international. The international dimension is being championed in the new European Commission's INTERREG agenda. The regional level of planning, however, is most critical because this is the scale at which most human activity takes place – in terms of work, rest and play. It also encompasses what is often referred to as sub-regions, relating especially to city regions, because of the need to distinguish them from administrative regions. The following review of strategic planning for the Glasgow metropolitan city region is one such case.

Context for metropolitan planning

The strategic planning of metropolitan areas has emerged over the last decade as a key tool in the delivery of national and international economic, social and environmental policies in the UK (see Chapters 2 and 7). Urban policies have always been vital to, if not synonymous with, the delivery of the social policy because of the concentration of disadvantaged communities within our great cities (EESC 2004). There is though a growing recognition that strategic territorial management (or spatial planning) is integral to the success of national macroeconomic policies to promote economic competitiveness. This is typified by the Treasury's involvement in housing policy (see Barker 2004). Similarly, international environmental obligations depend, amongst other things, upon managing energy consumption associated with urban travel. This renewed focus on metropolitan areas is reflected in a range of initiatives, for example the Organization for Economic Cooperation and Development (OECD) Principles of Metropolitan Governance (OECD 2001), the United Kingdom government's commitment to the Core Cities Agenda, and the Cities Review in Scotland (SEDD 2002a).

The future quality of life and competitiveness of metropolitan areas is also dependent on the effectiveness of strategic planning. A general constraint on achieving this that applies virtually everywhere in Europe is that the administrative boundaries of cities have little relationship to the area of the functional city region that requires to be planned strategically on an integrated basis, a point reinforced by Thompson in Chapter 13. Nor do city authorities (with the exception of London) have comprehensive powers to implement such a strategic plan. It is, therefore, almost without exception that effective strategic metropolitan planning requires joint planning arrangements which depend upon a sharing of power and responsibility.

In this context, the following case study of the joint strategic planning by the eight unitary councils in the Glasgow and Clyde Valley area (also referred to as the Glasgow metropolitan region) is presented. The first section reviews the three main periods of strategic planning of the area, with their contrasting institutional contexts. The second seeks to draw out some common lessons in the light of recent peer group reviews. Finally, some wider implications are drawn in the third section for the future development of metropolitan planning based on this practical experience in the context of the issues raised by Dimitriou and Thompson in Chapter 5.

Strategic planning of the Glasgow metropolitan region

The Glasgow metropolitan region (see Figure 16.1) is an area of some 3,385 square kilometres with a population of about 2 million. It is sometimes referred to as West Central Scotland and has an almost unbroken 60-year tradition of strategic planning. Wannop has declared that, "Of all the regions in the United Kingdom, the West of Scotland has had the most varied experience of regional planning and governance" (1996: 114). This can be considered in three distinctive periods of planning relating to the dramatically changing economic fortunes. These can be characterised as: the Clyde Valley Plan era of centrally planned industrial and urban expansion; the period of retrenchment and deregulation which the Strathclyde regional plan addressed; and the period of managed post-industrial restructuring and growth which has been the focus of the Glasgow and Clyde Valley metropolitan plan. Each has had a seminal plan which related to the needs of the era and the prevailing administrative and institutional arrangements. They each provide key insights into the needs of strategic planning in practice.

The Clyde Valley Plan (1944–75)

The post-war period up to 1975 was dominated by the need to tackle the severe concentration of Victorian slum housing in parts of Glasgow, particularly Cowcaddens, Dalmarnock, Govan and Maryhill. The plan estimated a need to decentralise 555,000 people from redevelopment areas, of whom 250,000–300,000 would move beyond Glasgow's periphery. The period dominated by the plan was associated with highly interventionist and centralised policies for promoting economic growth within the region – what is described in Chapter 5

Figure 16.1 The Glasgow metropolitan region

as "old regionalism". This was complemented by a regional economic strategy published in 1963, the Central Scotland Programme for Development and Growth (SDD 1963). The Clyde Valley Plan of 1949 (CVP 1949) set out proposals for the decentralisation of over half a million people from the inner-city areas in almost equal proportions to peripheral estates and to new or expanded towns.

Unfortunately, the developments promoted by this plan failed in delivering what would be described in current planning jargon as "sustainable communities". The inner-city renewal ran out of steam in the 1960s and left a legacy of vacant and derelict land from the early 1970s. The new communities housed in the four major peripheral estates in Glasgow (Easterhouse, Drumchapel, Pollok and Castlemilk) became synonymous with urban poverty and deprivation. These failures in community development were to dominate planning during the last quarter of the twentieth century in West Central Scotland. Despite these failings, by the 1980s the Clyde Valley Plan had been highly successful by virtue of so many of its proposals having been realised, ranging from the clearance of the worst housing conditions in the United Kingdom to the creation of two new towns (Cumbernauld and East Kilbride) and major initiatives in countryside recreation and conservation (Wannop 1996).

There are some key lessons for strategic planning from the past, even within the culture of "new regionalism" that currently prevails. A key question is "How did the Clyde Valley Plan have such a lasting influence even though it had no statutory basis?" The answer lies in a range of factors set out by Wannop in his valuable analysis of the plan. These include:

- *The strength of technical analysis*: This allowed the new town programme to be sustained "despite the Conservative Government's general 'retreat' from this policy elsewhere in the United Kingdom in the 1950s" (Wannop 1996: 122).
- *The wisdom of crowds*: Proposals and ways of thinking that were not acceptable to the government of the day were supported because of the "non-party" lobby of Scottish interests that was orchestrated across commerce, industry, local politicians, unions, employers and academics, represented by the Scottish Council for Development and Industry, which has parallels with the new regional planning bodies in England.
- *The quality of leadership*: Quality leadership is essential to balance the "wisdom of crowds". Without it there will be a tendency to the lowest common denominator. The role of Sir Robert Grieve in particular cannot be overestimated. He not only helped write the Clyde Valley Plan but used his later position as Chief Planner in the Scottish Development Department and his collaboration with James McGuinness, head of what was to become the Economic Development Department, to maintain the commitment to "collective planning" and to increased public sector house-building targets in the plan.
- *The role of government ministers*: The rivalries between the departments of the Scottish Office during this period were strong. The Secretary of State for Scotland was, however, able to promote a collective Scottish interest in Cabinet in contrast to the functional role of other ministers.

Strathclyde Regional Council Structure Plan 1975–96

The strategic plan prepared by Strathclyde Regional Council (SRC 1979) represented a fundamental shift in policy away from urban expansion to one of retrenchment, with a focus on urban renewal to relieve social deprivation and improve employment conditions. This built on the joint advisory West Central Scotland Plan of 1974 (WCSP 1974) led by Urlan Wannop. The introduction of statutory regional plans in Scotland coincided with the reorganisation of local government in 1975 which placed strategic planning at the heart of the new local government structure. Regional councils were set up which related, in the main, to sensible areas of administration and had a wide range of powers and resources (approximately £2.5 billion per annum at 1996 prices) for the delivery of social and community infrastructure. This allowed the structure plan to be integrated with wider corporate policies and commitments through the regional report which was required under statute.

As Wannop explains (1996: 128), "it is possible to criticise the Strathclyde Regional Council for having failed to take full advantage of its political and financial muscle to achieve even greater impact in terms of urban renewal and regeneration". The fact is, however, that the plan was instrumental in helping channel private investment (especially by volume house-builders) into renewal locations. The rate of urban expansion was reduced from 400 hectares per annum in the 1970s to 50 hectares per annum in the 1980s and 1990s, even though house-building rates increased by about 50 per cent over this period. The net effect was that the plan increased the rate of brownfield housing development within five years from around 30 per cent to between 65 and 70 per cent – a level which has been sustained for over 20 years. It has been estimated that this secured approximately £6 billion of additional private investment for urban renewal, over the plan period.

The Strathclyde Structure Plan, however, had other important policy impacts. It challenged successfully the trend to out-of-town retailing that prevailed elsewhere in Britain. The plan was also innovative in other policy fields, particularly the environment, for example creating regional parks and pioneering urban fringe and river valley management initiatives and the use of indicative strategies for rural land management. The plan was, though, more limited in its ability to guide economic development and prevent the continued decentralisation of employment from inner urban locations to peripheral motorway-oriented locations that were being promoted by the Scottish Development Agency and its successor, Scottish Enterprise (GCV 1998a).

Because of its far-flung boundary, the regional council had one major advantage over the English metropolitan councils in terms of its ability to redistribute resources, and cross-subsidise the provision of services from the more affluent to the less favoured areas. This was particularly important in terms of education and social services, not only for inner-city areas (e.g. in terms of pupil/teacher ratios) but also for remote rural communities (e.g. in terms of the subsidised bus services). It was also able to harness about £1 billion in from the European Regional Development Fund (ERDF) funding, including for environmental programmes (Bachtler and Turok 1997). The council was not, however, as effective in terms of core infrastructure provision or the rates of the treatment of vacant and derelict land.

Early in the life of the council it took a strategic approach to major transport investments by developing the connection of the rail networks north and south of the Clyde following the reopening of the underground, and by abandoning 17 major road schemes. This was not maintained with the deregulation of transport and the growing constraints on delivering new major public transport schemes, as was demonstrated by the failure to attain approval for a light rapid transit project in 1995/6. Even when schemes are agreed they invariably take over 15 years to implement, which is typically beyond the planning and financial horizons used by government. This is still seen as a major weakness in strategic/ sub-regional planning problems in Scotland (Begg 2002: 297).

Similarly, the rate of environmental improvement being achieved in the early 1980s curtailed as the funding agency, the Scottish Development Agency, cut programmes by 90 per cent. This was associated with its shift in priorities under the Conservative government away from major regeneration and "place making" projects, except where these were linked to enterprise zones, to business development and promotion of specific sectors (e.g. electronics and food and drink clusters).

The achievements of Strathclyde Structure Plan were recognised in the European Council of Town Planning awards in 1991 and it still remains one of the most successful examples of planning in post-war Britain, despite the criticisms that have been levelled at it. The four key factors considered to under-lie the impact and success of the Strathclyde Plan, which have a lasting relevance, include:

- *Willingness to tackle "wicked problems"*: Preceded by government action establishing the GEAR renewal project in Glasgow in 1976 and abandoning Stonehouse new town in 1977 (three years after its designation), the first structure plan, published in 1979, resulted in a quantum shift in the direction of policy from urban expansion to renewal. It did not adopt the easier political option of a gradual incremental shift, despite pressure from house-builders and government. For example, at the examination in public into the plan, there was significant debate about the feasibility of delivering the significant scales of owner-occupied housing on brownfield land in inner Glasgow that the plan proposed. In the 1970s, this was contrary to all historical trends and market evidence, but the council insisted that it was feasible and that no transition was allowed for the phasing in of brownfield options. Subsequent levels of brownfield development have demonstrated that the private sector was able to respond to a radical change of policy and to new market conditions as long as the rules are being applied even-handedly to all developers.
- *Evidence-based policies*: The regional council's success in arguing for a radical policy change was possible because of the quality and extent of the evidence base that underpinned the policy argument. In addition to the core annual monitoring of land supplies (housing, industry, business and vacant and derelict land), the regional council undertook its own market research on matters ranging across housing markets and preferences, shopping habits and the needs of business. Its economic and demographic forecasts were also consistently proved to be more accurate than "official" government ones, whilst urban capacity studies were undertaken as early as 1986.

- *The management of uncertainty:* The period of the Strathclyde Structure Plan was dominated by rapid de-industrialisation. In 1973, manufacturing accounted for about 40 per cent of the workforce. By 1995, this had dropped to about 20 per cent because of the loss of around 200,000 manufacturing jobs. It was important for a strategy based on urban renewal to be responsive to the continuous fallout of land from economic uses, whilst guaranteeing an effective five-year land supply to sustain the house-building industry. This flexibility was achieved by the forecasts being rolled forward on a two-yearly basis. As a result, over the 16 years following the 1979 plan, there were *seven* formal updates. This was possible not only because of the efficient management of the process by the council's directors, particularly Robert Maund, Roger Read and Jim Parke, but also because there was no public examination. The Secretary of State in effect dealt with objections on the basis of written representations. The two-year review process also took away the imperative to get the plan right in every detail which bedevils debates where plans are not kept up to date on such a regular basis.
- *Region-proofed policies:* The regional council never saw itself as hidebound by government guidance. Whilst official policy or advice was not challenged for its own sake, the council had the confidence and ability, where necessary, to promote an alternative view to the "official" policy attitudes more appropriate for the prevailing conditions and needs of the communities in the region. This applied, for example, to its promotion of brownfield housing sites in the 1970s, the opposition to out-of-centre retail proposals during the 1980s or the presumption in favour of development in the countryside in remoter rural areas.

Glasgow and Clyde Valley Joint Structure Plan (1996–   )

After 1986, Strathclyde Regional Council was the sole remaining metropolitan planning authority in Britain. Its abolition in 1996 was therefore, on the face of it, merely putting in place the final piece in the Conservative policy to break up all the large Labour-dominated mega-councils that had been pushed through in England a decade earlier. It was, however, made easier by a convergence of political agendas of all political parties and the Civil Service. In particular, it removed a hurdle to the creation of the Scottish Parliament, which could not operate effectively with a single council responsible for half Scotland's population. It also allowed, in theory, the promotion of a more community-based provision of local services through smaller all-purpose "unitary" councils. It furthermore permitted the transfer of strategic services (e.g. water) to central government, quangos or independent boards, allowing much greater control by ministers and the Civil Service. It strengthened the central executive by reducing the lobbying power of local government which a council of the size of Strathclyde exerted for example in securing funds from Europe or in running the referendum against the privatisation of water services. There were, therefore, strong proponents for the removal of the strategic planning authorities. The momentum for change was intensified by the fact that there was little love lost between the regional and lower district levels of local government, which would also gain power and functions by the proposed abolition of the regional council.

It was, however, generally accepted that the main risk of local government reorganisation in 1996 was to the effectiveness of strategic planning that the regional council had enabled. This was accepted even by the Conservative government of the day, which made one change to the Planning Act to require joint structure planning. This placed a requirement on the new unitary councils to exercise their strategic (structure) planning powers jointly, where directed by ministers. In fact 21 of the 32 councils were required to work together in six joint planning arrangements covering most of lowland Scotland, containing 73 per cent of its population. Joint statutory planning was therefore the norm under the new arrangements that came into force in 1996. The largest of these was for the Glasgow metropolitan area (see Figure 16.1), which is referred to as the Glasgow and Clyde Valley area, involving eight councils, although its area was more restricted than Strathclyde, relating only to the core metropolitan area, excluding the former Strathclyde areas of Ayrshire and Argyll and Bute. Elsewhere in Scotland joint arrangements varied, with between two and four councils being required to work together.

The detailed arrangements for joint planning arrangements were left to the individual councils. In the Glasgow metropolitan area the eight councils set up a statutory joint committee with delegated powers to prepare the structure plan and a dedicated non-seconded technical team to prepare, monitor and review the plan. In other city regions the joint arrangements were informal liaison arrangements. All have been able to carry out joint strategic planning. It has, however, been possible to achieve a higher level of collective working in Glasgow and the Clyde Valley despite, or some commentators would say because of, the larger number of councils involved – there being safety in numbers (Begg 2002: 297). The Scottish Executive's review of strategic planning concluded that this success was more related to the existence of a formal decision-making body (the joint committee) and the dedicated technical support (a core team) for Glasgow and the Clyde Valley area, which had worked "extremely well" (SEDD 2004a: 15). It, therefore, has used these arrangements for joint planning as the model for its proposals to modernise the planning system in Scotland (SEDD 2005).

The biggest challenge to strategic planning posed by the reorganisation of local government was the loss of powers of local government. Prior to 1996, decisions on servicing new development lay within the corporate powers of the regional council. The transfer of strategic functions away from local government control created uncertainty about investment in new infrastructure and therefore represented a real threat to effective strategic planning. As a result, the decisions on trunk road issues, water services, public transport priorities and affordable housing issues were increasingly dependent on government agencies. These concerns still persist and are reflected in the findings of the Scottish Executive review of cities, which concluded that "The unavoidable mismatch of administrative boundaries with patterns of activity means that collaboration/co-operation between authorities, agencies and partnerships will always be necessary to ensure planning, effective delivery and monitoring of the impact of services and infrastructure" (SEDD 2002a: 221). This reinforces the importance of the greater emphasis placed by the joint committee on reintegrating the capacity to take strategic decisions (Cars *et al.* 2002).

The output from the joint committee has been extensive. Since 1996 it has prepared a new 2000 structure plan (GCV 2000a), replacing the former Strathclyde Plan. This was approved in 2002 by Scottish ministers, after a two-year delay resulting from legal challenges. This plan was updated in 2006. Both these major planning exercises have taken about two years, including extensive periods of public consultation. In addition, three structure plan alterations have been prepared – two have been approved, dealing with major industrial sites for inward investment (GCV 1998b) and for the safeguarding of development options around Glasgow International Airport, including a second runway (GCV 2004a). The third alteration (see GCV 2003) has been approved by ministers but their decision is being tested in the House of Lords. The time-scales for producing these were comparable to, or faster than, those achieved by Strathclyde Regional Council. Joint working of itself, therefore, has not slowed down the planning process. The main delays have arisen from the legal challenges that are now arising because of the increasingly litigious approach to resolving disputes.

The scope of the 2000 structure plan was radically different from that of its predecessor, adopting innovative approaches to the preparation and format of the plan. The following points summarise some of the key components of this paradigm shift in the approach to strategic planning in the West of Scotland:

- *Joined-up policies:* The fragmentation of functions and powers for strategic planning was the key challenge for the joint committee. The 2000 structure plan was as a result prepared with the support of a range of new networking arrangements (Cars *et al.* 2002). Of particular importance was the Strategic Futures Group, which ensured that all statutory agencies were party to the assumptions, scenarios and targets in the plan and thus had a sense of ownership of the plan itself. This is considered to have helped the task of government ministers in approving the plan in a relatively short timescale. It also proved critical to the readiness of key agencies to promote the implementation of the key regeneration priorities.

- *Clear development priorities:* A general criticism of planning in the UK, especially strategic planning (reiterated by several of the contributors to this book), has been the lack of vision and clear direction. The plan sought to overcome this by being proactive and setting out a clear set of spatial development priorities in eight strategic policies. This was reinforced by the identification of three metropolitan flagship initiatives for the Clyde Waterfront, Clyde Gateway and Ravenscraig as the key regeneration priorities.

- *Minimal criteria-based planning:* The corollary of being more proactive was to get away from the regulatory focus that characterises most of the earlier development plans. There was a desire to have no control policies and solely to set out development priorities. This was not acceptable legally, despite the terms of section 25 (54A in England) for a plan-led system. The 171 policies and recommendations in the former Strathclyde Plan were, however, replaced by eight strategic policies, while development control criteria-based policies, which dominate most plans, were consolidated into two policies.

- *Linkage to implementation mechanisms:* To be effective it was considered that the core policies had to be linked to delivery mechanisms. Local plans were as a result prepared in tandem, such that seven of the eight councils had finalised or adopted plans within a year of the approval of the 2000 plan. In addition "common perspectives" were prepared jointly with key economic, transport and health agencies, which explicitly linked the policies and strategies of these agencies to the development priorities in the plan. These were submitted for approval by Scottish ministers. The 2005 plan seeks to extend this into thematic "joint action programmes" which link the plan more clearly to the programmes of the implementation agencies and to delivery mechanisms.

The effectiveness of the 2000 plan has been reflected in a number of ways, in terms of:

- *Promoting urban renewal:* The level of renewal has been sustained since 1996, with brownfield land take-up being maintained at about 66 per cent even though there has been about a 10 per cent increase in the average rate of house-building in the period 1996–2004. The three flagship initiatives have been taken up by the local development agencies and are now reflected in the national planning framework as key priorities. These collectively will promote 25,000 houses and a comparable number of jobs.
- *Harnessing additional resources:* The 2000 plan was adopted as the spatial development framework which underpinned the ERDF single programme document (1999–2006). It was also one of the core source documents used to harness £70 million additional resources through the Scottish Executive's Cities Growth Fund. More recently, the plan was being used as the basis of a bid for a £60 million five-year rolling programme for the treatment of vacant and derelict land and a £50 million multi-agency greenspace partnership.
- *Widening strategic cooperation:* The collective action achieved through the joint strategic planning arrangements has encouraged wider collaboration in other areas across the metropolitan area. As a result, the joint committee has been used as the mechanism for extending the level of cooperation between councils by preparing complementary joint transport and greenspace strategies, as a result of which equivalent dedicated teams are being set up to deliver these strategies. The structure plan has also been one of the core source documents for the City Vision Report, which forms the basis for a newly established strategic Clyde Valley Community Planning Partnership across all eight council areas in the metropolitan area.

Assessment of strategic planning in the Glasgow metropolitan area

Two separate recent peer group reviews help in this regard. The first draws upon the InterMETREX project (InterMETREX 2006), led by Glasgow and Clyde Valley to establish a systematic approach to benchmarking strategic spatial planning in Europe. The second review in 2002 was undertaken by the OECD. These are considered below, together with reference to other commentators on the planning system which have also considered the experience of strategic planning in the Glasgow area.

The InterMETREX project

The InterMETREX project was funded under the INTERREG IIC and IIIC programmes by the Glasgow and Clyde Valley Joint Committee. The first pilot exercise sought to establish whether it was possible to establish a self-assessment benchmarking system. This study was undertaken in six North West Europe metropolitan regions – Bradford, Brussels, Dublin, Glasgow, Lille and Rotterdam. In view of the positive outcome from this process it was later extended to 30 other metropolitan areas in Europe. This exercise was considered important to the Lisbon Agenda as it is accepted that national economies are critically dependent on the competitiveness of metropolitan areas and their management (i.e. planning regimes). At the heart of the InterMETREX study was the desire to establish a system of assessment that was capable of being applied across the diverse range of social, political and developmental conditions that are found in Europe and elsewhere.

The approach drew upon business models for assessing organisational effectiveness. Five groups of factors in summary were considered critical. The study concentrated on three of these which it was considered possible to systematically evaluate and that were capable of being detached from political judgements. The first relates to the ability of the planning arrangements to take effective decisions, i.e. what your "powers" or "competences" are. The second relates to the ability of the organisation to take informed decisions, i.e. what your technical resources or "capabilities" are. The third relates to the ability to make decisions which are accepted by those affected by them, i.e. what opportunities are provided for engagement in the plan-making "processes". Two other factors are important to explaining the variations in the effectiveness in different strategic planning arrangements. These relate to the quality of political leadership and the quality of the plan itself and its vision, which have been critical to explaining the more successful cities, such as Boston, Frankfurt or London. These were considered too difficult to measure on a comparative basis so they have had to be left to ad hoc assessment locally.

Although the project concluded that it is unlikely that any single metropolitan authority will achieve a perfect match with the benchmark, there are common issues which help explain the differences in the effectiveness of metropolitan spatial planning, including the following:

- *The coherence of the area as a functional urban region (FUR):* More coherent areas in terms of social economic geography are less dependent upon decisions taken by adjoining areas, and have greater scope for resolving conflicts locally. This is a particular strength of the Glasgow metropolitan area, comparable with such places as Stockholm, Copenhagen and Barcelona. The less coherent a region, the more critical are the consultative arrangements with surrounding areas, as was found to be the case in Rotterdam and Bradford.
- *The ability to deliver large projects, in terms both of financial resources and of organisational skills:* Large projects are often introduced for the transformation or re-engineering of a region's infrastructure and for stimulating public interest in the plan. If, however, they are not deliverable this can generate blight and loss of credibility in the plan generally. The "contrat de

plan" used in France was seen as a valuable model for the Glasgow area as a way of formally committing national and local government to large-scale infrastructure projects, which currently is missing.

- *The existence or not of a national planning framework*: Increasingly, local decisions are dependent upon national policy and commitment. This is particularly important in metropolitan areas which are not "coherent", such as Brussels, or where major projects are proposed which require national support, as in the case of Glasgow's airport rail proposals.
- *Planning for uncertainty*: Strategic planning seeks to set out the vision to provide longer-term confidence for and safeguard the interest of communities affected by change, and for those who risk their investment in new development. The practical response to this dilemma lies within the phasing, monitoring and commitment to review which is built into the structure plan with an annual monitor of the land supply for housing and industry, two-yearly updates of demand projections, and a rolling five-year tracking of market perceptions and aspirations.

The main strengths of strategic planning in the Glasgow metropolitan area that were highlighted in the final INTERREG IIC report were:

- The high level of "coherence" of the structure plan area in terms of labour and housing markets meant that decisions on specific development outside the area were unlikely to undermine the strategy.
- The measures to generate stakeholder involvement in the development of the plan had been very successful.
- The working arrangements to share power between the constituent authorities have been highly effective.

These conclusions are consistent with those of the Scottish Executive in its review of strategic planning (SEDD 2002b).

The key weakness in the prevailing arrangements in the Glasgow area is the need to develop improved linkages between plan making and plan implementation through better integration with the projects and programmes of national agencies. This has also been recognised as a weakness of the planning system nationally. The Scottish Executive is proposing to fill this gap by requiring action programmes for *all* development plans, not only strategic development plans for city regions. Producing action programmes should improve the level of commitment to the plan by the other public and private sector bodies responsible for delivering much of the plan. This will require more effective engagement and understanding of, and by, these interests in the plan-making process. While it will be a statutory requirement to include an action programme, the intention is that it will not be formally approved by the Scottish ministers, thus making updates (on a two-yearly basis) simpler.

OECD *review*

The OECD is investing a great deal of effort into encouraging better metropolitan governance as a key mechanism in promoting economic competitiveness. It has set out a set of principles which are similar in spirit to the basis of the InterMETREX benchmarks (see Table 16.1) and those set out in Chapter 5. The

Table 16.1 OECD Principles of Metropolitan Governance

Cities for citizens: Cities should be developed not only to meet the needs of the economy but also to help fulfil the aspirations of people for a higher quality of life through measures that can also maintain and enhance the attractiveness and liveability of cities.

Coherence in policy: The objectives and institutional frameworks of metropolitan governance should be adapted to and focused on key local problems such as economic development, affordable housing, congestion, sprawl, safety, environmental quality, and the regeneration of older areas, which should be tackled simultaneously, taking into account linkages and trade-offs.

Coordination: Metropolitan governance must reflect the potential and needs of the entire urban region. The roles and responsibilities of each level of government in respect of metropolitan areas should be clearly defined in order to facilitate policy coherence and cross-sectoral integration. Given the administrative fragmentation of metropolitan regions, coordination is also necessary among local authorities across jurisdictions, and between elected authorities and various regional boards or agencies with functional or sectoral responsibilities.

Endogenous development: Rather than basing economic development mostly on attracting investment through financial and fiscal incentives, emphasis should be put on investment in infrastructures and human development to take best advantage of local resources. Metropolitan governance can help to set priorities, taking a coherent approach to development based on the strengths and opportunities of a region.

Efficient financial management: Metropolitan governance should allow for the costs of measures to be reflective of benefit received and assure complete transparency, accountability and monitoring. It should also guarantee that all parts of the urban region are considered in assessments of the appropriate level for, and the costs and benefits of, public services.

Flexibility: In order to adapt as necessary to economic and social trends, technological innovation and spatial development, institutions have to be open to changes. A forward-looking, prospective approach is also indispensable to allow for flexibility as well as sound strategic planning.

Particularity: Except where the case for standardisation is justified, policies and institutions of government must be crafted to fit the unique circumstances of various parts of the country and to achieve the best cost efficiency of measures.

Participation: Given the growing diversity and size of metropolitan regions, governance must allow for the participation of civil society social partners and all levels of government involved in the metropolitan area. New technologies and methods of communication can encourage and support more interactive policy environments, bringing government closer to people.

Social cohesion: Metropolitan governance should promote a mix of population, non-segregated areas, accessibility and safety, and the development of opportunity, and facilitate the integration of distressed urban areas.

Subsidiarity: Services must be delivered by the most local level unless it has not sufficient scale to reasonably deliver them, or spill-overs to other regions are important.

Sustainability: Economic, social and environmental objectives must be fully integrated and reconciled in the development policies of urban areas, as reflected in the concepts of the healthy city and the ecological city; in the context of the wider bio-region, this implies greater cooperation between urban and rural areas.

Source: OECD 2001

OECD report *Urban renaissance: Glasgow – lessons for innovation and implementation* (OECD: 2002) was part of series looking at the problems of restructuring the core of large metropolitan areas.

The OECD focused particularly on the regeneration of the Clyde and referred to Glasgow as a "laboratory for implementation". The report looked in detail at the role of the structure plan as one of the principal mechanisms for guiding territorial development. This concluded that:

> the planning, transport and environmental management to realise social cohesion and economic growth are well articulated. A holistic policy context has evolved at the strategic level which demonstrates the broader trend away from sectoral policy approaches towards a more cross-cutting territorial approach on which sustainability is dependent. The Plan is a sound demonstration of intra-governmental co-operation and co-ordination thus establishing appropriate framework conditions to realise its goals. The Plan has made particular progress in establishing a framework which effectively addresses the social dimension of sustainability . . . The Glasgow and Clyde Valley Joint Structure Plan have successfully integrated the three core strands of sustainable development in its metropolitan strategy.
>
> (OECD 2002: 53)

This assessment confirms the potential of the new generation of spatial plans to contribute to urban renaissance if they can break away from traditional land-use-oriented zoning plans. One major OECD concern relating to the structure plan is how transport is treated and the limitations created by the fragmented administration and privatisation of transport services. The OECD report also identified factors that could frustrate the vision that has been set out for the area in the structure plan and other similar documents, such as the joint economic strategy. Amongst those factors which have wider implications are included the risks that arise from:

- organisational proliferation, "clutter" and institutional competition locally;
- tensions and rivalries between Glasgow and Edinburgh;
- the failure to translate the broader principles of sustainable development in the structure plan into the design of specific projects;
- the problem of ensuring that the benefit of urban renaissance is shared with all communities, especially the most disadvantaged; and
- national policies and programmes which have a negative impact on the development of the areas, in particular local government funding regimes.

Other commentators

In many respects the InterMETREX and OECD reports reinforce other independent reviews about the strength of the joint planning arrangements in the Glasgow metropolitan area. Keith Hayton, despite his general criticisms of structure planning in Scotland, considered the Glasgow and Clyde Valley Plan most effective at addressing social issues. He claimed it leads the way with its holistic strategy that makes linkages between regeneration and land-use patterns (Hayton 2001). The Urban Task Force, citing the Glasgow area as an example of best practice, claimed that "The disaggregation of Strathclyde Regional Council put at risk the capability to maintain a strategic planning overview." The task force was however impressed by the joint committee to reconcile targets over a wide area and went on to state: "The important contribution that the Structure Plan has made to the process of urban regeneration in Glasgow and the Clyde Valley has been recognised by Europe and the British Government" (Rogers 1999: 215).

Wider implications

There is a high level of convergence in the approaches that are being promoted for more effective strategic planning. Examples quoted here have drawn on those which have been used for the Glasgow metropolitan area. Some of the wider perspectives are evaluated in Chapter 4. The editors identify in Chapter 5 the central issues facing strategic planning in the UK. Because of its length and diversity, the history of metropolitan or strategic planning in the West of Scotland provides some valuable insights on the practical issues involved in tackling these challenges, which are considered below.

Issue 1: the need for an institutional capacity with a political mandate to address regional issues

There is a growing separation of powers and responsibilities for strategic plan making and delivery in Scotland. This makes the recent experience of joint planning in the West of Scotland by fragmented, under-resourced unitary councils particularly instructive, since it was based upon building new institutional capacities and new governance arrangements to take strategic decisions. This has been achieved by repositioning the statutory development plan from its regulatory role to a form of strategic community plan (Cars *et al.* 2002) linked subsequently to a formal Clyde Valley Community Planning Partnership.

It is evident from this experience that strategic planning can still be effective if there is a genuine sharing of power. Initial concerns in 1996 about the willingness or ability of eight unitary councils to work jointly have, therefore, proved unfounded. There was a concern that "bottom-up strategic planning" was an oxymoron. It was feared that the plan would be distorted by horse trading between competing authorities or that their individual parochial interests would dominate and lead to a dumbing down in decision making. There was also a concern that the process of joint planning was necessarily slower and less efficient. This has not proved to be so, but always remains a threat if not addressed directly.

The constituent councils of the joint committee sought to reduce these areas of potential tension and discontinuity between local and strategic planning by a range of actions. Amongst the more important was the equal sharing of the costs of the joint arrangements, irrespective of the size of the council, even though Glasgow City is six times larger than the smallest member of the joint committee. The joint committee carefully avoided adopting a policing role in development control decisions adopted by others, and substituted it by proactive consultative procedures. A culture for engagement was therefore set whereby all parties were seen as equal partners that were being strengthened by not being circumscribed by joint planning. This sharing of power was also embedded in the decision to set up a Strategic Futures Group to allow partners to set out the objectives, scenarios and targets of the plan, even though the final responsibility and accountability for them lies with the councils.

Issue 2: the need to integrate regional economic planning and regional spatial planning

It is not too great an exaggeration to see spatial planning as managing the derived demands for development that arise from the condition of, and changes in, the economic position of a region (see Chapter 7). This applies particularly to the aggregate level of demand for housing, levels of wealth and therefore consumption of goods and services, or levels of mobility. In addition, there is a strong correlation between economic and social conditions in terms of poverty and health. Similarly, the consumption of natural resources, whether land or energy, is also a direct function of economic performance. Although integration is a general goal for strategic planning, the linkage to economic strategy is critical.

Although the need for integration is generally accepted, it is not normally translated into action. Not only are separate (sectoral and geographical) strategies produced but the linkage in the main tends to be a matter of cross-referencing rather than genuine integration. One of the most telling examples in Scotland of this separation of economic and planning policy is contained in what is generally accepted as a ground-breaking and innovative national planning framework for Scotland. To make clear the demarcation between the development and the economic departments of government, the first paragraph of this report makes it clear that it is *not* an economic development strategy (SEDD 2004b: 1).

The approach to strategic planning in the West of Scotland has been very different in this regard. The councils have sought to go beyond the rhetoric, in terms both of policies and of programmes, through joint research into scenarios (Scottish Enterprise 2006) and mobile firms (GCV 2000b), common databases (e.g. in terms of marketable land), "common perspectives" and proposed joint action programmes. It has resulted in the priorities in the plan being taken up by the development agencies. This level of integration is reflected in the support by the national economic development agency, Scottish Enterprise, acclaiming it as providing a strong basis for collective action and investment to realise the economic potential of the metropolitan area. The agency especially "welcomes the ambition behind the Structure Plan and in particular its awareness of the needs of a growing and dynamic metropolitan city region". It goes on to recommend that "the Plan should act as catalyst for economic development, providing sufficient development space and connectivity for this growth" (Scottish Enterprise 2005).

It is generally relatively easy to achieve between planning and economic development bodies an alignment of general policies, objectives and even key projects for which there is a joint bid for additional resources. The more problematic area is the lack of integration between economic and planning assumptions, as illustrated in Chapter 7. This is particularly important where national demographic assumptions, which planning bodies are directed to use, are driven by historical trends which do not relate to potential or desired economic changes. In the Glasgow metropolitan area this had particular significance in the 2006 update of the structure plan, which sought to reposition the area in terms of its economic role, to meet Scottish, UK and European policy aspirations expressed in the Scottish national planning framework, the Treasury PSA targets and the Lisbon Agenda, respectively. There was, however, no specific guidance for any of these higher-order policies which translates them into usable development targets locally.

The joint committee, therefore, made its own assessment of the levels of sustained growth that were possible (GCV 2004b). It was expected to be challenged on these assumptions and therefore commissioned jointly with Scottish Enterprise an independent assessment to test the credibility of the planning and macroeconomic scenarios under which the proposed levels of growth would occur (see Gudgin 2005). This approach is a quantitative econometric exercise that can be described as "retrofitting strategies". It was complemented by "wind-tunnelling" tests of the strategy using more traditional scenario work with opinion formers in Scotland to strengthen the technical base of the plan (Scottish Enterprise 2006). This highlights the importance of developing more systematic technical bases for integrating economic and development policy analysis, and has implications for national planning considered elsewhere.

Issue 3: the need for dialogue and collaboration with the private sector

The globalisation of the world economy suggests that strategic planning policies must be based upon creating markets rather than determining them, except in the case of politically ratified publicly funded schemes. Advocates of this approach consider that planning in general, and strategic planning in particular, *ought to be* more sophisticated in dealing with free markets. They argue that economic conditions are today entirely different from those that applied in the immediate post-war period, for example, as the context for the preparation of the Clyde Valley Plan suggests. On this basis, they call for strategic planning and economic policy making that are more enabling and less directive.

As Dimitriou and Thompson explain in Chapter 5, this calls for the public sector to engage in greater dialogue and collaboration with the private sector. The structure plan joint committee has sought to achieve this through a range of initiatives within different sectors, including: house-builders, retailers, mineral operators, commercial interests and telecommunications, property and energy interests. This translated into: dialogue with private companies and focus groups representing specific industrial associations; market research initiatives of consumers and developers; market "tracking" efforts through the private sector monitoring and advisory bodies and companies; and receiving advice from specialist economic development agencies and key representatives of industry in identifying future economic scenarios and drivers of economic change. These have *all* proved invaluable in dissemination of information and identifying issues.

There are, however, practical problems in obtaining a "coherent" private sector input to the strategic planning process, especially in terms of its willingness to commit time and resources to the strategy or to share data and analysis (Cars *et al.* 2002). The ability to establish a common "industry view" is constrained by conflicting cultures in which private sector interests enter into discussions as a set of negotiations rather than collaboration, as discussed in Chapter 5. This is demonstrated in the *inability* of house-builders to commit to a collective view of demand, since any "ceiling" for newbuild will generally prejudice the interests of some of their members. Similarly the "retail industry" is *not* a single entity but a grouping of competitors who each will vary from being gamekeepers or poachers in terms of planning aspirations, depending on whether they are trying to safeguard their investment in a town centre or shopping mall or trying to promote a new one in competition with these established locations. This is illustrated in recent years by the desire by developers to obtain town centre status for major out-of-centre retail schemes which they built contrary to strategic spatial policies which sought to protect town centres.

The experience in the Glasgow metropolitan area would also indicate that it should *not* be assumed that the private sector view has the "best" perspective on which to determine policy about the long-term direction of the "marketplace". The private sector perspective of the market, apart from that of the major house-builders, is generally shorter-term than that required by strategic planning. Thus, for example, the typical time horizons of the retail industry are only three to five years, yet this sector is one of the major drivers of change in the urban structure and travel patterns.

Issue 4: the need for greater flexibility within plans to cope with uncertainty, including protection against failures of the market system

There is an inherent tension between, on the one hand, the need for a longer-term vision which lies at the heart of strategic planning and, on the other hand, the need for flexibility to accommodate changing circumstances and the short-term (three- to five-year) horizon used in public financing and by many private sector development interests. The practical response to this dilemma, as illustrated in the InterMETREX evaluation, lies within the phasing, monitoring and commitment to review. Real flexibility, however, is achieved by choosing industrial and business development locations that are robust in terms of labour markets, transport and clustering, and therefore able to meet a range of future scenarios, and *not* seek "niche" designations for locations (as in inward investment sites).

Issue 5: the need for expertise to handle transnational, national, regional and local issues simultaneously

The interaction between the various scales of planning is one of the main challenges that lies at the heart of the complexity that characterises strategic planning. Currently, there is limited integration between them, especially in England. Integration of regional and sub-regional planning is restricted by the rhetorical nature of much European policy, the lack of a national spatial framework and out-of-date local plans. Joint planning in Scotland has sought to bridge these gaps by unpacking the Lisbon Agenda with help from Scottish Enterprise, linking to the national planning framework for Scotland and by synchronising the preparation of local plans with the reviews of the structure plan, so that they are not out of sequence. There are, however, two general issues that need to be considered if the need for integration of the levels of planning is to be met.

The first relates to the need for plans to be based on true spatial – and not just locational – analysis. Many "so-called" spatial strategies are *not* truly spatial. They may have strong locational policies and spatial concept diagrams but they are often no more spatial than the old-style static land-use plans, albeit differently packaged, as many of the previous chapter contributions to this book imply. The key factor that differentiates spatial planning is its *understanding* of the spatial dynamics and interactions between social, economic and environmental systems. This needs to be reflected in planning methodologies. Local administrative boundaries should not, furthermore, be used as units of analysis, since they rarely relate to the socio-economic geography of the area (i.e. the areas in which people search for homes and jobs, work, play and shop). Experience in Scotland shows that geographical information systems (GIS) can allow research and analysis of housing, retail and employment needs to be related to the market areas, which cut across local authority boundaries. This fact reinforced the political commitment to joint working.

The second issue relates to the need for better national planning guidance. The greatest constraint on effective strategic planning at the regional or sub-regional scale is the lack of linkage between the plan and the policies and programmes of implementation agencies. This, however, is dependent on having more effective national development frameworks. National planning has a major role in shaping our metropolitan areas. The national spatial strategies have played a significant role in strengthening the Dutch planning system for more than two decades (see Chapter 14) and more recently at a transnational level as well.

The InterMETREX project highlighted the importance of clear longer-term national spatial priorities, expressed in an integrated national planning framework. The local councils have, therefore, been strong advocates of a Scottish framework, the first being produced in 2004. The Scottish planning framework has limitations, but this has also been the case for similar frameworks for Wales and Northern Ireland. Its preparation represents a major step forward in strategic planning, whereas the lack of a development framework for England is a major challenge, as highlighted by several earlier contributors to this volume.

Experience in Scotland suggests that the following principles should be applied to the preparation of *any* such national framework:

- It should focus exclusively on matters that require a national spatial perspective, and on the key development issues, rather than seeking to be comprehensive.
- It should be based on setting out a long-term infrastructure programme that links sectoral policies and investment programmes, taking an integrated overview of the priorities identified in regional and departmental programmes, and employing a process that ensures regionally differentiated policies.
- It should be light-touch in nature, a framework rather than a set of comprehensive and detailed policies, leaving as many decisions as possible at a regional level, if they are to flourish. This is *essential* if the process is to be credible. This requires the framework to be focused on those

key overarching issues that cannot be addressed through the regional or departmental structures. The sheer complexity of the exercise makes the development of an England-wide perspective highly desirable, especially if it is to be a flexible and responsive document. The framework should seek to open up opportunities rather than be prescriptive and close them down.

Issue 6: the need to adapt strategic planning practice to the needs of individual regions

The willingness to take a local strategic policy position, even if at odds with national policy, was a strength of the Strathclyde Structure Plan. This was possible because of the ability of the authority to undertake its own research. This commitment to technical independence has been maintained in the successor joint planning committee. The most recent examples of the local "adaptation" of national policies relate to the promotion of the metropolitan flagship initiatives and the debate on affordable housing. The flagship initiatives were promoted locally in the absence of any clear national spatial priorities for regeneration. These are now, however, built into the national planning framework.

In respect of affordable housing, there is a general national policy in Scotland to encourage the provision of affordable housing, with a 25 per cent allocation being suggested in the most recent national planning advice note. This generic level, however, has not been accepted by many parties, since the problems relative to affordable housing in Glasgow are very much localised in nature, affecting specific communities but not distorting regional economic development overall. General regional targets are therefore *not* seen as appropriate. Despite this opposition, there is a tendency for a formulaic approach to policy formulation and expression in regional strategies. This is due to the fact that advice given by central government tends to be considered "to be" policy, whilst most planning departments are unable to commission independent research. However, without clearer national spatial policies, the criteria-based emphasis of current national guidance creates a greater need for central government intervention in the final approval process (in terms of confirming interpretation of this guidance), with the result that uncertainty will continue to inhibit local creativity for fear of abortive efforts.

Conclusions

Metropolitan areas account for over 60 per cent of the European population. This has been referred to as the inescapable reality around which the challenges of economic competitiveness, social cohesion and sustainable development in Europe will be resolved or founder (EESC 2004). Cooperation and integration across metropolitan areas are essential to tackle urban sprawl and social exclusion, and to integrate land use and transportation. Spatial planning is an expression of this shift in culture that we need to achieve in the effectiveness and, therefore, the role of planning, with the planner as a ringmaster in bringing people, activity, resources and development together within a vision for the benefit of communities.

At its heart, spatial planning is concerned with the interdependence of communities (whether neighbourhoods or nations). With the growing plethora of statutory plans and strategies being produced by an increasingly large number of agencies in the UK, there is an urgency to find some means to integrate them spatially in terms of individual communities. Within this context and the lessons that have been learnt in Scotland from its longer tradition of strategic planning, there are some key concerns that need to be addressed in the emerging strategic spatial planning arrangements in Britain.

Spatial planning requires us to recognise that administrative areas and political constituencies do *not* reflect people's "real" community of interest. The introduction in England of statutory regional spatial strategies (RSSs) for administrative regions was welcomed. However, if there is to be sufficient focus on the economic, social and transport problems of the core cities, sub-regional plans for these metropolitan city regions should be an essential requirement of the new system, and *not* an option. The quality of the RSSs should be judged by the extent to which they will help resolve these problems. Similarly, the lack of a UK-wide spatial planning framework remains an impediment to our economic competitiveness. Without it there is no clear view of the relative role of each region. Without it, there is also no confidence about future infrastructure network development, upon which economic investment relies, as it will inevitably underperform.

Within Europe, metropolitan authorities are being promoted. Administrative arrangements for metropolitan development in the UK require joint working between councils, strengthened by a new national planning framework, as has been the case in Glasgow and the Clyde Valley. The primary lesson from this metropolitan area is that it *is* possible to have effective strategic planning, despite the limitations of the prevailing formal administrative arrangements, and political and legal systems. This is achievable by compensatory action. The lack of formal powers is often compensated by the "power of the argument" and the "sharing of power" – that is the strength of the technical analysis and the "inclusiveness" of the planning processes. There, however, remains a concern that, if the lessons learnt from elsewhere are not applied in England, the RSSs will not achieve the aspirations of those of us who support the new planning system.

References

Bachtler, J. and I. Turok 1997. *The coherence of EU regional policy: contrasting perspectives on the Structural Funds*. London: Jessica Kingsley.

Barker, K. 2004. *Delivering stability: securing our future housing needs*. London: HMSO.

Begg, I. 2002. *Urban competitiveness policies for dynamic cities: ESRC*. Bristol: Policy Press.

Cars, G., P. Healey, A. Madanipour and C. de Magalhães 2002. *Urban governance, institutional capacity and social milieux*. Aldershot: Ashgate.

CVP 1949. *The Clyde Valley Regional Plan: 1946*, P. Abercrombie and R. Matthew. Edinburgh: HMSO.

EESC 2004. *European metropolitan areas: socio-economic implications for Europe's future: draft opinion*. ECO/120. Brussels: European Economic and Social Committee.

GCV 1998. *Glasgow and Clyde Valley Structure Plan: issues report*. Glasgow: Glasgow and Clyde Valley Structure Plan Joint Committee.

GCV 1998b. *The structure plan: large single user high amenity sites.* Glasgow: Glasgow and Clyde Valley Structure Plan Joint Committee.

GCV 2000a. *Glasgow and Clyde Valley 2020: structure plan – collaborating from success.* Glasgow: Glasgow and Clyde Valley Structure Plan Joint Committee.

GCV 2000b. *Survey of industrial and business floorspace 1997,* and follow-up 2001 survey, Technical Report 2. Glasgow: Glasgow and Clyde Valley Structure Plan Joint Committee.

GCV 2003. *Ravenscraig: strategic planning role – first alteration.* Glasgow: Glasgow and Clyde Valley Structure Plan Joint Committee.

GCV 2004a. *Glasgow Airport: strategic role – second alteration.* Glasgow: Glasgow and Clyde Valley Structure Plan Joint Committee.

GCV 2004b. *Discussion document: the future for Glasgow and Clyde Valley 2025.* Glasgow: Glasgow and Clyde Valley Structure Plan Joint Committee.

GCV 2005. *Glasgow and Clyde Valley 2025: consultative draft structure plan.* Glasgow: Glasgow and Clyde Valley Structure Plan Joint Committee.

Goodstadt, V. 2001. The need for effective strategic planning. *Planning Theory and Practice* 2(2), 215–21.

Gudgin, G. 2005. Unpublished report by Regional Forecasts for Glasgow and Clyde Valley Structure Plan Joint Committee, Glasgow.

Hayton, K. 2001. Urban regeneration and strategic planning in Scotland. In *Strathclyde papers on planning,* P. Booth (ed.). Glasgow: Strathclyde University.

InterMETREX 2006. Unpublished findings by Eurometrex on INTERREG IIC and IIIC InterMETREX projects (accessible from Glasgow and Clyde Valley Joint Committee, Glasgow: contact info@gcvcore.gov.uk).

OECD 2001. *Cities and citizens: improving metropolitan governance.* Paris: Organization for Economic Cooperation and Development.

OECD 2002. *Urban renaissance: Glasgow – lessons for innovation and implementation.* Paris: Organization for Economic Cooperation and Development.

Rogers, R. 1999. *Towards an urban renaissance: final report of the Urban Task Force.* Department for the Environment, Transport and the Regions. London: HMSO.

Scottish Enterprise 2005. Unpublished response to GCV 2005 report.

Scottish Enterprise 2006. Unpublished work on scenarios and visioning.

SDD 1963. *Central Scotland: a Programme for Development and Growth* (Cmnd. 2188). Scottish Development Department. Edinburgh: HMSO.

SEDD 2002a. *A review of Scotland's cities: the analysis.* Edinburgh: Scottish Executive Development Department.

SEDD 2002b. *Review of strategic planning.* Scottish Executive Development Department. Edinburgh: HMSO.

SEDD 2004a. *Making development plans deliver.* Scottish Executive Development Department. Edinburgh: HMSO.

SEDD 2004b. *National planning framework for Scotland.* Scottish Executive Development Department. Edinburgh: HMSO.

SEDD 2005. *Modernising the planning system.* Scottish Executive Development Department. Edinburgh: HMSO.

SRC 1979. *Strathclyde Structure Plan 1979.* Glasgow: Strathclyde Regional Council.

Wannop, U. 1996. *The regional imperative: regional planning and governance in Britain, Europe and the United States.* London: Jessica Kingsley.

WCSP 1974. *West Central Scotland: a programme of action.* West Central Scotland Plan Team. Glasgow: West Central Scotland Plan Steering Committee.

17 Conclusions

Robin Thompson and Harry T. Dimitriou

Introduction

Contributors to this book have found many faults with the principles and practice of strategic planning for regional development in the UK. If we hold up the practice of regional planning against the more theoretical coverage of strategic planning outlined in Chapters 4, 5 and 6 we see that there have been numerous failures: for example, of short-term reactive planning, trend planning, the lack of integration of planned actions, conflicting objectives and policies and weak implementation. These failings are confirmed by the chapters which look at the recent UK history of regional planning, at planning for sectors such as housing and transport and at case studies.

The contributions of this publication collectively reveal six significant conclusions that interestingly reaffirm some of the same conclusions arrived at by Haughton and Counsell in their book on *Regions, spatial strategies and sustainable development* (2004). Firstly, both publications acknowledge in their own way the importance of how regional planning practice and procedures offer invaluable opportunities for debates as well as opportunities for examining competing priorities. Secondly, they expose the considerable absence of applied strategic thought in regional planning of the kind that other strategic planners would recognise and value. Thirdly, both books highlight a prevalence of conceptual confusion in the use of some important underlying principles and visions, which compromises the success of many a planning exercise from the very outset. Fourthly, they illustrate the widespread existence of inconsistencies in aims and policies pursued (both among sectors *and* between levels), made worse by problems of the multiplicity of aims and policies generated by a seemingly ever-growing set of organisations and stakeholders. Fifthly, they expose the frequent and sometimes shameful use of concepts and visions as rhetoric that have "tipped" into favour and political parlance that are often defined in such a bland manner that it is difficult to progress beyond the rhetoric.

Finally, and most importantly perhaps, both books imply there is an underlying desperate search by different and often competing parties for the true meaning behind many of the planning concepts and principles advocated, most especially in the context of the pursuit of the new regionalism agenda. This appears to take place almost in the form of a preparation for battles ahead for a dominance of ideas, visions and paradigms that might ultimately determine the future landscape of regional planning, of which new regionalism appears to be the current favourite. This observation is crucially important, for, as Haughton and Counsell point out, the "control over the meaning and truth of concepts and words can be a means of altering power relations and power possibilities" (2004: 200).

Any responsible critique of strategic planning for regional development must, however, be tempered with consideration of what regional planning *can do* in any given context as much as what it *ought to do*. In these terms, lessons from strategic planning discussed in Chapters 4 and 5 not only uphold the critical importance of context and highlight the significance of uncertainty and risk but also stress that making strategic choices systematically is not a matter of abstract theoretical concern but a reflection of effective decision making, a point particularly emphasised by Yewlett in his review of strategic choice theory in planning in Chapter 6.

One clear message from the book is that the context within which regional planning has taken place in the UK, and is currently taking place, is changing with very great speed and with many of the key forces of this change sourced outside the affected region's sphere of influence. The pace and the scale of such change have particularly accelerated since the Second World War and especially during the latter part of the twentieth century. These changes have brought with them greater complexity and interdependency of decisions and actions, fuelled by globalisation, technological developments, greater access to more rapid forms of movement, climate change fears, concerns about terrorism and security issues, and increased levels of migration. These are drivers that create complex and uncertain environments for policy makers, not least because they interact with each other, making it impossible for them to be comprehensively managed by regional agencies acting alone and in a non-integrated manner. These are facts that are sometimes overlooked by parties that harbour expectations that are not always realistic, wishing for speedier delivery of regional planning initiatives and outcomes than contexts in reality permit.

It is true, of course, that policy makers at other spatial levels and in other sectors face similar sets of "wicked" problems, but there are some distinct differences. Regional planning has peculiarities in terms of its complex political, institutional and policy contexts. Expectations of transparency in decision making and multiple goal achievement are, for example, greater in regional planning than for corporate and commercial enterprises. It is helpful here to summarise what the various contributors to this book have shown these peculiarities to be and how they have ultimately influenced regional planning. This is valuable because we can only reach conclusions about how regional planning might work better in future if we understand the contexts that will continue to shape it.

The political context

Dimitriou looked at the origins of strategic planning in military and corporate practice and at theories about its successful implementation. He found that effective strategic planning is characterised by relatively clear hierarchical structure with strong vertical and horizontal communication and a limited number of clear and well-understood objectives. It is facilitated by awareness and "sense making" of the operational context and an ability to assess the origins of change with the intention of making transitions to accommodate change in appropriate ways. Uncertainty is accepted as inevitable and something to be managed through flexibility, scenario planning and contingency planning. Dimitriou also acknowledges the importance of contexts previously deemed "disorderly" but which at closer examination are seen to possess an "emergent order" and that host important incubators of innovation. This is a phenomenon recognised by both regeneration and Regional Development Agencies in their increasing appreciation of the importance of the contribution of the cultural and arts sectors of cities and regions to the economy.

Corporate strategic planning does not always deliver the best outcomes. Indeed we can see that much of the effort of regional planning (and other forms of planned public intervention in spatial planning) has been intended to rectify the failures of the market. This is true, for example, of the post-war attempts to achieve more regional balance in the UK, discussed by Hall and Roberts, and of failures of labour supply considered by Turok. Corporate policy makers usually work to maximise a small number of objectives that promote their organisation's own (shareholder) interests, particularly in the short run. These often conflict with the objectives of other organisations, particularly non-commercial agencies, in both the short and the long run. Even under "new regionalism", in which the private sector participates more actively in regional policy making, its concessions to other interests are generally made because these are ultimately seen as unavoidable or because the longer-term interests of the private sector can be better fulfilled by engagement with the public policy-making process rather than any real concern for corporate social responsibility. What is a significant development, however, is that the corporate sector is now increasingly valuing long-term strategic planning, notwithstanding its traditional preoccupation with short-term returns.

This development is being facilitated by its greater understanding and awareness of the complex causes and possible outcomes of a number of major global developments, such as climate change and the emerging global energy crisis. Such challenges (albeit too slowly) are obliging commerce and industry to be more conscious of the need to address multiple objectives and to take strategic action jointly with the public sector. It is also now better understood that the success of regional planning does not rest on the binary (misleading) question of whether regional development should be public or private sector-led but on whether there is in place an efficient and adequately managed and funded public sector that offers effective institutional frameworks for all sectors, including the private sector as the key generator of wealth, to operate, plan and speculate for all horizon dates. This necessitates the establishment of joint public–private partnerships and experimentation in the design and management of delivery agents of the kind currently being pursued but with strong performance monitoring mechanisms so that lessons of success and failures can be learnt and acted upon.

Regional planning is and will continue to be an intensely political process, as Roberts observes. It concerns the long-term distribution of large resources in an arena in which there are competing objectives and in which stakeholders have sharp differences of priorities. This political context creates a very different set of conditions for policy making, which, although it prevents some of the corporate strategy-formulation methods being employed in the same manner, does highlight the need for strategic clarity and thought in the presentation of alternative courses and proposals to politicians.

One important consequence of the political climate in which regional planning has been implemented in the UK over the years is that aspects of uncertainty have been poorly managed. This is because, regrettable though it might be, political institutions have a strong propensity towards projecting an image of strength and certainty – and the main agents of regional change are essentially politically driven. They are so ultimately because of the accountability to voters, in a way that does not affect corporate decision makers, and the need to persuade voters that their political representatives are not weakened by doubt. Mason and Mitroff's (1981) assertion then that all strategic plans should have a healthy regard for "doubt" does not sit comfortably with the politician's way of operating, for politicians typically engage in the kind of debate where each political party needs to claim that its way is the only and best way. This desire for strong government has led to the creation of the new office of mayor in order to create greater clarity, speed and certainty in decision making. The Mayor of London, therefore, projected a strong vision for his region and effectively rejected the idea of scenario and contingency plans as confusing and as giving uncertain messages.

In other regions, where political representation remains indirect, there has been a search for "strong" leadership. The case studies suggest that the North West was perceived as suffering from parochialism and divisions within its regional agencies. Some of these perceptions are related to the concept that regions have to project a strong and distinctive "image" if they are to compete successfully in the global era. The North East appears to have benefited from a relatively clear identification of its territory, whereas the North West, with its two competing conurbations of Manchester and Liverpool and vague boundaries, has struggled to achieve the same acceptance of its area. In the new South East and Eastern regions there has been an enormous investment in the creation of new identities, despite in reality the lack of coherence of both territories and the manifest fact that both are more realistically part of the wider London metropolitan region. This political need for identity and boundary is a severe limitation in an age when drivers of change, such as global investment, pay little attention to institutional boundaries and when the complexity of decision demands flexibility in defining the appropriate territory for each decision.

The accountability of regional institutions, however indirect, also influences their decision-making capacity. The crowd may very often have wisdom in considering single issues. The evidence may not be so compelling, however, when it is asked to consider the complexity of objectives that regional policy making faces. If we consider, for example, Gallent's account of housing policy in the wider South East, we see a particular interest group dominating the debate and steering decisions that are multi-dimensional into the confines of a single issue. We also see stakeholders that have better access to political influence exercising their strength. Other members of the regional "crowd", such as those in need of affordable housing and those who will enter the housing market in the next generation, have relatively weak access.

There are some indications that the constraints that are imposed by the political nature of much regional planning in the UK are being addressed. It is now a requirement both of government guidance and of the strategic environmental assessment (SEA) process that alternative scenarios must be considered, discussed with stakeholders and assessed: this process is intended to address some uncertainties regarding alternatives and to facilitate the management of the risk of deviation from long-term strategies. Indeed the new system of regional spatial strategies (RSSs) has been introduced to encourage a more strategic and spatial approach that capitalises on these characteristics. The early evidence from the case studies and elsewhere is that they do represent a substantial advance from the previous system of regional planning guidance.

Some of the most effective planning in recent years has been done by bodies which are not associated with rigid administrative boundaries. These organisations benefit from not being tied down by executive responsibilities and by being more flexible in nature. One example, cited in Chapters 14 and 15, is the Northern Way as an informal coalition of regions. Another is the success of much sub-regional planning in the Greater London and Glasgow areas. In the Glasgow and Clyde Valley case study, a coalition of partners has been able to take a more confident approach to uncertainty and has shown a greater willingness to address "wicked" issues. Many have placed their confidence in the growth in cross-sectoral partnerships and agencies, expected to result in a cross-fertilisation of good practice between the private, public and voluntary sectors. Thompson argues, for example, that the Kent Thames-side partnership has benefited from the self-interested but highly strategic and long-term approach of the main land-owner and developer. Others, however, lament the institutional fragmentation of agents of change and warn that without strong coherent strategic frameworks for planning this can lead to further ad hoc outcomes.

The institutional context

Dimitriou's review of strategic planning thought suggests that there are institutional characteristics that can significantly assist in the achievement of successful policy and delivery. These characteristics include most importantly a capacity for learning, supported by openness and flexibility and by strong research and monitoring capabilities. This enables the early identification of sources of change and an ability to make transitions as well as to anticipate and respond to growth and change over long time horizons. Other contributors have emphasised that successful strategic planning flourishes in institutions that are well integrated both internally and with key stakeholders and associated bodies. They have executive powers, resources and tools appropriate to the tasks in hand and demonstrate institutional "thickness" as described by Tewdwr-Jones and Allmendinger.

However, a common theme throughout the book, beginning with Hall's historical review and concluding with the case studies, is that the institutions of regional planning and development have demonstrated few of these characteristics. There has been a clear absence of institutional sustainability (see Dimitriou and Thompson 2001): institutions involved in strategic planning for regional development have changed frequently and, under the Thatcher government, were systematically undermined. Overlaid on this is the tendency for political institutions to alter political orientation and to change their membership, especially on bodies that nominate representatives. The result of this well-documented sequence of change in the nature and role of regional planning institutions (see the chapters by Hall and Roberts and the example of Thames

Gateway in the chapter by Dimitriou and Thompson) has been a loss of continuity and of knowledge. In such a turbulent environment, learning is difficult both to institutionalise and to retain. In the North West we see that strategy is severely impeded until a process of region-wide studies is established and the constituent bodies begin to understand the region's collective issues and needs.

There is additionally a heavy fragmentation of institutions and up until recently a weak institutional framework for strategic planning for regional development. At present each region has three main agencies: the assemblies, Development Agencies and Government Offices. Tewdwr-Jones and Allmendinger illustrate some of the conflicts and confusions created by overlapping responsibilities and different accountabilities and objectives, notably in the case of the Development Agencies, with their focus upon economic competitiveness, and the assemblies, with their wider objectives of sustainable development. Williams and Baker suggest that in the North West the narrower aims of the Development Agency took precedence over wider considerations of spatial planning.

These institutions are described by Tewdwr-Jones and Allmendinger as institutionally "thin", lacking the resources and networks needed to manage complex regional systems. They have, furthermore, limited executive powers and rely to a great extent upon other agencies, such as those for health, transport and education, to collaborate with them on policy, and to gear their own executive powers to the delivery of that policy. In policy arenas of first importance at the regional level, such as climate change, the planning authorities *must* rely on the collaboration of many agencies to support their policy, and the mechanisms to do this are still to a large extent in their embryonic stages of development.

All the authors concur that central government has *consistently* denied the regional tier the powers and authority it needs to exercise effective strategic planning for regional development. Although devolution in Scotland and Wales has certainly created real regional autonomy, as Goodstadt shows, the situation in England can be described as "centralised decentralisation". Outside London, regional planning agencies do not even have the right to approve their own regional spatial strategies. The role of the Government Offices is essentially to secure the implementation of national government policy. However, at the national level there has been chronic fragmentation of policy throughout the post-war period: Roberts illustrates the consistent pattern of the lack of coordination between government departments responsible for economic policy and for regional policy. This feeds through to the regional level as a major inhibitor of horizontal policy integration. There is also a weaker vertical integration between local and regional agencies than successful strategic planning can tolerate. The case studies suggest this by revealing that the integration between the regional and the local level is often compromised by the ambitions of local government, whether this is in the form of powerful cities in the North West or protectionist districts in the wider South East. Even in Glasgow and the Clyde Valley, as Goodstadt points out, there is the continuing challenge of coordinating implementation agencies.

The policy context

The military and corporate sectors, which provide the clearest guidelines for strategic thinking, have long grappled with multiple objectives that have to be evaluated and prioritised by the exercise of strategic choices. As already pointed out, however, their operational contexts have a much narrower set of aims than public sector policy making and planning. For example, companies have an over-riding objective of profit making and an obligation to shareholders where they exist. While the objectives of commercial enterprises may be in conflict on occasions and need to be reconciled, for instance in determining prices, overall the range and degree of conflict are likely to be relatively contained.

In contrast, public policy making at the regional level has to deal with a very wide set of aims indeed, many of which at first glance at least appear to be in direct conflict with each other. The simultaneous pressure for development and conservation provides an example of this, as Glasson shows. Roberts notes that there have been many unresolved tensions between the objectives of economic planning and physical planning throughout the post-war period in the UK and argues, like Hall, that this has been to the serious detriment of coherent policy direction. Benneworth and Vigar, furthermore, observe that the Sustainable Communities Plan has the objectives both of achieving a better balance of England's communities *and* of supporting the growth areas of the wider South East. They point out, however, the contradiction in this approach and note that the vast majority of sustainable communities funding actually goes towards the costs of development in the South East, thereby fuelling the North–South divide.

An objective that appears to be largely uncontested in efforts at achieving regional development that is common to all regional plans is the promotion of the concept of sustainable development. Glasson shows that this contains three sub-objectives that are often in conflict: economic competitiveness, social inclusion and environmental improvement. However, as already suggested in the opening paragraphs to this chapter, "sustainable development" has "tipped" into general acceptance as an essential aim of policy *without* any rigorous and generally accepted definition of what it really means in operational terms. Thompson points out that at the examination in public of the London Plan, for example, different groups were able to make entirely conflicting claims in its name. The same lack of clarity and vagueness can be attributed to a number of other underlying concepts frequently referred to or aspired after in strategic planning efforts for regional development, such as polycentricity, social cohesion and mobility.

What is clear from the various contributions to the book is the importance of understanding the diversity and complexity of regional policy making and planning and that policy and planning implementation can quite often lead to unintended consequences. Vickerman, for example, shows that regions aspire to ambitious spending programmes on transport infrastructure as a means of stimulating their economies. However, he suggests that the evidence that such investment necessarily produces significant economic benefits is inconclusive at best and that the results may often be quite different from those originally envisaged. An example of this can be found at Canary Wharf, where major new public transport infrastructure has actually enabled higher-skilled workers from

West London to access jobs in far greater numbers than the more local, less skilled East London workers for whom it was initially intended to provide employment.

One of the sources of unintended and uncertain outcomes of regional policy is the weak coordination of policy clusters. Decision makers in sectors such as health, education, transport and housing are often insufficiently aware of each other's intentions and priorities. A notable advance in cross-sector collaboration has been the vigorous use of a spatial strategy for the Thames Gateway as an input to the long-term strategies of the two East London health authorities. The Mayor of London has produced a set of sub-regional development frameworks as a means of identifying the spatial implications of the policies of all the main stakeholders. This has widened mutual awareness of respective policies, though some sectors (most notably education) remain rather isolated within their own silos.

Several of the contributors to this publication lament the fact that regional planning in the UK has tended towards the lowest common denominator in order to minimise conflicting objectives. This was seen, for example, as a way of keeping the main protagonists in the North West on board by Williams and Baker. To the extent this outcome is prevalent elsewhere one could argue this is partly the consequence of the relative transparency of regional planning in the UK in which representatives of different places and interests want to be seen to have secured at least some success. Another consequence may be the tendency to conservatism in some regional planning efforts. Good strategic planning should explore and evaluate a full range of long-term options, as Dimitriou observes. Nevertheless, there are some shibboleths in public planning. There is, for example, a respectable argument to be made for a radical change to the green belt policy, which arguably largely reflects the world of more than 50 years ago. However, at both national and regional levels this option is currently effectively closed, as it is perceived as too controversial because of the opposition of powerful interest groups, notwithstanding the fact that these may represent a minority of the electorate. Having said this, other shibboleths such as road pricing have now "tipped" into acceptance. Road pricing is being introduced for possible implementation outside its place of introduction in London.

Successes and failures

Even if we make full allowance for the political, institutional and policy contexts of regional planning, the book has demonstrated that there have been significant disappointments in strategic planning for regional development in the UK. Some of these are problems of process; others are problems of outcomes.

As regards shortcomings of process, too much thinking and action has been short-term and insufficiently attuned to strategic dimensions of current and future change. For example, responses to major contextual shifts such as climate change and predicted energy shortages have been episodic and very belated. We have in particular seen that much, if not most, regional planning in the UK has been resistant to the acknowledgement of *uncertainty* as a critical dimension of strategic planning. We have also seen change agents obsessed with problems of appearing politically weak or indecisive that an acknowledgement of this kind is deemed to cause. Perhaps most damagingly, the case studies have reinforced the message in the earlier chapters that there has been poor coordination of policy and implementation both horizontally across agencies and vertically between different tiers.

Partly because of these weaknesses in the way regional planning has been carried out, there have been major failures of outcome. At the most basic level, the UK remains heavily imbalanced between its regions in terms of relative wealth and resources. The fastest-growing regions in the South East ("the mega-city region") experience the highest standards of income and skills, but also suffer from high costs, widespread congestion and signs of "overheating". In regions to the north, and in Wales and in Northern Ireland, there are unacceptable rates of unemployment and deprivation as well as an extensive underuse of resources of land and infrastructure. There is little evidence in current strategic planning practice for regional development that these imbalances are likely to be redressed in the foreseeable future, as, among other things, expenditure appears to continue to favour the growth areas (which are predominantly in the South) rather than the regions with greatest needs.

It is hard to say whether regional planning has mitigated the extent of the regional imbalance because, as Roberts points out, there is an insufficient database with which such judgements can be made. Hall suggests that the early post-war focus on regional redistribution did have some effect, and there is evidence that the more recent focus on inner-city regeneration is succeeding in several provincial cities. It is perhaps easier to recognise the clear physical and geographical symptoms of poor spatial planning. A lack of incisive strategic spatial planning has bequeathed us too much urban sprawl and too many instances of urban growth being parcelled into small packages and distributed around the region in an attempt to minimise pain and spread gain.

If we are to improve performance, however, it is important also to recognise what has succeeded. In terms of process, the current round of regional spatial planning stimulated by recent central government legislation is certainly shaping up better than the previous rounds of regional planning guidance (RPG). All the regions in the UK are now paying serious attention to "place" and their own cultural and socio-geographic context. RPGs often read like almost identical repetitions of national policy guidance. The new RSSs, on the other hand, are more distinctive in their identification of particular characteristics of their own region, as our case studies suggest. This is partly because they are based upon more rigorous information: regions like Yorkshire and Humberside have developed strong monitoring systems founded around clear targets. It also reflects a more transparent consultative process. In the South East and in Glasgow and the Clyde Valley, for instance, there have been rigorous processes of stakeholder involvement at the early stages of identification of alternatives, as well as at the more formal consultative stages.

The widening of processes to involve the private and voluntary sectors is also a major source of improvement, notwithstanding the doubts expressed regarding the genuineness of corporate social responsibility initiatives cited by *The Economist* (2005). This is expected to broaden the "reach" of planning and provide a better awareness of corporate planning methods and techniques, as well as priorities, along the lines advocated by the editors in Chapter 5. The London Plan, for example, reflects a substantial process of engagement with the private sector to understand what contribution it could realistically make and what interventions the Mayor could enter into. Adapting the plan to accommodate the proposals of the successful Olympic bid is likely to accelerate this collaboration and accentuate the need for strategic thought.

It can be argued that there are some advantages in the relatively modest powers of regional planning. Strategic planning as an exercise does run the risk of becoming over-prescriptive and of driving down innovation and entrepreneurship if it becomes too systematic and bureaucratic. Some of the most effective and innovative planning has in fact been done by relatively informal associations of public and private partners as well as by collaborations between agencies, as in the case of Glasgow and the Clyde Valley. This reflects Kurtz and Snowden's argument (2003) that major benefits come from harnessing the energies of less structured liaisons in contexts of what they called the "emergent order". In these informal arrangements, there is less anxiety about boundaries, territory, perceptions of weakness and other characteristics of formal governance.

There have also been successes of delivery. In particular, many UK cities (e.g. Glasgow, Manchester, Newcastle and Leeds) are exhibiting vigorous evidence of regeneration, and London is performing strongly as a world city. There is also evidence of considerable strategic thought in putting together and implementing the infrastructure-led sub-regional planning proposals for the Thames Gateway. Overall, without regional planning in the UK it seems probable that the unconstrained market would have exacerbated the degree of inter-regional and intra-regional imbalance, although the acid test could well be Thames Gateway.

Lessons for the future

A number of important lessons emerge from this book, which are summarised below as the concluding part to this chapter and indeed the book. The recent strengthening of regional, strategic and spatial planning could be consolidated by taking on board these lessons.

Planning as learning

There would be great benefit in a shift towards strategic planning as a form of ongoing learning rather than as a cycle of plan production. Change is swift and continuous, and both policy and planning responses need to be adaptive. There is evidence that a more regular process of learning and responding is emerging: for example, the London Plan has been updated twice in five years after its publication, in large part in reaction to becoming more aware about the possible impacts of critical developments such as climate change, ozone depletion, energy shortages, etc. Government guidance, though, still tends to focus heavily upon the plan itself as a product rather than on the processes of policy formulation and discussion. Simplification of some procedures would assist in highlighting the strategic qualities of a plan and enabling greater flexibility and looseness in the plan-making process.

Longer-term planning

Many of the challenges facing spatial planning either are long-term or have their roots in possible long-term changes, including demographic developments, climate change developments, demands for energy and other resources and infrastructure investment. Regional planning is by necessity adopting a more strategic and long-term approach, if only because some of the major infrastructure projects can take a couple of decades from their inception to completion. Infrastructure developments have particularly influenced the horizon dates adopted for the RSS for the South East and for London, as well as for some other regions. The South East Plan and the London Plan review have 2026 as their end date. The former in particular has begun to invest considerable effort in developing scenarios for its timescale.

Integration of policies and action

The shift towards spatial planning and territorial impact assessment emphasises the need for better policy coordination between sectors and joined-up action. While this has to be led by central government, there is too much evidence in this book of failures of collaboration in Whitehall, especially between economic and spatial planning agencies. Government Offices in the Regions have assisted in policy coordination, but their remit does not include key sectors such as education and health. These problems are exacerbated by the excessive ambitions of many regions, especially in the economic development strategies. If added together these amount to a vastly greater set of aspirations than the national economy and than the national resources can realistically accommodate. The time is well overdue for calls for a national spatial strategy for England, made by the RTPI and by several authors in the book, to be heeded. This would provide a badly needed strategic framework for both integrated national policy making and the determination of priorities between regions. Goodstadt also argues that there is still too much spatial planning activity that is not truly spatial, but locked into the narrower land-use planning of the past.

Clarification of roles

The excessive fragmentation of administration and policy making in regional planning and development in the UK, and with this a lack of clear responsibilities between the main regional agencies and stakeholders, poses major dangers. There would be much sense in strengthening the role of the regional assemblies as the most accountable bodies and even in giving clear primacy to the RSSs as the overarching cross-sectoral strategies. This however can only be successfully accomplished when such organisations are suitably staffed and resourced, and once the current "centralised decentralisation" model of devolution has become less directed from Whitehall.

Clarity and simplicity of objectives

Successful strategic planning exercises exhibit a bold and simple approach with a few dominant clear principles, even if this creates friction, despite the complex problems they address. In this way, they become more accessible to the community and to other stakeholders responsible for the implementation of their outputs. This logic is illustrated by the Mayor of London's contentious policy of requiring 50 per cent of all new housing to be affordable. This is an ambitious target and one that has been unpopular with many house-builders. It is, however, clear and understandable, and there is now emerging evidence that performance is gradually moving towards the achievement of this desired target. This example also underlines the importance of unambiguous operational targets in regional plans.

Acceptance and management of uncertainty

Dimitriou has in this book made much of the need to bring uncertainty into the milieu of strategic planning and policy making for regional development. The strength and volatility of the key drivers of regional change mean that strategic planning must incorporate flexibility and the capacity to reappraise. One example is the emerging imperative to include issues of security and safety in spatial and transport planning in a way that would have been inconceivable a few years ago. This suggests that reliance on "directed order" through rigid and top-down processes will be insufficient and that regional planning needs to exhibit "emergent order" in which less tangible factors such as cultural factors, leadership styles and even gut instincts have their place. It also suggests that temporary processes can be valuable as a means of dealing with particular problems in individual places at discrete times: multi-agency partnerships have often proved to be an effective way of tackling issues that may cross physical boundaries, require cross-sectoral approaches or benefit from more rapid timescales.

Adequate and appropriate resources

Last but not least, there has been a substantial increase in the allocation of resources to regional development in recent years, particularly to the RDAs and to the Sustainable Communities programme. Vickerman highlights the risk that regional agencies may lobby for resources *without* proper analysis of their potential effects. In the East of England, for example, the regional assembly has made the provision of additional resources a precondition of its approval of the draft RSS. In some cases, regional bodies appear to be demonstrating their virility to their populations rather than engaging in systematic analysis of what is needed, where, when and from whom. Having said this, there is a strong case for more delegation of decisions about resources: currently, regional planners find themselves seeking to make long-term plans *without* any long-term guidance from central government on the availability of resources. Another very serious gap in capacity is that of professionals with knowledge of regional issues across a range of sectors, and training and experience in strategic planning, including strategic planning techniques and methodologies. The diminution of strategic and regional planning in the Thatcher years, both in practice and in education, has left a situation in which demand for skills currently far exceeds supply. We hope that this book makes a contribution to redressing this imbalance.

References

Dimitriou, H. T. and R. Thompson 2001. The planning of sustainable urban development: the institutional dimension. In *Planning for a sustainable future*, A. Layard, S. Davoudi and S. Batty (eds). London: Spon Press.

Economist 2005. The good company: a survey of corporate social responsibility, *Guardian, Economist*, 22 January, 3–17, London.

Haughton, G. and D. Counsell 2004. *Regions, spatial strategies and sustainable development*. London: Routledge.

Kurtz, C. F. and D. J. Snowden 2003. The new dynamics of strategy: sense-making in a complex-complicated world. *IBM Systems Journal*, Fall.

Mason, R. O. and I. I. Mitroff 1981. *Challenging strategic planning assumptions: Theory, cases and techniques*. New York: John Wiley & Sons.

Index

Note: *italic* page numbers denote references to Figures/Tables.